1885

Bryn Mawr College

1- Taylor Hall

2. Merion Hall

3. Physics Laboratory

4. Gymnasium

5. Old Farm House

6. The Deanery

7- Yarrow [Betweenery]

8- Keiserhof [Greenery]

9- Cartref

Carey Thomas of Bryn Mawr

Carey Thomas

OF

Bryn Mawr

By EDITH FINCH

Harper & Brothers *Publishers*

New York *and* London

10-7

CAREY THOMAS OF BRYN MAWR

Copyright, 1947, by Harper & Brothers
Printed in the United States of America

FIRST EDITION

I-W

CONTENTS

ILLUSTRATIONS

PREFACE

S O MANY persons have aided in the making of this biography
that I am unable to express my gratitude to them adequately
or even to mention them all by name. I am indebted especially to
those who asked me to write the book and placed at my disposal
the material collected by Carey Thomas for her autobiography—
of which, unhappily, no trace remains: the executors of Carey
Thomas's will, her friend Mrs. F. Louis Slade and her niece Mrs.
Rustin McIntosh, as well as her sister Mrs. Simon Flexner. They
have all been most kind in reading the manuscript and in giving me advice and encouragement, and most generous in bearing
with delays. To others who have read the manuscript I am also
especially grateful: to President Katharine McBride of Bryn
Mawr College, to the president of the Board of Directors of
Bryn Mawr College, Mr. Charles J. Rhoads, to Carey Thomas's
nephew and niece, Dr. Henry M. Thomas and his wife Dr.
Caroline Thomas, and to her friends Mrs. Adolphe Borie, Mrs.
Learned Hand, Mrs. James Chadwick-Collins, Resident Director
of Bryn Mawr College, Professor Helen Taft Manning of Bryn
Mawr College and her husband Professor Frederick J. Manning
of Swarthmore College. To Mr. Manning are owing both the
idea and the execution of the maps of Bryn Mawr College that
form the end papers of the book.

I wish, also, to thank other members of Carey Thomas's family
who have helped me with information and advice: her cousin Mrs.
Alys Russell and her nephews Mr. Harold Worthington and Mr.
James Flexner. Some, alas, to whom I should like to acknowledge
my debt are now beyond reach of my words—Carey Thomas's
sisters Mrs. M. G. Worthington and Mrs. Morris Carey, her
cousins Mrs. Frank H. Taylor, Mrs. Oliver Strachey, and Mr.
Logan Pearsall Smith, and her brother-in-law Dr. Simon Flexner.

To President Emeritus Marion Edwards Park, Carey Thomas's successor, I am grateful for her encouragement and for permitting me to see certain letters to her from Carey Thomas. Many alumnae of Bryn Mawr and other persons have helped me by talking with me of Carey Thomas or by permitting me to see letters in their possession. But I should like, in particular, to acknowledge my debt to Carey Thomas's friends Miss Sophia Kirk, Miss Abby Kirk, Miss Isabel Maddison, and to Dr. Rufus M. Jones and Mr. Thomas Raeburn White of the Board of Directors of Bryn Mawr College. I am indebted, also, to Earl Russell, and to Professor Gordon Gerould of Princeton University. I wish, too, to thank Miss Dorothy Macdonald, Assistant to the President of Bryn Mawr College, for her help in looking up certain facts about the college which would have remained dark to me had it not been for her knowledge of the intricacies of the college archives gained during her work for Bryn Mawr under three presidents; and Mrs. Alice Nash Coffin for typing successive versions of the book.

To Carey Thomas's friend Lucy Martin Donnelly, Professor Emeritus of Bryn Mawr College, I owe a debt so great as to be beyond recording. It is with deepest gratitude that I dedicate the book to her.

EDITH FINCH

Carey Thomas of Bryn Mawr

CHAPTER I

Whitalls and Thomases: Early Years

I F I EVER live and grow up my *one* aim and concentrated purpose *shall be* and *is* to show that women *can learn, can reason, can compete* with man in the grand fields of literature and science and conjecture that open before the nineteenth century, that a woman can be a woman and a *true* one without having all her time engrossed by dress and society."

So wrote Martha Carey Thomas in her diary in 1871 at the age of fourteen, voicing the cry of every true Whitall woman. Indeed from her earliest days she showed all the earmarks of those dynamic women of her mother's family, the Whitalls and their connections. In their veins ran the blood—potent to the last drop—of that indomitable old Quakeress, Carey Thomas's great-great-grandmother, Ann Cooper Whitall.

For Ann Whitall,[1] the industrious, capable wife of a well-to-do New Jersey farmer in the second half of the eighteenth century, the mother of six sons and three daughters, there was no time for nonsense had she had any inclination toward it. But she felt none. She saw, as through the eyes of an ancient Hebrew prophet, the placid community of rural Quakers among whom she lived beset by all the wickednesses and abominations of Egypt and of Babylon. Her "medditations," as she called her diary, ring with vivid phrases of warning and lamentation and reproach worthy the Old Testament. She might mourn over "the poure dum creters" in the winter's snow and cold, wondering what would become of them for want of hay. She might apply sumach root boiled in hog's fat, and chestnut leaves, with tender care to the burns of

I

her youngest son John, Carey Thomas's great-grandfather, when he doused himself with scalding water, for she took particular delight in prescriptions and cures. She might rejoice with heartfelt relief when her husband escaped being killed in an accident while making a cider-spill: "O what a great favour he is still liveing among his children, O wonderful indeed: it is won of the grattest blessings that his children and I can have a this side the grave to have him a long with us." But she was too well endowed with "the Cooper snap" not to attempt unremittingly to rule her husband and "pasal of children," and even her neighbors, as well as herself with a rod of iron. Her "medditations" castigate their misdeeds and their levity with a kind of awful joy—and her own failings with a plangent, solemn rapture.

"Eating tu much," she wrote, "is the root of all evil in me, I du believe, O had I aminded it when I was young; but O this enimy of our poure souls always adriveing of us into sin—O that his chain moute be shortened won link!" She laughed too much, too, she believed: "I often thinks if I cud be so fixt as never to laugh nor to smil, I shud be won step better." The cardinal sin, however, of not going to meeting she never willingly committed. In this respect, as perhaps in others, her family were a sore trial to her, "running about of a firs day for to git bad compiny," all company except that of staid old Friends being "bad" in her opinion. To sit among "the poure moarnful gang of worshippers" at meeting on First Day was the greatest of all pleasures to her as well as a bounden duty: "What is all the week of turmile," she asked, "to the consolation and comfort of such a meeting?"

Her husband, Quaker though he was, failed to see things in the same light. "I am alone," she mourned, "like a Phenex, none of my mind." James Whitall preferred fishing as his relaxation from working on the farm. In this his children followed him and First Day found them all "a gading a brod," as Ann noted. "O what is more rong in my mind, all ways a gading abrod when firs day coms; there father is not at hom won firs day in a hol year if he can halp it." Their defection filled her cup continually with "wormwood and goll to drink at." And she was troubled by the gay fashions of the young Quakers. "But I a mani times think," she wrote in desperation, "what signifies my being concarned a

bout fashings? Where is won frinds child or children but some
doddry fashion or a nother on there backs or heds. . . . O the
calico! We pretend to go in plain dres and plain speach but where
is our plainness?" The straw bonnet lined with pink silk which
she herself wore to meeting is said by her more charitable descendants to have been in the accepted plain style and so permis-
sible from the strictest point of view. However that may be, hers
was clearly no spirit of acceptance of the wrongs she saw about
her, but of active reform.

In action she was no less downright and hardy than in phrase.
If the mare threw her on her way to meeting, she went home,
mounted another mare and started out again. If, alone in the
house, she spied a burglar creeping up the stairs, she followed
him, hauled him by the scruff of his neck from under a bed where
he had taken refuge, and marched him out the front door, ad-
monishing him the while to be thankful that she had been in time
to save him from sin. Whatever untoward occurrence might
arise she met with energy and intrepid common sense. In 1777
the newly formed revolutionary government in Philadelphia built
a series of forts along the Delaware River, one of them, later
called Fort Mercer, in the apple orchard of the Whitall farm at
Red Bank. Little consideration was shown the Whitalls by the
French engineer sent to strengthen the garrison, who regarded
their Quaker principles against war as tantamount to sympathy
with the British. He used the timbers of their barn and their fruit
trees to build the stockade. A few months later Sir William
Howe, after defeating the Continental troops at the battle of
Brandywine and occupying Philadelphia, found it necessary in
order to obtain supplies, to open river communications with the
British fleet under his brother Lord Howe. Fort Mercer was
attacked late in October in what is known as the battle of Red
Bank. The Whitalls prudently had left their house and taken
refuge nearer the town of Woodbury, but on the second day of
battle, Ann Whitall grew impatient. She felt that she must see
what was happening to the farmhouse. Besides, following her
Quaker principles, she felt that war should be ignored. During a
lull in the fighting on October 21, she returned with her eldest
son and when, the following day, two British frigates again

besieged the fort while the fighting raged within a few hundred feet of the house, Ann Whitall sat down quietly to spin. The uproar of the firing and screams of the wounded were deafening. Suddenly a stray ball crashed through the room directly over her head. Unperturbed, Ann Whitall arose, took her wheel, and retired to spin industriously in the cellar. The battle over, she emerged to care for the wounded and the dying, tempering kindness with stern moral reproof for fighting. From this episode she emerged "the heroine of Redbank." In all ways she showed herself the true progenitor and matriarch of Whitall women, "these vehement, powerful, Penthesilean women," as one of her descendants, Logan Pearsall Smith, calls them.

In her granddaughter Hannah Whitall Smith, Carey Thomas's aunt, a widely known preacher of charm and conviction, a philanthropist of energetic common sense, and a writer of fluent, vivid Christian books that have been translated into many languages and still bring in their royalties, Ann Whitall was reborn. To her own generation and its children she is the Whitall woman above all others, the standard and measuring rod. To a still younger generation her place has been usurped in family annals by Carey Thomas. If she followed the pattern in less accurate detail, turned her zeal into different channels, Carey Thomas inherited to the full her great-great-grandmother's most striking characteristics.

Not that the Whitall men were negligible, only less startlingly individualistic in contributing to the family inheritance.[2] The pioneer founder of the family, who came from England to New Jersey sometime before 1688, bequeathed to his descendants a sturdy character that enabled his grandson James to hold his own even against the outspoken buffetings of his wife Ann Whitall. Redoubtable as she was, she could not subdue his humor or restrain his independence. A story is told of him rivaling that of her imperturbable behavior during the battle of Red Bank: In 1780 the Marquis de Lafayette and the Marquis de Chastellux visited the battlefield accompanied by the French engineer of Fort Mercer. Uninvited, they entered the Whitall farmhouse. James Whitall, sitting in the chimney corner scouring herbs, neither lifted his head to look at the Frenchmen nor spoke to them. They were, in his eyes, marauders and, what was worse, warmongers to be ignored. Baffled by this snub, they retired in a huff.

The grandson of James and Ann Whitall, and Carey Thomas's grandfather, John Mickle Whitall, exemplifies at their best the pre-eminent Quaker characteristics: honesty combined with exceeding shrewdness, simplicity both of heart and of manner, tolerance of the lapses of others combined with rigid personal discipline. He was a kind, jolly man, quite unintellectual, but with a naïvely direct approach to life that endeared him to people and made them trust him. After his marriage to the gentle and capable Quakeress Mary Tatum and the birth of his five children, his life is a fairly conventional tale of struggle and ultimate prosperity in business, of domestic happiness, and of civic and, especially, religious interests and philanthropy. But his youth, before he settled down in Philadelphia, brought a touch of adventure into the family history.

In 1815 when he was fifteen years old his father lost his money, moved the family from their old home in Woodbury, New Jersey, to a near-by farm, and took his three sons out of school to work there. John Mickle Whitall, the youngest of the boys, infected by two sailor cousins with longing for the sea, sailed in 1816 as apprentice on the ship *William Savery*, the first of eleven long voyages made on different sailing vessels to England and India or China. During this first voyage a passenger gave him a Bible which he set about perusing from cover to cover. Before the task was finished he found that his "inclinations were totally changed." Though brought up as a Friend, he had heretofore taken little interest in religion. Now, he began to keep much to himself "in seeking after God. I was a wonder to many," he wrote later, "but my fellow seamen treated me with great respect, appreciating in some degree, the cause of the change." His captain, doubtless equally impressed by so exemplary a subordinate, certified him to be "one of the smartest young men that has ever come within my observation during the whole course of my life." At twenty he was made second mate, and three years later, chief mate. At this time, also, he adopted the Friends' plain garb and speech and developed the habit of meditation, of waiting for divine guidance, for half an hour before breakfast and half an hour before sleeping. A year later, on becoming captain of the *New Jersey*, the largest sailing ship in the port of Philadelphia, he forbade his officers and sailors to use profane language. "The result was," he wrote, "we had a quiet, orderly crew—my own respect for religion acted on all hands. The authority I had over the men seemed wonderful to me" —as indeed it was. Such piety must have been spiced well with the more liberal and humane virtues to make it acceptable. However that may be, doubtless his seafaring history later widened the mental horizon of his family; it might have done so to a greater degree had it been less consistently pointed, in support of Quaker ideals, toward the morals to be drawn from it.

2

It was left to their father's side of the family to bring a more worldly tradition into the lives of Carey Thomas and her brothers and sisters. Among the homely, solid Whitall virtues gleams of riches and high origins in the Thomas chronicle lighted up occasional vistas of romance for the children.[3]

When very young, to be sure, Carey Thomas was shamed by a dilapidated little wooden house pointed out by her father on the banks of Jones Falls stream that ran through the center of Baltimore as the dwelling of his great-great-grandfather Carey, the first of the Careys to come to America. Later, she felt considerable pride in "a family that took only two generations to bridge the gap between the little riverside shack and Loudon the delightful country estate where my great grandfather James Carey kept open house for all Baltimore." But before so sophisticated a view developed, she delighted to dwell upon another of her father's forebears, Philip Thomas, who came to Maryland in his own sailing ship from Bristol in 1651 bringing with him, as well as a large family, a gold-headed walking stick and a set of table silver, both engraved with the arms of the Welsh Sir Rhys ap Thomas K.G. of Carew Castle, Pembrokeshire. In family legend Philip Thomas is descended from an illegitimate son of the great Sir Rhys, who, at Bosworth Field, commanded half the army under the Earl of Richmond, afterwards Henry VII, slew King Richard in hand-to-hand fight, and later was appointed to attend King

Henry VIII at the Field of the Cloth of Gold. Although the line of descent has never been clearly established and the gold-headed stick and silver service had disappeared before Carey Thomas's day, their reputed ownership by earlier generations clinched the matter in family tradition.

Philip Thomas himself cut no mean figure in the family annals. A well-to-do businessman, after landing at West River in Maryland he acquired five hundred acres called Beckley, where he lived on the west side of Chesapeake Bay, and gradually became one of the largest landed proprietors of Maryland. He was one of the two leaders of the Puritan rebellion in Maryland against Lord Baltimore's Catholic government and, after the Puritan victory, became one of the six high commissioners of the Provincial court.

In 1672-73 Philip Thomas, probably, and many other members of the landowning families of Maryland, certainly his wife and children, were converted to Quaker belief by George Fox. From that time on, Quaker sobriety tempers the family history, the slaves on the Thomas plantations were freed, and the family's worldly fortunes dwindled. Mediocrity settled down upon them.

To the lively imagination of Carey Thomas, however, color was brought into the story again by Thomas alliances with Maryland families of some note: the temperamental Careys; the Ellicotts, inventors and engineers and merchants who helped to found Ellicott City and to lay out Washington; the Chews; the Hopkinses; and others. The marriage to his cousin Mary Snowden of Carey Thomas's great-grandfather, John Chew Thomas—a man of some ability and the first of his family to enter a profession, the law—especially stirred the fancy of their young descendant. Mary Snowden was a great lady, an heiress, inheritor of the estate of Fairlands and of many slaves. If in the end the slaves were freed, the wealth was lost, and she and her husband were obliged to move to Baltimore, they had for a time lived a gay life at Fairlands. Two of their daughters, Henrietta and Julia, delighted their small great-niece Carey Thomas with tales of life on the plantation, where each little girl had a little girl slave and each little boy, a boy to play with them, wait on them, and sleep outside their doors. Many important people attended the brilliant parties at Fairlands, among them George Washington, then President for the second time, whose ceremonious manners were more than the twelve-year-old Julia could bear. As he bent over to kiss her mother's hand, she stole up behind him and was about to tweak his august pigtail when she caught his eyes gravely watching her in a mirror. Terrified, she crept away and refused ever again to appear in his presence. Long afterwards, when Carey Thomas was thinking of writing her own reminiscences, she found great-aunt Julia a bright light in the dimly glowing galaxy of her other relatives. A remarkable if somewhat awe-inspiring old lady, energetic, spirited, and witty, she lost her temper royally when things went wrong. "Nothing was ever dull where she was," said Carey Thomas. She "talked about things," about ideas as well as people. And she had known a wider world than most of the other relatives.

For the Thomases had become as entirely Quaker as had the Whitalls. Less tempered by common sense perhaps than the Whitalls, their fervor rose at times to fanaticism, sank at others, as in the case of Carey Thomas's grandmother, for whom she was named Martha Carey Thomas, into religious melancholia. But they belonged with equal zeal to the self-contained group formed by the Society of Friends, separated from the community about them by the beliefs and interests and customs deriving from their religion.

Their plain dress—often of the richest stuffs—marked them out: the long gray or plum-colored skirts and tight bodices, white kerchiefs and caps or large bonnets of the older women, the swallow-tailed coats with stiff high collars and wide-brimmed hats of the orthodox older men. Even the dress of the younger generation, as in the case of Carey Thomas's parents, was impressive in its simplicity. Their speech, too, was different, their use of "thee" and "thou" or of expressions such as being "led" to do this or that by "Heavenly Father" and of "having a concern" for someone or something. And their views on many controversial topics were distinctive. Unlike most of the other inhabitants of Maryland they were Republicans, their affiliations closer with the northern than the southern states, especially with Pennsylvania, the stronghold of Quakers, and New Jersey. They disapproved of slavery.

They even regarded women as the spiritual and mental equals of free white men, capable of being "moved to speak" with authority in meeting, often ranking as ministers with power equal to that of men.

To be sure, Quaker women were not expected to enter either business or the professions; their work, though different, was quite as important. They added to the duties of wife and mother such religious and philanthropic efforts as could be carried on within the accepted restrictions of womanly reticence. Women, like men, were in direct relationship with God, directly guided by Him, and everyone's duty was to live according to His guidance. Small wonder, then, that among the Quakers are to be found many fearless individuals. Though their individualism lies within the bounds of group morality and ethics, and follows a profound conviction of righteousness, it demands strength of character and independence and calls, also, for a certain amount of self-analysis and self-expression. And herein lie pitfalls, for delusion is all too easy in searching personal motives, and facile expressiveness too often aids delusion. Moreover, the training needed to act by conscience—deliberate training it must be for the children of Quakers since it involves a cardinal point in their belief—may easily warp a sensitive and introspective temperament. For an executive temperament, on the other hand, such as Carey Thomas's, bent toward action, it is in many ways useful.

Since the Society of Friends was relatively small, the ruling, active until well on in the nineteenth century, that Quakers should marry Quakers, resulted in constant intermarriage. This inbreeding, Carey Thomas was fond of pointing out, had two effects: physical and mental instability was frequent, and interests, already limited, were still further narrowed. *Hebraising*, as Matthew Arnold uses the term, came to the point of almost wholly exorcising liberal culture. Whatever aesthetic appreciation the elder Quakers of Carey Thomas's youth possessed they did their best to ignore. Music was a sinful indulgence. In later, more liberal days, the younger members of Carey Thomas's family, it is true, owned and played a piano but they were warned not to speak of it and to push the instrument into a dark corner when their Grandmother Whitall visited them. Though on the dining-room

wall hung a painting of brightly brindled cows in a meadow of
violent green, painted by that John Chew Thomas who married
an heiress, his son was regarded by his kin as a failure largely
because he, also, indulged in painting pictures.

Apart from these two outbreaks, the family repressed any inclination toward the arts it may have had. There were, however,
clear glimmerings of intellectual interest. The Quaker mind
turned almost wholly toward practical and religious matters and,
in so far as it bore upon these, fostered education. A certain
amount of scientific learning was approved by all Friendly circles,
for science obviously could be applied to alleviate human misery,
and Carey Thomas's grandfather, like her father and her favorite
brother, was a distinguished physician in Baltimore. Her lawyer
forebears, too, show intellectual leanings in their choice of a profession. But the interests of Carey Thomas's father appear to have
been markedly intellectual. Something of a classical scholar like
most gentlemen of his generation, he enjoyed his Horace, prop-
ping the book before him during his bath to read the Odes in
almost the only quiet interval in his busy day. And his love of
English poetry he transmitted early to his children. He stands out
among the Friends of that time as one of the leaders of enlighten-
ment.

As for Baltimore at large, during the last half of the century,
it had little more intellectual life than existed among the Friends.
There was, of course, a thriving institute of music founded and
endowed by the philanthropist George W. Peabody, and a circulating library—but no one read much in Baltimore. Carey Thomas
was reminded of this many years later when she went to make a
speech in Richmond, Virginia, where there existed at that time no
library that she thought adequate. She labored in vain to divert
to the building of a library the funds then being raised for what
would be a third statue in Richmond to General Lee.

The hallmarks of Baltimore were southern leisure and hospitality and gaiety. "Baltimore belles" were far famed. At intervals, a Baltimore aristocrat would gather himself and his family
together to make the grand tour of Europe in a stately and
expensive way. But the city remained provincial, its peace, until
the clattering horsecars came, broken only by the comfortable grind

and squeak of carts and the quick clip-clop of horses' hoofs. The broad streets were lined with trees and neatly white-trimmed brick houses on whose front steps the less aristocratic inhabitants sat gossiping on warm summer evenings—a quiet pleasure denied the little Thomases. Fine houses rubbed elbows with poor hovels of negro servants and laborers and wastrels. There was only surface drainage and, when it rained, torrents of water ran down the paved, hilly streets. High stones at the crossings enabled pedestrians to step from one sidewalk to another without wetting their feet. A childhood memory graved on the mind of Carey Thomas was of her mother's abandoning her, during a summer shopping expedition, to run across the stones to speak to an acquaintance. The little girl, letting herself down laboriously into the dry road-bed to follow her mother, found herself in a kind of canyon, hemmed in by the steppingstones that towered above her. A feeling of utter desolation overwhelmed her such as she never experienced again until, long afterwards, her "intimate friend and house companion died in the early morning."

3

Into this quiet southern town Dr. James Carey Thomas, aged twenty-two, brought his twenty-year-old bride in 1855. Carey Thomas's father, a handsome, genial man of a temper as quick to forgive and forget as to erupt, made valiant efforts to be fair-minded, and was indulgence itself toward those whom he loved. His world revolved about his wife Mary Whitall, a radiantly lovely person in both looks and character, gay and good, with a fresh, straightforward, quick mind and a rare combination of courageous integrity with gentleness of manner. Few of the many who were led by her ready sympathy to confide in her went unrewarded by an illuminating response. No wonder that she was the bright star of Carey Thomas's youth. Nor is it astonishing that she and her husband drew about them in Baltimore not only the large group of their relations but an ever widening circle of acquaintances.

They lived at first with Dr. Thomas's father and his family. The house was small and money not too plentiful, but Mary

Whitall infused into the life there the warmth and cordiality that characterized her own home in Philadelphia. She also brought to it the financial backing of the comfortably well-to-do Whitalls. The tie continued to be very close between Mary Whitall and her parents and between the Whitall brother and sisters, inevitably bringing the Thomas household much under their energetic sway.

Mary Whitall was so young at the time of her marriage that her mother consented to it only when Dr. Thomas, of whom she highly approved, promised to relieve his wife of the daily care of marketing—a promise that he kept throughout her life the more enthusiastically because of his own love and knowledge of good food. When things got out of hand as they occasionally did after Carey Thomas's birth, and young Mrs. Thomas despaired of the rooms and cupboards ever again being in order, her mother would come from Philadelphia, whisk everything efficiently about, and set the household straight again. When, later on, it seemed impossible that the bills, rapidly increasing with the ever growing family, could be paid from the doctor's relatively slight earnings, a check would conveniently appear from Mrs. Thomas's father or, still later, her brother Jim—a check always accompanied by no restrictions other than the charge to spend it wisely.

The Whitalls followed the ample tradition of hospitality of wealthy Quakers. Whatever Friend chanced to come along they welcomed at their table, always groaning beneath hearty nineteenth-century meals, and begged to stay in their house as long as he or she desired. There was always room to tuck away one more somewhere in the Whitalls' big Filbert Street house. With equal generosity, the Thomases carried on this tradition and, though their means were less, the food was simpler, and the quarters were shabbier and more cramped, the welcome was no less warm.

The Thomases followed too the precept often enunciated by old Mr. Whitall that "every child should have a happy childhood tucked under his belt." Happiness and goodness, he thought, go hand in hand; and his children, having benefited by this belief themselves, knew its value and carried it out in their own families. The little Thomases owed much to it. Carey Thomas, the eldest of them, had a happy childhood.

From the moment of her birth, January 2, 1857, though she had

older cousins, Carey Thomas, or Minnie as she was called in those
days, became the center of the whole family, one of those gay,
strong-willed little dynamos who win hearts by their very egotism.
A sturdy, bright-eyed creature with pink cheeks and a mop of
shining brown curls, she engaged everyone's attention—even her
odd physical clumsiness in childhood had all the charm of a
puppy's blundering. From dawn till dusk her clear voice chattered
and her "milk and porridge stumps," in her mother's phrase,
tapped like little pistons up and down through the house. She was
quite fearless and direct; her curiosity was insatiable; her determination, not to be diverted. "I feel as if I needed help and advice
in training little Minnie," wrote her mother anxiously, "she is
such a handful."

Among the most uncomfortable of Minnie's tyrannies was her
habit of stroking her mother's eyebrows to put herself to sleep.
Mrs. Thomas, worn out by bending over the despot's crib at all
hours of the night, sent for her sister Hannah. Minnie never
forgot the menacing figure entering the darkened room where she
lay screaming insistently for her mother. "Minnie," said Aunt
Hannah, "thee might as well keep still. Thy mother will not come
if thee cries all tonight and all tomorrow." And, popping a large
white mint-drop into the astonished child's mouth, she departed.
After this impressive as well as characteristic proceeding, Minnie
lay so still that her mother thought she must be dead and lingered
outside her door sobbing, forbidden by the adamant Hannah to
enter the room. Never, even in old age, could Carey Thomas
taste a mint-drop without recalling this episode of her second year,
grown sharper doubtless with innumerable retellings.

Her parents' gentleness of manner and kindness impressed itself
upon Minnie, for they had her confidence and she wanted to be
like them. Often as their restraint irked her, still more often she
bemoaned her misdeeds heartily. From the beginning her parents
respected her as a reasonable human being, explaining things to
her, tacitly expecting her to face the world on her own two feet.
Stinting neither praise nor blame, they permitted her to learn by
trial and error. She grasped a point with exceptional rapidity, of
course, learned eagerly, and showed great pride of accomplishment;
also, explanations were easier for her parents than for many who

have not always "Heavenly Father" and His inexplicable ways to fall back upon.

The belief in "Heavenly Father" and His ever watchful care being the central point in the family teaching, everything must be done with reference to His wishes. In childhood she accepted this; as she grew older, the discrepancies between her early religious teaching and its possible literal interpretation inevitably surprised her. Though she puzzled over these lapses and took hard the discovery that the kindliness of God's care showed itself in devious ways, she had no time to brood upon them, for she found life vastly interesting and action a necessity.

Yet, active as she was, she would sit for hours listening to stories. She longed to read them herself, galloping through her first instruction with the greatest enthusiasm and impatience. At the age of three she trotted about with a huge cushion almost as big as herself on which were pinned scraps of paper each with a letter of the alphabet printed on it, imploring her mother to call out the letters so that she might stab them with a pin. It did not take her long to master them. And from this, it was no step at all to putting them together and spelling out words—not that she ever, at any age, could spell correctly. Though her mother was reluctant to teach her, having been warned of the dangers of intellectual stimulation, she could not hold the child back. Climbing up her father's stretched-out legs, she would comfortably ensconce herself in his lap with a large book and read him, willy-nilly, long passages full of difficult words that she could not understand.

Although by her sixth birthday her grandmother Whitall urged that she be sent to school—"She most certainly needs the regular pursuit and occupation"—her life was already fairly full of responsibility. As baby brothers and sisters appeared on the scene, one every other year, she quickly adopted an elder-sisterly attitude. She regarded herself as her parents', and especially her mother's, right hand in bringing the children up as they should go—a point of view accepted perforce by her juniors and indulged by the grown folk. She was given household duties that demanded intelligence, not only the dull dusting and tidying but "helping" to cook and make things. Sewing she did not take kindly to; but rolling out cookies and stirring pots seemed delightful. Generally wise as may have been this policy of employing her with responsible tasks, it brought disaster in its wake, for Minnie was far too headlong not to need constant supervision.

One day toward the end of January, 1864, when she was seven years old, shortly before the birth of her fourth brother, Minnie announced to her mother her intention of helping Eliza, the cook, with lunch. Enjoined to wear an apron and be careful, she rushed down to the kitchen. Eliza was not there, but a pot boiled on the stove. Trying to reach up to stir it Minnie stood too near the stove. Her frock caught fire. Terrified, she snatched a shawl, tried to roll it round her, and in flames ran shrieking up the stairs to her mother. Mrs. Thomas, tearing the blankets from the bed, put out the flames. "Then," she wrote later, "I cut her clothes off and wrapped her in cotton soaked in lime water and sweet oil and laid her on the lounge and tried to comfort her with assurances that she would soon be well." But the child was burned all over her body and in some places very deeply. For a time she complained only that "Heavenly Father was with Shadrach, Meshak and Abednego in the fiery furnace, and she thought he would have been with her." Toward evening, fever and delirium came on and the struggle for her life began.

For many days it was touch and go whether the child could live. Her mother hardly left her for an instant, for she could bear no one else to touch her; her father slept on a little cot in the corner of the room; another doctor stayed in the house for two weeks; and they pulled her through the first fight. But it was still a question whether the taut little bundle of pain she had become could stand the strain of prolonged tension. The dressing of the sores was the worst. She screamed at the doctor called in consultation, "Go away, go away, with your eyes."

The deepest sores on her arm and especially on her right thigh showed no signs of improvement for four or five weeks. Her mother devoted herself to her. The Whitall grandparents rushed to Baltimore. Aunt Hannah, kept at home by the expected birth of another child, wrote and illustrated two long series of "the Wagtail stories by Sir Edward Little Bull-Frog, a near neighbour of the Wagtail Family" and of "the Tales of Four Mischievous Children, Frank, Whitall, Bessie and Minnie, and their cross old

Aunt Wispelteedum." She chafed and worried, as Minnie was her especial darling, taking the place of her first little daughter, who had died at about the time of Minnie's birth. Prayers were sent up in Quaker meetings for "the little Christian sufferer" and many Friends all over the country sent messages of sympathy to the afflicted parents—astonishing though typical compilations of sympathetic distress and exhortation. "Everything comes *direct* from the hand of our Father," wrote her sister Hannah to Mrs. Thomas, "and there is no peace except in realizing this. His will is sweet even though hard to bear, and He is giving thee a blessed chance to manifest thy loving submission to it: Dear sister, I shall pray for thee continually that thee may just lie passive in thy Father's hands; and may realize vividly that thy precious daughter is dearer to Him than many sparrows."

For weeks Minnie cared not a straw for visitors or stories. At last one day, to her own consternation, "little Aunt Mary," Dr. Thomas's half sister not much older than Minnie, sitting beside Minnie's bed on her way home from market, dropped the basket of eggs she held in her lap. The spell was broken. The awful smash made Minnie chuckle for the first time since the accident. But when in the spring Aunt Hannah brought her new baby Mary to Baltimore, she wrote, never mincing matters, "Minnie's sores look to me *perfectly hopeless.*"

Dr. Thomas devised a large, flat basket that would hold a crib mattress and fit into the carriage, in which Minnie, after a few test drives, was transported to Philadelphia and thence to "the Cedars," a near-by estate in New Jersey which old Mr. Whitall had bought with his usual benevolence to be a summer refuge for his children and grandchildren. It was a farm with a big, rambling house surrounded by gardens and fields and with a stream running through meadow and woodland. Much to old Mr. Whitall's amusement his energetic daughter Hannah at once uprooted the peach orchard that grew in front of the house and landscaped a smooth and shady lawn to make the place perfect for children in the summer.

The following six weeks were a great success. Everybody put himself out to cheer and entertain the sick child. The Nicholson and Pearsall Smith cousins gave up anything for her. Her grandmother planned delicious meals, especially her favorite "chicky dinner" to persuade her to eat. And her grandfather took her driving in her basket every day, letting her hold the reins herself.

After two years of enforced quiet, Minnie and everyone else began to forget her burns, and the months of suffering began to be looked upon as all in the day's work. They left strangely little mark on her even physically. Only the burn on her thigh ever troubled her and that not till years later when the scar tissue broke down and the limp, so slight as not to bother her in early years, became pronounced and painful.

The following summers were spent mostly at the Cedars where, owing to the pressure of the constantly increasing number of children, "the Barracks" was built near the big house in accordance with Aunt Hannah's design—a long narrow building with nurseries at either end of a big room on the ground floor and bedrooms on the second floor. The summer before it was built, the Pearsall Smiths and Thomases kept house at "Storm Tide," the grandparents' cottage on the edge of the sea at Atlantic City. And one late summer, for an extra holiday, the Thomases, taking their cousins Bessie King and Frank Pearsall Smith with them, went on from the Cedars to the Catskills where the Nicholson cousins were summering: "Minnie was in her element climbing rocks and mountains and taking long trips with her father and all the young folk."

Periodically, children were born. The family went through bouts of measles and whooping cough. And, for a few dreadful days, Mrs. Thomas was desperately ill of typhoid fever. Minnie, the only one of the children old enough to realize what this meant, hid under her mother's bed in an agony of grief, refusing to come out till the crisis was passed. And in the spring of 1868 Mrs. Thomas's father, with despotic benevolence, insisted upon the Thomases' moving to a more spacious house in Baltimore at 1228 Madison Avenue. They left with regret the old house where generations of Thomases had lived contentedly, but were whisked away by old Mr. Whitall, who said, "Too many angels have died there."

During the two winters, 1865-67, after her recovery from the burn, Minnie and her brother John went to a little dame's school kept by Eleanora Coale, and then for a year to Miss Norris's school. Minnie, with her passion for new ideas, enjoyed it hugely. The first school did more good in the way of discipline, as her mother remarked, than in learning. But at Miss Norris's she studied Latin and fractions, and wrote innumerable essays. She and one other little girl were the only two in the school to sympathize with the North in the Civil War. They were strong Unionists; the others, all rampant Southerners, contrived each morning to destroy the pictures of Lincoln that Minnie and her friend, possessed of an apparently unlimited supply, stuck daily in their desk tops. Minnie felt obliged to have a good many fist fights during recess in defense of Lincoln. Needless to say, she invariably won.

CHAPTER II

Childhood

I

A GROUP of Quaker parents under the leadership of Mrs. Thomas had for some time thought of starting a Friends' school rather more efficient in its instruction than either of those to which the little Thomases had gone heretofore. They persuaded to head the school Miss Rebecca Marble, a Baltimore Friend of much tact in managing children and some learning, who won Minnie's heart almost at once. And when, two years later, Miss Marble married the eldest of Dr. Thomas's young stepbrothers, a professor of history at Haverford College, Minnie rejoiced mightily. She had spied out each step in the courtship with huge delight, noting down in her diary each blush and hesitation. "Romance," she observed, "enlivens up this prosaic world of ours a heap."

As for Miss Marble, she fell in love with the whole Thomas family. They were her refuge during her two years' teaching, Mrs. Thomas her guiding angel, Minnie her naughtiest, cleverest, most beguiling pupil. Any mischief in the school could be safely ascribed to Minnie Thomas. Her enterprise seemed endless, particularly in leading the girls in valiant warfare against the boys. Many a hand-to-hand tussle was only broken up by Miss Marble's entrance, when the boys "scattered like chaff" leaving the girls, Minnie in the forefront, to receive the reprimand. The worst "blow up," as Minnie called it, happened during one recess when the boys squirted water from little pop guns at her and another girl. The girls retaliated with spit blowers and tumblers and buckets of water, drenching boys and girls alike, steps, walls, and furniture. "It was the jolliest fun I've had for ages."

Hotly as she resented any real restriction of her liberty or any injustice, she took reprimands for the most part lightly. They rather surprised her and momentarily checked her headlong career. Only once did she prove entirely recalcitrant. After an egregiously ingenious exhibition of misbehavior, during which the girls, led by Minnie, covered ceilings, walls, furniture, and even their own right shoulders with chalk, Miss Marble threatened to complain to their mothers. Minnie stormed. If her mother did not know all about it she would tell her herself. Thereupon Miss Marble showed her acumen by appealing to Minnie's heart and vanity.

For some time thereafter, Minnie concentrated on studying. But she found lessons too easy to deserve much attention. "I didn't have time to look at my lessons" occurs frequently in her diary. The family verbal facility—a gift encouraged by Quaker training —enabled her to rattle off recitations more glibly than most of the other children and helped her in writing themes. She saw through this easy fluency herself: "I wrote a composition today which she [Miss Marble] liked about Paris. It had a lot of palaver about principle and that sort of stuff. I wish I felt as good as I can write." Sometimes it seemed as if she really wrote well; then, later, reading through the themes coolly, she recognized the same old hollow work—"mere romancing," "climbing over the clouds," "an ordinary schoolgirl's composition."

Though she heartily disliked admitting her failures to anyone but herself, she faced them honestly and made innumerable good resolutions. The challenge of difficulty or opposition, as well as encouragement, and praise if she thought it deserved—she was critical of it in those days—spurred her pride and ambition. Outside school hours she and Bessie King felt they must try to learn Greek, since the study of Greek was regarded as harmful to girls and fitting only for boys; and the promise of "going into Caesar" in school, if she did well in her first year's Latin, aroused her to energetic effort. She had the unbounded satisfaction at the end of the school year of winning four prizes.

Her tastes, like those of most children, were catholic—she went through the usual phase of making collections, one summer pursuing "bugs" with the aid of all her cousins and the next amassing a hoard of "minerals"—but the zest with which she arranged insect boxes and built a mineral cabinet was characteristic of her own lifelong delight in paraphernalia. The energy and perseverance with which, interested by scientific lectures at the Peabody Institute and encouraged by her father's permission to use a corner of his laboratory, she and her cousin Bessie King "did experiments" was perhaps also exaggerated above that of most children. They wanted to build a telegraph like that constructed by one Willie Roberts, a college boy who told them about his own telegraph instrument, and were outraged when Mrs. Thomas remarked, "Oh you can't, you're only girls." "When I heard that," wrote Minnie, "I ground my teeth and swore (affirmed) that no one should say that of us—as if we hadn't as much sense, invention, and perseverance as boys."

But her favorite illustration in later years of the ardor with which little girls as well as little boys pursue knowledge was the unpleasant tale of their dissection of a mouse, the result of an avid perusal on a winter Saturday, 1870, of "a glorious book called Boys Play Book of Science." Her diary tells the story vividly: "Set a mouse trap last night in case Bess [her friend and cousin Bessie King] and I might want to get his skeleton. Caught him. But he wasn't dead. Neither Julia nor Netty will kill him so I heroically dropped the trap into a pail of water and rushed out of the room. Then took my slippers into mother's room and *sewed* and *sewed* and *sewed*. Oh the monotony of worsted work!" Luckily, Bessie arrived to free her. After roasting chestnuts, they proceeded to work on the mouse. "The poor little creature being drowned by this time we took our victim out in the yard, bared our glittering knives and commenced operations—but the horrid little mouse's fur was so soft that we couldn't make a hole in it and besides it made us sick and our hands trembled so we couldn't do a thing, but concluding it was *feminine* nonsense we made a hole and squeezed his inside out. It was the most disgusting thing I ever did. We then took off his skin . . . and put it on the fire to boil. . . . When it had boiled some, we took it again and picked all the meat off it and saved its tongue and eyes to look at through the microscope and then the mouse looked like a real skeleton. We then put it out the window to bleach."

Exalted by success they decided to invest all their pocket money, thereafter, in instruments, instead of candy, "and then we will invite our friends to see our experiments." But—"Oh my, we are unfortunate"—while Minnie walked home with Bess, the maid threw away the mouse's tongue and eyes and, worst of all, the skeleton fell out of the window and smashed. "When Bessie's father heard of the experiment he looked grave and said 'Bessie, Bessie, thee is losing all thy feminine traits.' I'm afraid I haven't got any to lose for I greatly prefer cutting up mice to sewing worsted"—a point of view from which she never wavered.

Reminiscing years later, Carey Thomas observed that she had spent most of her childhood in reading. "I cannot remember a time," she wrote, "when I did not read at every available moment." It is true that she read very fast and, her taste being romantic, went through a good many novels in spite of her parents' disapproval. She bemoaned the fact that she read sixty-five in 1871 "and only eight useful books." Among the latter, Carlyle's *Hero Worship* interested her "more than any book I ever read almost." Ruskin on architecture at that time left her cold. Not unnaturally at thirteen, she preferred *Tom Brown at Oxford* and still more enthusiastically *Jane Eyre*. "It [*Jane Eyre*] is perfectly burning and full of concentrated passion and oh so powerfully written! My throat was parched while I was reading it and cheeks fairly scorched. Oh, though I dare say it isn't a good book, yet it seems to me as if it were something worth while to be able to write something that should have power to excite and intensely interest to such a degree. The part of it where it tells about the mad woman has a perfect fascination for me."

Fortunately, for she loved it, the reading of poetry was permitted to Quakers and encouraged by Dr. Thomas. Minnie learned Shelley's "Cloud" and long passages from Mrs. Browning by heart, and spent her "currencies" on a volume of Tennyson. With Bessie King, she climbed to the housetop and, sitting in the shade of a chimney, recited "High Tide on the Coast of Lincolnshire." The literary lectures at the Peabody Institute seemed to her even more enjoyable than the scientific ones: "Lowell's lectures are worth all the other lectures put together. . . . He talked in poetry about John Milton. Oh it was elegant!" Moreover, she wrote verse herself.

Among other poems, she wrote one about a long talk on their ambitions that she and Bessie had had in the firelight before the Kings' open grate. But of all her effusions she preferred seven stanzas—all her pieces were metrically similar—called "Snowflakes," beginning:

> Softly fall the little snowflakes
> On the hard and frosty ground
> Quietly covering over foot-steps
> Making all look white around.

"Prettier than any of the others," it also pointed a satisfactory moral—

> Little snowflakes you can teach us
> In your simple childlike way
> That what ere our Father tells us
> Only straightway to obey.

This so impressed Aunt Mary that she sent it "anonimously" to a Friends' magazine, *The Leisure Moments*, where it appeared a month later, leading Minnie to hope that she had considerable poetic talent, a hope that she never entirely relinquished. The story and poem that Minnie herself sent to *Harper's*, however, were "respectfully returned"—"but il n'importe. I shan't try again."

In spite of these more or less intellectual labors, both Minnie and Bessie King gave their best energies to outdoor sports, as manly sports as possible. Parental restrictions based on propriety seldom troubled them. Bessie's mother had died and Dr. and Mrs. Thomas, occupied by manifold duties and five small children, permitted Minnie to do almost anything. After one dashing exploit in which they drove the Thomas carriage around town at a riotous pace, frightening even to themselves, Mr. King forbade his daughter to drive in the carriage, let alone manage the reins. But in skating they followed their own tomboy wills unhindered, rejoicing in cutting figures of eight and backward circles, skimming over cracking ice, venturing on ponds forbidden to skaters as dangerous. "All the rowdy ponds in the city of Baltimore are frequented by us. All the skating roughs in the city know us by sight. The upshot of it all is that when other 'ladylike girls' (if such there be that skate) have one skate, we have twenty, and so rowdyism pays in this instance as it *always* does. For my journal, the result of the cogitations of my fifteen 'summer suns' resolves itself into this advice—Go ahead! Have fun! Stop short of nothing but what is wrong (and not always that)! Respectability," proclaimed Minnie, "is nothing."

Even the quiet of Quaker meeting itself did not subdue them. Nor did the fact that they were appointed to prepare supper for forty or more members of the sewing circle or of other Friendly gatherings prevent their cutting capers, making tea with one and a half cups of green leaves instead of the customary tablespoon of black and sending the ladies home with parched, sore throats to a sleepless night. Nevertheless, the future that they planned together was a serious one. Walking up and down the aisle of the empty meetinghouse after a sewing meeting, they talked of what they intended to do and be. "We would devote ourselves to study, live together, have a library with all the splendid books with a bright wood fire always burning, dark crimson curtains and furniture, great big easy chairs where we could sit lost in books for days together, a great large table covered with papers, for we would be authors; adjoining this should be a laboratory where far into the night we would pore over crucibles mixing our mystic ingredients and perhaps making discoveries which should affect the whole world; and there we could live loving each other and urging each other on to every high and noble deed and action till all who passed should say 'their example arouses me, their books ennoble me, their deeds inspire me, and behold they are women.' "

That Minnie was the instigator of their pranks is hardly to be doubted since, during the summers at the Cedars or with her cousins in Philadelphia, she led an equally rowdy life. Her boy cousins early gave up daring her to do things because she always had a try at them even at the risk of her life. One summer when she was thirteen or fourteen, on a visit to friends, the children took turns riding a pony. Minnie had no sooner mounted than one of the boys approached waving a stick that he intended to give her for a whip. The pony shied and reared. To Minnie's withering scorn, the boy had not sense enough to drop the switch. Still he came on brandishing it. The pony reared again—"and tumbled backwards on me and there we lay rolling together. Sue and I just before had been talking about women's rights so I determined to let them see a woman didn't scream, so I didn't say a word and at last crawled out all right much to their astonishment, for they were ever so frightened. I then got on again and rode nicely. . . . The next morning after a ride on that delightful pony we went home." The entire account is highly characteristic.

During the New Year's holiday, 1871, her cousin Frank Smith confided in her that he was in love with one of her Philadelphia acquaintances, Anna Shipley. Up to this time Minnie had paid no special attention to Anna; now, her interest whetted by the problem of what Frank saw in Anna, she put her to the test, proposing that they climb the Philadelphia roofs as she and Bessie King climbed those in Baltimore. At first Anna refused; then, doubtless seeing Minnie's scorn, agreed. Not content with so hesitant a mark of Anna's courage, when they reached the roofs Minnie ran from that of one house over the next, till she "came to a very high wall below which was another roof. . . . Though I was terribly afraid, I hung and dropt so as to see if Anna would, and she, though I know she hadn't been used to climbing, did it without the slightest hesitation. Hurrah for her!"

To these escapades the grownups paid little attention, wanting the children to be independent and self-reliant and, above all, to have a good time. They had delightful times themselves on winter visits and in the summers at the Cedars. Weeks spent at the Cedars were holidays for parents as well as children, especially for Hannah Smith and Mary Thomas. They had leisure to gossip then and to discuss happenings among the Friends and their own religious views as they did the mending or strolled together over the wide sun-flecked lawns. It never occurred to Hannah Smith, entirely redoubtable herself, that any misfortune could befall the children. She put her trust in Heavenly Father, set things going according to the dictates of her own common sense, and expected them to turn out right. Mrs. Thomas, equally trusting in God but more sensitive, occasionally grew anxious. After all, responsibility

·for the enterprising Minnie fell on her shoulders. Even Aunt
Hannah had written early in the summer of 1871, when Minnie
left her brothers and cousins at the Cedars to rejoin her parents
in Baltimore, "The boys are almost too good for boys. The wild
element has taken its departure in Minnie." Bolstered up by her
sister's hardier spirit or when she was where she could see for
herself how things were going, Mrs. Thomas did not worry
unduly, but when she and Minnie were parted her imagination
got the better of her. She wrote Minnie then, "Suffer thyself for
once not to think of the most unheard of things to be done and
take thy pleasure in a quiet way."

But to Minnie, whose courage was indomitable and who gloried
in combat and movement, quiet seemed hardly desirable. At rare
intervals she might be found, her mop of dark curls tangled, her
eyes bright and intent, her body tense, crouched over some book
or problem. More often, she was seen by breathless comrades
climbing the highest trees and crags and roofs in sight, exploring
the wildest streams or woods, racing over the fields, hair flying,
cheeks pink with excitement and exertion, and, usually, clothes in
tatters. She delighted in stretching her muscles, pitting her mind
against intellectual obstacles, testing her vigor in reckless ex-
ploits, defying the brilliant sun or the gusts of icy winter wind—
all to the greater glory of womankind.[1]

2

At this date the young Thomas children were seldom permitted
a share in Minnie's rampageous life. Earlier, of course, when there
were still only three younger members of the family—John, born
in 1859; Harry, in 1861; and Bond, in 1863—they had all played
together. Long afterwards, Carey Thomas liked to recall with
tender amusement the peculiar misfortunes of young Harry, a
fair-haired, gentle little boy with a twinkle in his brown eyes.
None of the grownups, neither the parents nor the old nurse
Mama Adgee, who cared for all the children in turn, realized that
Bond, the most brilliant child of the family, the handsomest, and
later the best at sports, especially skating, spent much of his time
devising small hypocrisies to exhibit his own angelic goodness at

Harry's expense; and of course none of the children explained. But Minnie, from that time forth, became Harry's champion. Nevertheless, she led him into mishaps. As one of Minnie's hens in a fine barnyard game of her invention, he went to roost at her command on a high beam in the stable hay loft. He tried to stand on one leg in proper hen fashion, toppled off straight on the sharp steel prongs of a rake which pierced his foot and made him lame for a long time. Still worse, one day when the children were climbing the eight-foot iron fence between their house and their uncle Galloway Cheston's, Harry was caught on one of the iron prongs, which pierced his side, and swung slowly round and round as on a pivot. The other three children, who had got over safely, screamed. The negro servants rushed about helplessly. At last a passer-by fetched a ladder and lifted off the unfortunate Harry.

Dr. and Mrs. Thomas, while at their frequent meetings, often left her *in loco parentis*. On these occasions Bessie King came to supper with her and the two eldest boys. "Thee ought to be very thankful that thee has two such good brothers," complacently remarked John, whose flaming red poll and hot brown eyes betrayed his quick temper. Johnnie almost always started a quarrel. Minnie and Bess would thereupon throw him to the floor and, together with Harry, take turns sitting on him until he promised to be calm. He was obstinate and Minnie, ensconced on his head, would read aloud, usually "The Rhyme of the Duchess May" by Mrs. Browning. They would burst into tears when the lovers leaped the parapet on their roan horse, Johnnie crying no less sympathetically than the others.

But Johnnie's rages were exasperating. One day when Minnie was ten and the little Thomases were playing with their cousins on the beach at Atlantic City, he fell into a great fury, raging at the top of his lungs. It was too much. At Minnie's suggestion the others dug a hole in the wet sand just above the breaking waves and, putting him in with his arms tied to his sides, filled in the sand up to his neck, stamping it down hard. There they left him, only his head, his shock of orange curls and bright red cheeks and open mouth roaring for help, rising out of the sand. It never occurred to them that the tide was coming in and anyway they intended, after giving him a good fright, to dig him out. But they forgot. The waves began to break over his head before some people farther up the beach heard his cries and rescued him. It is not surprising, in view of the probable family reactions and her own remorse, that Minnie's diary for the next New Year, 1868, contains the following entirely uncharacteristic resolve: "I am going to be more gentle to the boys this year. I have asked Heavenly Father to help me."

By this time the family had increased. In 1865 another brother, James, who lived only a few months, and a year later a sister, Mary Grace, were born. Three years afterwards another sister, Margaret Cheston, known to the family as Daisy, was born and was followed, at two-year intervals, by a little girl, Helen Whitall, and a boy, Frank, the one named by Minnie for Helen of Troy, the other for her cousin Frank Smith, and spoken of often as "us" because they were inseparable. Finally, three years later, in 1876, still another girl, Dora, was born who lived but a year. Toward the end of the list Minnie accepted the arrivals as inevitable, if not particularly noteworthy: "I have a baby sister Helen, and Whit [her cousin Whitall] has gone to Providence and school has commenced and I have begun Vergil." Although the name "little boserations," by which the two youngest of her family went, had considerable truth in it from her point of view, she got on well enough with younger children. Her training with them had begun too early for her to put up any artificial barrier of self-consciousness. And when they were not too ever-present little botherations, they amused her.

During the summer at the Cedars, in any case, she was freed of all responsibility for youngsters. To be sure, the young Thomases and Smiths were there and the young Nicholsons came over with their elders almost daily from their near-by summer house, Linden, but the groups of cousins, massed according to age, went each its own way. In infant days at Atlantic City there had been bitter rivalry between Whit and Minnie for the leadership of their group. But as the children grew older Minnie effortlessly became the unquestioned chief.

Of young people outside her family she saw little and was far from being at ease with them. Bessie King's accusation that she felt herself superior to other Baltimore girls might have been

justified later but at this date was "very unreasonable." Shyness
and a feeling of insecurity unfamiliar to a child so safe among her
family were almost wholly responsible for Minnie's clannishness.
And with plenty of cousins always to make up a good game of any
sort the family remained for a long time self-sufficing.

Her cousin Frank Smith was the first to make any real break
in the ranks by falling in love with Anna Shipley. Their courtship,
a callow, however tenderly felt, affair, added to that of Miss
Marble and her Uncle Allen, greatly interested Minnie. Moreover,
various others of her friends began to fancy themselves in love
and, though she experienced no such tender emotion herself for
any young man, she felt a little out of the swim in having no
affair of her own. But a difficulty arose: "Suppose I should want
to fall in love . . . who on earth would there be to fall in love
with?" One thing she determined—if she fell in love, she would
do so, not tamely like most of her friends, but "with fiery overwhelming passion." Meantime, to uphold her self-respect she must
try her hand at flirting and at least outwardly equal her enamored
friends.

Yearly meeting gave her her chance. She made herself so agreeable that one of the two young men staying with the Thomases
became "right devoted and I went to meeting several times with
him." On the last evening, she was able to record gloatingly that
he asked for her picture. "I told him I didn't give my picture to
young men and so on but he was real serious and I do believe
thought I would give it to him, the goose." Having so successfully
led him up the garden path she felt no need further to prove her
prowess.

Years later, looking back on her youthful adventures, it seemed
to Carey Thomas that, whatever they had thought at the time,
Frank Smith must have been in love with her and she with him.
When preparing to write her autobiography she jotted down two
different versions of a sailing party they planned for the summer
of 1872. Between them they had saved enough money—one hundred and fifty dollars—to hire, without consulting their parents,
a boat with sleeping cabin, captain, and one sailor, in which they
proposed to sail for three weeks down the Delaware and up the
Atlantic coast. In one version of their plans she pointed out that

they were in love; but in the other, which corresponds in detail more nearly with contemporary accounts, she mentioned nothing of the sort. Very possibly, given more time, they might have fallen in love. But even the sailing party was never to take place.

Minnie's last adventure with Frank that summer, or indeed ever again, was a driving trip made by the society—"the SSS" from its motto *Primus Ludus, Supremus Ludus, Semper Ludus* —started two years before by Minnie and her older Philadelphia cousins and one or two of their friends. Packed into three carriages and a provision wagon navigated by Minnie and Anna Shipley, one managing the reins while the other held an umbrella over them both, they explored the upper reaches of the Brandywine in Pennsylvania, driving twenty-five miles a day, stopping the night at various villages, having the to-be-expected number of adventures, and doing "whatever rowdy things" they could think of. Finding the door of the meetinghouse at Ephrata locked, Minnie and Frank Smith took out a pane of glass, opened the door, and led them all in to examine the architecture. No locked door ever prevented Carey Thomas from entering any place she had determined to enter. In her late sixties, stout and handsome and very lame, on a motor drive in Sussex, finding a little flint church that she planned to visit locked, she sent the youngest of her party scouting for a window to climb through. The young friend, hesitant about breaking into churches, failed. With scorn Carey Thomas herself set about examining locks, found a window that could be opened, and dispatched the young woman through it to unlock the door from within. Then the rood screen proved to be locked. Undaunted, Carey Thomas ferreted out a space in the grill through which, by mounting a bench, she could climb. At last, quite fresh, her enthusiasm only quickened by obstacles, she found the floor brasses that she had come to see.

3

On the whole, except for Frank whom at the time she took for granted merely as a friend and the best of companions, boys seemed to Minnie less entertaining than girls and generally inferior. If she wrote "boys and girls" in her diary she quickly crossed it out, substituting "girls and boys." More and more she was becoming jealous for woman's equality to man. It bowled her over to hear, during a lecture on Joan of Arc, that the parents of a girl and boy of precisely similar abilities and early training would encourage advanced education for the boy but would put under lock and key the girl who wished for a like opportunity. "Oh my," cried Minnie, "how terrible, how fearfully unjust. A girl certainly should do what she chooses as well as a boy. When I grow up—we'll see what will happen." Fuel was added to the flame by a friend of her father who walked home from a meeting with her talking all the way about "the sacred shrine of womanhood." He said that "no matter what splendid talents a woman might have she couldn't use them better than by being a wife and mother, and then went off," wrote Minnie indignantly, "in some high faluting stuff about the strength of women's devotion, completely forgetting that all women ain't wives and mothers and they, I suppose, are told to fold their hands and be idle waiting for an eligible offer. Stuff! Nonsense!"

All her life, of course, she had to combat similar complacencies, the more galling because they never ceased to give her an uneasy feeling, as she confessed in her old age, that they might contain a grain of truth. Uncertainty, then as later, doubtless contributed to the overemphatic statement of opposing arguments. "If our brains *do* weigh less," she fumed after a lecture "on Soul and Body" in which the speaker had announced that women's brains weighed a few ounces less than men's, "what does it show? Why, that for hundreds and thousands of years women haven't had the same education as men, they have not had the same chances for developing, that with all their force and power men have been keeping them down and forcing them to remain in the narrow sphere of *household* duties and anything beyond that was in the highest degree 'indecorous, unrefined, coarse, unladylike.' What a burning shame! . . . Well! one thing I am determined on is that by the time I die *my* brain shall weigh as much as any man's if study and learning can make it so and then I'll leave it in the hands of some physiologist to be weighed so as after that no miserable man can stand up on a platform and tell a miserable audience that my brain weighed 'a few ounces less than any other man's.' Just wait till equal education takes place and see if that remark can be made!!!"

Worse still, she discovered that her own father shared this masculine arrogance. When she remarked that she disbelieved St. Paul as far as she possibly could anything in the Bible because he seemed to her very unjust to women, her father replied that St. Paul had been right, "that *sweetness, gentleness, gracefulness, beauty, love* belonged to a woman; that power, strength, force, intellect, to a man; that a wife must reverence her husband; that the man always took the lead and was made by God to do so"—a homily well calculated to stir Minnie's anger. "Oh it is too unjust, too horrible, that things should be so. Of course I don't believe it. I believe that I have as much sense as any boy I know . . . and more too. And if I live we'll see who'll be worth the most. It seems to me I'd die if I could do *anything* to show that a woman is equal to a man."

Minnie had long since grasped the fact that her father, in spite of his belligerent faith in man's power, by no means ruled the family. No man, however orthodox his opinions upon this subject, married to a Whitall woman could hope to carry out such doctrine. To be sure, with his quick temper, Dr. Thomas laid down the law impetuously. When it agreed with the dictates of her conscience and intelligence, his wife saw that it was obeyed: she had learned what she called "woman's lesson, to give up her will to the lords of creation." When it did not, she quietly overlooked it or supported the opposition patiently and tactfully until her husband inevitably capitulated. She knew quite well that after the first explosion Dr. Thomas, definite as his pronouncements might be, was too warmly humane to act on them. This state of affairs hurt Minnie's pride in her parents. To Mrs. Thomas, however, the situation seemed merely the way of the world, regrettable perhaps but to be borne with grace. She had seen enough of the injustice caused by convention, both to the poorer women among whom her charitable enterprises led her and to her women acquaintances in their marital relations, to be wary of it. Slower to pass judgment, more flexible by nature than her husband, she felt convention less binding. She believed that women should be given independent legal status and, also, that each woman was entitled to an unprejudiced judgment of her individual case on its own merits, refusing to condemn a woman who obtained a divorce under such circumstances. Conventions were, to her mind, useful and necessary but not to be accepted untested. She could understand Minnie's desire for a good education since she too in her youth, as her diaries show, had longed for one and had continued to deplore its lack, believing that it would help rather than hinder her in fulfilling woman's obligations. Never sympathizing with the belief in the equality of the sexes to which her sister Hannah was rapidly coming, she upheld the doctrines of feminine propriety largely because one lost more than one gained in flouting them.

Experience convinced Hannah Smith, on the other hand, that women were much like men and should be given equal opportunities to develop. She welcomed eagerly new points of view and believed in crusading for what she found right in them. Though Mrs. Thomas besought her to stick to religion and not enter upon the questions of equal suffrage and women's rights in preaching from the public platform, she discussed these topics with her sister at length. From their voluminous letters and from summer talks at the Cedars her aunt Hannah's unconventional ideas filtered through to Minnie and, being directly in line with what she wanted, encouraged her natural bent. Moreover, Dr. Thomas himself fed grist to Minnie's mill. He was on the directing boards of several male institutions of learning and anxious to examine new educational theories. Failing to perceive where his daughter's proposal to take part herself in educational advancement might lead, he discussed matters openly and with enthusiasm, never thinking to check her interest at a point where perhaps it might have been checked.

Minnie's aspirations, thus fostered by her elders, were quickened by association with Frank Smith. Since from earliest childhood Minnie's spirit of competition had been spurred by efforts to keep up with Frank, four years older than she and four years richer in experience, nothing could so stimulate her desire for advanced education as his assured achievement of it. A boy, he would be sent as a matter of course first to boarding school, then to college. To uphold her own, and to make her individual contribution to their friendship, she needed a background of equal learning.

Temperamentally opposite, Minnie and Frank played into each other's hands, Frank's caution and quiet intelligence often bringing her down to earth and setting her straight, her fire kindling him. The family, recognizing this, encouraged the friendship, calling her "Frank's girl." When, in 1869, Frank went to West Town school and missed part of Minnie's visit to the Cedars, Aunt Hannah wrote her mother, "I myself regret exceedingly her missing him for I really believe her companionship would have done him far more good than the whole of West Town. She has already been a great advantage to him in developing his poetical tastes etc. and I prize her companionship for him more than that of anyone else." Frank on his side influenced Minnie equally for she greatly admired him. Indeed to the whole family, elders as well as children, Frank most nearly of all the cousins approached the ideal in mind and character—a fact of which he was well aware, since the family never spared either praise or blame. The other children might be docile enough young Quakers, following their parents' lead, but Frank was independently "a Christian."

To the Smiths religion formed the foreground as well as the background of their lives, providing a conscience-free outlet for the abounding vitality of both the downright Hannah and her more mystical husband, Robert. In their energetic search for religious sustenance they grasped at various faiths and doctrines outside the Quaker fold and heralded to the world each fresh aspect of the truth as it was revealed to them. Careful as they were to respect the reserves of their children, whose self-reliance they cherished, the unconscious eagerness with which they hailed any manifestation of religious grace inevitably exerted pressure. It speaks well for both the Smiths' physically wholesome way of life and the sturdy thoughtfulness of the elder son Frank that he became neither a nervous wreck nor an unbearable prig. He accepted without question his early teachings and did his best to comply with Heavenly Father's wishes—as he himself interpreted them. His relations to Heavenly Father were his own affair. He rarely spoke in the constant prayer meetings led by one or the other of his parents; he looked with a tolerant rather than a sympathetic eye upon the revival and camp meetings to which they frequently took him. Such outpourings might be very well for others; they were not for him. His parents knew, nevertheless, that however "normal" and game-loving and boisterous he might appear, he spent much time in solemn examination of how to become a good Christian and, as far as a boy might, had achieved balanced perfection.

Minnie had been subjected to no such spiritual gymnastics as he. Doctrinal discussions, to be sure, especially when riddled with inconsistencies, piqued her curiosity. She was enchanted to learn that her parents did not believe literally all that they had preached to her. "I don't see how people can be content to live without studying all about it," she wrote with enthusiasm upon learning that "Miss Marble and Uncle Allen and even Father won't positively say that Adam and Eve were created all at once." But the interests of her parents lay less in such problems then in philanthropy. Equally desirous as the Smiths of living the good life, they turned to action rather than to religious speculation; and good deeds, which often interfere with personal freedom, are apt to arouse rebellion in a child. It irked her that her mother's attention should be diverted from herself by a woman whose only claim not to be relegated to the kitchen with Eliza, the cook, was that she happened to be a Friend; and she resented the fact that she had to listen in Bible class to a woman preaching about simplicity who must have spent an hour or two arranging the "horrible little curls" that adorned her head.

In spite of these natural if rebellious reactions, she still held to her parents' standards and admired wholeheartedly Frank Smith, who fulfilled them with such success. To him, more often than to anyone else, she confided her dreams of noble deeds. His commendation of her suggestion that they apply the legends of King Arthur's knights to their own lives gratified her. Frank wanted to be a lawyer though he doubted, as he wrote her, his ability to become a great lawyer because he lacked the necessary eloquence—an uncommon deficiency in one of his family. Doubt of her abilities seldom troubled Minnie. Only at rare intervals did she fear that her daydreams might come to nothing: "I'm so afraid I'll be just like everyone else in the end." Her real difficulty lay in settling on one line amid the many that interested her. At one moment she decided to take up a science, geology or chemistry; at another, to become a writer of first-rate books. Then again she said: "More and more every day I'm making up my mind to be a doctor for when I grow up I can't be dependent on father or mother and I ain't going to get married and I don't want to teach school, so what can I do. I can't imagine anything worse than living a regular young lady's life and I have a taste for doctoring and could study at Philadelphia and mother and father would *have* to let me if I was determined. I don't care if everybody would cut me. I despise society and I *detest* girls"—presumably "young ladies."

Both she and Frank were convinced that, whatever they might do, they needed the best education obtainable. "Day by day," wrote Minnie, "I'm more and more waking up to the fact that an awful amount of drudgery and study *must* be gone through before you can write of, or understand, a solitary thing." Frank's parents, of course, approved of his entering Haverford in 1870, the Quaker college on whose Board of Managers sat two of his uncles, Minnie's father and James Whitall, as well as many family friends. And when he became disillusioned with the life and the academic standing of Haverford, they agreed to his transfer to Princeton. The managers of Haverford and the faculty seemed to him to be turning the college into a boarding school fit only for little boys instead of a place where people lived an intelligent adult life. Worst of all, there was nowhere to study in quiet and, he observed petulantly, never could be. "Each fellow," he told Minnie, "ought to have a room for himself so as to study rightly; the collecting room [the common room] here is a perfect hubbub all the time."

Frank's difficulties, all discussed at length with Minnie, can be seen influencing her even years later when she was faced with establishing a college for women. In the seventies, however, her major interest lay in obtaining an education for herself—a good deal more complicated problem than for Frank. Education beyond that given in the secondary school was not regarded as necessary or even advisable for girls. A few individuals, on their own initiative, obtained further instruction through private tuition. No one in Minnie's circle had broken convention by going to any one of the few institutions of learning then open to women.

This educational discrimination whetted her natural desire to fly in its face. "My firm fixed purpose is to have a thorough knowledge of French, Latin, Greek and German," she asserted, "and then to read and study carefully all the principal authors especially the old German metaphysicians and to go high in mathematics, for even if they ain't of any 'practical' use they strengthen the mind. I think I would like to take some science for my specialty and then my greatest hope and amibition is to be an author —an essayist, an historian—to write hearty earnest true books that may do their part towards elevating the human race." Having formed this somewhat expansive program, it behooved her to find ways of carrying it out. Action always followed directly on the heels of Minnie's thought.

Miss Marble had a friend who had been for a year at Vassar College. "Oh my," exclaimed Minnie, "I *must* go to Vassar. Miss Marble says she thinks I might possibly be prepared to enter the Freshman class by next summer if I study real hard till then. . . . And I really think mother might possibly let me go." No one of her elders opposed her new amibition; but the hopelessness of making them take it seriously filled her with despair. "I do want to go to Vassar," she groaned, "for there is one thing I can do and that is study. There's nothing else worth doing and how can I do it at home." Fortunately, Miss Marble's friend appeared in Baltimore and persuaded Mrs. Thomas that the plan was feasible.

Frank Smith, of course, had been the recipient of each new burst of aspiration, each fresh moan of anxiety. He might twit her about her "equal suffrage and all such huffage" and remark witheringly when asking her advice, "not that I value it, but just to see what thee says." He might chill her ardor with salutary doubt: "Now, why should thee or B. [Bessie King] or I, be any more likely to succeed than the thousands of others who have been just as ambitious and just as talented?" He might exhort her "to put a little practical" into her dreams. But in all this he was quite certain of her comeback. No doubt of his would weaken her determination or quench her fire. She had no fear of failure. Passionately, she hurried on—"Oh," she wrote, "I despise every-

body for living along so quietly and here I go and live along humdrum like all the rest of the world. I wish the air were pure
oxygen and then, as it says in our chemistry, our life would sweep
through its fevered burning course in a few hours and we would
live in a perfect delirium of excitement and would die vibrating
with passion, for anything would be better than this lazy sluggish
life."

And so Frank egged her on. "Do hurry to the Cedars," he
urged. "The Philadelphia Library will not be shut up, so we can
have that all summer. Do you know yet what books we want? I
think abstract subjects afford an endless field of fun to us. We
have hardly ever thought about them before and they have the
charm of being fresh. It is a perfect joy to me to talk about them."
Abstract subjects attracted Minnie only if they might be translated or applied to her own action, for act she must: "I must *do*
something," was her constant cry. To produce a list of books,
however, suited her admirably.

The list, alas, was never to be used, for that summer brought
the abrupt end of the two cousins' companionship. Shortly after
their return to the Cedars from the driving trip in Pennsylvania,
Frank fell ill. He grew worse so rapidly that, almost before the
family realized that he was down with typhoid fever, his life hung
in danger. "Today [August 4th] at 4 o'clock," wrote Minnie,
"Frank died. . . . I had *no idea* of his dying till today as I was
asleep on the sofa they waked me up and said 'Get up. Frank is
dying.' I went in his room. . . . I never knew what death *was*
before. I hardly knew there was such a thing. But now—oh it
seems too dreadful. I can hardly believe it. Frank's and my lives
have been so intermingled ever since we were children and we
planned all our future together and everything and to think that
I'll have to go on alone." "For the first and last time in my life,"
she wrote long afterwards, "I had illusions when Frank died. I
imagined that he was not dead. I saw him breathe in his coffin
and I begged my father not to let him be buried alive." There was
no one to whom she could pour out her intimate feeling or with
whom to pick up her life, as Bessie King had been in Europe
since May. She could only vow to carry out her plans, to do some-

thing worthy of Frank, to become a "real Christian." For the time being her zest was gone.

Toward early autumn *Frank, The Record of a Happy Life*, Hannah Smith's biography of her elder son, was published. At once it had great success among Friends and, before the year was out, had been republished in England and, in translation, in France. Its influence, as all the letters that came to Hannah Smith testify, was phenomenal; and the book still brings royalties to her heirs. She schooled herself to be thankful that Frank had escaped possible unhappiness and to rejoice that through "his book" he carried on the work that he had longed to do of converting and helping his fellows to a purer Christian life. Minnie, too, found some comfort in this, though by no means as much as she had been taught she should. In her less disciplined reaction the account of their happy relationship, recalling her loss, made her even more lonely. She could take little pride in her inclusion in *The Life* as the confidante of so admirable a youth, since her family as well as her own honesty pointed out the discrepancy between Frank's state of grace and her own lack of it. "I am glad there is nothing in the book that makes thee out better than thee is," remarked her mother, gently indicating room for improvement.

Largely in an effort to distract her and help her to start afresh, her parents arranged with Bessie King's father on his return from Europe to send the two girls to a Quaker school in northern New York.

CHAPTER III

Boarding School

I

WHEN, in the autumn of 1872, the question of what school they should go to came up, both Minnie and Bessie plumped for the Howland Institute, a girls' school recently started at Union Springs on the eastern shore of Lake Cayuga near Ithaca, New York. They were impressed by the adult character and the intelligence of its catalogue, shown them by Hannah Smith; it promised sound and hard work and no namby-pamby cherishing of young ladies. The program must have influenced Carey Thomas later when she herself was laying plans for schools. Even in the 1940's it would be up to date. History, for instance, was to be taught to the younger girls by means of games and to the older girls, in part, by dramatic representations arranged by themselves. The heads of the school did not believe in rules or coercion. They intended to make the work so interesting that the pupils would wish to learn—and, moreover, to learn not only facts but how to weigh facts and to think for themselves. Modern methods were to be applied in the courses preparatory for college: in science, laboratory experiments were to be made, field trips organized, microscopes, telescopes, and other apparatus used; in the classics, the philological and historical as well as the literary approach would be followed. In the final term of the senior year a course in the history of civilization was to be given. Although competent teachers of the fine arts would be provided, pupils wishing instruction in either music or painting must agree to add an extra year in order to complete the curriculum. The health of the students, too, was cared for: in the gymnasium, pupils were required to take half an hour's calisthenics daily; and outdoor exercise, such as walking or boating on Cayuga Lake or skating on the near-by ponds, was encouraged. Each term a series of lectures on hygiene was given; and once a week a woman physician visited the school not only to attend the sick but to talk with the pupils about their individual problems. Finally, the catalogue pointed out succinctly the harmful effect upon pupils' work of visits to family or friends during term time. "A little forecast during vacation," it concludes, "will obviate the necessity of calling pupils away from school to replenish their wardrobes or to visit the family dentist."

Dr. and Mrs. Thomas and Mr. King, hardly less impressed than the two girls by this stern educational regimen, and knowing both the founder George Howland and the president Robert Howland to be good Quakers, agreed to their daughters' choice and in October escorted them to Union Springs. The school proved to be delightful—the teachers interesting, the pupils "very polite," the buildings spacious and dignified, set in pleasant grounds that ran down to the lake. Minnie and Bessie were established together in a large, comfortably furnished room, to be swept and tidied daily by themselves and heated by a small stove.

The stove, which with the oil lamp caused extreme anxiety to Mrs. Thomas, who knew her daughter's headlong awkwardness too well, hardly served its purpose. As the first winter drew on the house grew cold and damp and by the second, steam heat had to be installed. But the stove remained useful for cooking the oysters and bacon and other food sent from home for between-meal snacks. With the food often came other gifts, a black and scarlet table cover, or much needed clothes—the two thin lawn dressing sacks that Minnie wore while studying on hot June afternoons on the balcony; a balmoral short enough to wear under her black gymnasium uniform; a smart dress-up polonaise; an apron to cover the rent made in her dress as she struggled to free herself from the mud into which she had sunk four inches above her knees while on an early spring walk by a stream.

Sometimes gifts for Minnie were packed among Bessie's things because the Thomases could not afford to send her a whole boxful. "Thee must remember," wrote her mother, "that thee is a *costly* girl, and a very *dear* one. If we had the money thee knows we would not grudge it, but we have not got it." The Whitall family, as usual, stood behind the Thomases with timely gifts for necessities. But it was a constant trial to Mrs. Thomas to have nothing left over with which to give her children all the fun and luxuries they wanted, and she longed to save her beloved eldest daughter from any need to scrimp especially during her first terms away, when she thought her a little homesick. Minnie herself had been horrified by the amount her school wardrobe had cost—seventy-four dollars—but, helped out by an occasional five dollars or so from her Whitall grandparents, she took her parents' adjurations fairly lightly. When there was anything she really wanted, she made no bones of saying so clearly. For the most part she was too busy with work and play to think of money.

The "classical course," upon which the two girls entered as juniors, was really the equivalent of the first two years of college work. The family expected Minnie to do well; even Harry in his one short letter asked, evidently sure of his answer, "Is thee first in thy lessons?" Almost at once her alert eagerness to learn drew the attention of her teachers, especially of Miss Slocum, teacher of metaphysics and political science, and of Dr. Zaccheus Test, who taught her Latin and Greek. She worked, she said, "like the mischief," though it was not easy for her to buckle down: "Oh I do love fun so much and I do really like to study too and they don't gee I'm afraid." This dilemma, added to a very real interest in the subjects she was studying, led her into excesses most alarming to her parents. "Last night," she wrote them, "I sat up until a quarter to three and read Paley"—which immediately drew from her mother the reply: "But how terrible it was in you to sit up all night to study! I don't think Paley can digest at the rate of so many pages a day—thee will have gone through the book, but it will take another reading to make its ideas thy own—if indeed its ideas are worth making thy own. Not having read it I cannot say." For all her disarming, amused tolerance Mrs. Thomas constantly urged Minnie to be careful not to work too hard, pointing out that "it does not pay." By her second year the whole family had become alarmed lest Minnie break down from overstudy, and her uncle Jim Whitall offered to finance an extra year at the school if she would spread her work thinner.

The anxiety was quite superfluous. Minnie was extremely healthy. Even the effects of her childhood burn were disappearing. The slight limp with which it had left her was so little evident that her mother exhorted her to "be mindful of thy walk. There had been such an improvement I want to see it go on to complete success." With her abounding energy unabated, Minnie had been quick to take her place in the forefront of all the activities and pranks in the school and was long remembered as the promoter of all the mild devilments in which the girls indulged. The class prophecy, written by one of her schoolmates at the time of their graduation, in which her ambition is achieved, as her fellows had no doubt it would be, gives their view of her. In it she is a brusque, efficient, if absent-minded and kindly, middle-aged doctor who welcomes patients gruffly, blusters, grumbles, and cures any ailment in no time with strong measures. Her face is red, her hair insecurely "knotted up à la professional" with a single hairpin. After a twenty-minute search she claps a monstrous hat on the back of her head, drags "from under an immense pile of books, tin boxes, preserve jars, dresses and umbrellas, a pair of big buckskin gloves." She is always late; and her expletive is, "Great Zeus."

The family doubtless recognized the essential harum-scarum, energetic likeness of this caricature, for they knew the hurly-burly in which Minnie lived. They expected her, however, to be prominent among her fellows and, more than that, to influence them for their good. "Who among the girls are Christians?" queried Mrs. Thomas in an early letter, for she felt that association with other young Christians would be "a real stimulus" to Minnie. "I like thee," she said, "to cultivate Friends." She wondered how the others could ever "come to the knowledge of the truth—their ideas are so mixed up," and warned her daughter, "You will find it much more profitable to think about what you *do* believe than what you do not believe. Just observe if this is not the case." She thought that Minnie in her talks with the other girls "could help them to definite and clear and decided views on some points," and suggested her holding a Bible class on First Days. Knowing Minnie's love of argument, however, she urged her not "to start any questions which are only vague ideas in your own mind—everybody might not understand you."

Long as were the letters that Mrs. Thomas wrote giving her reasoned disagreement with them, she was not alarmed by Dr. Test's "extraordinary religious views." Others, however, were less confident. "Dr. Rhoads," she wrote, "says he would not have a daughter at Howland's under Dr. Test's influence and Miss Slocum's. He would prefer the conservatism of Haverford—this is a secret though." But she was sure that Minnie was too right thinking to be affected by Dr. Test's errors. In actual fact, though she was not conscious of it at the time, they did affect Minnie, showing her the naïveté and certain inconsistencies in her own youthful acceptance of the faith taught her at home. She wanted to be a Christian, but, as she told her aunt Hannah, "I ain't consecrated yet a bit. I think it's harder for me than anybody else." She was quite frank in her letters home about her religious failures. Indeed, she wrote frankly every week to her parents about everything that went on in the school and in her own head. She hardly needed her mother's encouraging assurance that "every detail interested" them and that she might "write as freely and grumbly" as she liked.

2

The arrival of Minnie's letters was a great event in the Baltimore family's week. After the parents had read them, and read them again to each child in the family and to the old nurse, they were sent off to the Whitall grandparents and Aunt Hannah. "Blessed be the man who invented letters," exclaimed Mrs. Thomas, though she was occasionally obliged to delete certain passages in Minnie's. In reading to the boys she skipped Minnie's account of a cider party. "Indeed," she admonished her daughter, "I am doubtful about the propriety of it for thee. Thee knows the dangers of getting a fondness for such things are fearful. And for the sake of the *example* if for nothing else I would most *decidedly* avoid the *cider* in the future. Buy cream."

Carey Thomas was wont to say, in later life, with the often ill-founded consciousness of superiority of one possessing scholarly training topped off by a certificate of learning, that she never heard discussed at home any books or any intellectual subjects. Yet her mother's letters to her, and still more her father's, attest their interest in literary, scientific, and educational subjects. It may have made her squirm with scorn to hear that while her mother wrote her, her father was lying on the sofa laughing over the child's book entitled *Pet*. But she should have welcomed the following letter from him concerned with the Johns Hopkins University of which he was a trustee: "This morning I went for the first time with Uncle Galloway to Clifton to look a little into the situation of the future college domain. We found it much neglected. . . . . I have been much engrossed and deeply interested in reading up University subjects. . . . Do find out," he added, in what proved for Minnie to be a pregnant sentence, "about the success of Cornell and whether it is true, as has been alleged, that in order to get students they were obliged to lower the standard for admission." Dr. Thomas rarely missed a lecture at the Peabody Institute. Even Mrs. Thomas found time to hear Tyndall speak, though it grieved her that "a man who had such a profound admiration for the beautiful working of the laws of nature should be so profoundly ignorant of Him who set them all in order."

Minnie rejoiced whenever her mother was able to indulge herself in an intellectual pleasure of any sort and was dismayed when Mrs. Thomas wrote, "I am kept so busy all the time that I do not even get time to think." She began to blame her father for the many children and—though she was fond of them—to resent the children themselves. But Mrs. Thomas's frequent complaints of time consumed by household cares and children seem to resolve themselves into the usual longings felt by most spirited people to be something other than they are and to do something more than they can do. Expressed with the Whitall family eloquence they sounded more serious than perhaps they were, for her letters show her as both being eminently happy and finding time for what interested her most—religious and philanthropic activities. The fact that neither these pursuits nor the public affairs of which her mother wrote in the least interested Minnie doubtless contributed to her growing feeling that her mother's was a dog's life. Mrs. Thomas herself sometimes twitted her daughter about this indifference: of Dorothy Trumbull's faith cure, she remarked, "if thee is sufficiently informed about the facts and realities of the times in which thee lives to know what that is. If she were a fictitious character, one of George Eliot's heroines, thee would doubtless know all about her."

In spite of Minnie's often preoccupied response, Mrs. Thomas continued to write of all that lay nearest her heart. She told Minnie of the prayer meeting at which Caroline Talbott made Daisy and Gracie cry abundantly—"Does thee remember her last visit here when thee and I cried so much?" she asked. She had, she said, a *wonderful* time visiting and praying with Caroline Talbott in the worst drinking houses in Baltimore. She had been drawn into the temperance movement almost unconsciously and was as "busy as a bee putting it on the right foundation." During the rest of her life it was to be one of her major interests. "What do you think of the woman's movement in Ohio against rum?" she asked Minnie. "I think it's grand!" With two other ladies she paid "a real touching visit" to a murderer in jail: "a really sweet looking young man, most courteous and attractive, very grave and respectful. We talked to him and prayed and wept and he thanked us and we told him we should go on praying for him and then came away." Of the frequent prayer meetings she was wont to say with considerable satisfaction as well as amusement, "The Thomas family as usual exercised their gifts." They were good speakers, all of them fluent and emphatic. And to improve them, Mrs. Thomas wrote, "we have an elocution class just in the family, for practice, on 6th day nights—we have a capital book about it." A remark which showed a trust almost as complete as her daughter's was to become in the printed word.

But Mrs. Thomas was by no means entirely unworldly. Her gossipy letters were weighted with Chesterfieldian advice: "Be sure to behave like a lady under all circumstances, do nothing that will attract the least notice"; "above all don't show any disgust at table"—this, in response to the not uncommon complaint of school meals; "remember *not* to cross thy wrists—but lay thy hands quietly and reposefully in thy lap." Accepting human frailty, she frankly countered it: "You will get hints from the girls about certain ways of avoiding strict obedience to the rules but I advise you to be very cautious *whose* advice you follow. You will find there is a great difference in the standing of the various girls."

She gently pointed out that the girls upon whom her daughter looked down were doubtless in some things her superiors—besides, she added, "few people are remarkable." "I think, my darling, thee has got a little up into the airy mind in thy opinion of the teachers and girls. . . . Avoid a critical judging spirit. . . . *Manifest* a real interest in people."

On the other hand, when the girls, under Minnie's leadership, rebelled against an examination suddenly dropped upon them, she wrote with a sympathy that many years later might have made Carey Thomas, with the shoe on the other foot, shudder: "We all concluded that you quelled the insurrection among your teachers with great promptness and efficiency. Really it was expecting a great deal of you to remember every book without cramming." But she knew too well her daughter's occasional wish to *èpater le bourgeois* to be drawn when reports came of much relished escapades. "I'm afraid thee will not be well long," she remarked in amusement, "if thee wanders off without any wraps, and sits down romantically on rocks beside babbling brooks."

When two friends go away to school together almost always they make new friends and the old tie is loosened. In this case Minnie, shyer, much less experienced in the world than the mother-less and traveled Bessie, responded freshly to new influences and was the first to break away. Soon after her arrival she and another girl "smashed on each other," as she put it. Bessie was extremely annoyed; a bitter quarrel ensued during which neither roommate spoke to the other until Aunt Hannah, warned by Mrs. Thomas, visited the school and patched matters up. "Bessie and thee must agree to disagree on some friends," wrote Minnie's mother, "but do it gently and courteously." Somewhat later she observed, "I think you are rather lovesick this term. I would do as little of that as will go down for I think it must be rather sickening. I never had any fancy for it. Real nice earnest talk is another thing." But—in answer to a further letter from Minnie—"I guess thy feeling is quite natural. I used to have the same romantic love for my friends. It is a *real pleasure.*"

Mrs. Thomas's sympathy was as unfailing as her practical wisdom. Feeling strongly the value of friendship, she told Minnie to invite her new friends home with her for the holidays. By a little doubling up they could always be stowed somewhere in the Thomas house. Only when Minnie, her heart wrung as it always was by the plight of her friends, asked her parents to lend two hundred dollars to a penniless girl who longed to follow the career of a singer, did Mrs. Thomas protest. The girl, she remarked tartly, had a family of her own to appeal to; and the Thomases could find barely enough money to finance their own children. "I expect thee dear daughter to keep thy common sense, and thy private judgment."

Usually in matters of conduct she set the alternative before Minnie and left the decision to her. To Minnie's request for permission to buy a class ring, she replied: "If thee ever wears a ring on thy finger, or earrings in thy ears it will not be with my consent. Father seems to care less about it than I do—and it is possible that he may choose to give it to thee if thee asks him. . . . If it cost but a trifle I should not object to thy getting it, and wearing it on thy chain, but I cannot think it right to spend $15 for it. Now thee has my deliverance on the subject and thee must decide for thyself." Minnie, of course, did not buy the ring. Such generous and reasonable placing of the responsibility on her shoulders might have resulted, had Minnie been less honestly determined to be admirable, in strengthening her selfishness and teaching her to rationalize her wishes in the pleasantest possible manner. And it might have embittered her when, nine years later, her mother, mellowed by experience, accepted from Aunt Hannah a ring for Grace, saying that she did not disapprove of anything "except nose rings perhaps." But by that time Minnie accepted the fact that her mother's judgments might change and relax with change in circumstance.

Only once did this method of coping with Minnie's headstrong career fail, and that was when Minnie was swept into an escapade on the spur of the moment, carried away by excitement and fun. Her mother commented upon Minnie's dressing as a man in an "opera" given by the schoolgirls: "Thee knows how I feel about thy dressing up as a man. It is repugnant to my taste. I do suppose it is great fun but I think it is not nice. It would be simply disgusting if any men were present and I don't like it anyhow. Thee must not mind my criticizing darling, thee knows I have to be perfectly truthful with thee." But the charms of dramatic representation exceeded Minnie's self-control. Not many weeks later the girls gave "a wedding" and she could not resist taking the part of a man. Innocent of guile, she wrote a full description of the affair to her parents. The reply came promptly: "I am both surprised and mortified," wrote Mrs. Thomas. "After such a positive and unqualified disapproval of it—I had entire confidence that thee would not do it again. I shall now be forced to make it a *positive command. It must not* be done again." Indeed she felt so strongly about it that in her next letter she said that she could "no longer recommend the school to a creature" if it continued to be the custom for the girls to masquerade as men. "If you scholars care for the reputation of the school one iota, you will put a stop to it, as far as in you lies." No more was heard of Minnie as an actor of male parts. And Mrs. Thomas's doubt of the good influence of the school evaporated. Both parents felt that Minnie had benefited by her two years at Howland, and when Dr. Thomas was asked to make the commencement address he accepted readily.

His speech was a strong one, and informing from the point of view of his own psychology as well as of the history of women's education. In founding the Howland Institute for the training of girls with college preparatory courses, George Howland, he said, had been carrying out the traditional policy of the Society of Friends. From the first, no religious community had ever accorded to woman higher position, both in the church and in the family, than was accorded to her by the founders of the society and their successors. "Given equal traits of character and mind, surely that woman is most fitted to be useful who has most highly developed and trained her intellect. . . . The power to gain such culture constitutes the undoubted right to its attainment, and why should culture and intellectual training, in its highest sense, do other than intensify a woman's noblest power? Surely in this day we need trained and cultured woman," he concluded, "we need her aid in the vast struggles that today are arranging the good and evil forces of society. . . . But nowhere does the need of the purifying and ennobling influence of culture and refinement more prominently appear than in the present home and social life of our country."

"Well," Miss Slocum was overheard to say when he had

finished, "I know the reason Dr. Thomas could talk so grandly about women—look at the women he has known," nodding her head toward Mrs. Thomas, whose charm had as usual subjugated everyone. It was true enough that his admiration for her had been the inspiration of his reasoning. Undoubtedly he believed all that he said. But his question, "Who shall deny to women the opportunity of obtaining advanced intellectual training," remained for him merely rhetorical—an abstract proposition. He was far from realizing the fact that in commending the opening of all avenues of learning "to the feet of all comers, whether shod in man's sandal or women's slipper" he was committing himself to a particular line of action in regard to his daughter's future. Mrs. Thomas, on the other hand, to whom, as to her daughter, pronouncements of faith were of little importance unless acted upon, realized the implications as well as the sound reasonableness of her husband's speech and held him to them when the time came. As for Minnie, all that he said fell in with her beliefs and desires, and she accepted his good faith at face value. The family stage was, in fact, set for struggle.

The commencement, however, was wholly satisfactory to both parents and daughters. All available accounts of it were kept carefully by Dr. Thomas in the scrapbook where he was to paste equally laudatory clippings reporting later episodes in his daughter's career. Minnie wrote the class poem and replied to the toasts at the class dinner, and on the day of the exercises received much praise for her essay—as indeed did every member of the graduating class for their essays. One by one, "in spotless robes of white with here and there a floral ornament and immaculate white kid gloves, each member read an original essay of considerable length and moral purport." Upheld by the presence, among the dignitaries on the stage, of her parents, of whom, as she confided later to her aunt Hannah, she felt very proud, Minnie was able to read her essay aloud without her accustomed shyness in public—"I did not mind speaking at all." The local paper in its proud paean of praise of school, teachers, pupils, and exercises, said that "Miss Thomas' essay on the subject of 'choice' was a valuable contribution to the rich literary feast enjoyed thus far and she was deservedly complimented with numerous bouquets at its conclusion"—each performer was showered with bouquets. "The scholarly essay produced, combined with its originality and the keen perception of human nature manifested by the reader, betokened a well schooled mind, capable of expressing itself in the choicest language. Man's tendency to seek after earthly happiness and pleasures alone, to the exclusion of all else, was rightly deprecated by the essayist among other things, and the audience seemingly appreciated her effort." The depth of thought and practical wisdom of all the essays, observed the enthusiastic journalist, showed "that the young ladies at Howland are made to think as well as learn."

Before Minnie left for home, Miss Slocum called her in to receive the suitable farewell benediction. She had watched Minnie carefully and discovered that she could go to the roots of things and understand them. In a word, Minnie was the only girl she had seen with "the power of mind" to advance women's position in the world. "What we want in the cause of women," she concluded, "are not doctors and lawyers (there are plenty of those). We want scholars. You have, I think, as fair a start as any boy of seventeen in the country and now I want you to be a great scholar. I don't think you will be content to merely receive and not originate. . . . I want great things of you."

Needless to say, Minnie was impressed. Miss Slocum seemed to her "the noblest woman next to mother and aunt Hannah" whom she knew. "What could I say," she wrote with awe in her diary, chronicling the episode at length, "except that I cared more for her opinion than anyone else's, that the thing she wanted was the one thing I had dreamed of, that I would try to show her that I was worthy of her confidence and trust. And so I will. I will devote my life to study and try to work some good from it." In a trice, the old plan of becoming a doctor went by the boards and Minnie's purpose was bent toward the cause with which her name is associated—education.

3

In after years Carey Thomas said that at the Howland Institute she first discovered that she was clever. But, as her diary amply testifies, she had in actual fact learned long before then that she was exceptionally "bright" and "quick." At Howland, however, largely owing to Miss Slocum's special interest in her, she ceased to look upon her cleverness merely as a gift like another, to be accepted and exploited. She learned to think of it with pride and began to feel that it implied a superiority which she must exert herself to live up to. This new self-consciousness, combined with greater independence of mind, had its drawbacks: "I have not come back from Howland," she observed sadly, "as happy or as *faithful* or as confident as I went. How vehement and headlong and positive I was two years ago! I think I am as *vehement* now, perhaps more so, only it is a stiller kind. As trusting I am not." The analysis is acute as far as it goes. A certain reserve begins to show in her diary and the rather bewildered sense of frustration natural to an objective and "vehement" temperament when restrained by self-consciousness.

In the autumn, in Baltimore, she turned the little room next her bedroom into a study and set to work to prepare herself for college entrance examinations in the early summer. But the winter was broken by the usual family demands and visits. She preserved quinces with her mother, and reupholstered an old sofa for the new study, tied its springs, picked over its hair, restuffed and covered it. She took enthusiastic part in the usual family New Year's gathering at Philadelphia; she helped to entertain the constant stream of family and friends who visited the house; and she wrote exalted essays in her journal. At first—though she did more as the winter wore on—the only systematic studying she could manage was in Latin and Greek and algebra three times a week. She could settle to nothing. Doubtless she believed her own too frequent protestations of the joys of study, but her heart was not in her work. For the first time in her life she felt despondent for a prolonged period.

The summer at Atlantic City and the Cedars had been unhappy, for she had missed Frank sorely, and now, when she wanted to study, she missed the stimulus of schoolfellows. Bessie and she, though still friends, had grown away from each other. "There is not anybody I care to be with particularly," she cried dismally. Moreover she had a distressing sense of failing her parents because, as she knew they were aware, she could sympathize little with their religious efforts and meetings. They dubbed her love of study "an enthusiasm." But "May not Christianity," she asked herself, "be a deeper purer enthusiasm than any of the rest, yet be an enthusiasm? What have Christians in their infatuation to oppose to that of the Hindoos? Their personal delight, their lives, the nobility of the Bible, the gloriousness of Christ's life and creed —yet His creed teaches that all save a small portion of His creatures shall be damned. And His followers carry His love down to such concreteness that all the godliness is gone; at best nothing but a narrow human man is left. God is high as Heaven and deep as Hell. How dare they speak of Him with a familiarity which his own most beloved disciples dared not use." The emotionalism of some of the Quakers, whom her parents took seriously, offended her: "When Christians talk of such a manifestation of their Saviour that they tremble and swoon it may be wrong but I feel like crying out, 'away with this importation of *nerves* into religion making it a byword to all intellectual people!' It is simply another form of the trances of the neo-Platonists and of the absorption of the Buddhists into Brahma and an exact parallel to the rapturous visions of St. Theresa." Intellectually, the whole thing irritated her. She was torn by the condemnation of her parents implicit in her skepticism.

Along with all these distractions, the wall of opposition erected by her father to her plans for college prevented her working with real zest. Her standard of scholarship had risen at Howland. She had come to feel that Vassar College could give her little more serious training than was obtainable at a young ladies' seminary, and what she still wanted was an education quite as good as that given to young men in the best of their colleges. A few midwestern colleges were coeducational but only the University of Michigan, as she was to explain many years later in her *Monograph on the Education of Women*, could even hope to rank with the great eastern universities in scholarship for men, let alone women. In the East there were no coeducational colleges until Cornell University opened its doors in 1868 to both men and women. Its Quaker founder, Ezra Cornell, wished to provide a nonsectarian place of learning where, in his own words, "any person can find instruction in any subject." The first halls, of course, were dedicated to the men students. Women, though permitted to follow the courses and to work for a degree, were given no living place on the campus. In 1875, however, owing to the generosity of one of the trustees, Henry W. Sage, a special building, Sage College, was built to house them; in return for which, "Cornell University is pledged to provide, and forever maintain facilities for the education of women as broadly as for men."

Minnie's father was greatly interested in the experiment especially in relation to the plans for founding the Johns Hopkins University about which he had considerable correspondence with Cornell's first president, Andrew Dickson White; and he much admired President White as a gentleman of wide culture, learning, and liberal mind. Perhaps it was his request to Minnie, while she was at Howland so near Ithaca, to find out all she could about Cornell, that first turned her own interest in that direction. But in any case she would have heard much of Cornell, for the faculty of the school kept in close touch with near-by centers of learning, Cornell University and Wells College. At Minnie's school commencement there had been representatives of both these institutions among the dignitaries on the platform. Minnie looked at those from Cornell with special curiosity, having made up her mind that Cornell, not Vassar, was the place for her.

It did not take her long after returning to Baltimore to see that her rosy dreams would encounter plenty of opposition. In spite of his commencement address, her father could not bring himself to approve of Minnie's wish for continued systematic instruction. She had been given a good foundation upon which to build for herself. Further training was unnecessary and might even be detrimental, making her into a mere bluestocking and, far worse, undermining her Christian faith. It would be expensive, moreover, and such money as he had he felt should go toward his sons' education. They must have training in order to follow the professions necessary to their livelihood. This brought up the often argued question of "our duty to ourselves and others." Even Minnie acknowledged that she was under no religious obligation to go to college. "Many and dreadful are the talks we have had upon this subject," she wrote later. "Father was terribly opposed and last Christmas when Miss Slocum was at our house said never while he lived would he give his consent." All the Baltimore relations took sides, all except Bessie King, against Minnie. Sometimes the opposition was so strong she doubted whether she could persist. Her father felt it all no less deeply than she; and they both suffered tortures.

Fortunately, Minnie had her mother's sympathetic support. Why, asked Mrs. Thomas reasonably, should an advanced education destroy Minnie's faith and not the boys'? She had found her husband's speech at the Howland graduation sound and she saw the logic of supporting it with action. As for financial difficulty, she was a firm believer in the old saw, "Where there's a will, there's a way." So, gently convicting her husband with his own arguments, removing obstacles tactfully, one by one, she backed her daughter up. Her ingenuity and firm patience, combined with Minnie's persistence, were impossible to withstand. Three weeks before the examinations, Dr. Thomas gave his consent to Minnie's taking them.

At last Minnie could apply herself to study with a free heart and all her native zeal. "I never did such terrible studying—every moment for those three weeks and on the way up in the cars— Geography, Grammar, Arithmetic, Algebra, Plane Geometry, Latin and Greek, all to be reviewed in that short time. . . . The strain was terrible—because it was my first experience and I could not have endured failure."

While she took the examinations, her parents, who had accompanied her to Ithaca, explored the university. They talked with the president and various professors; they plodded about the campus on its hill above the town, appraised the fine old trees and the still rather new-looking halls of stone and the big wooden laboratory. They examined with especial care Sage College, not yet finished, where Minnie was to live. They took a walk or two to view Cayuga Lake and Cascadilla Gorge cutting one side of the college hill with its wooded cliffs and tumbling stream. And they found it all satisfactory. Indeed, as the reports on their daughter's papers came in, they found everything delightful. For Minnie, to her "inexpressible satisfaction," passed well. "Almost all the professors," she announced with gusto, "complimented father and mother upon my passing so well." The night before they returned to Baltimore her father said to her, "Well, Minnie, I'm proud of thee but this University is an awful place to swallow thee up." Despite his capitulation he upheld his point of view. All rifts were healed at last.

The next months were a period of unalloyed joy to Minnie. She had won her heart's desire triumphantly and could give herself up entirely to the pleasure of camping with Aunt Hannah's family in the Adirondacks. She shot and fished and rowed with her boy cousins and made long expeditions into the mountains. And in September, in robust health and high fettle, she set off for Sage College. Almost twenty years old, she embarked on the "advanced education" of which she had dreamed and which, whatever its disappointments and vagaries, was to carry her far.

CHAPTER IV

Cornell and the Johns Hopkins Universities

I

MINNIE THOMAS entered Sage College with *A Purpose* backed by a strong will and an acute sense of everything bearing upon women's position in both education and society. She saw her fellow women students as crusaders, taking it for granted that they, too, had won their way to Cornell for reasons similar to her own; and, since heretofore she had been a successful leader, she saw herself in the forefront of their militant ranks. To this end, one of her earliest acts on arriving at Cornell was to use her second name, Carey, instead of Minnie, as she persisted in doing even in the face of family irony for the rest of her life. The added dignity and especially the sexlessness of the name were symbolical.

Alas, she soon found that no militant ranks existed. Though the women at Sage College, it is true, felt themselves to be pioneers striking out in the new field of women in institutions of higher learning, they were unaware that their responsibility went beyond doing their academic work adequately and committing no indiscretion likely to bring criticism upon their sex. Many of them had achieved college against odds but few of them had been obliged to thresh out with such thoroughness as Carey the reasons for the fight they had made. The Thomases, with their Quaker habit of searching the heart, had laid bare the motives and probable results of Carey's determination. Without changing her purpose, this showed her that she must not merely do well in her studies, she must do better than the men; she must behave not only with decorum, but with marked decorum.

Before she had been long at Cornell she realized that her dream of the university woman was far from the fact. Sage College was the disillusionment that colleges are apt to be to young people who enter them from families where talk is lively and good on questions of the day. With high hope of wider interests, more brilliantly stated, they find what appears to them frivolity and narrow pedantry. Her fellow students, Carey thought, were either earnest grinds or too intent upon having fun in this, to them, "elegant garden of young men." Only one of them seemed really clever, and she worked solely to win approbation. Neither she nor any of the others had any true intellectual interest. There was no life of the mind, according to Carey, at Sage College.

If Carey herself was not, perhaps, more intellectual than many of the other students, she fully believed that she was. Her keen mind and her vitality deceived her by encouraging that disease of youth, a thirst for universal knowledge. She wanted to know and understand thoroughly all sorts of things. Unconsciously, nevertheless, she measured their worth by their power to stir her emotions or, owing to her inherited bent and training, by their ethical purport. What she loved to discuss were not so much intellectual questions as questions concerning the good of society. What she liked to read were Emerson's essays, which in one way or another she could apply to the daily life about her, or rousing stories such as *Thaddeus of Warsaw* and poetry like Tennyson's "Maud" that awoke in her an almost wholly emotional response and made her cry out, "I think I enjoy poetry more than anything else." "Paradise Lost," however, left her cold, and "Dante," she pronounced, "is stupid."

Mistaken though she may have been in thinking that her interest in things of the mind sprang from her own intellectuality, she was none the less right in thinking that she had that interest. Nor would it be true to say that she did not understand intellectual matters. She missed the true intellectual's joy in purely mental gymnastics but she was quite capable of doing the gymnastics and found other reasons for her failure to delight in them. So sincere, indeed, was her belief in the joys of the intellectual life that she could impart a sense of them to others as if she had tasted them herself. To Carey Thomas to believe in a way of life was not only to try to live it but to preach it with the utmost, and sometimes illogical, enthusiasm.

This bending of native tastes into unnatural channels was a strain. Her purpose involved, for a nature so instinctively forthright and impulsive as hers, conscious and unremitting care in matters of conduct. When unhampered by the need of keeping up the show, her jollity broke bonds and she had "an utterly elegant time." As her purpose developed, the conflict between deliberate and natural behavior made her a little *farouche*. Her reactions were sometimes unshaded and her strictures on her own, and other's, doings burst out with unexpected vehemence. Luckily an inner fire robbed her determination of its grimness, and lighted in many people an answering spark. On some, she exerted a kind of magnetism to which they instinctively responded; in others, her fervent conviction bred equal conviction. It was no uncommon experience for her to receive letters such as the one from a young lady with whom she had trudged about Machinery Hall at the Philadelphia Centennial: "I admire your honesty and strength and enthusiasm and am truly glad to have known you even for so short a time." Many, on the other hand, were put off by her aloofness. Her consciousness of being awkward added to her shyness, and played its part in her growing scorn of those who had different manners and ideals from her own.

Her fellow students, the women anyway—she paid little heed to the men—at first thought her, she knew, haughty and cold, for she viewed them with an appraising eye, measuring them up against her expectations. Many of them continued to dislike her since she did not hesitate to show that she scorned them. The first arrogant months were lonely, alleviated by fortnightly trips to the Howland Institute in search of congenial companionship. Gradually, she permitted herself to make friends with the seven young ladies living nearest her in Sage Hall, far as they fell below her standard. Deplore though she might the waste of time involved, she had not yet schooled herself to resist the temptation of "joining in" and of setting things straight.

In spite of the fact that the young ladies observed a certain formality—they never dropped the "Miss" and their manners toward each other were those of polite acquaintances—they en-

joyed themselves tremendously and often riotously. Carey, unable
as a Quaker to attend the College germans, saw her friends off to
them sympathetically—"Miss Tilden looking elegant in shimmer-
ing green satin with waist terraced in puffs of lace"—and threw
back her head in laughter when they returned to her room, all
chattering at once about who danced with whom and who was
handsome or awkward or clever or dull. "Even the university
women can't stand a German," she remarked good-naturedly. She
herself had sat upstairs "reading Schlegel's *Dramatic Literature*
and feeling virtuous" while the dance progressed.

She was obliged, also, to abstain from the occasional dances
among the young ladies themselves after dinner in the gymnasium.
But as often as not the dance turned into a game of blindman's
buff in which she took tumultuous part. One evening as the
blindman, she ran, long skirts and hairpins flying, full tilt into a
wooden post, giving herself such a crack on the head that she
almost fulfilled a lifelong ambition to faint. The parties she most
enjoyed were those where she and her seven friends played the
uncomfortable though often salutary game of truth or discussed
questions of vital moment while consuming maple sugar and
oranges. No subject escaped untouched: politics, literature, conduct, and religion. Argument went to her head like wine. She
always had a point of view which she supported tooth and nail,
though she tried to act upon her mother's caution—"Thee must
not be too fierce in argument. There is much greater strength in
a calm fair presentation of the truth, than in any heated antagonism of others." Of the poem "Aurora Leigh," she contended
emphatically that Aurora's mission as "a poet to raise the few and
inspire them with heaven-sent visions, was higher than Romney's
to be a raging philanthropist and give soup to the masses." One
Sunday with her friend Miss Hicks she had "a terribly earnest
discussion as to whether Unitarians had the full benefits of
Christian doctrines," pointing out that a man must either believe
in Christ as God or believe all "stories of His birth and resurrec-
tion to be old women's fables—between these there is no middle
position." There rarely was a middle position for Carey. It took
an hour of cajoling to restore to equanimity Miss Hicks, who
had been reduced to tears—"a great waste of time." In fact Miss

Hicks was the cause of much of Carey's lost time and a source of perplexity to her.

When Carey Thomas came up to Cornell to take her entrance examinations she had noticed a very pretty girl in gray with a wing in her brown hat. She had talked to her at President White's at tea and, finding her "smart" and well prepared for her examinations, "rather hoped" to see her again in the fall. Sure enough, the first person she spied on arriving at Sage College was Alice Hicks. They chose rooms on the same corridor, "hall 3," and after Carey's first shy, scornful weeks saw more and more of each other. They read Homer together and "Atalanta in Calydon" and, "in a lovely place above Cascadilla gorge," "Tintern Abbey"; when it grew dark they "would sit under Miss Hicks' blue shawl and talk." They climbed down Trip Hammer Falls "to get a glorious view." Carey taught Miss Hicks to row on the lake and they sold their old textbooks to hire a carriage in which to drive about the countryside.

But they quarreled a great deal—"All our ideas were opposite" —and Carey's strictures on the charms of her "Clytie" were severe. "Miss Hicks' literary criticism and conversation disappoint me," she announced to her parents, "and she is so commonsense it is impossible to rouse her to talk with any sort of generous abandon." Except when angry, she gave no impression of speaking from the heart. Having "not the least bit of fastidiousness," she liked anyone and cared for everyone's opinion. So, though she was "bright," she would be turned aside too easily to make a success of her proposed career as an architect. She would probably marry. Owing to these unfavorable characteristics, as Carey Thomas termed them, she did many things that Carey thought unsuitable. "I would object and say more than I ought and Miss Hicks would fling herself on the lounge in a passion of tears and sometimes we would both cry. Altogether it was dreadful. . . . This high tragedy," added Carey with truth, "seems ridiculous written but I know I shall forget the possibility of such things unless I do write it."

Though constantly aware that in wasting her time with Miss Hicks she fell far below her standard of the purposeful life of a university student, she did her academic work well. As at Howland, she impressed professors almost at once, and Professor Byerly offered to give her special instruction in calculus to fill in a yawning gap in her equipment. Hearing of this, her mother wrote agitatedly: "I do not at all like thy having the lecture *alone*. . . . Is there no one in the room but thee and Byerly? If that is the case I think it is *objectionable*." And in consternation she outlined the exact pattern of repressive behavior to be followed by her daughter, who felt no need whatever of the warning. Professor and student remained on decorous terms—"Professor Byerly would not dream of taking liberties"—and when, called to Harvard in the following year, Byerly became the first member of the Harvard faculty to co-operate with the committee that in 1879 was planning "collegiate instruction for women," Carey was confirmed in her belief that he would always prove his worth.

The difficulties that Carey overcame in her studies at Cornell were not slight. Joining the class of 1877 as a junior, she missed the two years' training they had received in methods of study and in the idiosyncrasies of the professors, a lack noticeable especially in Latin and Greek, in which she was least well prepared. As usual, however, difficulty stimulated her. Professor Flagg remarked in her senior year that, owing to the presence of Carey Thomas and another young lady, he had never had so satisfactory an advanced Greek class—a tribute in which Carey gloried since it reflected honor upon the whole of womankind. During the second term of that year she had become so proficient that she tutored a less industrious member of her Latin class. Toward commencement time, the lecture she delivered to the Latin class, obligatory on all its members, was the best of all those given, "a real success." In fact she was in a fair way to become a good speaker for, called upon suddenly in a debate in the literature class she managed, though cold with fright, "not to lose her train of thought" and was much complimented afterwards by Mr. Milford, the president of her class. Oddly enough, considering her later scorn of it as a subject of academic study, she became much interested in history in her last term, swallowing great gulps of Grote's Roman history and doing exceedingly well in the class: "History is after all more interesting than anything else."

Her scholarship apart, she was marked out among the women

of the university by other attributes. Though not beautiful—her features at that time seemed too pronounced and a little heavy—she did not look like a college "grind." Her shapely head was held so proudly and she radiated such vigor that she at once caught attention. In spite of her slight limp she moved quickly. There could be no doubt of either her mental or her bodily alertness. She had made a name for herself, moreover, soon after her arrival by her athletic prowess. The baseball played with her cousins in the past enabled her to explain the points of the game to the young ladies as they sat on their shawls critically watching the university team practice; and when it was necessary she could talk even to the less cerebral of the athletes on their own ground. More than that, she proved herself able to row and skate with the best of them.

During her first year at Cornell Mr. Gardiner, the university's most accomplished skater, chose to skate with her and in her second year Professor White, upon whom Mr. Gardiner's mantle had fallen—a distinction especially welcomed by Carey since Professor White had "the reputation of being very smart. He has been abroad," she told her parents impressively, "and is going again in '78 and knows Lowell and Fiske and all those Harvard literati." She was flattered, too, by being one of the university young ladies to be asked to Mrs. Schaefer's sedate evening party of Ithaca dignitaries, and by being singled out, in her "long-skirted gray silk trimmed with rosebuds and smilax," for talk and supper with the president of her class at the reception given before commencement by the president of the university.

She immensely enjoyed her success and, equally, the feeling that through her the women of the university were at least slightly more respected than they had been. Largely by her efforts her group had become the self-constituted guardians of propriety, a fact annoying to the other women but admired by the men. "The gentlemen," she noted complacently, "seem to draw a distinction between us and the rest of the girls, and several remarks have been repeated to us: 'oh their table is the aristocratic table'; 'the third hall clique would not think that proper.'" She was delighted when they invited six of her group to visit their chapter house—the first young ladies to be accorded the honor—but fearing possible gossip she argued the other five into refusing with her. With civilly cloaked but perceptible jeers she sent the young man packing who, in accordance with the men's custom of bribing their young lady acquaintances to vote as they desired, drove up to the door of Sage Hall to escort her to the election of officers to *Era*. And when at the end of her senior year the question of class photographs came up, she at first stoutly refused to have hers taken. She could see no reason why the young ladies of the university should permit even the most boorish campus nobody to own their photographs; and to withhold them, she realized, set a higher value upon both pictures and originals.

Such aggressive independence insured her being observed even more eagerly than were the other young ladies for a solecism with which to feed college gossip. And the observers were rewarded when, in her second year, she happened to return to Baltimore for the Christmas holidays in the same train with Professor Boyesen, one of the few men of the university whom she allowed to be "cultivated gentlemen" and with whom she liked to talk. The train broke down near a small town and the passengers had to spend the night at the hotel. Naturally, Professor Boyesen took Carey Thomas under his gentlemanly wing and, foreseeing awkwardness, tried to persuade her to sign her name in the hotel register as Mrs. Boyesen. She refused. A month or two later Cornell burst into a roar of laughter. One of the undergraduates had seen the register and returned, enchanted, to spread the news. The unfortunate professor in great confusion stumbled through ineffective explanations. But Carey was highly amused. The situation was too egregious to be anything but uproariously funny, and she laughed as loudly as the undergraduates.

"There is much," she wrote, "that is very hard for a *lady* in a mixed university and I should not subject any girl to it unless she were determined to have it. The educational problem is a terrible one—girls' colleges are inferior and it seems impossible to get the most illustrious men to fill their chairs and on the other hand it is a fiery ordeal to educate a lady by co-education. . . . It is the only way and learning *is worth it*." She was thankful to be at Cornell, for she had become "enamoured of life there" in her senior year and had learned much. She had widened her horizons by breaking out of the old ruts and mingling with different sorts of people; and she had learned enough to know that she wanted to learn far more than she had dreamed there was to learn.

The subject of her final thesis puzzled her—should it be "The Song of Deborah and the Persians of Aeschylus, Illustrating the Lyric and Dramatic Tendency"; or "Catullus and Tacitus"; or "The Medium of History Changing, the Aims Remain the Same"?—but the writing of it did not trouble her much. Nor did her final examinations; the general fuss about them amused her. She rejoiced over her bachelor's degree, taken in June, 1877, for it represented, she congratulated herself, far more than a Vassar degree would have done; and eighteen years later when she was elected the first woman trustee of the university, her pride was gratified. At the moment, not merely the desire for scholarship but a longing for culture—that attribute so lamentably lacking to the students of Cornell—had begun to assail her with improbable dreams.

2

Behind these years at Cornell—the brightly lighted forefront of the stage on which Carey played her daily part—the busy family life in Baltimore formed a shadowy background. Important only when suddenly, for a moment, its activities coincided with her interests, it none the less framed and warmed for her the scene in which she moved. At any instant she could find support in it; into it she could retreat. And the figures chattering, gesticulating —often, it seemed to her, so unreasonably, with such trying unconcern—became buffers or confessors or lawgivers as she had need of them. It provided the taken-for-granted security that the life of the family usually gives its youthful members who have gone off in pursuit of their own ambitions; and was, in turn, accorded the usual rare and egotistic attention.

In the letters that went to and from Baltimore everything was set down higgledy-piggledy, as it occurred to the writer's mind, with perfect faith that the recipient would be interested. But Carey had been away from home a long time. Unconsciously, her parents had slipped into accepting her as an independent individual apart from themselves, more or less capable of managing her own affairs. Their exhortations, though still present, were fewer. On Carey's part, the observations on family news occurred more rarely, though when anything startling happened her interest was immediately caught.

The news of the disaster that had befallen her uncle Robert Pearsall Smith, which came during her first year at Cornell, aroused her at once. For several years he had been evangelizing in Germany and, especially, in England where, in 1873, he had persuaded his wife to join him and with her held many extremely successful revival meetings, preaching, according to their granddaughter Ray Strachey, "the needs for the Higher Life and the quickening of the religious impulse." Their teachings spread like wildfire, and a great number of people from all over the world gathered to hear them at Oxford and Brighton. At the height of their success, as is often the fate of the prime movers in such revivals, scandal fell upon them—or rather, upon Robert Smith. "Aunt Hannah," wrote Mrs. Thomas, characteristically thinking first of her sister, "has had some trouble about some very disagreeable things which have been in some of the papers about Uncle Robert. A young lady who came to him for spiritual help complained of impropriety in his conduct and conversation, though at the time she did not manifest the slightest displeasure which was very remarkable if there was any real ground of complaint. Some papers in England which have been persistent opposers of holiness and very severe on the teachers of it, have made a good deal of it and some in this country like-minded have taken it up. This is very disagreeable but I think it will blow over soon." Needless to say, Carey replied at once, for she was devoted to her aunt Hannah and fond of her uncle Robert. "Do tell me *what* the papers say about Uncle Robert," she demanded, "I am *so* sorry for Aunt Hannah." Though Mrs. Thomas was right in thinking the affair would blow over, it made a deep impression on Carey's mind, contributing to her own mistrust of religious zeal.[1]

The accounts from her parents of the opening of the Johns Hopkins University also impressed her, and her father's doings on the Board of Trustees, especially in regard to "the woman question." Such matters were right up her alley. From the beginning she had been informed concerning university affairs. The will of the philanthropic Quaker, Johns Hopkins, its founder, appointed three executors of his estate—Francis White, Francis T. King, and Charles J. M. Gwinn. One was Carey's cousin and father of her oldest friend Bessie King, and one was the father of her acquaintance Mary M. Gwinn. They settled the estate with phenomenal intelligence and efficiency and handed over the Johns Hopkins' University bequest to the already appointed Board of Trustees, which included themselves, to exercise its own discretion as to the precise kind of university to be founded.[2] Appointed to this first board were not only Carey's uncle Galloway Cheston and John Garrett, the father of another of her non-Quaker acquaintances, Mary Garrett, but, most importantly for Carey, her father.

Like the other members of the board, Dr. Thomas took his duties seriously; perhaps more than the others, with the exception of Francis King, he was interested in general questions of education and, like King, from experience on the Board of Managers of Haverford College knew a good deal about educational problems. From a mass of information gathered in institutions both in America and abroad, they and the other trustees were inclined toward setting up an institution that, somewhat like German universities, would give a really advanced education to its students. Neither President Eliot of Harvard, nor President White of Cornell, nor President Angell of the University of Michigan, whom they consulted as being the best-known progressive educators of the time in the United States, thought such a plan feasible, however desirable. Unanimously, though independently, nevertheless, they advised the trustees to offer the presidency of the Johns Hopkins to Daniel Coit Gilman, then president of the University of California. And Gilman, with whom they opened negotiations in October, 1874, had already thought out and was anxious to put into effect plans for a university just such as, more vaguely, they had wished for—a university concentrating upon postgraduate work, rather than upon the usual undergraduate college work of most universities. Such an institution, admirable and desirable as it seemed to most enlightened educators, was almost unprecedented in America. No sooner did plans for it leak out in April, 1875, than a storm broke over the upright heads of the trustees, heralded by the opposing arguments of the conservative Baltimore *American* and the progressive New York *Nation*.

The former was stirred to vindictive horror by the proposed

concentration upon postgraduate rather than undergraduate work. It pointed out that the postgraduate school organized by Professor Louis Agassiz on Penikese Island, the one wholly postgraduate institution in the country, was petering out, and that few or no students attended the postgraduate courses at Princeton. Apparently ignorant of the fact that German universities were in truth schools of advanced study, they threatened the trustees with dire consequences if they refused to follow the admirable example set by German universities. The *Nation*, on the other hand, hoped for a university unlike any other educational institution, unhampered by state or religious denomination or established precedent. "Considerable waste of skilled labor," moreover, might be saved if the trustees, who had been given a liberal endowment and a free hand, founded a university in which the professors need not teach the rudiments of any subject. It might solve the problem that university reformers had striven to overcome ever since John Stuart Mill's famous attack, forty years before, on the English universities—the problem of how "in the interests both of economy and culture to reserve the highest teaching power of the community for the most promising material." In fact, the *Nation*, envisaged the new institution, not like the Baltimore *American* as a glorified high school for Maryland hobbledehoys, but as a university refining and elevating the whole country by diffusing a taste for study and research, spreading faith in the powers of knowledge, forming social and political ideals, and "making a small though steady contribution to that reverence for 'things not seen' in which the soul of a state may be said to lie, and without which it is nothing better than a factory or insurance company."

Needless to say, the trustees concurred with the *Nation*, sympathizing especially with its editor's remark that the value of a university does not depend solely on the proportion of students to the amount of revenue, and, in spite of the acrimonious and strong pressure of both provincial and conservative thought, persisted in carrying out their plan. The pros and cons of the debate and the facts that it brought up made their impression on Carey's mind, concentrated though it was on her own particular problems and activities. Sooner or later they reappear as grist to her mill.

In September, 1876, the Johns Hopkins University officially

opened with the inauguration of President Gilman. Carey at Cornell was kept informed of its progress. Her mother told her of sending, with President Gilman's approval, a letter to the New York *Observer* in reply to its scurrilous attack on the university for failing to introduce Huxley's inaugural lecture with the Lord's Prayer, and of persuading Dr. Thomas to stir up the trustees to buying the Academy of Music, which was for sale. And the following November, Carey pricked up her ears in good earnest: "They had the woman question up at the J.H.U. Board the other day," wrote Mrs. Thomas, "and had a most interesting·discussion. Johnson set his foot against it—totally unwilling to let women in anyway. Frank White and Gwinn agreed with him. Father, Judge Dobbin, Garrett and F.T.K., and Uncle Galloway all strong on the woman side. Finally Gilman asked them to leave the matter to his discretion with power to make such arrangements for special cases as seem best. Johnson opposed this but the yeas finally had it. Johnson insisted on his protest being recorded in minutes and would have resigned the chairmanship of the executive committee if father had not dissuaded him. Johnson said Bessie King would be applying to enter in the morning but father said she had made other arrangements for the present and the matter might not be put to the practical test for a long time." Carey replied to her mother's letter with the question, "Why don't Gilman come right out and tell the trustees what he thinks—it would have a great effect. . . . I do not think I could stand it," she declared, "if father were on the other side." Again the doctor, as innocent of complicity as Reverdy Johnson himself, had helped to prepare the way for his pioneering daughter to become one of an entering wedge of women, this time into the reluctantly opening doors of the Johns Hopkins.

At the time, however, Carey had no intention of studying at the Johns Hopkins University. Only as it was borne in upon her that two years of ·undergraduate study would not carry her far along the road to scholarship did her thoughts begin to turn toward future possibilities. Occasional talks during the summer holidays with two young Quakers, Richard Cadbury and Francis Gummere, had encouraged her desire for learning. Francis Gummere had sat on the green sofa and she in a rocking chair at

Atlantic City discussing his plans for Harvard and hers for Cornell. "We had a talk upon study and men and women's work. He said Tennyson just expressed it. I got him my green copy and he read that part (from 'The Princess') 'not like in like, but like in difference.' We agreed of course." Then she saw him at a Philadelphia party—"we talked about books and stood by the mantle piece and I had a fan." After that they saw a good deal of each other. She learned that both he and Cadbury were as dissatisfied with Harvard as she was with Cornell. They found "no earnest companionship there"—a dismal observation corroborated by Professor Byerly, who wrote that he found the intellectual tone of Harvard far below that of Cornell, largely, he thought, because of President Eliot's policy of "free electives" which lowered the standard to the level of the rich idle young sons of Boston. Since Carey's opinion of even Cornell culture was low, she was delighted to hear that Francis Gummere was going on from Harvard to a German university. He knew, he wrote her, that he could depend on her understanding his hope of becoming "something more than a physico-mental machine," for he had never met her "without feeling the inspiration of pure and noble intellectual aims."

She did better than sympathize. She set about following in his footsteps. It was all very well for her to write in her diary, "I hope he will persevere and go to Germany and I wish I were a man for that; because *Germany is shut* to ladies along with the J.H.U. and a few other of the very most glorious things in the world. Yet I would not be a man." She was incapable, however, of placidly accepting the closing of any door against her. The very fact that doors appeared to be unyielding tempted her to test them. Before she left Cornell, she had determined to try to enter the Johns Hopkins University.

3

The death of her grandfather Whitall just before her commencement and then of her baby sister Dora overshadowed her summer after graduation. But by September she was full of happy excitement over her own winter's prospects. "Yesterday I made application to the Johns Hopkins University to study for a second degree. Mr. Gilman was very polite and it will come before the Trustees in a month and I (oh I hope there is some chance for ladies!) am in great anxiety to know whether all these advantages are to be shut forever, or even for a time, to us." And ten days later, when given permission to study there on certain conditions for a master of arts degree: "Oh, this year does look very pleasant ahead and life seems a very delightful thing. Bessie is so satisfactory and to come back to our old studying together and our old talks is lovely. . . . I wonder what it is, this love of study—it seems far removed from active life and yet—."

The swift dying of Carey's elation under the load of work leads to the suspicion that "this love of study" was an idea, part of the conception of her ideal self toward which she strove with such wholehearted desire that it seemed real. In actual pursuit of study her spirit flagged, her mind became distracted and bored, but, treasuring the belief that the scholar's road leads to the end she wished to reach, she struggled to endure its rigors. Already, in the first entry in the journal after admission to the Johns Hopkins, joyous enthusiasm had departed. "I am studying," she wrote soberly, "three mornings in the week from nine to three with Bessie. We read Classen's Thucydides and La Roche's Homer; the other three mornings I study German and Greek; in the afternoons, drive or ride or walk, except two when Gildersleeve lectures. German, Professor Gildersleeve said, was a *sine qua non* and gave me till Christmas to master (?) it. I am very discouraged. Now that I have entered upon a three year's course of work I feel the recoil and I feel how absolutely impossible is my knowledge of Greek and it does seem hopeless and then after all—there seems something degrading in the minute study Classen's notes require—what difference can it make if a second aorist is used once or twice in a certain writer? I cannot bend my mind to it and yet—I must. I must now be a good scholar or nothing."

By the new year she had discovered that, for a woman, work at the university meant merely the privilege of attending certain lectures and of being instructed once a term in the amount of study to be done.[3] The condition, "without class attendance," upon which she had been admitted was interpreted to exclude her both

from work with other students in the seminars and from instruction in stated private tutorials. The burden of working without
such stimulus and assistance weighed heavily upon her. She was
"utterly discouraged. . . . Is this trouble after all worth it," she
asked herself, "is it not a waste of one's life? . . . I have no time
to read, no time to see people—not that that amounts to much, but
still it is a kind of living death. But then," she added stoutly, "if
I had my choice at the moment I know I would choose nothing
else"—only to repeat, "Perhaps my studying is all a mistake—if
only I were more master of the subject I could tell better." A
week's visit from an old Howland friend refreshed her, the enforced idleness making her resolve to study "passionately" when
the visit ended. But with the return to work, blackness again
settled down upon her: "I have to put wax in my ears and with
my own hands keep myself to the mast—a living death—and do
nothing but devote myself to Greek. But I have been putting it off
too long and I shall *fail*—I who care so much for women and
their cause—will *fail* and do them more harm than if I had never
tried. But it is so hard."

A fortnight later her friend Mamie Gwinn introduced her to
Godwin's *Political Justice* and changed, Carey thought, her whole
point of view toward life. Her past attitude seemed to her now
to have been very limited. She set about reading Godwin and, with
greater pleasure, Shelley and discussing them with Mamie Gwinn
and Mary Garrett and Julia Rogers. These three had long been
close friends of Bessie King's, but they belonged to a group in
Baltimore society with whom the fairly Quaker-bound Thomases
came in contact only on special occasions. Carey had been shy of
them and, to Bessie's distress, held aloof. Since her return from
Cornell, however, bolstered up by two years' independent life
among people of various social backgrounds as well as by the
prestige of a learned degree, she had met them with less awkwardness. And having met them, soon fell under their sway.

Their lives had been different from Carey's and, from her point
of view, worldly. They had been to plays, seen pictures, heard
music, as Carey had never done; belonging to families far richer
than hers, they had moved in circles she had never touched; and
they had traveled much more widely—as indeed had even Bessie

King. All this cast an enchantment over them in her eyes; and in their turn, they saw Carey surrounded by the glamour of academic achievement. Like her they hungered for knowledge—and here lay the solid basis of congenial tastes—but unlike her they had not been able to win their way to established instruction. In consequence, their learning, sometimes deeper than hers, followed more desultory and less orthodox lines, and depended more nearly than hers on individual taste. The fact that they approached similar preoccupations from different angles and with different equipment made them interesting and stimulating to each other.

It was not long before Carey, with energy and enthusiasm burning so high as to make her at times amusingly naïve, at times startlingly perspicacious, became an indispensable member of the group. The five friends met once a fortnight at one or the other of their houses to discuss literature and to write a novel, a long, somber, highfalutin' romance to which each in turn contributed two chapters. Carey's chapters tell the main story and are the only ones that move with any life; the others, though equally characteristic of their writers, deal with setting or minor matters. But even in Carey's, the plot is obscured by verbiage and flights of fancy. She omitted nothing in the way of embellishment: fairies, dryads, Titans, "Christ's sweet parables," the Greek gods, "the great elemental genii," even "Thor with his hammer smiting down the Jotens"—an up-to-date touch since, in 1877, the Norse gods were just coming into American notice.

The story, set in England during the intellectual disturbance following the French Revolution, is told in the first person with no ray of humor and no evidence of actual experience behind it. Indeed it passes on a Shelleyan plane so high as to transcend all reality, but seems to center on the contrast between the degradation and suffering consequent on carnal passion and the nobility of love upheld by a true desire to succor humanity. To what mankind is to be helped is never vouchsafed; nor is it precisely stated how the aid is to be given—although Carey's chapters suggest that the means is literature, and more especially poetry.

Possibly the sententious vagueness is owing to the fact that the five authors were not altogether clear in their own minds. They could not decide what they thought about "the whole question" of love and marriage. Industriously, they read Shelley and Godwin and Mary Wollstonecraft and after serious discussion concluded that there was "something wrong about the present relations of marriage." Only Mamie Gwinn, however, accepted Godwin's view of free love and she refused "to consider the bringing up of children." Carey's contribution to the talk was that the question must be judged from the point of view of expediency. Free love, she felt, would "derange matters and above all women." But, she added with unwonted prudence, "I really think that I personally do not know what to say about this matter—I must wait till I see and know more to decide." She was delighted by the liberality of her friends' opinions—and her own—and the keenness with which they, especially Mamie Gwinn, saw points. "Looking at it abstractly," she wrote, "it did seem an anomaly to see five girls, brought up in the most carefully guarded homes, whose whole ancestors would shrink in horror from the mention of a doubt of 'the sacredness of the marriage tie,' discussing gravely and with the most liberal views such subjects. I do wonder what will become of us all."

Such discussions were most profitable, Carey felt, as were her first adventures at the play. On her twenty-first birthday Mary Garrett gave a theater party in her honor to see Modjeska play *Camille*. Carey's parents, of course, had always disapproved of her going to the theater, but, at twenty-one, she took the responsibility upon her own shoulders. The play "came up to and went beyond anything I had imagined. I utterly lost all idea of locality and just saw Camille in her magnificent longings after a better life. . . . The play might have been made a disagreeable one but the whole thing was raised by the purity of the passion and I could see no imaginable harm in it and oh it is such a mighty pleasure." She felt defrauded by having missed such pleasure "all these years." What, she asked, can be the objection to it? To her amazed embarrassment, and the glee of Mary Garrett, who pointed out the oversight to her, she had quite failed to observe the fact that Camille was Arnaud's mistress. She never ceased to be grateful to Mary for not giving her away. Since "the risqué situation" upon which *Camille* centered had escaped her, she concluded that plays could not be morally harmful and set out upon what was to be a lifelong career of theatergoing. Before the end of the next winter she had seen Booth in most of his important Shakespearean roles as well as Henry Irving, Ellen Terry, and Salvini. The years 1878-79 were good Shakespeare years in the United States. Booth, she wrote later, "was the greatest Shakespeare actor of my generation. . . . Irving's shocking enunciation and uncouth mannerisms seemed to me a travesty after Booth's fire and tenderness." As she had read little Shakespeare, the plays came to her quite fresh through these interpreters and seemed "all glorious."

Though it opened to her this new delight, the experience of her first play also chagrined her, showing her as it did the unexpected innocence with which she viewed life. She began to suspect that there were depths in the relations of men and women of which she and her friends were quite ignorant. To remedy this unscientific state of affairs, she brought from her father's office one evening when Mary and Julia came to supper—"tea" as she called it—fifteen of her father's medical books. If they cared, as they did, to work for the good of humanity they must not go about it blindfolded. If passion and sensuality were real factors in life they should understand them. Otherwise, Carey observed, what could they do against them? It is every woman's duty to face things, she announced. But having faced them, having read the books, the three friends were appalled. "Religion, philanthropy, may as well cease; *Sense* remains." Carey was "more thankful than ever to be a woman" for "the time a man has to spend in struggling against his lower nature she has to advance in."

Apart from these gratifyingly educational events and discussions which she shared with them, Carey found that her mind constantly strayed into idle reflections on the doings and opinions of her friends when it should have been on Greek syntax. They presented her again with that old bugbear, the wasted time entailed by friendship. She had become fond of Mary Garrett. She admired her character, "a sort of sweet strength about her," and her fearlessness on horseback; and she felt her sympathetic on almost all points. Worst of all, Carey found Mamie Gwinn so delightful that she wished constantly to be with her. "Have I the time?" she asked herself. That the answer was a mournful negative did not change the course of affection, nor did her realization of the faults of her friend: "She is now too self-centered; she is too fantastic in many ways; she represents all the side of my nature I am trying to suppress—the roving through literature and study, seeking out whatever the bent of my fancy leads to, the complete contradiction to the steady working spirit that I am endeavouring to summon." At one moment she "really liked and trusted" Mamie Gwinn, "and found pleasure in her"; and the next, thought her "not particularly nice."

The truth was, she was "fascinated by her." Mamie was what Carey admired, a true intellectual. The practical, the moral, indeed the human aspects of life interested her not at all except as subjects for abstract theorizing. She did not necessarily believe the printed word to be the final one, but she went to it naturally as the fountainhead of sustenance and enjoyment. Her mind was subtle, even tortuous—the antithesis of Carey's—and brilliantly keen. To talk with her exhilarated Carey. In appearance, too, Mamie charmed her irresistibly. She was slender and delicately boned, white skinned and black haired, and her dark eyes were intensely alive. Her movements were light and languid. Again, she was the opposite of the robust and instinctively headlong Carey.

Through these differences they gave each other much that offset the disadvantage of "wasted time." Following Mamie Gwinn, Carey read *Pendennis*, interested especially in Thackeray's treatment of women and thinking him sympathetic; found the arguments in Lecky's *History of European Morals* "splendid"; and discovered the Wordsworth of *The Prelude*: "He spoke right to me. . . . I was almost frightened as I found thought after thought there that had come to me so often. He gives real spiritual help which I need so much and I am so glad to have him to turn to now." She studied *Hamlet* carefully in order to refute "Mamie's wrong theory about it"; and read Rossetti's poems—"He is a perfect poet within his scope"—and Henry James's *French Poets and Novelists*. Gradually, under Mamie's influence, she began to approach her reading from the aesthetic and technical points of view, studying not only its meaning and emotional effect upon herself but the methods employed in achieving them. She began to think that she "cared more for literature than for anything else." And her own writings underwent a change. She tried to write not merely effusions but experiments in technique, inditing her first sonnet to Mary Garrett, and also worrying over her lack of prose style. Once more her mind was filled with large ambitions. She wondered if she could not be a poet, a great poet, or perhaps a novelist or story writer. "My style is *wretched*. . . . I think I shall, upon the chance, devote myself to improving it and reading, broad wide reading."

Here again Mamie's influence told. It supported the belief, consciously fostered by Carey, in the general and unfailing efficacy of the printed word. By the very act of reading she would magically absorb the secret of writing. Yet how could she read and read? She had bound herself "in this University." Having put her hand to the plow she must carry on. In order not to fail—and failure was intolerable to Carey—she must "bend her whole thought, eight hours a day at least, to grammatical points and minute examination." In fury she wrote: "When there are so many books, when the noblest literatures, Greek as well as any other, are waiting to unfold their treasures I must learn to write correct lifeless Greek. Why it will not tell in what I want to do!... A degree is a mere toy if I do not care for the work beneath it. I do not care for it." Under the pressure of drudgery, freshly encouraged in bright dreams of literary achievement, her thoughts grew vast and misty and turned back to meditation upon Culture —by which uncertain term she seems to have meant a comprehension of the spirit and forms of antiquity.

Such was her turmoil of spirit, beset by indecision and distractions, that she was incapable of any work. Added to other demands upon her time, the profoundly disturbing and humiliating suspicion dawned upon her that she had fallen in love. The young man who caused this distressing complication was very congenial with her. They agreed with special enthusiasm on theological and literary subjects. He was not only "a passionate worshipper of poetry" but a writer of it, and was "struggling with the same old problems of life and religion" that haunted her. She had known him for upwards of five years and increasingly admired him, for he seemed to have "a little of the divine fire" which "removed him utterly from all other people."

The story of their meetings and growing attachment follows

the pattern of the usual youthful idyl. While Carey was still at Howland his dearest comrade had fallen in love with a Philadelphia friend of hers at whose house, during the summer, the four friends often met, under the benignly simple Quaker rule untroubled by chaperones. They rode together and Carey's young gallant, who had ridden only once before when he had been thrown, filled her with forbearing amazement by his "magnificent disregard of his horse. He let the reins hang so loose," she wrote in tender reminiscence, "that my foot caught in them once or twice. We had a lovely talk." In the evening, the air sweet with honeysuckle, the fountain dripping on the lawn, they sat on the porch in the moonlight and quoted poetry to each other. Carey's young man recited "The Garden of Prosperine" and "The Hymn to Prosperine"; and Carey herself "got intolerably frightened in the midst of 'The Last Ride Together.'"

In the summer of 1876, as Carey's beau had sailed to Europe, they did not meet; and the following year when he returned, Carey's feeling had somehow changed, perhaps owing to Cornell, or merely to growing up. In any case she felt "embarressed" for the first time in his presence. They wound hammock cord together —"which helped us through"—and made lemonade, looked over a volume of Tennyson's poems, and discussed Wordsworth and Pope. They found themselves in "such a ridiculously novel-like position" that Carey became more and more self-conscious and provoked. She resolved to be "as cold and careful as possible and show him that [she] did not care for him. . . . He sat in a great big rocking chair and moved it nearer and nearer as he talked," and he was "so splendid" that every now and again she forgot her resolution. When they met again the restraint was even more noticeable. Carey blushed; which made her snub him. Their relations preyed upon her mind all through the following autumn and winter months.

She was well aware of the irony of her falling in love—she, who had "declared against" such weakness. Other men, she said grandly, were of no interest "except as studies or to amuse myself with." But this one young man was "so brilliant and so cultured in many ways that I am not—and yet I feel that I can give him some culture too—I could help him to have a steady aim which is the only thing he needs I believe." She heard, moreover, that, as she honestly confessed she had suspected, he admired her but "looked upon it as something unattainable" and was prevented asking her even to write to him "by a sort of awe." Marriage or nothing were the alternatives. But marriage, she was becoming more and more convinced, meant the wife's playing second fiddle, giving up her own work and life to her husband's, and that she could not accept. Then there was the appalling possibility of children: "If a woman has children I do not see but what she will have to, at least for some time, give up her work, and of all things taking care of children does seem the most utterly unintellectual."

When it had first swept over her that she "cared for him," she had cried and cried. "It was an awful trial," she wrote; and with uncommon shrewdness added, "You see, I never came to anything before I could not, partially at least, manage." It irked her unbearably not to be able to control her thoughts. Irresistibly they dwelt on him. To vow to forget him merely gave him the added fascination of a forbidden subject. What with this absorbing preoccupation and the excitement of friendship, she was reduced by the end of the spring to a feather pillow-like condition. "Truly reading and poetry and being out in the sunshine seem the only desirable things."

Then, as so often happened to Carey Thomas, her forces were revived by the sudden looming of an obstacle ahead. Miss Christine Ladd, who also was working at the Johns Hopkins, wrote that President Gilman was doubtful if she would receive a degree or a certificate after her examination. "Wretch," wrote Carey wrathfully, "he *knows* the motion stands 'Resolved that Miss Thomas be received as a candidate for a second degree,' and of course her case is the same as mine. . . . I will take the degree in their teeth—if only I have *fair play*."

She passed her yearly examinations with commendation from her professors; but she was worn out. Two months of novel reading and rest with her grandmother Whitall in Atlantic City were needed before she again felt "energy enough to jump over a house." She had convinced herself by that time that she had never been in love with her young man; she was free of her friends; Atlantic City provided an admirable place and plenty of time for study if only she could make use of it. As usual, she set the stage, "fixing up" the nursery, with her aunt Hannah's help, as a study. Then, suddenly, disconcertingly, immersion in the religious pre-occupation of her relatives again disturbed her equilibrium.

4

As an old woman Carey wrote, "From the time when my mother told me God was love and could not torture people in hell, I never gave the future after death another thought"—a statement far from accurate. When her baby sister Dora died the condolences sent her parents by devout Friends moved her to speculate about the after life. "Your children," read one letter, "have only to think of her as glorified and roaming in delight through the green pastures and beside the still waters of everlasting life. It will bring Heaven very much nearer to them." Carey was little disturbed that she could not see Dora as either glorified or roaming in delight. Separate individualities, she decided, did not exist in "the other world" although there must be another world, "or all our struggles here and our real intellectual life go for worse than nothing." Now, however, her grandmother's and aunt Hannah's certainty of a heaven where, freed from earthly sins, one lived forever a blissful Victorian idyl, revived her doubts. With both of them she was on the best of terms—Carey, wrote old Mrs. Whitall, "knows how to turn things to good account and is *very satisfactory*"; aunt Hannah, said Carey, is "the most completely honest woman," "grand and noble in many ways" and "only deluded in two things, her slavish devotion and real selfishness for her children and her christianity"—but talk with them, when not merely cheery gossip about people, remained largely upon religious subjects. Her in-ability to meet their assurance made her feel isolated, a kind of pariah, sorely in need of the congenial theorizing of her young Baltimore friends. Although she had received several letters from them—the two from Mamie Gwinn "without beginning or end, a regular essay cut off in the middle"—letters by no means gave the support of companionship. The prospect of a visit from Mamie therefore was doubly welcome.

Before her arrival Carey, divided between trepidation and

curiosity, had wondered how her friend would "stand the Bible and preaching every morning." To give Mamie the best of what in any case must be endured, she arranged for her grandmother's friend Eliza Gurney to preach, if, when the time came, she could possibly feel herself moved to do so; and to provide more mundane and probably more welcome entertainment, she persuaded her father, sending him details of prices and methods of freightage, to ship his horse Annie and phaeton to Atlantic City. The visit went off with no visible hitch. All day and half the night Carey and Mamie read and talked together and Carey, smitten again with admiration for the keenness of Mamie's literary sense, began to toy once more with the idea of giving up work at the university and taking to a literary career. Mamie evinced a kindly tolerance of Whitall religiosity and to the best of her ability conformed in every respect with its standards. In fact she went so far as to remark to Carey, "I want to know everything so as to be good." This was most gratifying, especially as Mamie was so "gloriously clever." Nevertheless, she succeeded in making Carey more unhappy than ever about religion: "We sat on the balcony at sunset and read Swinburne's 'Hymn of Man' in *Songs Before Sunrise*. It is a poem of triumph over the vanishing of the Christian religion. To Mamie it was elixir, to me, poison; though I could not help the bewildering beauty of it carrying me away."

Soon after Mamie's visit, Carey followed Aunt Hannah to the Adirondacks where she joined the rest of the Pearsall Smith family on Long Lake in Hamilton County. There, one clear starlit evening as she rowed down the lake over a mile from shore, thinking of her quandary about the university, she had an experience that she never forgot. She felt forsaken with "no god to pray to . . . no shrine of Apollo to go to." Suddenly, "as suddenly as a possession," the temptation to upset the boat swept over her. She came so near doing it that she could not think of it later without trembling. Then, as quickly as the desire to drown had seized her, a sense of "use and purpose and beauty in living stole over" her. "All the old fighting to believe died away." She clearly perceived that "all religions are 'part of the hunger and thirst of the heart,' good and noble so long as they do not shackle, but only notes in the chorus. The core of Godwinism, the heavenly secret of Shelley 'to fear himself, and love all human-kind,' are all one. It is worth working for, worth living to work it out." She vowed that she would dedicate herself to humanity.

The decision made her happier than she had been for a long time. She swam and rowed, climbed and hunted. Her spirits soared so high, her energy and enterprise became so marked that the elders of the camp were kept in a constant flurry and the young people agog with admiration. "I was *thankful* to get Carey off with whole bones, and all her limbs!" exclaimed Aunt Hannah to Mrs. Thomas. Carey, it was obvious, had enjoyed herself to the fullest. On her return to Atlantic City, however, announcing with ungrateful snobbery that intellectual pleasures were far beyond physical enjoyment, she rushed in to Philadelphia four days on end to read in the Mercantile Library—"The hours were seconds, I was thirsty with an unquenchable thirst."

Having slaked her thirst, she turned to work on the novel that she, like each of her Baltimore friends, had sworn to write during the summer, but after a few days' toil admitted that she felt no capacity for novel writing: "I sit and think and can find no satisfactory plot." In the nick of time to save her from facing the issue, Bessie King arrived to visit her. They had "an idyllic time," learning poetry; "rowing in the evening among the meadows," silently enjoying "the perfect stillness of the sea of grass, the soft grey light of the sky and the sails moving here and there"; sitting on the porch, their feet on the railing and, according to Carey's journal, smoking cigarettes in the starlight. Unfortunately, Bessie confided the tale of the painful love affair through which she was struggling—and Carey replied with hers. "After I went to bed I felt as if talking had undone the work of this summer," groaned Carey. The fear that she would be able to control her thoughts no better now than during the previous winter haunted her. "It lost me last year. I am ashamed to think of the hours I sat and did nothing or threw myself on my knees by my sofa and prayed against it."

She knew that she would never marry the young man; she had made up her mind to that a year ago. And this summer her aunt Hannah's journal, which she had been permitted to read, confirmed her in her view that marriage meant "a pulling down of the woman." But she would do her young man one good turn, at least, before setting herself again to forget him. It occurred to her that he would make an admirable president of the institution for the higher education of "female friends" that Dr. Joseph W. Taylor proposed to found near Haverford College. She had heard it much discussed by her parents and Francis King, one of Dr. Taylor's closest advisers. Cold as ice, hands and voice trembling with emotion, she sought out her cousin Francis and forced herself to make the suggestion.

At the Johns Hopkins, from a long talk with Professor Gildersleeve, she saw that she would be excluded during the coming year as in the past from the Greek seminarium and the advanced instruction given male postgraduate students, and would be dependent again upon Professor Gildersleeve's occasional advice as to reading. Her sole privilege would be to go up for an examination. It was not enough—or, perhaps, without instruction and competition, it was too much. Deeply as she revered Professor Gildersleeve, grateful though she was to him, and long though she did for a second degree, she went home and wrote a letter of resignation to the trustees.

The die once cast, she squandered no time in sorrow or anger at benefits denied her. More strangely, she seemed not to recognize the fact, which as a distant possibility she had feared, that by failing to put through the three years' course for an advanced degree, however many the difficulties, she had failed to prove her own and woman's power to do so. Perhaps she felt that her failure itself marked a step forward for women by proving that the trustees, in attaching so insuperable a condition to their admittance of women, were effectually excluding them from obtaining degrees from the university. She had at least clarified the situation. In any case, against accomplished fact Carey never wasted energy in vain regrets. Her face turned forward always; her courage rose against the future. Having rejected the crumbs bestowed upon her by the Johns Hopkins, she settled at once upon a new program which would satisfy her literary as well as her scholastic ambitions: "Writing I shall seriously try—two hours every day—read Greek two hours; German two hours; and in the evenings—four hours —French and English." Her new freedom elated her: "I feel the power to do something." Alas, within the week, work entirely under her own steam proved as impossible as it had under the slight incentive of desultory competition and distant examinations. She became "blue as indigo"; the novel would not progress; she felt she could never write: "Surely this is the test and it has failed."

In the midst of her despondency Mamie Gwinn, to whom her devotion had increased, spent an afternoon criticizing her scathingly: "She said I swung my arms very much, bowed too low, pushed away a person's hand and did not look at him—that is, turned half away—sat with my legs crossed and my arm over the back of a chair, and threw my head back when I talked. Could there be a longer list." She found herself in the same old grooves of the previous year, unhappy, uncertain, distracted, and quite unable to work. Worst of all, she and her family had got painfully on each other's nerves. The process of irritation had begun, indeed, not many months after her return from Cornell.

5

Carey, like so many young people, was fastidious and hotly resentful when anything connected with herself failed to come up to her standard. It offended her taste and hurt her pride. After the independence of college life the plunge had been severe into the easygoing communal life of her busy family with all its conflicting interests and habits. She was soon driven to write in her journal that the Thomas household "was not constructed right." There was too little ceremony and the small things, that to her seemed as important as the large, were neglected. Nothing, she felt, drives love away sooner than lack of care in personal manners and she determined never herself to be guilty of it. "I am *sure* that there is a possibility of everything about a house being managed—things cooked propperly and dusting and proper behaviour at the table—without precluding all outside interest." She bore the strain as best she could, but found it increasingly difficult not to show her irritation. "When father or mother do anything I don't like, it takes me hours before I feel like going near them.

Like Iago I am afraid 'I am nothing if not critical.' But I struggle against it and it does me no good."

The happy-go-lucky clutter of the Thomas household was the result, she decided, of too many children: "If people realized," she wrote severely, "that to have more children than they can afford to train and support properly, was a greater crime than anything else, I am sure it would be better. Nobody can tell—people are more magnificent frauds than anything else—how little sympathy can be hidden by apparently pleasant family relations." The evils in marriage, and especially in large families of children, she thought were the fault of husband rather than wife. Ignorant of much of Mrs. Thomas's deep happiness—Carey had naturally seen neither her mother's journals nor her letters to her father—impressed by Hannah Smith's diary, Carey thought that her mother's feeling must be what her own would be in similar circumstances. Increasingly she imagined her mother unhappy and put upon, and blamed her father bitterly. Her brothers and sisters, moreover, though she was fond enough of them, seemed to her boring and troublesome when she had to live among them. This dissatisfaction with the family, try as she might to hide it, inevitably made itself felt. Moreover, she seemed entirely self-absorbed, caring only for her own work and her own friends. Though for her parents' sake she tried to keep up the forms that were dear to them, attending meeting regularly and never voicing her doubts, her indifference to religion was apparent and to her parents alarming, both for her sake and lest it influence the other children, who regarded her with considerable awe. The older members of the family looked upon her with alternate tender sympathy and impatience. Gradually, impatience got the upper hand.

Toward the beginning of the New Year, 1879, things had come to such a pass that her parents could no longer restrain their disapproval. Dr. Thomas remarked vehemently "that he shuddered to think of her in the house speaking words against his Saviour." The next evening, Mrs. Thomas mounted to Carey's study and had it out with her. "I do believe I shall shoot myself," wrote Carey late that night. "There is no use in living and then mother would see in the morning that she had been cruel. She says that I outrage her every feeling, that it is the greatest living grief to her to have me in the house because I am a denier and defamer of the Christ whom she loves thousands more than she loves me, that I am merely selfish—a cipher, and worse, a finder of fault in the house—that she has ceased to love me except as a child, that I make the other children unbelieving, that I barely tolerate. father, that I am utterly and entirely selfish, that I use the house, of which I take the best of everything, and father and herself for my purposes and then care no more for them, that as for treating me as if she approved of me she will not be so untrue to her Saviour. Oh heavens what a religion that makes a mother cast her daughter off!"

The diary continues with pages of bewildered lamentation and rage. Carey was not averse to "scenes"; in fact she frequently generated and rather enjoyed them. But this was different. When the scene was over and she had cooled down, she was engulfed by desolation. It marked the nadir of the two unhappy disintegrated years since Cornell. Unconsciously, she had depended on her parents; she had been devoted to them, all but adored her mother; and now the prop was jerked from beneath her.

Doubtless Mrs. Thomas saw that in the emotion of the moment she had spoken too strongly, for the next day she explained and softened her strictures. "She was lovely," wrote Carey, "and we will be different, I will be different." They would "try again." "But it is hard to bring back a feeling," Carey added sadly. The incident left its mark upon both her religious views and her attitude toward her parents. Her doubts of Christianity were confirmed and her trust in family security was shattered. Though life at home soon appeared to follow its usual currents, she saw that she must stand upon her own feet, that it was necessary for her to make her own way in the world apart from her family. As the next months passed, repeating the experiences and distractions of the previous "wasted" year, it became clear to her that, if ever she was to do anything, she must get away from home.

She had tried to force an entrance into the Johns Hopkins University because that seemed the only possibility for further academic study. She had longed to follow the footsteps of her two friends Richard Cadbury and Francis Gummere to Europe, especially those of Gummere since they led to a German university, that Mecca of American students toward the end of the nineteenth century. But even Carey had hardly permitted herself to dream of a German university. Now that the Johns Hopkins had proved a failure for her and there was no other accepted way to turn, she began to wonder if after all Germany might not be possible. Cadbury and Gummere were both to be working abroad, the latter as an accredited student in a German university. Why should she not go too?

The more she thought of it the more feasible the plan appeared. Women were permitted to work at some of the German universities; in fact, there were American ladies attending courses in them. If they could do it, why could not she?—and go them one better by completing the work for a degree from one or other of the universities, as they were not attempting to do? She was twenty-two and able to make her own decisions. The difficulty lay in the fact that she depended upon her parents for money and therefore must have their approval for the scheme.

Mrs. Thomas, too, saw the impossibility of Carey's living contentedly at home and, as always, sympathized with her desire for learning. To Dr. Thomas the idea of Carey's going abroad alone to study in Germany was not only disconcerting but outrageous. His reasons differed little from the earlier arguments against Cornell, but were voiced with the stubborn reiteration of one who desperately sees himself losing ground. The family story, growing like a snowball in the tellings, runs that Mrs. Thomas, seeing that arguments availed nothing with her husband, remarked to her daughter, "There is nothing for it, thee must cry thyself to Germany." Whereupon they both wept and wept for a fortnight until they broke Dr. Thomas's spirit. However that may have been, certainly by pursuing the tactics of non-co-operation mother and daughter again brought him round, if not to their point of view, at least to agreeing to try it out. With somewhat pathetic humility and resignation he wrote his wife, "Minnie ought to be truly thankful she has such a mother to support her as thee. I feel that my instincts are so naturally opposed to a woman's fighting it out alone in a foreign land—and my natural timidity so great—that she owes this as other things to thy pluck and determination. I can only pray that the Divine guidance of the Holy Spirit may attend her and make it all work together for her good." It was little comfort to him that Mamie Gwinn, by inducing in herself hysterical fainting fits as well as by tactics similar to those employed in forcing his own hand, had succeeded with her mother's help in persuading her father to allow her to accompany Carey.

Having once consented to the plan, however, Dr. Thomas did all in his power to forward it. He wrote to various people to enlist their help and advice, among others to President White of Cornell, who was at that time the United States ambassador at Berlin. The idea of a young lady attending lectures regularly at a German university appealed to Mr. White little more than it had to Dr. Thomas, although he thought that Carey "could use a year or two in Europe to great advantage." He advised her to live with a German family long enough to learn the language, meanwhile attending certain lectures suitable to ladies, and then to travel. It was unlikely that the University of Berlin would admit a young lady but, he said, "at Leipzig there is already an American lady, Miss Eva Channing, attending various lectures." From an eyewitness he had learned that "all seemed to go perfectly naturally and easily, her coming in attracting no attention." On this slight encouragement it was decided that Carey and Mamie, after a preliminary canter in a German family, should go to the University of Leipzig where the way was already broken.

During the following summer months Carey walked in sunshine even when it rained, for she herself was radiant. She dreamed and planned and made preparations and farewell visits. Letters of encouragement and congratulation poured in upon her, only occasionally tempered by doubt of the wisdom of her crusading point of view. One Cornell friend voiced this uncertain sympathy most clearly, pointing out that it was possible to do splendid work and help the cause of women without making any protestation or fuss about it; she knew women who proved it. "I believe," she wrote, "the bounds are in many cases imagined. I think the least publicity that is possible for accomplishment is the best." Such tepid douches did not chill Carey. She was not only excited by the prospect of new lands and people, elated by the chance of obtaining Culture as well as learning in that home of all culture, Germany, but she was exalted by the vision of herself breaking down barriers set against the education of women. The parting from her family, and especially from her old grandmother Whitall, whom she feared never to see again, sobered her. But in July she and Mamie had not sailed away long on the little Baltimore liner before her spirits revived full strength. Her dreams were coming true.

CHAPTER V

European Universities and Travel

I

CAREY THOMAS'S first reaction in the autumn of 1879 to the European scene was that at last she had caught a glimpse of paradise. "It is as if a man were to meet his dream love," she wrote her future sister-in-law Zoe Carey. She was exalted by the paintings in the galleries of Antwerp, where they landed, and of Brussels—"in America we dream of color and find it here, in masses and piles in galleries that may be seen for the asking"; by the incredibly vivid green of the vineyards along the Rhine; and by the majesty of Cologne Cathedral—"before it everything unworthy and artificial fades away." Even the life at Stuttgart, later to seem so boring, led by the three maiden Grüneisen sisters, with whom she and Mamie had arranged before leaving America to spend their first German months, interested her breathlessly.

The Grüneisens were "really cultivated." Their father, at one time court preacher to the king of Württemberg, had been among "the first to start the new revival of art of which Lübke etc. are the aftermath." His youngest daughter Fräulein Mathilde, who took the two American girls under her special protection, had "read every one" of the five hundred books on art that comprised his library. Although she had never seen the originals, since she had never been outside Stuttgart, she "knew" almost every picture in existence painted by an Old Master; and although she herself painted, she had been given no chance to train her talent, being expected to devote herself to the domestic frugalities and to teaching her young American and English paying guests elementary

German. Most satisfactory of all to Carey, she was well enough acquainted through her father with many distinguished literary men to say *"du"* to them. In short, if the Grüneisens were fair examples, and Carey took it on faith that they were, Carey had come to the right place to achieve culture. She noted, to be sure, the strange customs and opinions of the country: the enormous quantity of food eaten; the elaboration and lack of taste of the ladies' dress; the buttoned gloves "which are kept on till the first bite of bread is taken at the tea companies"; the overwhelming power of family ties and the "equally hampering and far more degrading insane worship of Bismarck and the Kaiser and, above all, the Crown Prince"; and the injustice done France—"They deny it poetry and art, all." But not until she and Mamie had reached Leipzig and settled down to the routine life of students, unshepherded by the amiable Fräulein Mathilde, did the flaws in German culture trouble them.

For the first few months in Leipzig they lodged with Frau Doktor Metzge, to whom the Grüneisens passed them on. The bedroom and the sitting room, in which the maid Pauline served their meals, were comfortable enough, but it was not long before Carey and Mamie began to find the cost too great, the meals nearly inedible, and the Frau Doktor herself overcurious and mean. The chief argument against Carey's coming abroad had been financial and for her the problem of expense was serious. Mamie, on the other hand, had no need for extreme economy, since her parents were well off and her mother begged her to spend all that might be necessary to live in comfort and to travel. As Mrs. Thomas put it impatiently, "It is absurd for Mamie to be so miserly." Nevertheless, perhaps as a matter of pride, she was even more frugal than Carey and, when lending money to Carey for holiday travel, demanded full payment.

Nothing in the way of clothes, with the exception of the socially requisite kid gloves, was bought by either of them in the first year, and very little in the following years. When bodice seams split, as Mamie's did during a strenuous climbing holiday in Switzerland, Carey inked them; when darns were necessary, Carey sewed. Heavy winter woolens were packed carefully in camphor for the summer: "A terrible ordeal. . . . Mamie had to lie on the floor at intervals from exhaustion. We comforted ourselves by thinking that most women's lives were spent in clearing things out of one place to put them in another, and that we had forsaken that sphere." As the years passed, it was sometimes necessary to buy "fixings" such as a lace scarf to hide discrepancies, cuffs and collars, handkerchiefs, shoes, and even, owing to the gibes of friends and the urgent pleas of their families not to put them to shame, an occasional new dress or hat: a pretty brown hat trimmed with a band of feathers for $2.50 for Carey and a "sweller one" of brown plush with pompons for $5.40 for Mamie; a suit made "with a curious plaited basque like a French model" for Carey with a charming bonnet to match.

The real economic difficulty, which they succeeded in solving only momentarily and at intervals, and one that caused them to break with many a pension keeper, was the problem of food. The European climate made them as ravenously hungry as it does most Americans: "Mamie eats away like an industrious ant." Strange foods and new ways of cooking interested them not at all for, to such intellectuals, food was ignoble. But the ordinary student fare served them by Frau Metzge—"scraggly breakfasts," as Mamie called them, of tea and rolls; dinners of corned beef or rabbit—was so different from the plentiful and rich Baltimore food to which they were accustomed that they did not like it. Their complaints left the Frau Doktor amazed. She considered them "spoiled" and their strange ways bewildered her, their lack of interest in her conversational openings, their reticence concerning themselves, the freedom with which they pursued their own course. It upset her to have Carey receive a young gentleman—an American student whom she had known in Baltimore and almost her only caller in Germany—alone in the parlor. Since Mamie refused to chaperon them, the Frau Doktor herself entered the room. Carey and the young man were looking over a Gothic grammar, discussing grammatical forms, but Frau Metzge seeing at a glance that they were seated upon "the betrothal sofa" leaped to the obvious conclusion. After that, Carey could hardly bear to speak to her and Mamie entirely refused to do so. They concluded that she was neither "cultivated" nor "a lady" though, remarked Carey, "an excellent character for Balzac to work up."

They learned thankfully of rooms at considerably lower price to be had in the flat of Fräulein Pochhammer at the top of a tall stone house on a pleasant square five minutes from the university. From the big double-paned windows of the flat, gay with flower boxes in the spring, they had "a lovely sky view." And their three rooms were comfortable : a long narrow bedroom with the two beds, wardrobes, and washstands end to end; a small cubby hole known as "Mamie's study" with table and couch; and a sitting room furnished chiefly by an earthenware stove, so tall it almost touched the high ceiling, and a large table where Carey worked. When their steamer chairs had been set up and Carey had made lambrequins and table covers of cretonne and curtains of blue satin cambric, and Mamie had bought a bust of the young Augustus to stand on the bookshelves, the rooms presented a cozy aspect highly satisfactory to their occupants. Anna, the maid of all work, kept the place immaculate. The unsettled problem was, as always, the food.

Carey made breakfast, preparing the porridge the night before. At midday they went across the square to the *Schützenhaus* for an enormous meal of two sorts of meat and vegetables for nineteen cents apiece; at the end of the day they supped on chocolate or tea and eggs or cold cuts for thirteen cents each; and between them, unable to swallow the Leipzig water, they drank a "daily bottle of beer." Yet had it not been for the enormous boxes of food sent them by their families, they would have starved, they thought. Though their intentions were abstemious, they could rarely resist buying the cream cakes so enticingly exhibited in the baker's window and on one occasion indulged, almost fatally for Mamie, who gobbled, in six dozen canned oysters boiled in a chafing dish. It was a relief in the vacations when they were traveling to take their meals *en pension*. "As Mamie says, we live on our fat like bears while we are at Leipzig and then pounce down upon pensions and devour everything like locusts." Such were their reports from Leipzig of starvation that Mrs. Thomas's anxiety was allayed only by receiving a photograph taken during their first winter in which she could see that they were far from emaciated : Mamie looked "untragic" and Carey herself, though dissatisfied with the picture since it had been taken full face instead of from the side as she preferred, appeared to be quite stalwart and happy.

After a year they began to find Fräulein Pochhammer, who at

first had seemed "a most lovely person" with charming manners
and much cultivation, thoroughly tiresome. They suspected her,
as they did most pension keepers, of committing frequent and
unaccountable perfidies, even dishonesties. Like Frau Metzge before her, she found bewildering their penurious ways, unexpected
in Americans, and even more so the coldness with which they received her friendly advances. She retaliated, as she thought, in
kind. But by that time Carey and Mamie had become too intent
upon pursuing the purpose for which they were living in Leipzig
to pay much attention to Fräulein Pochhammer.

2

They had plunged into lectures at the university, buying themselves the regulation student paraphernalia, *Hefte*, ten sheets of
paper sewed together on which to take notes, and *Mappen*, little
oilcloth bags in which to carry them. Under the Grüneisens'
tutelage their German had become ready enough for them to
understand the lectures and to take voluminous notes. For four
hours or more daily during their three years in Leipzig, Carey
sat at one time or another under some of the most famous of
German professors. She attended Curtius's lectures on the Iliad;
Ebers', on "The Comparative Philology of the Romance Languages"; Wülcker's, on "Old English Literature" and on "The
Historical Grammar of the English Language"; Braune's, on
"Gothic, Middle and Low German"; Hildebrand's, on "Goethe's
Lieder"; Zarncke's, on "Old German Literature" and on "German
Grammar"; and, because Richard Cadbury told her that no one
could form a reasonable aesthetic appreciation or judgment without some knowledge of philosophy, Hermann's lectures on "Attempts at a Philosophy of History" and Heinze's "Ethics of
Philosophy." Francis Gummere first disposed her to look favorably upon Professor Friedrich Zarncke, whom, by October, she
had come to regard as a model to all other lecturers. "Not only
does he tell one everything upon his own subject, but he settles
all other subjects. . . . He is admirable, genial, generous in praising,
thorough in criticizing and fair in all his views. He is also sweet
and funny; he looks like a clever pig. . . . I have perfect trust in

everything he says—except upon women. . . . Mamie feels just the
same." She attended all his lectures that were open to her, reveling
especially in those on philology, a new field to her: "Zarncke on
German grammar is adorable."

There were two schools of philology at Leipzig, enemies to the
death—the new, headed by Zarncke, and the old, by Curtius.
"Curtius and the conservatives," explained Carey, "believe that
a, i and *u* were the original vowels from which all others were
derived, and the new school . . . that *e* and *o* are the aboriginal
vowels. . . . Of course I am a believer of the new school but in
one way it is very trying because all text books and grammars
are one and all incorrect, being of course upon the old standpoint.
. . . There is *no* certainty in *anything*. You have to try the theories
for yourself and the work is tough." This, however, did not dim
Carey's zest especially since in these experiments she was following
a brilliant leader of the newest fashion. She attended Zarncke's
biweekly quiz in Gothic, much amused by the heavy stupidity of
all the men students which, to her delighted mind, only made the
professor's wit shine more brightly. At the end of the year, she
entered his evening seminar of fifty-six men, six of whom read
and were examined upon passages of Middle High German at
each meeting. Carey declined to read and be examined, fearing
that the men might think her forward. So she sat back and
listened, laughing with pleasure when the denseness of the men
made Zarncke stamp and groan with impatience.

Her other professors she found less inspiring, though both
Curtius, whose learned publications she knew before coming to
Leipzig, and Ebers, whose novels of Greece and Egypt she had
read in Baltimore, had a "sleek scholarship" that was highly instructive. "Ebers," she wrote in her first semester, "has been
upon the Arthur and Charlemagne romances and this week has
drawn up great family trees for the different *geste* cycles. To be
sure his writing on the blackboard cannot be read and his pro-
nunciation of French names is atrocious, but still we are edified."
Many years later she remarked seriously to a distinguished professor of Bryn Mawr College, "The students tell me that they
learned a great deal from your lectures, but you speak so rapidly
they are unable to understand a word you say." Professor

Wülcker, editor of the journal *Anglia*, seemed unbearably stupid at first but by plowing along, she felt she derived a certain amount of information from him. And Professor Hildebrand, who had a large part in working on Grimm's Dictionary of the Germanic Languages, was almost equally dull, but at least picturesque and sometimes startling: "He is a travesty of the idea one usually has of a German professor. He looks very grisly and slipslop and dirty; he shambles into his lecture flourishing an enormous bandana handkerchief and spits tobacco, hawks and chokes several times before he reaches the stand. . . . He is an ideal *germanist*, he hates the *barbarische* influences of the French, he abhors classic methods; but the mere whoop of a German savage back in the *urzeit* moves him to tears."

Carey's way at the university had been in some measure prepared for her by letters from Ambassador White to professors Curtius and Ebers, through whom she and Mamie met socially in turn Wülcker, Zarncke, and others. To the envy of the one other American woman then studying at Leipzig, Miss Channing, they were asked, soon after their arrival, by Professor and Frau Curtius to an evening tea *conversazione*. The talk surpassed expectation—"It was a different thing from what one finds in America"—ranging over the latest books, the most recent lectures, Wagner and his music, and the merits and doings of Leipzig professors. And both Professor and Frau Curtius were more than polite, showing an amiability that, Carey suspected, he at least did not always show. "I had such an awe and reverence for Curtius that I can hardly believe I know him," said Carey, urging her father to thank Mr. White and tell him what a difference his letters had made in her reception at Leipzig.

Calling, by invitation, a few mornings later upon Professor Ebers, they were equally impressed: "We were shown into a beautifully furnished study and there sat Ebers on a Turkey rug, leaning back in an armchair with his feet on a cushion and an Eastern red rug thrown over his lap. He is lame and it was through this confinement that he first thought of writing his novels." Suddenly, alarmingly, into the room swept Frau Ebers, an imposing, pretty woman in lace and black velvet, followed shortly by a young man in white cravat and gloves. Carey and

Mamie felt shamed by their own dowdiness amid such grandeur and were relieved to have the morning call succeeded by an invitation to a large evening party. Many professors and their wives, and many sons and daughters of professors, appeared at this function but while they drank tea Professor Ebers devoted himself to Carey—rather underdressed, even this time, in her brown brocade. Later, when they moved to the dining room for an elaborate supper, she found herself sitting between Dr. Creizenach, one of the most successful of the younger men, and Professor von Noorden, a popular professor of history and an enthusiastic philosopher. Every ten minutes after supper "a very décolleté girl from the conservatory sang in a glorious ringing alto voice to the accompaniment of the piano played by the prettiest young man, and Mamie and I were in the midst of the most charmingly interesting comparison of lectures and hours with von Noorden when"—the maid from Frau Doktor Metzge came to fetch them home. "We were very much provoked we had to go. I quite enjoyed talking with some men again."

Practically, as well as socially, they were helped by their new acquaintances. It was Frau Ebers who found them lodging with Fräulein Pochhammer, and her husband who obtained them admission to a reading room hitherto forbidden to women, containing all possible learned periodicals; Frau Curtius helped them on every hand, and Profesor Curtius, Carey thought, took "a decided fancy" to her, only slightly cooled by her desertion of his lectures when she turned away from the classics to follow Zarncke.

Naturally, such consideration from the great made Carey and Mamie marked students in the eyes of the professors. "It is surprising how politely they treat us, one professor stopped his lecture, descended from his desk and closed the shutter" because the sun shone in Carey's eyes and on another occasion picked up Mamie's muff. Wülcker brought Carey her gloves, and "another professor placed his library at our disposal." Even the students seemed "much more polite" to them than to the other women. They often opened doors for them to pass through first—though sometimes they hesitated and then passed through determinedly first themselves; and after a year seemed to have developed "a sort of contemptuous affection" for them. "They observe us with a good humoured but by no means impertinent interest," reported Carey to her parents. "I suppose they accept us as established nuisances by now."

In spite of these ameliorations the lot of women at a German university was not easy. They were not wanted except by certain liberal professors who had found that they made good students. Almost no one agreed with Professor Ebers that women should be given degrees. Even as mere hearers, they had been admitted only on sufferance and without the knowledge of the minister of culture of Saxony, in whom lay the ultimate authority in such matters. When he learned of their presence, early in 1880, he ordered them at once to apply directly to him for permission to attend the lectures. The government feared, so Curtius explained to Carey, the entrance of Russian women and their spreading doctrines of anarchy and socialism as they were reported to have done at Zürich. It was highly probable, too, that the great Bismarck, whose hand lay heavy on all small German states, had himself urged the Saxon minister to oppose the admission of women. "They say," wrote Carey, "if he hears that Göttingen will grant me a degree he will find some means to stop it. He has no real power over any university outside of Prussia but a tyrant always finds means to enforce his tyranny."

However that might be, Carey was obliged halfway through her first semester to appeal to Ambassador White for help, asking for a letter to the Saxon minister of culture recommending herself and Mamie as university students. Professor Curtius wrote their formula of application and sent a letter about them to the university. And by the end of February they had received permission to continue work at Leipzig "until further notice." All the ladies— ten of them—then studying at Leipzig had been admitted, the minister of culture told Ambassador White, but all future applicants would be refused. Two years later, this archenemy of women students visited the university in attendance on the King of Saxony. Carey, informed that if he saw a woman student he would probably order her dismissal, took it upon herself to warn away all women students from the six lectures attended daily by the industrious royal party. Such difficulties, she felt, but enhanced her glory in being one of the few women students at Leipzig.

Tolerated though they were by the university officials, respected by the professors, and even treated with civility by the students, Carey felt that she and Mamie, as women, were obliged to put up with many trials. They had to run the gantlet daily—and painfully, until they grew used to it—of hundreds of interested eyes fixed upon them, so they thought, as they trudged through the dust or, more often, the mud of the great courtyard in front of the university. At the first possible moment each semester, they had to take seats for the term on the front row of their lecture rooms for, if they sat on a back bench, the men turned round and looked at them throughout the lecture—"which is disconcerting." Whatever motion they made in the lecture rooms was remarked with interest. When Carey spilled ink down the front of her gray stuff dress, as she inevitably did, the eyes of two or three hundred men fastened upon her, sympathetically but again disconcertingly. One morning as Carey and Mamie rose between lectures to go for a fresh supply of ink, every student turned toward them, anxiously thinking they intended "to cut," and murmured *"Sie gehen fort."* Carey observed that no students ever cut a lecture, although they had the right to do so. She was surprised, too, by their diligence in "taking notes without a breath between" and, before lectures, by their "talking only about books and notes." She approved of their custom of applauding any professor whom they especially liked—Zarncke notably—when he entered or left the lecture room, or of shuffling their feet when they wished something not understood repeated. But she lived in terror of being made the butt of their time-hallowed custom of echoing any student who coughed during a lecture, or of groaning or shuffling when any student entered a lecture room after quarter past the hour.

A good many American women were studying in Germany, and four at Leipzig before Carey and Mamie left there, so that Carey's and Mamie's painful consciousness of being lonely pioneers, the cynosure of all eyes, was somewhat overstressed. It was not, however, entirely groundless. Baltimore, like all provincial towns, kept severe tabs upon its inhabitants and, apart from one or two ambitious young women who followed their progress with envy, disapproved of Carey and Mamie for breaking the accepted pattern of young ladies' lives. In the course of gossip,

stories of their doings naturally grew to astonishing dimensions
and ill-natured things were said of them, some of which were
passed on to put them on their guard and some, told them as news
by fellow travelers. They were horrified to hear of the rumor that
the Gwinns' doctor had told Mamie that if she persisted in going
to Germany her mother would die, to which she had replied she
did not care. They besought their families to be silent about them.
But Mrs. Gwinn was incorrigible: "She probably does not see,"
observed Carey wearily, "that secrecy and guile are the only refuge
of a down-trodden sex." And even the circumspect Mrs. Thomas
could not refrain from sending Carey's letters to her sisters. Inevitably the sisters gossiped, for Carey's position as the daughter
of parents known at least by name to all Quaker circles made her
career of interest to a large number of people and especially to
the many liberal Quakers concerned with the problem of women's
education.

In their eagerness to avoid rumor that might jeopardize their
power to blaze a trail for women, as they believed themselves to be
doing, their observance of the proprieties went to the extreme.
After the unhappy affair of the betrothal sofa, as might be expected, they permitted no man to call upon them, in spite of Frau
Curtius's assurance that such social calls were customary. But
they went farther than that. Any student who showed the slightest
disposition to talk with them after a lecture, even though on
academic matters, was promptly quenched. They ignored the
civil *"Guten Morgen"* of students whom they met daily in lectures, until the students, shy themselves, gave up. And when a
young man accosted them as they were examining a ruined abbey
during a walking trip in the Thüringen forest and begged politely
to introduce himself as a fellow student at Leipzig, they snubbed
him royally: "We said," wrote Carey smugly, "we could not make
acquaintance so. He said he didn't mean that, but it was such a
lovely feeling to meet again in the midst of a forest (who but a
German could say such a silly thing). We thanked him for his
kindness and turned away leaving him utterly baffled."

Decorum carried to such lengths may have served its purpose,
but to Carey, in especial, it formed a serious drawback, since she
stood in real need of those useful tips to be gained only from talk

with other students, as Mamie, who had no intention of taking a degree, did not. Fortunately, Carey allowed herself to see something of Francis Gummere when he came to Leipzig and from him learned the answers to a few of her questions about books and academic ways and means. After Gummere's departure for Strassburg, she could talk with no one except Mamie and, on great social occasions, professors; apart from them, she spoke only to the bookseller and Fräulein Pochhammer's maid and little dog— "as for a man, never."

The worship of culture, according to their narrowly limited definition of the term, as well as the awareness of certain deplorable Americanisms, especially in ways of speech, both in themselves and others, only increased Carey's and Mamie's consciously fostered attitude of lonely superiority. Mamie was startled into remarking, when Carey read her a passage from one of Mrs. Thomas's letters, that she had never supposed anyone outside of their set of five girls could pronounce so intelligently upon writing. And when they met any woman on their travels, as they occasionally did, especially English women, who showed what seemed to them the proper freedom from conventional trammels and an intellectual keenness equal to their own, they were amazed. As for strange customs and ways of thought, observe them though they did, they were untouched by them and uninterested, remaining outsiders to the end.

3

Such complete satisfaction in each other's company was doubtless a misfortune. Had either been in Germany without the other, she might perforce have made a few friends, American or foreign, to rub away some of the crust of Baltimore. Indeed, later, after the weeks that she spent without Mamie in Zürich, where she developed a little independence and made friends with a number of women, Carey's natural warmheartedness was permitted occasionally to show itself. It was she who called a doctor and helped with the nursing when Edward Everett Hale's daughter, living with a friend and fellow painter in rooms above them in Paris, fell ill of typhoid fever. And a little later when Representative

Kelley's daughter, a Cornell woman whose legal thesis had been highly praised, turned up, Carey welcomed her cordially. But for the most part, Mamie, scornful of all that did not minister directly to her tastes and comforts, jealous of all that did, demanded Careys' full attention and acquiescence. Except when in need of them for some special purpose, therefore, they had as little as possible to do with either the women students at Leipzig or their fellow travelers, and even their introductions to the great they never followed up beyond the first formal civilities. The only real friend whom they made, Gertrude Meade, an American student in Berlin, merely confirmed them in their own ways and views. They asked her, since she was a friend of Julia Rogers, to spend part of the Christmas holiday of 1881 with them at Leipzig. Much impressed by the independence of their lives and the certainty and completeness of their opinions, she at once dropped into the endearing position of disciple, the only terms on which they would have accepted her, and the more gratifying to them since she seemed "to have real ability" and "a literary sense" and "knows," Carey said with vicarious pride, "such lots of people—Howells, Longfellow, Emerson and all their families, besides all the Concord people, and in Berlin she got to know most of the Art men and some great lights." Even she, however, never cracked the entity formed by Carey and Mamie.

Only Carey's family was permitted to intrude upon their haughty solitude. In this Mamie had to acquiesce, inclined though she was to resent the claims of a large family that presented so whole a front to the world as did the Thomases and Whitalls. Bent by Mamie's instinctive opposition, Carey did no more than her duty by the less dear members of her family whom she chanced to meet, merely calling upon the Braithwaites in England and on her father's stepmother when their paths chanced to cross in Paris. Once she went out of her way, largely because both she and Mamie wanted to travel through Prague to Vienna, to look up her stepuncle Dr. Richard Thomas and his wife Anna Braithwaite who were living there. Richard cured her of the painful lump that had grown in the scar tissue of her old burn and reassured her that it was not cancerous—she was nervous, dreaming constantly that she or Mamie or some member of her family had cancer or consumption or was sinking into a decline; Anna took them on various sight-seeing expeditions and won "even Mamie's stony heart" by her gentle gaiety and sweetness; but they left Vienna rejoicing that they were foot-loose and free of domesticity.

Carey herself, like most members of large families, believed in clan solidarity and was pleasantly conscious of the exceptional unity of hers. The situation was far from simple, however, when her parents proposed to visit her in the summer of 1881. For many years Mrs. Thomas had dreamed of journeying to Palestine, stopping on the way in England and Europe and Egypt. Now the moment had come when she could regard the first, albeit to her the least interesting part, of her journey a duty since Dr. Thomas, worn out, needed a change. The Medical and Chirurgical Faculty of Maryland proposed sending him as its delegate to the International Medical Congress that was to meet in London early in August; and the Baltimore Society of Friends urged both him and his wife to attend, on their behalf, the Friends' yearly meeting in London in May. The eldest children were away at school or college, only the youngest, Nellie, aged almost ten, and Frank, eight and a half, presented a vexing problem. The first plan was to leave them at home in charge of their nurse and two great-aunts; but, as many years later she explained in a book about her childhood, Nell was reduced to such a passion of tears at the thought of being left behind that her parents were forced to take her and her brother with them.[1]

When the journey was first mooted, Carey deluged her parents with advice as to how to conduct their travels: they must go to Italy in July—"It is never hot then and is entirely free of mosquitoes"; they must learn a little Italian so as to enjoy Italy; they must not spend all their time visiting institutions but must see, in especial, pictures; above all, they must not bring the children. "We have not seen one child in all our travels," she wrote. "There is *no* provision for children on the continent. I suppose that is what makes it so charming." In the first flush of enthusiasm, nevertheless, on hearing that her parents had sailed accompanied by Nellie and Frank, she suggested that the children stay with her and Mamie in July while her parents traveled. To her parents, who had been toying with the unsatisfactory idea of leaving the chil-

dren in England while they went to the Continent, Carey's suggestion seemed an admirable solution. They accepted at once. Meantime Carey discused the matter with Mamie—who was aghast.
The children would have to sleep in her bed in the room with
Carey, ousting her to the sofa in her study; worse still, they would
disturb her reading, since everything could be heard through the
walls between rooms. For herself, Carey was willing to put up
with anything: "Thee knows," she wrote her parents, "if I devoted myself to them [the children] a year or *five* I would then feel
that I had not done half enough to express my gratitude to you
for the benefits above and beyond your duties as parents which
you have bestowed upon me." But Mamie's suffering was hard
to contemplate. At last a compromise was agreed upon: Mamie
would put up with the children, indeed would take charge of them
while Carey attended lectures, if Carey would promise to stay an
extra week in Paris after her parents sailed and would "make
her presents to the amount of ten or fifteen dollars." The arrangement astonished Mrs. Thomas, who replied with the sensible suggestion that some German woman be hired to care for the children.

In the first week of July, parents and children arrived. "Minnie
looked just the same as she did when she left us," wrote Mrs.
Thomas to the children in America, "the same old things on and
all." Before leaving for Italy she condemned most of "the same
old things" to the old-clothesman and fitted out her daughter
afresh. Carey and Mamie, left with Nell and Frank, were mightily
amused by the stir caused in university circles when they appeared with two children. "It is lucky," remarked Carey, "the
children are no younger." The fact that their elders were busy
and not to be troubled had been impressed upon the children by
their mother. Though he tried to be good, the warning had no
great effect on the natural ebullience of young Frank's spirits,
especially as he disliked Mamie and cared not a pin to please
her; but it lay like a weight of doom on Nell's overtender
conscience. Her scruples made the few real difficulties that Carey
had to face with the children: her objection to listening to music
on First day, that led to the awkward compromise of walking
about with Frank in the Rosenthal gardens beyond the range of
the music that Carey and Mamie delighted to hear on Sunday

afternoon; her distress at eating food bought on First day morning; her qualms lest Frank act a lie when Carey dressed him up as a little girl in order to take him with her to the public baths. For the most part, however, the fortnight passed easily until they all four joined Dr. and Mrs. Thomas at Lucerne.

Realizing how torn Carey must be between her devotion to her parents and her desire to make Mamie happy, Mrs. Thomas had looked forward to an awkward time with them in Switzerland while Dr. Thomas went off to his medical congress in England. But Mamie, she reported to her sisters, accepted her and the children "as legitimate encumbrances," and she had "snatches of delightful talks" with Carey when the others were in bed. They spent a fortnight of hard traveling in German Switzerland, the children tossing to the peasants as they went religious tracts that their parents, before leaving home, had had printed for the purpose on pink or blue slips in German and French. Joined by Dr. Thomas at Lausanne they went on for more climbing in Chamonix. After crossing the *Mer de glace* Mrs. Thomas confided to the children in Baltimore, "I think I have graduated on glaciers." Carey's appetite, on the other hand, had been whetted. Not troubled, as was her mother, by the poverty of the peasants in the upland valleys or, as was young Nellie, by nightmare from the goiters of the inhabitants of the Rhône Valley, she enjoyed Switzerland to the full. The vigorous physical exercise in clear Alpine air filled her with a sense of well-being that held over to the following weeks in Paris and England.

All the same, it was a relief to return to quiet work—"A student's life is a lovely one," she exclaimed. "I feel as if it gave one eternal youth." Not only had the children's visit dislocated her life as a student but the family holiday had prevented her doing even the usual small amount of work accomplished in vacations. Lost time was hard to make up since her days in Leipzig had always flown, packed to the brim, beginning at six-thirty and continuing with unabated hurry until eleven in the evening. But it was the pace at which she liked to live. She was happy. "The days are so short I wish the sun would stand still and let me read all I wish to. But everyone is not a Joshua. . . . I wish I were sure of living to two hundred; then there might be time for something." Fortunately, they had reduced social demands to a minimum. And sight-seeing was no temptation, for Leipzig had little to offer in comparison with places visited in the holidays. Carey and Mamie went once or twice to see a play and sometimes heard a Wagner opera—the first, *Tristan and Isolde*, at the second Bayreuth Festival in 1882—and an occasional concert in the Thomas Kirche where Bach had been organist. But there were lectures to attend; the ordinary daily tasks to be done; the long biweekly family letters to write—"I am writing this," Carey told her father, "in intervals between rushing to Mamie's study to see that the tomatoes do not burn." There were walks to be taken "at great loss of time and tranquility of spirit" to avert the headaches that threatened her from want of exercise. And always, above all, there was Mamie, intellectually stimulating but, also, a time-consuming temptress.

4

Undoubtedly Mamie's interest in intellectual matters spurred Carey to work with an enthusiasm she had been unable to muster when living with her family in Baltimore. But Mamie was far from being an easy companion. All the practical arrangements of her life devolved upon Carey, as well as the tender cosseting she demanded during her frequent minor ailments and the illnesses that threatened whenever anything went contrary to her desires. Like Carey, she had the cause of women's education at heart—indeed, she was a more severe feminist than Carey, but a less practical one; action held no fascination for her. Whereas Carey looked upon herself as a future benefactor of the Cause by positive deeds, Mamie's idea of her contribution was to become herself an educated and cultured woman. She was under no financial pressure to prepare for a remunerative position of any sort and she saw no reason to slave for a degree simply in order to prove her equality with men in the academic world. It is not to be wondered, therefore, that she should have insisted upon traveling in the holidays, especially since her mother, who did not understand the sacrifice of scholarly work involved, begged her to do so. Besides, Mrs. Gwinn could not believe that the Thomases were really unable to afford unlimited travel for Carey. "She insists on think-ing," Carey wrote her mother, "it is because thee thinks I shall get all in Heaven anyway and earth makes no difference."

Passionately fond as was Carey herself of travel, and helpful as she recognized it to be in furnishing her mind, the expense of both time and money for as much travel as Mamie wished pre-sented an insoluble problem. Before each holiday she went through heartburnings, balancing the advantages and drawbacks of the proposed journeys. "I foresee," she wrote at the end of her first vacation from Leipzig, "we shall have to give up traveling en-tirely and just buckle to, fourteen hours a day right through vaca-tions as many of the men work." But her courage failed her when she thought of Mamie undergoing such discipline. Mamie, learn-ing as their third semester neared its end that Carey intended to stay in Leipzig during the spring holidays, cried all night: "She says travel in *the thing* in the world that she cares most about and that this is her only chance." During their first journeys in Europe, until Frau Curtius laughed them out of it, they had ar-ranged to have a chaperone; and even now, after four long jour-neys alone together, they did not think it right for Mamie to travel to Italy alone to join Mary Garrett and Julia Rogers in Rome. In the end, Carey succumbed once more, as she always did, to Mamie's wishes—in this case not unhappily, for Rome, after her first visit there in the previous spring, 1880, had become to her "the Venus-berg. . . . I left all my heart there." Her heart was to welcome many loves in the travels of the following three years but Rome remained its constant star.

"Rome, oh Rome is glorious as ever," cried Carey on their arrival in 1881, "the one city in the world." Its charm was only enhanced by the unexpectedly warm welcome of the Garretts and Julia Rogers. The Garrett courier made life easy, since he ob-tained the permissions to enter private galleries hitherto painfully sought by Carey; and, although Mary's maid somewhat abashed Carey by at once whisking away all her dresses to brush and re-furbish, Mary herself was entirely satisfactory: "She is above all antiquarian in her tastes—a hole in a delight. This just suits me." Mamie and Julia hated holes and were horrified by Carey's and Mary's intention of penetrating "to the very bottom of the catacombs," though, as Carey observed, they had not strength of mind enough to stay at home.

Mamie may have wished to travel, to "fill in the map" as she put it, but, once started, Carey led her a strenuous dance. For their first summer holidays she managed for them a meticulous tour of small towns in northern Italy, a journey made by few tourists in 1880 and so arduous that it taught them, once for all, to cut their luggage from the respectable amount to which they were accustomed to a minimum: "one soap cup, one sponge bag, one comb and brush etc., all crammed into Mamie's bag and one umbrella, one shawl strap and an armful of books." Carey arranged for starts and arrivals at five in the morning or at midnight and for night railway journeys on hard second-class benches among travelers who drank wine and ate sausages and gossiped steadily. She got them off for walks in rain or grilling sun. She dashed up the leaning Tower of Pisa; she threatened to ascend Mount Vesuvius even though it was in eruption; she scrambled up and down the roughest sort of paths in the Bernese Oberland, "over mountains covered with Alpine roses and ravines dark with firs and moss"; she rowed strenuously, and instructed Mamie in the art, on Lago Maggiore and Lago di Lugano; "I have," she said, "a troublesome desire to get to the bottom and to the top of everything." And Mamie, panting, blistered, and weary, followed after. Once only did she rebel: she refused to indulge in the "splendid climbing" in the Engadine where they were staying with the Garretts and where Carey gloried in "one and a half hours of 'rock work' as they call it, two hours of snow and four of ice work."

Carey's reluctance to forgo anything of possible interest overcame not only physical hardship but all other barriers. In England, after the departure of Carey's parents in 1881, they learned on reaching Leamington that, since the earl was in residence, no one would be admitted to Warwick Castle except on previous personal application. Mamie refused to take any measure; but Carey wrote, "Would the Hon. Earl of Warwick kindly grant the privilege of seeing his Castle to two ladies—Miss Gwinn and Miss Thomas—who live in Germany and who will be passing through Warwick tomorrow." To her delight, they not only were permitted to view the castle, but "had the satisfaction of seeing the Earl himself, a little dried up man of sixty, walk into his ancestral hall and take a cane from the rack and sally forth under his primeval trees."

Independent and forthright, within the limits of propriety, in practical matters, in intellectual and aesthetic, Carey was bound by the dictates of conscious "culture." The Baltimore and Cornell she knew all but starved aesthetic emotion, making her "stamp up and down her room with impatience." Though photographs and books had set her dreaming, and though Ruskin and Arnold had developed her bump of reverence for all that was hallowed by their own and their peers' accolade, Europe and England were a "revelation" to her. Sensitive to the atmosphere of places, she often became more than a mere observer of them and gloried in finding her reactions all they should be. The quiet intimacy of the English countryside touched her and she felt the "sentiment" of a view as she could not in America, understanding for the first time "how Wordsworth and Matthew Arnold could get so much out of nature as they do." In Siena she was mystical, on the Italian lakes "pastoral," and in Ravenna, "grim and early Christian." To painting, too, she responded with zest. She had all the passion for color natural to so exuberant a nature and as ready a response to the dramatic contrasts of light and dark, of chiaroscuro, as Ruskin himself might ask for.

In both nature and art her taste was that of mid-victorian romantics: intimate vistas from little balconies, glowing sunsets, moonlight on water and snowy peaks, horrid crags, and fir-clad ravines with streams foaming through their darkness; tall spires, intricate carving, dusky aisles touched with motes of color from stained windows—all the appurtenances of the Gothic—delighted her. The stupendous, the rich, the exotic impressed her, and, even more deeply, the flawless and the noble. Above all other paintings stood, in her judgment, Raphael's "Sistine Madonna," "the only divine thing left on this earth, or rather that has ever been here." Next to it, in her estimation, ranked the frescoes in the Sistine Chapel and Leonardo's sketch for the head of Christ in his "Last Supper" and his "Last Supper" itself. "One bows before them as by magnetism and immediately one's past life becomes a poor undeveloped thing because they have been wanting to it, and one's future full of longing without them."

Asceticism in any form, needless to say, made no appeal to her: she deplored the terra-cotta statue of St. Francis in his church at Assisi in which "the face was like that of a man worn out by fasting and prayer and scourging, and the blue eyes looked so tired and sad and fanatic that altogether it was a very dreadful statue." Yet moral goodness and integrity attracted her. Paintings without "sentiment or nobility," as she found Tintoretto's, seemed to her "simply tours de force." And Titian presented her with a problem. His "Assumption" she thought "glorious" and his other paintings enthralled her; but she disapproved of them: "I cannot help missing the soul in them, the ideal something." Her early training disposed her to carry Ruskin's precepts concerning the alliance of morality and art much farther than he pushed them. In literature as well as painting she had come to believe that nothing would "stand that does not appeal to the purely everlasting which is always noble." She deplored the sordid and the base that intruded into the "really lovely ideal writing" of Alfred de Musset and of Gautier in *Mlle. de Maupin.* As for Flaubert and Zola— unfortunately she draws no distinction—they made her think of "the terrible charnel houses filled with victims of the plague that Italian talent executes in wax."

"Noble" as "the soul of the artist" must be, she was not led into confusing the artist's morality in life with the morality of his work. The "soul," after all, was the ideal, not to be confounded with the puny fallible soul of daily life that inevitably exhibits derelictions of the ideal. "Now mother," she scolded, "how can thee argue that a profession is discredited because a man or woman of genius who pursues it happens to be like nine tenths of the rest of the world. . . . I believe the artist and his art, the poet and his poetry, the actor and his acting are as far apart as the heavens from the earth." The divorce came home to her at Oberammergau where she and Mamie felt as if they had looked on at "the real passion of the true Christ." Carey understood for the first time what "ideal dignity inspires actors who play dramas that embody their religious beliefs." Seeing Joseph Mayer walking down the village street in the evening, she perceived that he was "just the empty shell"; the inspiration given him on the stage by belief in his part was wanting. Henceforth the private life of Sarah Bernhardt or of any other actor ceased to trouble her. She and Mamie were conscience free to go to the play whenever opportunity afforded—and they often took considerable pains to get there, inconveniently hurrying away from Chester, for instance, because they heard of a new tragedy by Tennyson to be played in Liverpool that same evening by Irving and Ellen Terry.

Mingled with the worthier motives of Carey's devotion to culture was the not unnatural one of snobbery. Since culture as she understood it seldom appeared in the Baltimore with which she was acquainted, still less in the comfortable Society of Friends, to possess it was to be raised above the common herd; even to long for it marked one out as a person of rare understanding and knowledge. It was becoming, moreover, the cult of the advanced young American intelligentsia and to Carey, who intended to be an intellectual leader of women, was doubly desirable. Because the pride of the elite and the scorn of those of coarser clay are hardly to be avoided by the members of a cult, she shared with her aspiring fellows a rabid culture snobbism. She gives herself away in a passage written to her mother from Siena where she had found Hawthorne's notes useful, although "now no one would dare express such naïve opinions as his." He relegated to perdition frescoes, oils, statues stamped by her mentors as "the high water mark" of art. "At first one agrees with him but now Mamie and I are truly classical; we really admire what we should."

She was genuinely distressed to discover that one of "the five girls," one of her own Baltimore circle, was immune to the dictates of culture. Julia Rogers in Rome persistently held out against Ruskin's teachings. "I do wish," remarked Carey petulantly, "that she would become *converted* in my sense of the word." On the other hand, she was astonished almost more than she was pleased to hear that her Pearsall Smith cousins had made friends with that great anti-Philistine, Walt Whitman—"*I* of course should be charmed to entertain him." She herself stood out against cultural canons only in one instance, in her love for Milan Cathedral, and then she was careful to make plain that she knew she was being unorthodox: "Of course all art critics condemn the cathedral as a mongrel—Italian phantasy ruining pure Gothic; but it is like a fairy land and I had rather sit and muse there than any place I have ever been in." Why, she asked, will not a score of the rich men of America build a cathedral like it, "to which Americans could journey and on whose altar they could light their torches." She had also asked, after seeing the Olympian casts in Berlin, why Baltimore or even America had no such casts. In common with others of her cultural persuasion, she regarded them and their originals with almost equal admiration.

Where her own feeling or her judgment differed from that of the cultured, she was troubled, certain that she had failed in just appreciation. She must discipline her taste, look and look again until her eye and emotions found what her mentors, the cultured few, had found. It was well enough, since none of them particularly commended it, to condemn modern German painting, which she thought lamentably lacking in color, but the Italian primitives were another matter. With admirable patience she subjected herself to them until her eyes became accustomed to their simplicities and she began to take pleasure in paintings that had seemed "horrid and stiff" to her at first. Not until her fourth visit to Italy was she satisfied that her delight matched that evinced by the cultured. Florence, too, was slow in making its impression and Venice only less so. "But father," she wrote Dr. Thomas in bewilderment on her arrival, "I do not find Venice the Venice of Ruskin." The heat was withering; the water, foul; the marble palaces were blackened by age and damp, and interspersed with "many wretched plaster structures"; and, most disillusioning of all, there were pavements for walking through much of the city. Only the exhibits of human anatomy in the Natural History Museum, odd as it is, won her instinctive enthusiasm. "Even St. Mark's was disappointing." Both Ruskin and Howells spoke again and again of the dark mystery of the vast church "with its tiny windows glimmering like stars up in the dome," but she found it "one blaze of light" thrown by an immense window cut over the door the year before her arrival. "One might as well be in a barn," she cried resentfully. "I feel so sad and angry that I can scarcely bear to enter the church."

Eight days later, however, she had lost her bitterness. A great funeral that she witnessed from the balconies, priests and retainers and black-robed monks, white-robed sisters and crimson novices moving ceremoniously about the black and silver catafalque in the blaze of thousands of tapers, gave her a sense of the majestic and solemn pageantry of which the church was an essential part. St. Mark's, even in too stark brightness, became all that she had hoped; and she spent hours, as she was to do at intervals all her life, absorbed in studying the mosaics with the aid of Ruskin's descriptions. The moon, moreover, had come to the full and she had discovered "a pet gondolier—handsome as the morning"—who took them far out into the lagoon "as if we were sailing out into eternity. . . . Everyone—as they always are—is right about Venice in the moonlight." She was filled with well-being, exhilarated, interested, and beginning to feel the happy superiority of a tourist already familiar with the ropes. Even her own appearance, reflected in the windows of the arcades' shops, gratified her. A little more time, and Venice shared her heart with Rome.

Her satisfaction was complete when, returning with her brother Harry after several stays in Venice with Mamie, no shadow remained of her early disappointment. Her taste had been developed and she could play cicerone with enthusiasm. They went twice to the Lido to swim; floated in the gondola of the handsome "pet gondolier" out into the sunset, "a sunset far beyond any we had ever seen, all of Ruskin's most glowing descriptions would pale before it"; supped at Quadri's; took chocolate and rolls and Apollinaris water each evening in the Piazza or in Florian's rooms; and "did" the churches and galleries with the speed and thoroughness of familiarity. "I believe Harry thought Venice went beyond anything he had yet seen. . . . He delights my heart by caring about pictures as he should"—a great tribute, indeed, on Carey's part.

Though faithful to her first love, Italy, Carey's love for England was equally strong if of a different quality. In Italy she dreamed, she drank in loveliness, her imagination reveled in the past. But, however delightful, it was exotic, alien. England, she felt, was her spiritual fatherland. Like so many of her countrymen of her generation, she turned naturally to England to escape what appeared to her to be the gross Philistinism of America. The American sense of values seemed to her warped; the American scene, blankly glaring and desiccated. Never subjecting herself to English ways thoroughly enough to have them become part of her fiber or even to rub off her obvious Americanism, she adopted in so far as she understood them English standards, especially in all things literary and artistic. She accepted as incontrovertible the belief prevalent among the American intelligentsia that no painter or writer in America counted in the least with the exception of Walt Whitman, whose poetry was extolled in England and but little appreciated in his own country.

Carey felt that in visiting England she had achieved her birthright and "should at once become more mellow." No ripening softness is visible; but she quite evidently enjoyed herself as never before in "doing" the sights in London and throughout the length and breadth of the country from Stonehenge to the Trossachs. She "was perfectly wonderstruck" by Stonehenge, painstakingly, if surprisingly, tracing its likeness to an old Greek temple. But "Of all the sensations I have had in England"— England to her included Scotland—"the most decided thrill was upon coming suddenly upon Michael Scot's tomb in Melrose. I had been so horror struck by that part of 'the Lay of the Last Minstrel' as a child." Sentimental pilgrimages were a delight to her then as always. She and Mamie with a guide followed the route up Helvellyn taken by Wordsworth and Coleridge and Southey; tried to bribe their coach driver to go out of his way to pass Wordsworth's yew trees, "Fraternal four of Borrowdale"; climbed the garden wall of Rydal Mount to see the "truly beautiful" view Wordsworth had had from his doorstep; and visited Dove Cottage—"a little hovel" Carey called it, who preferred things on a grand scale and had been shocked by the miserable small rooms of Holyrood in which Mary Queen of Scots had been thundered at by Knox for luxurious living. The vicarage at Haworth, on the other hand, was no more desolate than she had imagined it; and the beauty of the Brontës' Yorkshire moors made her demand, oblivious of the fact that she had seen comparatively little American countryside, "Why has even nature put us in America off with second best, why are not our hills like the hills of England and Italy, covered with red and purple gorse, why have they no violet shadows?"

With more than the usual tourist's industry, Carey and Mamie visited many great houses. Of them all, Haddon Hall, to which they drove in a four-in-hand, caught their imagination: "It is splendid, almost the nicest thing we have seen in England." She was to return there again and again with Mamie and later with Mary Garrett, and to design the large room in her own house in Bryn Mawr in fond reminiscence of its hall. German palaces were cheerless, and even the lovely sixteenth-century villas of Italy were not for everyday existence. English great houses, however, might be and, indeed, were still lived in with comfort and delight. There was no divorce there between past glories and present charms.

This continuity in English life, added to the fact that she felt her roots lay deep in English soil, stirred her ambition as nothing Continental had done to take her place among the contemporary great—to her the literary great. Even in England, however, she labored unconsciously in the shadow of the past, for she knew no one especially interested in the arts to put her in touch with what was being done at the moment. Though she read avidly among the journals and slim volumes of contemporary verse, looking as she did for "a new prophet," she depended too heavily upon the verdict of the pundits of culture, who spoke for a past generation, to risk any discoveries for herself or to develop new loyalties.

Occasionally on her travels she met among her fellow *pension-naires* English people who knew Ruskin or Rossetti or Swinburne or others whose work she had admired even in Baltimore days. It made her miserable to think that probably she herself would never speak to a person of genius. "I despise myself," she said, "for not having the power to write things that shall force recognition from them—but think what an American and a woman would have to do to win it." When she first saw one of the great, however, she "felt vaguely disillusionized." Christina Rossetti at the exhibition of her brother's paintings at Burlington House in 1803, which Carey and Mamie had traveled eagerly over from the Continent to see, looked—only "much ennobled"—like one of the plainer members of the Baltimore Society of Friends. Dante Gabriel Rossetti's paintings, on the other hand, surpassed their hopes and would "make a difference," she felt, in her "whole life." Very much of her own time in matters artistic, Carey never outgrew this overestimate of Pre-Raphaelite art.

5

Carey's deep interest in the arts caused her mother considerable anxiety. She urged her daughter to mark the life of the people among whom she traveled, their political and, above all, their social problems. "If I had thy opportunities," she observed, "I should be so much more interested in the people with their aspirations than thee is. But thy time for people has not come yet." It was never to come, for to Carey the observation of human behavior was of little interest until distilled through the arts, especially the printed word—except, that is, as it bore upon her fixed belief in the necessity of freedom for women from financial and marital oppression. She paid no attention to the various movements for "women's rights" then in full swing in England, but she noted the evidence that piled up on her journeys of the shameful subservience of wives to husbands. Every woman, she concluded, in order to preserve any independence, must have a profession of her own and no woman should marry, if marry she must, a man with less than four thousand a year. Her observation of how pinched were the lives of professors' wives, and of even their husbands, led her to believe that "professors and teachers should take the vow of celibacy." The position accorded women in both German life and German literature was exasperatingly low: it "turned Mamie into such a woman's righter" that Carey "had to laugh at her." Carey's own feeling culminated in throwing over forever her once dear friend Miss Hicks on the announcement of her engagement, arousing not only Clytie herself but Mrs. Thomas to expostulation. "Thee ought to extend to others the same liberty on the subject thee claims for thyself." She welcomed her daughter's discretion, however, both in breaking off her friendship with Francis Gummere, who had become engaged, in spite of the fact that from him alone she was able to find out "how men think and feel"—a bit of information helpful to a crusader—and in closing, a year later, her correspondence with Richard Cadbury, with whom she found it impossible to keep the exchange on a purely friendly level.

On a different count, an article that Carey wrote after her first two visits to Rome about the galleries there increased her mother's fears that she was on the wrong track. Mrs. Thomas had accepted the fact that Carey would not be caught by the snares of Roman Catholicism and that in studying art she must consider the human body from an aesthetic point of view. She could joke about it herself: "I am very glad the King of Bavaria has proper ideas about fig leaves. I am afraid you will not be so protected in Rome." But to suggest publishing an article in which the author first confessed herself to be a young girl and then discussed the good points of the naked bodies painted or carved went beyond the pale. "There is nothing to be gained by it, but a *great deal* to lose." In the end her parents suppressed the article, finding it when purged of indecorum entirely empty. The lack of judgment shown in wishing to publish it confirmed Mrs. Thomas in thinking that Carey and Mamie ought to spend the next year in England where they might possibly make friends and, surrounded by people of their own kind, be brought into closer relation with their own world. Though pointing all this out to her daughter, she did not dwell upon it: "I have long since given up expecting entire satisfaction from my children. I passed through the bitterness of death on that point when I first became aware of thy views on subjects that were of the deepest moment to me, and from that day to this I have ceased to hope for much." She did, however, continue to warn Carey that if she wished to write well, whether with propriety or not, she would do better to live in England, where she would hear and speak and read her own language, than in Germany. "The obvious way to master our mother tongue is to study that and not the mother tongue of somebody else, Curtius to the contrary." German scholarship made no appeal to Mrs. Thomas. "The minute attention given to these vowels disgusts me with your German professors." It was a waste of time since someday, she believed, Carey could be a writer as she wished.

Carey's own mind misgave her. She saw that her work in

Germany was corrupting her use of English—"Even in writing to thee I have often to stop to think of an English word"—but the truth was that, though she talked a great deal about it, her desire "to write" was not an ambition of first importance to her. Only in letters to Richard Cadbury did she lay her emphasis on becoming a writer. He put her on her mettle, forcing her to find excuses for both her sight-seeing and her scholarly efforts, the former as "furniture for her imagination," the latter as "a provision for old age." She knew that he greatly admired her—her vitality and force of character "almost terrified" him—and thought her gifted, capable if she would of writing something that would count as literature. She believed him to be, moreover, if not a "true poet," certainly a "near genius" whose literary pronouncements and efforts were to be taken seriously. His poetic drama "Nero," which he sent her late in 1879 and in its subsequent revisions, she criticized minutely and with acumen; and rising to his expectations, she promised him repeatedly to try herself to write. With bravado inspired by his taunt that she would succumb to scholarship, she replied: "I shall write, to begin on, a love poem of the purest water—a lyrical drama and prove you in the wrong, Sir Poet." She "spent two days reading poetry to get her hand in," but the poem would not flow, let alone flow melodiously and with passion. The sum of her literary success rested on one or two "Letters from Germany" that her acquaintance Edward P. Allinson published in *The Alumnus*. Finally she confessed that to her a literary career was a "rainbow bridge" and that she would probably have to stick to scholarship, pointing out a more glorious career to others. "For a woman there always remains stirring up women to revolt, waking up girls; it is delicious to plant theories of independence and—oh all sorts of things—it has the excitement of revolution, the heroic thrill of martyrdom." But this cheerful mood of prophetic insight into her own character was followed shortly by one of gloom: "It is awfully degrading to mix oneself in reform."

Perhaps, unconsciously, she realized that she was not cut out to be a writer. Her speech, often eloquent, achieved vividness by the magnetism of her presence and by emphasis—sometimes grotesque exaggeration—rather than by precise or felicitous phrasing. And her letters often had a warmth and vitality that made them a delight to the recipient. Translated to the formal printed page, however, her words too often fell hollow and flat. The quick response brought by the spoken word, the imagined meeting of individual minds in letter writing, were needed to stimulate her effort. She rationalized the inability to apply herself seriously to a literary career by pointing out that she could not afford to spend her one chance of acquiring knowledge in Europe in trying to assimilate and produce as well as to accumulate. Probably, too, she avoided literary attempts with instinctive dread of failure. She shunned all deeds dependent on anything not to be influenced by her determination; and a literary career, if first rate, depended in great measure upon an innate gift, the presence of which had never manifested itself with any certainty. As a teacher, on the other hand, she had already had indications that she could succeed, for clearly she possessed the gift of inspiring enthusiasm in others; and scholarship she believed to be merely a matter of hard work.

Not that Carey had a very high opinion of the teaching profession, especially for women in America. It was, she felt, looked down upon; and she begged her mother not to mention the possibility of her joining it—a request that called from Mrs. Thomas a severe reprimand: "It is not a thing to be ashamed of at all, and if anyone chooses to hurt thee with less consideration on that account, I should dismiss their consideration as not worth caring for." After all, Carey herself had chosen a career in spite of her parents' wish for her to settle down at home, and to say that it would prevent her going into Baltimore society was "simply ridiculous." If she "broke out in a fresh place" and wished to enter society she would have no difficulty in doing so. "The fact is, thee shares the vulgar prejudice against self-supporting women and so helps to rivet the chains of dependence upon thy sex. . . . I guess however thee has too much pride, and too little true independence to play the part of pioneer and reformer." Thus goaded, Carey replied that she cared nothing for Baltimore opinion but believed that her plan of becoming a teacher would be attributed to financial need and lose its theoretical value. She intended, she said, to remedy the great failing of American women teachers, and most men—their want of scholarship—and to advance the cause of women by her own achievement, raising the standard of their education.

To do this she must take a degree from a German university. Increasingly as she disliked Germans and their "barbarous Germany," there was "no hope for a scholar unless he comes to Germany." Though England provided "the only criterion of success for all higher work," English scholarship, she felt, even in the study of English literature, was weak and inaccurate. Categorically refused a degree at Leipzig, Carey had hoped to be received as a candidate for a degree at Göttingen. Since all German universities demanded among other things, a thesis, she set to work on a subject given her by Professor Wülcker only to find after four months' study that the subject already had been thoroughly worked over by Jacob Grimm and others. Outraged, but undismayed, Carey sought a subject for herself and, armed with an outline of this new dissertation and her Cornell degree, her Leipzig lecture notes and other evidences of accomplishment, made definite application to Göttingen. A month and a half later the verdict came: Göttingen would give no degree to a woman.

Luckily, she had already ascertained that the University of Zürich granted women degrees and, though in Switzerland, might be counted as German in scholarship. So in the early summer, 1882, Carey and Mamie moved to Zürich, glad to shake the dust of Leipzig from their heels. Their rooms seemed much pleasanter than at Fräulein Pochhammer's and the views of the lake, especially from the university lecture rooms, constantly delighted Carey. Altogether they felt freer in Zürich—perhaps because they were making a fresh start with much experience behind them— and even went so far as to talk with their fellow *pensionnaire*, a young Swiss student who spent most of his time riotously drinking beer with his cronies and who gave Carey "extremely interesting" information especially about dueling customs. Even though there was no brilliant Zarncke there, the lectures seemed admirable and the professor of English commended the subject of the dissertation on "Sir Gawayne and the Green Knight" that she had nearly finished. But he demanded, as well as the dissertation that must be published, a study of some modern English poet written in German publishable form, though not necessarily to be printed. Happily he chose the very poet Carey would have wished; and she set to work at once on "an introduction to the study of Swinburne's poetry."

The requirements for a degree from Zürich, as Carey remarked, sounded savage, but "what other people have done I can do and I am sure that getting through must often be an easy matter." There was much work to be accomplished both during term and in the following vacation in Italy in order to do herself credit and demonstrate that a woman could vie with men on their own scholarly ground. By rising before six and working in every free moment of the holidays, she finished her study of Swinburne in spite of almost burning herself disastrously a second time because of it: One evening in Florence, taking out a volume of Swinburne's poems, she fell into a discussion of them with Mamie so heated that she knocked over a lamp. Instantly the curtains at the window and the portieres were all ablaze. Mamie rushed for help; Carey seized the other lamp and plunged it into a jug of water lest it explode in the heat; all the *pensionnaires* came running, pulled down the hangings and stamped out the flames.

When Carey returned for the final six weeks before the examinations in Zürich, Mamie, seeing for herself that she was a distraction from concentrated work, remained in Florence. Carey, who had left her dissertation on "Sir Gawayne and the Green Knight" to be read by the professors in the holidays, was welcomed by the heartening news that they not only accepted it but thought it a first-rate piece of work. The decan told her that "he had rarely, if ever, heard the chief professors speak in such high terms of any thesis, of the learning, or rather the wide reading and clear critical arrangement shown in the treatment of the subject matter." Conditions for work, moreover, were at last ideal. The pension was comfortable and without Mamie she made friends with four American women, a Mrs. Putnam and her two daughters, whom she found "a great consolation," and a rich Dr. Culbertson studying at the Medical School, who had already followed a career that mightily impressed Carey. Glowing with satisfaction, Carey felt that she might win high honors at Zürich.

The university presented four degrees: *rite*; *cum laude*; *magna cum laude,* so good as rarely to be given; and *summa cum laude,* almost never given. Besides writing the dissertation and the paper on Swinburne, in order to obtain even a degree rite, Carey would have to pass a three days' written examination on her particular field, German philology, and a three hours' oral examination in German before the assembled philosophical faculty of the University, whose vote that she had passed the test must be unanimous. In spite of this formidable array of obstacles Carey set her heart on winning a *magna cum laude.* The odds against her were great since she had to overcome the double handicaps of writing and speaking in German and of being examined by professors under whom she had worked for only a few weeks, whose idiosyncrasies she did not know, and who were not especially interested in her.

At the end of a few weeks' work her essay on Swinburne was formally accepted and she took the three days' examination which she was permitted to write at home. After it, she was ill for three days with a severe headache and fever, but Zürich's "most prominent woman doctor" and the Putnams, who took possession of her room, administered medicines, read to her, and generally cared for her. By the end of the week she was fit for the six hours' written examination which she was to take locked up alone in a room at the university. The professors said "all sorts of nice things" about her written examinations and begged her to be calm in the oral one, which was to come at the end of another week, telling her that "many students became unnecessarily confused from mere terror." Needless to say, this combined encouragement and warning worked her up to a high pitch of excitement. Two men, she knew, had failed and one obtained only a degree rite during the past semester; and she wanted passionately to do well, "to set a seal upon the last three years." She became more and more nervous, even fearing that she might die before getting her degree, and could neither sleep nor eat. "If it had not been for Dr. Culbertson's medical assistance," she acknowledged, "I do not know how I could have gotten through. . . . I took everything she gave me—strychnine, valerian, etc."

Early in the afternoon of November 25, 1882, Carey, dressed in the "brown brocade and velvet" that she had worn at her

Cornell commencement and "a pair of seal brown gloves to match," was made to drink two cups of strong tea without milk and escorted to the university by Dr. Culbertson. At three o'clock she was shown into a large room with a long center table covered with green baize, around which were ranged the professors and, at one end, the decan. As the time for each professor came to examine her in his field, the decan, opposite whom she was placed, struck on the table and the examiner took his seat next her, putting his questions while the others listened. She was examined on Anglo-Saxon philology, Anglo-Saxon historical grammar, and English historical grammar for a quarter of an hour each; on German, Gothic, and Old High German philology for three-quarters of an hour; on German literature for half an hour; and on Middle High German for a quarter of an hour; and finally, for half an hour, upon the development of English literature. As the clock struck six the decan asked her to retire.

She found the beadle and his wife waiting to support her while the faculty deliberated. They said they were sure she would get a *cum laude*. She thought possibly she might receive a *magna cum laude*. From the moment she had approached the green baize table she had felt perfectly calm and had been able to answer with perfect distinctness and, as far as she could tell, with almost no mistakes. "All the laws of the development of Gothic out of Indo-Germanic were never clearer to me than at the moment of the examination." But the five minutes of waiting with the beadle and his wife were torture: "I have never felt such a sensation of choking anxiety." The message came to re-enter the examination room. She stood at the foot of the table. The decan rose and said that he had the pleasure of welcoming her as a Doctor of Philosophy of the University of Zürich and of informing her that the faculty had bestowed upon her the highest honor in its power to give—*summa cum laude*. He handed her her documents and shook hands.

She had not even dreamed of taking the highest possible degree. Only one woman before her had taken a doctorate of philosophy of any sort. Now she, a woman and a foreigner, had taken a degree heretofore given only to men—and few of them—who had applied late in life after many years' study and original investigation. It seemed "too splendid to be true." Too excited to sleep, she wrote her parents that night a long paean of joy, warning them that they must frame and hang on the wall one of the twenty copies of her diploma on which the words *"summa cum laude"* appeared after her degree and *"doctor et admirable,"* instead of the usual *"accurate et diligente,"* in acceptance of her dissertation. "It is the very nicest thing that has ever happened to me except having such a nice home and such enlightened parents. I wonder if I shall care as much about my first book or if it will be received 'summa cum laude,' or if it will ever exist at all."

Four days later she joined Mamie at Spezia, having tasted some of the fruits of triumph and found them delicious. She had called on her three chief examiners the day following the oral examination and had been congratulated with unprecedented cordiality. One professor, whose scholarship she revered, said that he would not try to tell her how her philological knowledge amazed him; he had hardly ever had a student with such a clear and critical understanding of philology and never supposed a woman could show such philological talent. The professor of Middle English said that he knew she deserved a *summa cum laude* but could hardly believe it—it was so unusual—when he saw that the faculty were determined to confer it on her. During his whole connection with the university he had known of only one *summa* being given. Best of all, her triumph was thought to be a triumph for women: friends of coeducation at the university rejoiced; two women called to thank her in the name of the women students; one of them said she had only one wish, that Carey might become *"ein grosser mann der wissenschaft."* "For the first time in my life," wrote Carey, "I rather enjoyed being stared at." The fifteen students who dined at her pension could not eat for watching her, and when she rose to leave the room dropped knives and forks and preserved profound silence until the door closed behind her. People turned in the street to look at her. The papers of Zürich, as was customary when a man obtained the highest degree, published an account of her life and scholarly attainments.

News of her victory spread quickly in Baltimore. Her friends and her acquaintances among the professors and students of both Cornell and the Johns Hopkins naturally were interested. In the

Society of Friends her victory was heralded abroad. Mrs. Thomas, as "an American mother who had no opportunities for a higher education in her day, and who has always felt the loss and need," increased her daughter's reputation by writing an account of Carey's triumphantly crowned work in Germany and Zürich in order to awaken other American girls to worthy ambition and achievement in advanced learning. Rumors of her fame soon reached Carey. Accustomed as she was to the encomiums of her friends and believing though she did in her own high destiny—"I expect to shoot up like a rocket someday and cover thee with stars," she had written her mother from Leipzig in 1882—it was none the less gratifying to receive the letters of congratulations that poured in upon her now, "the nicest of all" from Mary Garrett. It was satisfactory to hear that Mamie's aunt had found an article at Gallignani's in Paris devoted to the Zürich exploit and to learn that Miss Susan B. Anthony and her traveling companion Miss Rachel Foster (later Mrs. Avery) wished to see her when they arrived in Paris. She even rejoiced in the clipping from a Philadelphia paper stating that she had taken a degree "after an examination lasting five weeks and is now going to study five years in the British Museum."

6

In spite of her happiness in the knowledge of this well-justified fame, the last ten months of Carey's stay in Europe proved to be an anticlimax. Together she and Mamie were content to dawdle along the Riviera, up the Rhône Valley, and to London for the Rossetti exhibition. It was their first "quite unintellectual holiday," broken only by the proofs of Carey's dissertation, which followed her in batches for correction and bored her excessively. "My dissertation looked at dispassionately, across the space of time, seems too stupid, too unimaginatively dull! It deserved *more* than the highest degree—to have an intelligent being for four months of her life eat dust and grovel in the mole holes of the earth to collect *such* data." She found it disillusioning that at Zürich they thought it "splendid." Oddly enough, neither this awakening nor the harvest of disillusionment that they reaped a few weeks later at Stuttgart, where life with the Grüneisens, once so exhilarating and enlightened, seemed tiresome past endurance, made them modify in any way their belief in a degree as the cachet of scholarship or their desire for culture as they had always defined it. Avoiding the obvious conclusions, they merely sank into gloom. Carey, unable to finish the article that she had begun in London on Rossetti, brooded on what work, if she had believed she were to die soon, she should have taken up—poetry and Greek probably, she thought, and not philology.

It was a relief to reach Paris where they were to spend some time before returning to America and to begin attending lectures at the Sorbonne, especially those of Gaston Paris. After a series of private lessons, Carey found that she could understand the language easily; speak it she never could, either then or later, even passably well though she had the power, largely one of energetic determination, of making herself understood in it. Partly because of this failure she maintained, for the time being at least, that no one not a native of France should attempt to teach the French language or even to work in the field of Romance philology. From the point of view of her academic education these months in Paris were unimportant, but inevitably they taught her much. She learned that Paris, far from being full of pitfalls for unchaperoned young ladies, was much more comfortable for them than any other place she had tried, save in America or England. She was accepted naturally at the university, no one stared at her in the street, even the reputedly wicked Latin Quarter turned out to be not only pleasant but the acknowledged place for respectable students to live. Paris, moreover, provided her to her heart's content with a theater worth going to: Sarah Bernhardt was playing—"The three occasions upon which I have seen her have been the most tremendous in my life I think"—and always there was the Théâtre Français, in her view then and later supreme among all theaters.

For a few weeks the summer heat sent them off with Gertrude Meade to the Channel Isles where, after a bad bout of gastric fever, the culmination of the past year's fatigue, all Carey's energy returned. Old friends remarked her carefree happiness and Mamie's aunt pronounced her "very pretty" and "strikingly handsome." She herself felt that she had grown "much nicer," and boasted that "Gertrude says she thinks I am one of the most even tempered and unselfish people she has ever seen." In truth, she was little different from the Carey who had left America four years before even in appearance. Time had perhaps sharpened the outlines, refined the features somewhat, but the slim stocky figure with its slight limp and quick abrupt gestures moved as energetically as ever, the proud head was as vivid. If her manner was more assured, her poise not to be ruffled, its cold aloofness was belied by the brilliance of her eyes. Her enthusiasm for what caught her interest burned as hotly as before, though the old shyness, increased rather than diminished by a sense of greater prestige, had taught her to control a show of feeling. And her resolution was as strong as ever. The gift that carried her triumphantly to her goal was only more marked, the gift of remaining undeflected by any experience or fact that ran counter to her course. Then, as always, albeit often unconsciously, she ignored unwelcome facts or, discarding the rest, turned what might be useful in them to her own account. And she drew support from unexpected, even most unlikely, quarters. In knowledge, of course, she had gained and in academic discipline. The foundations had been laid firmly for her not only to plan but to take definite measures to shape her future career.

She had seen for some time that the proposed new woman's college founded by Joseph W. Taylor at Bryn Mawr might offer her the best opening for a teaching position.[2] The suggestion that her father be appointed its president had filled her with trepidation lest the opening be closed to her, for she had observed too many unfortunate exhibitions of nepotism in staffing institutions to subject her family to the suspicion of it. Worse still was the possible appointment of Francis Gummere, whom she herself had suggested for president but whom, after talking with him in Germany, she now found hidebound by German pedantry, wanting in true scholarly vision and interest in culture. High academic standards could be neither established nor maintained, she thought, in any institution headed by him. And naturally she had no intention of becoming a member of a college faculty not possessing the highest standards. Even while still at Leipzig she had been engaged in

debating ways in which to liberalize and perfect plans for the
new college. Whenever she met any woman from one of the
American women's colleges, she examined her perseveringly as to
the flaws in her own institution; and, in spite of Mamie's bored
refusal to accompany her, she had insisted upon visiting Girton
where fifty-three girls were doing, with no ill effects, the same
work that won for Cambridge undergraduates a university degree.
"Doctors had begun prescribing Girton for the health of their
patients." The living arrangements there especially impressed
Carey. Each girl had two rooms, confirming her belief that Frank
Smith had been right when long ago he said that no student could
work well if obliged to do it in the room where he slept. She
wrote her father at once to emphasize the point. Indeed her letters
to her parents, especially to her father, who, with her uncle James
Whitall, her cousin Francis T. King and others, had been appointed a trustee of Bryn Mawr College, were filled with advice
as to how academic standards might be raised.

Her most cherished plan was that of a system of fellowships
"consisting of free board and two or three hundred dollars over"
to draw to the college graduate students who, as advanced workers,
would inspire professors and young students: "That is my idea
and I am proud of it and wish the credit of it when the fellows
of Bryn Mawr have become a power." She begged her father,
also, to urge the trustees to make attendance upon recitations
voluntary. Leipzig had taught her that "girls manage themselves;
they are only too anxious to work." And Leipzig had made her
"very anxious" that every professor should be "abreast of all
the newest research." Not that she wished the work to be too
hard for beginners. It should be clear and simple enough for them
but at the same time advanced enough for those who had already
begun: "Here is a chance of giving milk to the babes and strong
meat to the strong if the trustees are only wise." In reply to
some objection of her mother's, she replied stiffly that there could
be nothing in Dr. Taylor's will to prevent Bryn Mawr from becoming admirable—"It need not be any the less guarded because
it is good"—and nothing would so increase the power of Friends
as establishing a college admittedly in the front rank of women's

colleges. The great point, in order to make it first rate, was to appoint the right president.

The more she and Mamie discussed possible presidential policies the more enthusiastic she became in forming one. "Oh dear," she cried, "if I had the organization of the College I am sure I could make it the greatest success." She was certain that if given the chance, she could find suitable professors: her training had fitted her for just such a job. "I envied Miss Freeman her chance when I read of her appointment to the presidency of Wellesley and after all that is not a new college, nor to compare with what Bryn Mawr may become." She did not yet, however, seriously suggest herself as a candidate for the presidency. There were still two months before she should go up for her doctor's examinations and all future plans must wait on the results of those.

Their triumphant outcome gave the necessary fillip to her self-confidence to make her face her wishes frankly. From Spezia on November 30, 1882, she wrote her mother, "Of course I suppose it is impossible and that they would never give it to me, but I should love to have the presidency of Bryn Mawr. I believe that I could make it the very best woman's college there is, so that English and German women would come and study there—that is, I believe it could be so managed and I do not believe any other person whom they could get would have the interests of other women so at heart and, at the same time, would have the requisite training to enable her or him to see what was needed. . . . If it were not that father and Uncle James were on the Board and the other trustees more or less friends of yours, I mean if it were any other college about to open, I should write and propose myself as a candidate. In this case it is out of the question of course." The very adverseness of her conclusion warned her parents, who understood her, that she was about to take action. Though they wrote her discouragingly—whether because they thought her an unsuitable candidate or because they feared to disappoint her, she did not know—they consulted James Whitall, who replied directly to Carey that he saw nothing unfitting in her proposing herself. He advised her to write to Dr. Rhoads, the trustee appointed to the preliminary management of the college, and either to say that she wished to be considered for the presidency or at

least to prepare the way for a second letter in which she stated
her case.

It was not an easy letter to write, partly because she had so
much to explain and partly because she was not sure that she
ought to write it at all. On the whole she was fairly certain that
her appointment "would give the college an éclat which the nomin-
ation of a totally unknown man could not give among women and
women's colleges." This was neither conceited nor improbable,
she contended, since every woman who had known her would
understand that she would be unwilling to undertake such an
appointment were she not certain of making the college superior
to those already in existence. "The girls and women whom I have
met are not many but they are enough to spread about this report
among those little circles which are stirred by the opening of a
new college." Fortified by this belief she and Mamie painstakingly
worked out their ideas and while in Paris in June indited a letter
to Dr. Rhoads that was a manifesto. Before sending it, however,
they thought it advisable for Carey to write again to her uncle
James and, also, to warn Bessie King in strict confidence of the
situation "so that if anything comes of it she may be on my side
with her father." Not until September, therefore, on the very eve
of their return to America, did Carey finally dispatch the letter.
With a copy of it, she sent her father a plea not to treat the
possibility of her becoming president as a whim or out of the
question if anyone should broach the subject to him. "Thee sees
if *thee* does not discuss it seriously, no one will. I am a woman
now, nearly twenty-seven years old and I believe I could make the
College more of a success than anyone else they are likely to
appoint and I want thee at least to give me the benefit of the
doubt."

No reply came before she sailed for America in October. Carey
was on tenterhooks. She tried to soothe her impatience by thinking that if the trustees did not make her president they might
grant her a professorship. She would accept that—if they appointed as president someone of whom she approved. In fact she
would be quite happy if they could find and would appoint some
other woman who saw eye to eye with her. A woman, of course,
would be better fitted for the position than a man, though she

could put up with a man if he were young, trained in modern methods and theories, and knew what was demanded to satisfy the needs of the day. In any case, she supposed that her high academic degree guaranteed her a position somewhere in America where she could fulfill her desire to raise the standard of women's education and which would, incidentally, enable her to pay back the $3,833.07 that, according to her reckoning, her parents had expended on her European adventure.

Deplore though she did the necessity of returning to America, in her eyes so aesthetically unsatisfying, so intellectually thin, she accepted the necessity without repining. All she begged was that her family would not urge her to return for her brother John's wedding—"I am shy of going in among that Philadelphia crowd just yet"—or for the Friends' yearly meeting, the epitome of everything she knew as American, particularly Baltimorean. Earlier she had so decried all that was American in contrast to the cultural wonders of Germany that her mother had risen in defense of her native land. "Does thee mean," Mrs. Thomas asked her daughter with asperity, "that Dick Cadbury has started for the United States of America when thee says he is returning to the Indian Country?" But now she was obliged to agree with her mother's remark, "You may go to Germany to get your knowledge but you will have to come back here to have a chance to use it. What chance have women in Germany, I would like to know?" America's very faults, she now saw, provided opportunity for her to accomplish the reforms that she was determined to accomplish, and her departure for the United States was taken with a high heart.

CHAPTER VI

The Opening of Bryn Mawr College

I

THE excitement of the travelers' return soared to its crescendo for them in the hurricane through which their ship hurtled and tossed its way to Baltimore—Carey exulting in the bluster, Mamie reading Victor Hugo, the other passengers praying aloud in the little red plush salon—and for their families in the reports of storm and disaster causing the ship's delay. Though on disembarkation the discovery of the loss of one of Carey's precious trunks might have dampened her spirits, it but added to the hurly-burly of her welcome, a hero's welcome, prepared for and looked forward to for months, and to the interest of an audience agog to learn of her triumphs at first hand. The years abroad had surrounded Carey with a glamour that in the eyes of her friends separated her from the common herd. The younger members of her family, in especial, regarded her as a person apart and above them, slightly fabulous perhaps but gifted with a power to achieve whatever high ends she might desire. With the first great step in her career accomplished, their faith had been confirmed and their admiration was unbounded. And as such approval does, their belief in her spread to an ever widening circle like ripples from a stone dropped into still water. She herself, confident in her wider experience and acclaimed scholarship, if she took no measures to preserve her ascendancy, never questioned its justice. Nor was daily familiarity given a chance to tarnish it. Hardly a month passed before, in pursuit of her immediate aim, a position at Bryn Mawr College, she again left the Baltimore family never to return to them in future save for short periods.

She had found her father, one of the eleven trustees appointed by Dr. Taylor, in the thick of plans for the new college. His talk, the whole family's talk and that of their friends, teemed with the aspirations, theories, and practical measures connected with its organization. In no time at all she was fully informed of the latest developments and crosscurrents. A considerable number of critics, seeing the discretion and careful judgment with which the trustees advanced, cried out upon their illiberalism, suspecting that in the end they would cautiously open merely another glorified seminary for young ladies. To them the college seemed to have progressed little since Dr. Taylor's death in January, 1880.[1] At that time the main part of what is now the college campus had been bought and the foundations laid for the central academic building, Taylor Hall, and the dormitory, Cottage Number 1, later called Merion Hall.[2] Dr. Taylor had offered a sum of money to President Gilman of the John Hopkins, President Seelye of Smith College, and Miss Annie E. Johnson, Principal of Bradford Academy in Massachusetts, to write, each of them, "an essay" giving their suggestions as to the most efficacious way of attacking the problems to be considered in founding such a college as he proposed. These essays, along with suggestions from other sources and from the findings of James Whitall and, in especial, of Francis T. King, who visited the universities of Europe and England in search of information, provided the trustees with a mass of material from which to work. After Dr. Taylor's death, at their first meeting as an organized board under the presidency, according to Dr. Taylor's wish, of Francis King, the trustees decided to call the new college Bryn Mawr, the name of the near-by railway station and village, and appointed a committee to draw up the application for a college charter under Pennsylvania law. The charter being granted them in May, 1880, the college was scheduled to open in the autumn of 1882. But that autumn had come and gone, and skeptical critics saw little hope of the emergence of the liberal institution they had been led to expect.

The buildings that, according to Dr. Taylor's plans, should have been finished in 1881, were still incomplete in the summer of 1883, partly because the trustees, with the relatively small income of forty thousand dollars a year, were impressed, in the words of

Dr. Rhoads, "with the importance of preserving the estate intact in order to supply the future needs of the College." The plans for Cottage Number 1 had proved so expensive and its first site so unsuitable that it had to be begun again in 1881 and was not finished till four years later. The purchase in 1882 of one acre of ground adjacent to the campus raised expenses well above income. As a curb on expenditure, the trustees passed a resolution providing that whatever might be withdrawn from the principal should be refunded by annual appropriation from the income until it was repaid. Manifestly, it was necessary, in order to increase the income, to open the college as soon as possible. But still the opening was delayed.

During these years the academic plans had by no means been neglected—it was in them that men like Francis T. King and Dr. Rhoads were most interested—and by the late summer of 1883 the trustees drew up a circular describing the physical attractions of the college, indicating not only the financial terms but the academic requirements for admission and, broadly, the methods and kinds of instruction to be given, and announcing the opening of the college in 1885. The trustees and most of those in their counsels knew that they had lapsed in neither standards nor determination: they still intended to achieve for women an institution quite as advanced as the most advanced of men's colleges. But also they knew, from observation and their own experience with the other educational institutions with which many of them were connected, the necessity of deliberation and of taking a long view if they were to avoid not only immediate pitfalls but ultimate wreckage. With the quiet affirmation of righteousness with which Friends customarily achieve so many practical ends, they were willing to weigh possibilities at length before proceeding discreetly to take the next step in their uncharted course.

Into this steady progression, so slow as to be almost imperceptible, Carey Thomas now threw all her zest and the fruit of her experience, sharpening the edges of discrepancies and setting pros and cons in clearer relief. Her desire to be made president of Bryn Mawr or, if not that, then professor of English had reached boiling point, increased by the assurance that Francis Gummere, who had been called to Haverford, was out of the running, in spite of promises made him by Dr. Taylor and by the attention her views received from the trustees. The favorable impression created by her letter to Dr. Rhoads, added to what they already knew of her, led to a series of interviews with various trustees that seemed to her, at least, satisfactory. The way for her had been prepared by the natural interest of her relatives and family friends on the board. Their equally natural tendency not to regard seriously one whom they had known from infancy was outweighed by the fact that, being Quakers, they were accustomed to regarding even children as responsible human beings, and especially by the fact that she had, after all, succeeded signally in obtaining for herself what they wished to provide for all young women fitted to receive it.

After talking with her and discussing her merits it became evident to the trustees that she had qualifications desirable in a president, in purpose and academic knowledge as well as in background, looks, and address. In addition, most of them were inclined to agree with her in thinking that the appointment of a woman would have what is now called publicity value. But she was unproved. She was not quite twenty-seven and she entirely lacked administrative experience. Her youthful, energetic certainty and enthusiasm, moreover, left the more staid among the trustees uneasy lest her judgment prove rash and her loyalty to sound Quaker principles unsteady. Even her closest adherents were obliged to admit these possibilities. To appoint her, a woman, young and untried, to an authoritative position that had yet to be shaped and limited would be to run unwarrantable risk. The need of compromise was clearly indicated. At this point, as so often, fortune was with the trustees: a fact that does not lessen the honor due them for courage and clear-sightedness in recognizing and grasping their opportunity.

Dr. Rhoads, fifty-six years old, vice-president of the Board of Trustees and chairman of the Executive and the Buildings committees, who had been in charge of the college for the past year, presented all the attributes that Carey Thomas lacked: mature judgment, administrative experience, wide knowledge of human nature. They were complementary to an astonishing degree: his gentle kindness and charm of manner, his unfailing if somewhat remote courtesy, to her vivid, proud self-consciousness; his slow, carefully reasoning mind, to her hot zeal and quick intuition; his devotion to the tried principles of the Society of Friends—he was a minister of the society—to her emancipation from Quaker doctrine. On the other hand, they shared an intense interest in the struggle of women for advanced education and a determination to provide the best for them at whatever cost to themselves. Dr. Rhoads, moreover, was a retired physician and his training for general practice had given him the insight into scientific standards and methods which enabled him to understand the more recent and intensive scholarly training in which Carey Thomas believed. If she went farther than he in dislike of mediocrity, they both disdained pettiness in all its forms; and both were too intent upon their object to be other than personally generous. All this was evident to the trustees. And at their meeting in December, 1883, they appointed Dr. James E. Rhoads president of Bryn Mawr College and Martha Carey Thomas dean and professor of English.

2

Then began a collaboration rare in its harmony and unity of achievement. Too little, perhaps, has been known of the part played in it by Dr. Rhoads; too exclusive attention has been focused upon Carey Thomas's share—not unnaturally, since hers was the more picturesque. It has been accepted that Dr. Rhoads acted only as the check upon the youthful dean's enthusiasm, as her supporter and the smoother of difficulties permitting her to carry out her ideas. All this he did; but more than this. The ideas that were put into effect and the foresight that was acted upon were in large measure owing to Dr. Rhoads's grasp of the situation in all its details. Carey Thomas drew a long bow in saying fifty years later that, as it had been understood from the first she was to do, she organized the college on the academic side, nominated professors for Dr. Rhoads to appoint, and managed the students. Superficially speaking perhaps this was true; and it was true that she wrote the programs, planned the entrance examinations, adapted "the group system," and arranged the

courses of study. These things, however, were accomplished after
protracted discussion with the president and, largely through him,
with the trustees. They were done with his advice and only with
his full support.

It is significant that when Carey Thomas started, at the request
of the trustees, early in 1884 on a tour of inspection of the existing women's colleges, Dr. Rhoads presented her with a list of the
points that she was to study with particular care. These ranged
from methods of instruction and professional salaries to the number and kind of chairs for the dormitories and arrangements for
cooking and heating. And her report at the end of the tour was
made up almost entirely of the answers to his questions. This
does not mean, of course, that the answers would have been the
same had anyone but Carey Thomas made the inquiries. Nor does
it mean, even, that none of the questions on his list were her own.
Doubtless some were, for both she and Dr. Rhoads drew their
ideas from the common fount of educational ideas in the Quaker
and academic circles of their time. Few if any of their ideas, even
in combination, were original. Besides, she and Dr. Rhoads discussed fully not only the points upon which the questions bore but
the detailed purpose of her tour. That the list was in his writing,
couched in his words, means, however, that the president was no
mere gentle and compliant puppet in the dean's hands. Their collaboration was a true one in which the qualities of mind of age
and of youth were allowed full play in a nice adjustment of give-
and-take. Their relation was one of mutual admiration and affection and forbearance and, on the part of Dr. Rhoads, exceptional
generosity and broad-mindedness.

Whatever their respective shares in building up the college,
Carey Thomas played an invaluable part. In 1883, in spite of the
assurance of the trustees' circular, neither the physical nor the
academic organization was complete, the details of neither had
been formulated precisely. To resolve the uncertainties and the
discreet hesitancy of the trustees into practicable shape the combined irritation and magnetism of Carey Thomas's zeal was
needed. More precise and detailed information than even that
gathered by the trustees was wanted, moreover, before the final
shape was cast. "As no institution is theoretical," said Carey

Thomas, "but wholly practical in its working, before formulating anything it would be desirable to visit the different existing institutions, staying if necessary a week or so in each college, going into recitations, etc., and becoming thoroughly familiar with the working of each." With this point of view the trustees reasonably agreed; and they saw as clearly as she that, primed and cocked and youthfully capable as she was of the exertion involved, she was the person to undertake such an investigation.

Before starting on the tour proper she prepared the ground by a long talk with President Gilman, from which she gleaned a number of precepts that stood her in good stead. No college, he said, was worthy of its name that had not a strong man in each of its chief academic departments, and the literary qualifications of the professor of languages should be emphasized. And no professor should be appointed whose usefulness in ten or fifteen years was unlikely to be as great as in the beginning, since he might be difficult to get rid of. These and other of his suggestions seemed to Carey Thomas good, as did his pronouncements, in general, regarding fellowships since she had already modeled her plan for Bryn Mawr fellowships upon that of the Johns Hopkins. But she found less palatable his warning that a postgraduate school had its dangers: the professors often had to work so hard to keep ahead of the fellows that their best energies were absorbed, leaving nothing for the undergraduates; and even more often, the professors, yielding to the fascination of postgraduate work, scorned teaching undergraduates. Though she was to live to see the wisdom of these warnings, at the time she had an answer that seemed to her final to both objections: the danger that, without the incentive of a postgraduate school, the undergraduate teaching would become humdrum outweighed that of too exclusive an interest in advanced students.

A month after this instructive talk, toward the end of April, 1884, armed with Dr. Rhoads's comprehensive list of questions, she set off to Vassar. She was amazed by the interest in her problems of everyone from President Caldwell, who received her "in his private parlor and was charmingly kind," and the lady principal, who gave up a whole day to showing her about, down to the less important women teachers. She attended classes, examined building arrangements, and talked with the faculty and staff. Her position as dean seemed to open all official doors. Better still, what she did not learn of the inner workings of the college as dean, she learned in private conversation with the friends of Gertrude Meade, who had given her introductions to many of the Vassar teachers which removed the discreetly formal barriers to free criticism. Since the importance of her mission lay, as Dr. Rhoads already had pointed out, largely in the discovery of criticisms and suggestions regarding the established order, she at once wrote to various friends for letters of introduction to women in the other colleges that she planned to visit— a precaution that contributed much to the success of her trip.

On the whole, Vassar impressed her more favorably than she had been led to expect it would, and the buildings, she confessed to her mother, "are far better than we can hope to have." Main Hall, designed after the plan of the Tuileries, she found especially impressive in spite of its dark inner rooms. On the advisability, however, of a dormitory to house three hundred instead of several smaller ones, each for about fifty students, as in "the cottage system," she was doubtful. It would be more difficult to govern three hundred students under one roof than in separate groups of fifty; and even were the single dormitory fully occupied, the fee of three hundred dollars paid by each student would not cover its upkeep. Vassar had to run a preparatory school to make up the needed sum; and the presence of young pupils added to the complications of governing the students. But if the rules savored to Carey Thomas of boarding school, she spent no time in finding fault but gravely jotted them all down in her notebook for future comparison with those of the other colleges.

In academic matters she was as favorably surprised as in the buildings. The mathematics lecture that she heard struck her as "brilliant" and many of the others as "good." The teaching requirements were severe for the seven professors, four men and three women—among them the distinguished astronomer Maria Mitchell—who each received a salary of twenty-five hundred dollars and either living quarters or four hundred dollars extra; and for the sixteen teachers and the many corridor teachers, all women, whose salary was much lower, the teaching excessively heavy.

But their unexpectedly liberal views delighted Carey Thomas. They welcomed the idea of an elective system, or, as Carey Thomas named it, a "group system" of studies such as the Johns Hopkins University had evolved, which both she and Dr. Rhoads were inclined to adopt.[3] According to this system, each student must elect, apart from certain subjects required of all, any one of a number of groups of studies consisting of two "major subjects," and then would be free to fill out her program with any courses— "free electives"—that she chose. The constituents of a group were determined by the authorities as giving the necessary basis for specialization in its central subject as well as the background needed for a liberal education. It was a costly method, as President Gilman had pointed out, but one that allowed the student to satisfy her needs and tastes without danger of futile scattering or superficiality. Such a system, said the Vassar teachers, was "just what they were working towards."

At her next stop, Smith College, she found in the faculty no such stimulating individuals as the astronomer, the mathematician, and the physician of Vassar—perhaps, she thought, because there were no women professors there. Smith taught her little academically. Though in many ways it was not as much like a glorified boarding school as Vassar, the teaching seemed to her less good and the intellectual standard no higher than she had expected it to be. The criticism most often made to her, she observed, by the few students with whom she talked was that none of the professors could lay claim to "original scholarship" or were fit to guide a student in "original work." And with President Seelye's complaint that it was almost impossible to find women properly educated to teach and that the few who might be found usually married and left the profession, Carey Thomas had little patience. Perhaps he was right; but certainly, she felt, insufficient effort was made at Smith College either to find or to produce good women teachers.

Given her opinion of the intellectual standard at Smith—a standard higher in word than in deed—it was hardly strange that she should have been chagrined by the view prevalent among the Smith teachers that Bryn Mawr could hardly be accounted a college at all since the entrance requirements announced in the trustees' circular were so low. Though Carey Thomas had herself made this stricture and was obliged to combat it throughout the rest of her tour, she had not before heard it stated. She was divided between satisfaction in having her own belief upheld and humiliation for Bryn Mawr. The requirements should be high in the beginning, remarked President Seelye, providing her with ammunition to be used later in combat with Bryn Mawr trustees. If preparatory schools balked at the amount of Latin and Greek required, they must be forced to comply; and they would comply, because students themselves desired the highest and best no matter how difficult to achieve—a point heartily endorsed by Carey Thomas. The importance of Greek, in especial, President Seelye insisted upon since, regarded as a manly prerogative, its study gave a woman self-respect besides providing her with a discipline that made her, he had observed, better able to cope with other subjects than was the student of only Latin or modern languages.

On the nonacademic side, the matters concerned with the physical plant and domestic arrangements of the college, Smith and President Seelye had everything to teach her. "I have never seen better managed external details than here," she noted. The college was arranged according to "the cottage system," which everyone at Smith extolled—four cottages of which each was a complete unit, having its own dining room and kitchen, its own lady-in-charge who was at once bursar, housekeeper, and matron, and its own staff of servants with the exception of five men who were in charge of the college as a whole: an engineer and his assistant, a janitor, a gardener, and a night watchman. Since no one would give money to a college for food or repairs, each cottage must both support itself and pay interest on its debt for building and furnishing. President Seelye had managed this "by balancing each item of expenditure against the special sum received for it" and by building and furnishing with the utmost frugality. As even the workmen of the college and of the town of Northampton attested, he had succeeded admirably because he knew more about their jobs and materials than the skilled men whom he employed. "He has learned to be fireman, architect, builder, stone mason, gardener and all the rest," said Carey Thomas. "It is the only way." And she set about her apprenticeship at once, filling her notebook with minute details concerning building and furnishing, running expenses and wages, and tidbits of all sorts of practical advice.

The very fact that Smith College made clear to her numberless difficulties that could be overcome only by hard work on her part acted as a stimulant. She was in the best of spirits, facing plenty of definite action: "I never felt so strong a capacity for managing anything—oh, if I had it all to do!" Besides, she enjoyed the visit itself. The weather was perfect: "The hills look purple and green and gold in the splendid sunlight." The tang of the New England spring air, so different from her own soft Baltimore climate, invigorated her. And she had that sense of personal power than which nothing is happier. Though she had not a minute to herself at Smith, since the president and the faculty and staff were so generous in their entertainment and readiness to talk things over with her, she had met relatively few of the students. Those few, however, had heralded her fame and her words throughout the college. Before she left she observed, "The college girls say I have stirred them all up to do better work, though how, I can't tell." Her conviction of being able to influence students was vindicated and she left Smith College with an increased self-confidence that carried her triumphantly through the rest of her trip.

It was soothing, too, at Wellesley College, her next protracted stopping place, to find that the professors and teachers were almost all women, and to hear President Freeman say that if women were less constant to their profession they were more valuable than men as long as they remained professors because they devoted themselves more disinterestedly to the college. Softened by the evident right-mindedness of the Wellesley authorities, Carey Thomas viewed the organization of the college and listened to the precepts of that "most able woman" President Freeman with warm attention. In the absence of an endowment fund, the yearly deficit was reduced by having all domestic work outside the kitchen done by the students themselves, a deplorable arrangement, Carey Thomas thought, though offset by the more important fact that no professor or teacher was required to teach more than one subject, a system that not only attracted good teachers but made it possible to have specialists in each subject.

Every statement printed in the college circular, said President Freeman, should be upheld without exception; no student should be admitted without a doctor's certificate; and if students were admitted on school certificates alone they must be dropped at once if they showed themselves unable to keep up with their classes; all admirable maxims from Carey Thomas's point of view. "Seventeen girls were sent home from Wellesley last Christmas in spite of agonies of tears," she wrote with approval, adding in capital letters at the foot of the page, "THE SECRET OF WELLESLEY'S SUCCESS IS HER INEXORABLENESS." And successful Wellesley appeared to be. Even the separate department for training teachers, drawback in many ways though it seemed to Carey Thomas, she was assured by President Freeman stood so high as to be called upon yearly to supply more teachers than was possible. The buildings, too, were imposing; and she was gratified to learn that the cottage system met with approval. In the other colleges she had found the libraries to be inadequate. Wellesley's library, on the other hand, appeared to her ample and its arrangements admirable. The distinguishing merit, that made it "perhaps the greatest attraction of Wellesley," was that in spite of a yearly endowment of only two thousand dollars, it took in "all the French, German and Italian periodicals." None the less, in Carey Thomas's scale of values, the Wellesley gymnasium under a gymnastics teacher trained by Dr. Sargent of the Sargent School of Physical Education in Cambridge rivaled the library and was equally unusual among the women's colleges. Much struck by its efficiency and charm, she noted down its measurements and arrangements and apparatus and, on the advice of her old Zürich friend Dr. Culbertson, sought out Dr. Sargent himself in Boston. He was not encouraging: in the plans proposed for a Bryn Mawr gymnasium too much had been expended on useless decorations and the want of a gallery to be used as a running track was lamentable; women gymnastics teachers, moreover, were mostly cranks and had little general intelligence whereas they should be college graduates, preferably holding a medical degree. But Carey Thomas was undismayed. Now that the model of perfection had been made clear to her, plans could be changed and a suitable teacher found.

Carey Thomas thought at the time that her stay at Wellesley had been the most profitable of all her visits; but Boston, the last and most varied lap of her tour, from which she visited Cambridge, was the most enjoyable and not lacking in profit. Radcliffe, or the Harvard Annex, as it still was called, not being a separate women's college, could teach her little in the way of organization. Nevertheless she examined it with especial interest foreseeing that, with academic aims similar to those of Bryn Mawr, it would become Bryn Mawr's most formidable rival. She learned that it had "the tacit promise, conditional only on raising a sum already three-fourths secured, of incorporation as a separate entity within Harvard University." When that union took place, the Harvard Annex would be comparable for women to Harvard itself for men. President Gilman had advised her against copying exactly any of the men's colleges: "They have made many mistakes. Evolve something new and suited to the times, women, America." This was all very well but, as Carey Thomas observed, the men's colleges after working so long on problems of education must have more nearly solved them than any other guide she was likely to find. Now, with the prospect of Harvard University, through its women's annex, becoming Bryn Mawr's chief competitor, it behooved her more obviously than ever to inspect Harvard and make inquiries of its professors.

"The Harvard professors," she announced with a credulity later repudiated, "are charming in regard to women's education." They gave her many odd bits of advice and warning. Professor Childs fulminated against the tendency he had descried in Bryn Mawr's trustees to stress buildings rather than professors and a library, "the important parts of a college." Clement Smith's suggestion she never forgot and found in her own experience wise: "In engaging professors do not take people who apply. The people you need are already busy. *Go out and look for them.*" Professor William Elwood Byerly, her friend of Cornell days, urged her to see that Bryn Mawr professors were given time to carry on their own work. He also advocated appointing them for a period of three years with permission to leave during that time if a better position were offered them—a suggestion against which Carey Thomas wrote in her notes, "too just." Worried, perhaps, by the zeal with which she was pursuing the best possible means of perfecting every aspect of the college, he warned her that women wore themselves out by being too conscientious. Oddly enough, she did not resent this slur upon the feminine sense of proportion. It was probably true, she conceded. But she found entirely misguided his remark that "it is not necessary that all things should be done well—do not make that mistake." She was a perfectionist and all things, she felt, should be done well; the real problem in proportion was to survey the whole field in order to discover which things were the most important and could best be done by oneself, then to do them and to arrange for the less important things and the details to be carried out by other people competent to accomplish them.

Since starting her tour she had met plenty of doubts concerning the academic standard of Bryn Mawr, based chiefly on the entrance examinations proposed by the trustees in their first circular; but no one had expressed himself to Carey Thomas as strongly as did Augustine Jones, head of the Providence Friends' School to which she paid a visit of two days during her stay in Boston. "At Providence," she wrote her parents, "I found organized disapproval of Bryn Mawr and it took all my enthusiasm for higher education to soften Augustine Jones." He had been proud and happy about Bryn Mawr at first, but now was quite disillusioned by the illiberality of certain of the trustees. Not one Providence graduate, he declared, should go to Bryn Mawr; his interest was "in higher education and not in a boarding school college." "I told him," reported Carey Thomas, "that mine was the same, that unless we gave a better education I too would try and persuade everyone to leave Bryn Mawr and should leave myself." She put up a stiff fight and in the end, by the conviction with which she spoke, won him "from studied coldness to real warmth." He became so interested in the college that he began to offer advice, particularly urging the installation of electricity for lighting. He even told his wife in private that his first pride and trust in Bryn Mawr was returning since he had seen Carey Thomas. To her suggestion that she speak to the juniors and seniors he agreed with alacrity and rejoiced in the favorable impression she made. "Altogether," she congratulated herself, "I believe the current is turned towards us, two scholars were almost promised before I left." It had been a personal victory but she was sure that neither

Augustine Jones nor the pupils who followed her enthusiastically would ever regret their conversion. "I am certainly in my right place so far," she remarked with satisfaction.

Her college tour, she thought, had been "invaluable" and also, by her careful management, inexpensive to the trustees. Its one failure lay in her discovery of singularly few teachers whom she wished to call to Bryn Mawr, which was not at all unexpected. She had at least achieved a long list of professorial possibilities to canvass and had amassed a great number of practical suggestions that should prove of inestimable help, as indeed they did. They can be seen cropping up at every turn in the shaping of Bryn Mawr, evidence of Carey Thomas's power to recognize, even in circumstances other than those with which she was to deal, points and details that might be useful to her, and to combine them in a fresh pattern. The last days in Boston went off, therefore, in a happy glow of triumph, the happier since Mamie Gwinn had consented to join her. In between Carey Thomas's appointments they visited the art gallery with only a slight nostalgic twinge for their sight-seeing abroad, made an expedition to Concord, and attended a reception at which they met several young professors who had heard lectures with them at Leipzig, and "Greek and Latin grammarians, Sanskrit readers, etc., disported themselves about the room." In fact, Boston proved such a whirl that they retired to a quiet Friends' boardinghouse at Newport where Carey Thomas could gather herself together and, doubtless with Mamie Gwinn's help, plot out her report. They bathed and sailed and made a few pleasant excursions, though Carey Thomas found it difficult to think of anything but Bryn Mawr—"I am only afraid of getting too much interested in it."

The mass of details concerning building and furnishing she wisely decided to gather into a separate memorandum for the use of the trustees' Buildings Committee and to put into the report itself, asking the trustees to regard them as confidential, only her conclusions about methods of organization with adequate supporting detail. Understanding that the report must not only set out the facts for the trustees' consideration but must bring the trustees to adopt her way of thinking about them, she proceeded tactfully. Willing to give way in matters of secondary importance, she was uncompromising in regard to those, such as entrance examinations, which she felt really mattered. In her preamble, having stated the purpose and scope of her report, she pointed out that Bryn Mawr, much more recently founded and more largely endowed than either Smith or Wellesley, "ought to be an epitome of woman's education as hitherto conceived and attained to, and a model for her education in the future, so that, while we learn from our predecessors, we may not have, in our turn, to learn from those who come after us." She spoke of the cordial welcome given the new college, not only by Friends—and here she administered a well-timed threat by citing Augustine Jones, whose disillusionment she had seen to it that the trustees heard of—but by others who were not Friends who knew both of Bryn Mawr's endowment and of the trustees' wise policy of building only out of their income.

Since it was manifestly necessary to run the college on paying principles in order to derive a real advantage from the endowment, she first discussed its "financial organization" and introduced a series of resolutions: that every department except the academic department be at least self-supporting; and that the fees for tuition, board, and lodging be fixed separately—the whole sum to be from three to four hundred dollars a year. From her findings at the women's colleges she deduced that there need be no deficit in running expenses. Nevertheless, she pointed out, Bryn Mawr must not be too sanguine. And she ended this part of her report with two resounding aphorisms: "Nothing really pays for itself which does not somewhat more than pay" and "Nothing which is not conducted upon paying principles, is conducted upon business principles."

The academic organization, taken up next, she based less on what the women's colleges were doing than on what they seemed to wish to do and on what the men's colleges had accomplished. Having discussed professors' salaries, hours of work, and terms of appointment, she proposed that each subject in the curriculum be put under the charge of a specialist chosen for his knowledge and his ability to impart it and whose schedule was not so heavy as to impair his freshness either in teaching or in that continuance of study so necessary to good teaching. "Upon the personal ability and the training of its instructors the entire future of Bryn Mawr depends." The trustees naturally had an eye to the harmonious running of the institution as a whole and were interested in the character of the teachers rather than in their intellectual equipment. As Dr. Rhoads said, the proper working of a college faculty calls for "unity, cooperation, mutual consideration, and a magnanimous regard not for the prosperity of one department only but for the whole process of character building." To Carey Thomas, however, although she increasingly recognized the importance of character, the essential requisite of the faculty was its power to uphold a high standard of scholarship. Therein lay Bryn Mawr's first chance of contributing to the cause of women's education. But such specialists as she desired could be procured only by making the positions desirable by limiting the hours of work, freeing the teachers from extracurricular duties, making the salaries attractive, and, especially, seeing to it that the students were worthy of good professors.

In order to assure the college of a certain number of advanced and stimulating students, she suggested the establishment of at least one graduate fellowship in each department of study. And she noted the necessity, for both professors and fellows, of a good library. "The scope of a college," she remarked grandly, "is declared in its library." She urged that three thousand dollars, in time possibly five thousand, be appropriated yearly and expended under the immediate direction of the heads of departments, with the understanding that the library be not one of general literature but, "as is proper to a college library," a collection of specialists' tools.

Since Bryn Mawr's first duty under Dr. Taylor's will was to "young women of the upper classes" most of whom could afford to pay their way, and since "scholarships are the most frequent form of private legacy," Carey Thomas advised the founding of only one full undergraduate scholarship, the Dr. Taylor Memorial Scholarship for a member of the Society of Friends, and of a loan fund on which any poor students there were might draw for help. Most important of all seemed to her to be her own cherished scheme of establishing a fellowship of five hundred dollars to be given each year to a member of the graduating class to be used for study abroad. She had seen on her tour the reactions to such a proposal; it would repay itself many times, since no measure would attract more students to the college.

All the trustees, she knew, agreed to the wisdom of adopting the Johns Hopkins University's elective, or group, system of studies. As to departments of study, Bryn Mawr could not, if for no other than financial reasons, spring full-panoplied into action; but its limitations must be those of number, not of quality. A college that is required, as Dr. Taylor's will required of Bryn Mawr, to send out "teachers of a high order" must undertake to teach only what it could teach well, and its standards of whatever might be established in the beginning must be as high as was ultimately desirable. A broad cultural training would obviously be most useful to the "young women of the upper classes" for whose education Bryn Mawr was to be organized; few of them would wish to specialize in a science—luckily, since the equipping of laboratories cost dear. Carey Thomas proposed, therefore, to limit the departments to those teaching the classics and the modern languages, metaphysics, mathematics and history, and only such sciences as contributed directly to a general training: elementary physics, chemistry, biology, and hygiene.

As her private notes show, Carey Thomas in this choice of subjects was in agreement with the trustees, though her reasons for making it differed somewhat from theirs. She was as staunch a supporter as they of the classics, though she found superfluous the explanation given later by Dr. Rhoads in his inaugural address that Greek was of especial interest because it "enshrined the New Testament." She agreed with the trustees' more unusual stress upon the modern languages particularly because, after all, training in them constituted her own stock in trade. She had included a department of philosophy because it was a *sine qua non* in any respectable academic institution, whereas to the trustees it was a matter less of convention than of particular importance. "The too exclusive direction of modern research," said Dr. Rhoads, "to the natural sciences, to that which can be seen, handled, measured and weighed, and the great increase of comfort and luxury arising from the practical application of discoveries in them, have had a tendency to divert attention from metaphysics, and to produce results which would be amusing if they were not pitiful": to his mind and that of the other trustees the central problems of metaphysics were those related to Christian ethics. Both she and the trustees accepted mathematics and, in at least elementary form, the physical sciences as obvious necessities to a college curriculum. But in the creation of a department of history she submitted entirely to the trustees' judgment. In spite of her enthusiasm for it at Cornell, she had discovered, she thought, during her stay in Germany that it neither gave nor demanded a stiff enough intellectual discipline to be of value as a subject for college work, and was a subject to be read at will without professional guidance. Nevertheless, since history formed the subject of reputable, if recently established, departments in other colleges and most of the trustees expected it, she included it in her curriculum. If it suffered later from her lack of interest, it had as fair a start as any other department for, according to Dr. Rhoads, "from the beginning of the organization of Bryn Mawr, it had been a matter of solicitude to the Trustees that history should be so taught as to bring into prominence the great laws which underlie historic movements and events, and to display the moral lessons they afford."

Whatever the grounds of agreement, the trustees would almost certainly concur with the proposals of these first two sections of her report. The last, dealing with entrance examinations, would be less palatable. Carey Thomas attacked it none the less directly. "It is useless," she began, "to have excellent professors if the students still need schoolmasters; and useless to have an excellent library if the students are ignorant of the commonest languages in which learned books and books of reference are composed. . . . A college is ranked among other colleges by the difficulty of its entrance examinations." If the unfavorable impression already created by the requirements announced in the first circular were not removed, "even graduates of the Friends' School in Providence will continue to go to Smith and Wellesley." To set the requirements high would be a good policy, also, because preparatory schools liked to prove themselves by preparing students for the most difficult examinations. "There are studies," she said, "proper to schools only, and studies to be begun at school which are to be continued at college or are instrumental in college work.

The Sargent Portrait of Carey Thomas

Minnie Thomas and her Brothers

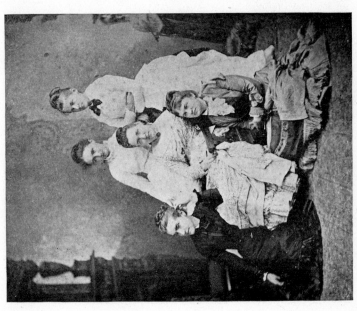

Five Baltimore Friends: Carey Thomas, Mary Garrett,
Julia Rogers, Mamie Gwinn and Bessie King

Dr. Thomas

Mrs. Thomas

Hannah Whitall Smith

Dr. Rhoads

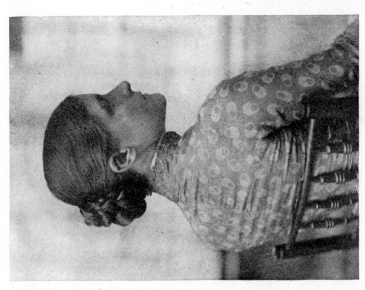

Carey Thomas as Dean

Photo by
Ida W.
Pritchett

Photo by
Ida W.
Pritchett

Looking past Taylor
Hall toward Pembroke
Arch

The Old Chapel

The Old Deanery

Dorothy Vernon Room of the New Deanery

Carey Thomas in
Academic Dress

Photo by Underwood & Underwood

The Garden of the
New Deanery

Photo by Ida W. Pritchett

Photo by Ida W. Pritchett

Academic Procession Forming before the M. Carey
Thomas Library

Photo by Ida W. Pritchett

The Cloisters

Only these latter are the natural subjects of entrance examinations." By confining the demands to them—as did Harvard, the Harvard Annex, and the Johns Hopkins University—the college relieves the student from cramming for numerous petty examinations, the material for which she will have studied in any case, and permits her to concentrate on more advanced work. She ended her report with the suggestion that the publication of a leaflet instructing schoolteachers how to prepare pupils for the Bryn Mawr requirements would be a useful measure.

3

The report was finished and sent off to Dr. Rhoads on June 7; and Carey Thomas returned to her family at Coombe Edge, the country house at Blue Ridge Summit where the Thomases now spent their summers. After the death of old Mrs. Whitall while Carey was still in Germany, there had been no gathering place for the family in the summer and, as Baltimore in the warm weather seemed intolerable, Mrs. Thomas and her sister Hannah decided to expend part of their legacy from their parents on buying a country estate. Hannah Smith and her family being in England, the Thomases were left to choose the location and, after much discussion, decided in 1883 on Blue Ridge Summit. Within easy commuting distance by railway from Baltimore, deep in the country yet with friends near by, it seemed an ideal summer center for the family. The rambling shingled house they built on the brow of a hill looking out over a lovely valley folded in by wooded hills was appropriately named Coombe Edge. Though the days were warm there, the large sitting rooms and dining room were shadowed and cooled by the broad veranda, and the evenings were often chill enough to make an open fire welcome. Upstairs there were small bedrooms enough not only for the family but for the young guests who liked to come where life was simple and carefree and gay.

Almost all the young people were preparing for school or college examinations and, especially her younger sisters Grace and Daisy, constantly sought out Carey Thomas for advice. As early as 1881 their mother had written Carey in Germany that Daisy had set her mind on going to the new college when it opened. Grace, whose ambitions at that time were all social, showed no interest then in Bryn Mawr; but when her elder sister was made dean and things began to hum, she became hardly less ardent than Daisy. Carey Thomas had little time, however, to help aspiring sisters. She was plotting the organization of the college and discussing it with her father and her cousin Francis King; or she was away in Philadelphia talking over her report with Dr. Rhoads before sending it to the trustees and preparing with him the second circular, based on her report, to supersede the first sent out by the trustees in 1883.

That the trustees accepted the second circular at their first meeting in September bore witness not only to their breadth of view but to the force both of her reasoning and of her personality, for it was entirely different in tone and interest from their first circular and omitted much that was dear to them. Where they had been tentative and conciliatory, she was vigorous and challenging; where they addressed parents and Friends, she addressed every student impartially; where they stressed the appearance and comfort of the buildings and the health of the students, she stressed the intellectual demands and advantages of the college; where they agreed to accept on certificates candidates who lived too far from the college to take the entrance examinations, she refused. The matriculation requirements had been stiffened and concentrated according to the recommendations in her report and were the equivalent of those demanded by men's universities of highest standard. Every candidate, to be accepted, must pass either the Bryn Mawr examinations or those covering equal ground given by Harvard or the Harvard Annex. By refusing to accept certificates in lieu of entrance examinations except for students honorably dismissed from another "college of high grade," Bryn Mawr at once set herself with the Harvard Annex apart from the other women's colleges—a position that was for many years a source of pride as well as of difficulty to everyone connected with Bryn Mawr.

Perhaps nothing that Carey Thomas forced through had such wide and cumulative an influence as these Bryn Mawr entrance examinations. The idea was not a new one: the Harvard Annex had already thrown down the gauntlet. The trustees were willing to support it—though only after being convinced by Carey Thomas of its importance. It was she who saw its possible value not only to Bryn Mawr but to all women's education; and to her voice, constantly stressing its value, was owing the carrying power of the examinations' challenge. If they were overstressed in the beginning—as the facilities for postgraduate work at Bryn Mawr were overdrawn—and lent themselves to later abuse, they guaranteed at least a minimum basis of capability and training uniform enough to insure the possibility of advanced work on the part of both students and professors, and stirred the ambition of all those interested in scholarly achievement. Students longed, as the popularity of intelligence tests and information quizzes show that people always do, to prove their powers against a standard of recognized superiority. The pupils in girls' schools began to demand, not vaguely to be given work equal to that done in boys' schools, but specifically to be prepared for either the Harvard or the Bryn Mawr examinations, the highest test, rumor had it, open to them. Even the more conservative teachers in preparatory schools gradually were moved, by the rivalry among schools if by nothing else, to try to meet this growing demand. The Bryn Mawr examinations, therefore, played no small part, as Carey Thomas intended them to do and, by constantly reiterating their great accomplishment, largely made them do, in raising the academic standard both of secondary and of advanced education for girls— a step forward that naturally had its effect upon the education of boys as well. In fact American education, directly or indirectly, benefited for a long time by the rigors of the Bryn Mawr examinations.

The shrewdness of Carey Thomas's appeal to students is shown, also, in her paragraphs in the second circular on courses of study. Addressing the students as mature and serious people, she took it for granted, as she always did, that they wanted not the easiest but the best. She did not minimize difficulty. To her, as to most young people, difficulty was stimulating if the stakes seemed worth it. Here, she said in effect, will be courses planned according to the best educational tendencies of the time, taught by professors trained in modern methods; here will be well-equipped laboratories and a library that will take in the leading scientific, philological, and literary journals of Europe and America; here students may avail themselves of these facilities with the utmost freedom practicable. If a student persevere, and it will be entirely up to her whether or not she does so, she will achieve an A.B. degree of the highest standard, evidence of the sound basis that she has acquired, even the specialist's basis, for further work. Each postgraduate, moreover, will become acquainted with the progress already made in her field and will be enabled to become an independent investigator. In short, if the student pulled through—and there was no reason why she should not—she would be at the top of her particular tree.

The circular then lists fellowships—Bryn Mawr resident fellowships were the first ever to be given women in the United States—and scholarships, and comes to the physical details of the college plant of which the trustees' circular had been almost wholly composed. Again the details are astutely chosen, avoiding solecisms, like "Merion Hall is a home," which occur in the first, and giving only the necessary facts and such appealing items as that each single room and study in Merion Hall has an open fireplace. The circular ends with the stimulating advice to candidates to apply at once since rooms would be assigned in order of the student's application.

After the circular had gone out there remained less than a year before the scheduled opening of the college, in which not only a multitude of decisions were still to be made about the buildings and their administration, but teachers must be appointed in time for them to equip their departments with books and laboratories. A large part of all this work fell upon the willing shoulders of the young dean. It was she who journeyed about interviewing professorial candidates and making the preliminary eliminations. She had, of course, canvassed the field in a general way during her tour of the colleges, finding only one teacher up to her standard of qualifications not too happily entrenched to accept appointment at Bryn Mawr. The obvious, indeed the only, thing to do was to draw either from abroad or from among the young men who had recently taken their doctorates of philosophy with honor. For Carey Thomas to turn willingly to these novitiates was not sur-

prising since then, as always, she sympathized—in the most exact
sense of the word—with youth and was a firm believer in its
advantages. At that time, moreover, she could hardly quarrel with
their lack of experience in teaching since she herself, though
equally inexperienced, had a profound conviction that she could
master the art without difficulty. For the trustees, however, to
have acquiesced is another instance of their genuine broad-mindedness.

By March, the usual time for completing appointments for the
following year, a skeleton faculty had been appointed, and in time
for the opening of the college all the positions on the faculty and
staff had been filled. There was but one full professor, Carey
Thomas herself, who held the chair of English as well as the
deanship, the two together at the salary of three thousand dollars
to be paid all full professors. Among the five associate professors,
at a salary of two thousand dollars there was only one who had no
German training—an English mathematician, Charlotte Angas
Scott, graduate in honors at Girton College, Doctor of Science
from London University and, for three years, lecturer on mathematics at Girton. Of the others, Edward Washburn Hopkins,
appointed associate professor of Greek, Sanskrit, and comparative
philology, Edmund B. Wilson, of biology, Edward H. Keiser, of
chemistry and physics, and Jean Jacques Sturzinger, of Romance
languages, all had at least a year of training in Germany, a doctor's
degree—two of them from the Johns Hopkins, one from Leipzig,
and one from Zürich—and two or more years' teaching experience.
Of the three associates, Emily Gregory in botany and Paul Shorey
in Greek and Latin had just taken their doctorates in Germany
but had had no teaching experience. The third, Woodrow Wilson,
appointed to the Department of History and Political Science, had
neither advanced degree nor experience as teacher but had shown
himself so promising as a student at Princeton, the University of
Virginia, and the Johns Hopkins University, and as an occasional
lecturer and writer of articles that, backed by the advice of the
Johns Hopkins, Bryn Mawr risked appointing him. To this faculty, remarkable in that almost all its members became pre-eminent
in their profession, was added the staff of two instructors, a
gymnasium directress, and a lady-in-charge of Merion Hall.[4]

Forty-seven candidates for entrance as undergraduates took the matriculation examinations at the end of June or in September. Five fell by the wayside; seven, after having passed the examinations, dropped out; and in mid-September the remaining thirty-five, along with seven graduate students of whom four held fellowships, established themselves in Merion Hall. The college buildings had been made ready for them in the nick of time. In Taylor Hall at the east end of the campus, the central point about which future academic buildings were to cluster, the golden oak interior woodwork was just finished, the biological and chemical laboratories just equipped in essentials, the library just stocked with one thousand of the books ordered by the different professors. In Merion Hall to the northwest of Taylor toward the old Gulph Road down which Washington's men marched to Valley Forge, the fire escape had been attached and the fireplaces properly constructed only a short time before the influx of its inhabitants. Additional plumbing had to be installed at the last minute. During the summer the running track, dressing rooms, and showers had been added to the little red brick gymnasium to the west of Merion as well as the apparatus demanded by Dr. Sargent's methods. Even at the last moment the college water supply was not entirely secure. And the president's house, Cartref, across the road to the east, as well as the dean's house and the two faculty boarding-houses that stood in a row along the southern edge of the campus, had been patched and refurbished only in time to receive their inhabitants before the advent of the college students.

Time had had no chance to soften the raw new ugliness of the Bryn Mawr buildings. The gray stone walls of Taylor and Merion, unmitigated by the shrubs and the ivy of later growth, glittered in the soft September sunlight, their gaunt ungainly outlines stark against the sky. Gray stone posts marked the entrance to the college, standing where the gateway of Rockefeller Hall now arches. Between them a narrow path led diagonally from the intersection of Merion and Yarrow streets up the slope to Taylor Hall, cutting across the merest indication of future smooth green lawns. Two or three weeks were to pass before, in the autumn haze, the flickering copper and bright yellow radiance of the cherry tree south of Taylor and the avenue of maples marching over the hill, relic of a long-past farm road, cast its enchantment over the campus, and the air became delicious with the sweet indescribable autumn smell of dry and burning leaves.

But the bare ugliness of the buildings was no greater than that of other institutions built in the same architectural era and shocked neither faculty nor students. Their minds, in any case, were set on other things. Most of the students had had to struggle against prejudice of one sort or another to get to college and some against faulty preparation: they arrived intent on intellectual matters. Most of them had chosen to come to Bryn Mawr thinking that in this new institution of high standards they might obtain what they wanted according as they demanded and worked for it. The professors, too, felt this and to an even greater degree. Young and energetic and full of theories as to the rights and wrongs of educational methods and aims, many of them saw a chance to develop not only their own careers but a whole educational system according to their ideals.

If the hopes of both professors and students were high, higher still were those of Carey Thomas, who had lived in a dream of an academic Utopia during many months—and toiled to prepare for it. The quiet, dignified manner of the young dean could hardly conceal the vitality and excitement that she tried to suppress. Her happiness, her profound conviction of success, her faith in the achievement of ultimate aims, even though she was beset by a multitude of subsidiary details pertaining to her double office of dean and professor of English, polarized the enthusiasm of students and faculty. No student left her office after the first interview without a warmer determination to strive not only for her own ends but for the good of the college itself.

4

The very air of the college was electric when on September 23, 1885, Bryn Mawr formally opened its doors with an inaugural ceremony in Taylor Hall. Early in the afternoon the first carriages swung up to the opening of the path from Merion Avenue to Taylor Hall, disgorging the notables of the countryside into the blustering wind that swept across the campus; and the steady stream of visitors who had arrived by the Pennsylvania Railroad from Philadelphia began to move sedately toward the college, the black frock coats of the gentlemen and the dark-cloaked, full-skirted dresses and modest bonnets of the Quaker ladies making almost as gravely decorative a procession as if they had been in academic dress. On the platform in "the handsome assembly room" at three o'clock sat the college trustees, its president, dean, and faculty as well as the heads of various older academic institutions and a number of other dignitaries. In the front rows, facing the platform, sat the students backed by parents and friends—so great a crowd that even the adjacent corridors and classrooms were packed. Unfortunately, since much that was best in Bryn Mawr was owing to him, the chairman of the Board of Trustees, Francis King, was ill and his place as presiding officer had to be taken by Philip C. Garrett, who, "following a prayer offered by Dr. Thomas," opened the ceremony by reading verses 1-17 of the twenty-ninth chapter of I Chronicles and introduced the speakers: President Rhoads, President Gilman of the Johns Hopkins University, President Chase of Haverford College, and, finally, James Russell Lowell.

Dr. Rhoads, as was to be expected, gave a brief account of the character, intentions, and achievement of Dr. Taylor, its founder, and spoke of the scope and aim of the new college. The speech was skillfully woven, closely packed with information, impressive in the thoroughness and farsightedness with which the scheme of the college was thought out—a plan intended to permit growth in certain directions. The trustees, accepting the definition of education as "the equable development of all our faculties by means of use and knowledge," believed that Bryn Mawr must take an especial part in that development. In the three questions that Dr. Rhoads named as essential for the trustees to settle in order to prepare for this may be grouped the questions that the college is still called upon to face; and his answers were in general outline those that, with two possible exceptions—the Carola Woerishoffer School and the Department of Music—the college continued to give.

President Gilman warned Bryn Mawr that, though being new and free she was "a likely leader of kindred establishments the world over," she must guard against slavishly following the example of other colleges and against the self-imposed bondage of precedent, obligation, law, and other fetters. Bryn Mawr must discriminate and save only what "is of value now." This plea for progress contrasted markedly with the conservative conception of Bryn Mawr outlined by President Chase, whose ideal for the college was, by teaching all the accepted studies and concentrating upon the classics, to fit women "for life, the glad bright life of the pure and healthy body; the noble, unwearying, ever expanding life of the mind; the undying life of the intelligent, feeling, willing soul." Mr. Lowell—though some of the undergraduates, possibly following the dean's lead, later suspected him of being "a shocking anti-feminist"—again was more liberal, and seemed the personification of the qualities that those who aspire to culture most admire. His Bryn Mawr audience must have agreed with him when he said that American education, the merits of which Americans were inclined, he thought, to overestimate, has two faults: "a want of thoroughness and a disposition to value learning chiefly as a means of making a livelihood." But they could not have accepted wholly the summary statement that followed—the cry of a dyed-in-the-wool upholder of liberal culture against the rising tide of specialized training: the object of a university education is not to help man as a breadwinner, "but to be the lifelong sweetener of all the bread he ever earns." Though Bryn Mawr intended to give no direct vocational training, she was committed by Dr. Taylor's will to fitting young women "to become teachers of a high order." Carey Thomas, at any rate, must have been gratified to hear him deplore American indifference to the use of English and rejoice that at Bryn Mawr the study of English was to be emphasized: it gave him hope that Bryn Mawr might produce "truly civilized women" capable of discriminating between literature, even contemporary literature, and mere printed matter. And his audience acclaimed wholeheartedly his final precept that teaching should be "given life," should be always "The New Learning."

With Lowell's speech the formal exercises closed and "the audience of unusual intelligence," in the words of the press, dispersed to inspect the buildings before reassembling for "a collation" in the gymnasium. Far from being a merely perfunctory ceremony, the exercises proved not only to have clarified the issues and reassured and stimulated the audience in general, as such exercises should do, but to have enlarged the vision and ambition of the students. The conviction with which the speakers had stated their ideas, the keenness with which they had disclosed dangers as well as ideals, and especially the clearness with which Dr. Rhoads had explained the reasons for the college's aims and organization, roused them to think deeply about the whole subject of advanced education. They had come to Bryn Mawr hoping to achieve for themselves education like their brothers', more advanced than they might find at other women's colleges. Now they began to think in broader terms.

Each step in the history of the progress of women's advanced education, from the founding of Mt. Holyoke on, had been attended by students who felt themselves to be pioneers. The Bryn Mawr students, in their turn, felt themselves pioneers in the final step, as they regarded it—education like that of men. Now they began to see themselves in the vanguard of the forward movement of all education. There seemed no reason why Bryn Mawr should not give them an education better than that obtained by their brothers, no reason why it should not lead men's as well as women's colleges. This possible superiority they grasped at with delight and guarded jealously, examining and criticizing their college minutely, comparing it continually with the other colleges in order to make and keep all possible advances. It was the beginning of that attitude of superiority associated for many years with the students of Bryn Mawr, and also of that critical vigilance and outspoken advice with which students and, later, alumnae watched each move on the academic chessboard.

Deanship; Family and Friends; Bryn Mawr School of Baltimore; Johns Hopkins University Medical School

I

IN FOSTERING the pride of Bryn Mawr students in the college and their vigilant care of all its aspects, Carey Thomas played an important role. Her burning interest in everything pertaining to Bryn Mawr, when allowed to express itself, was of almost volcanic force. Her words were those of complete conviction, her actions quick and decisive. Neither could be overlooked, both aroused immediate reaction. And as dean she held a strategic position, not only in official relation to students and faculty and trustees and the outside world in their various twofold combinations, but in personal relation to each member and part of the college. No one connected with the college and no phase of its life went untouched by her. No one could remain indifferent to her.

With the Board of Trustees in the early years she had little direct contact. Not that the trustees were a remote body interested only in the finances and larger policies and the physical upkeep of the college. On the contrary, they were deeply interested in all sides of the college, and even well informed concerning the academic phase. After all, it was they who had planned the college and set the machine in motion and it was for them, they felt, to see that it progressed smoothly in the right direction. In her official position the dean was to them merely one cog in the great wheel. She was not a member of the board; such of her reports, requests, and recommendations as were officially made to it went through the president. Her only direct official connection with the trustees was with certain of the committees, notably the Buildings and Grounds Committee, to whom she was supposed to report the building needs of the college and, when requested, to say how far the proposed plans and the completed buildings met these needs. The problems themselves of building were not thought to be her affair. But her faith in the trustees' ability in building matters had been impaired by what seemed to her the relatively poor results and unnecessary expenditure in the case of Merion Hall. She had taken to heart, moreover, the precepts of President Seelye of Smith College: in order to run a college with requisite economy it was necessary for the president to oversee with a trained eye each detail of its physical plant. If the president did not do so— and President Rhoads clearly intended to leave such matters to their authorized overseers, the trustees—then it was, she felt, up to her to do it herself. Had the trustees been other than they were this determination of hers might have created considerable friction. Fortunately, most of them welcomed advice whencesoever it came and judged it upon its merits, not its source. And equally fortunately they found her advice good. Even so, she approached them at first through unofficial channels, through her father and uncle and President Rhoads himself. Diplomatically, one or other of them passed on to the board or the committee in question her findings, her words of wisdom or desperation, until gradually the trustees' building committee came to seek her aid directly.

A fortnight after the opening of the college, in answer to President Rhoads's plea for more provision for resident students, the trustees proposed that plans be drawn for a "cottage" for fifty-five students to be begun as soon as arrangements could be made. This was Carey Thomas's chance to bring her dreams into being. She knew, or thought she knew, the influence of surroundings upon the minds of the young. How much less wear and tear of spirit would there have been for her had she not been starved of all aesthetic satisfaction amid the raw, ugly, and utilitarian aspects of Baltimore and Cornell that surrounded her own youth. Naturally as a disciple of Ruskinian Neo-Gothicism, and dependent upon the aesthetic judgment of her "cultured" contemporaries, she did not recognize the beauty of American colonial building. It is doubtful if she had heard of the charm of the universities in Virginia. Academic beauty could lie only in the halls of Oxford and Cambridge. In this opinion she was supported by most of the cultivated elite of her generation, who accepted it unquestioningly. Even the trustees, who without Carey Thomas's impetus would have continued to multiply forbidding structures like Taylor and Merion halls peculiar to the architecture of the "Main Line", turned their eyes wistfully toward the established triumphs of the older institutions across the Atlantic on any question related to education. Precisely how far her wishes counted in the choice of architects for the new building it is impossible to tell, or precisely how far her wishes influenced their plans. Suffice it to say that Radnor Hall was the first of a long line of collegiate Gothic buildings—bastard Gothic, they were termed by Roger Fry—which the firm of Cope and Stewardson designed for Bryn Mawr College, Princeton, and other universities.

If the trustees were complacent on the score of Merion's appearance, they were far less so in regard to its costliness. Their anxiety over its initial cost was not allayed by the first year's running expenses. Carey Thomas's arguments as to the necessity of making a residence hall more than pay for itself and the ways of doing so, based on her study of Smith College cottages, found more and more favor. The trustees soon felt the cogency of even those precepts nearest her heart, that not only should there be a separate room for each student but there must be rooms of different sizes, and even suites of rooms, at various prices in order to provide enough revenue over the bare board and upkeep to pay back gradually the initial cost of building and to contribute toward academic expenses. In the building of Radnor Hall, finished in January, 1887, the mistakes of Merion, as Carey Thomas saw them, were rectified. Although it was by no means wholly satisfactory, its mistakes, in turn, formed part of the cumulative experience that went into the building of future halls.

Two years later it became evident that a third hall of residence for sixty more students would be needed. Denbigh Hall, of dark gray stone like Radnor "in the collegiate style of the Tudor period," gave "universal satisfaction," announced Dr. Rhoads upon its completion in February, 1891. Carey Thomas agreed, though ostensibly she had not had much more to do with its planning and construction than with that of Radnor. But behind the scenes, partly because her relatives among the trustees recognized her as the probable instigator of the demands for a new hall and partly because they could vent dissatisfaction more readily upon her than upon either President Rhoads or each other, she had been obliged to bear a large part of the brunt of their financial anxiety. The president of the board, her cousin Francis King, had also begun to find both her practical advice and her willingness to drudge over plans very helpful. From his experience on the Johns Hopkins Hospital Board, of which he was chairman, he had devised a plan whereby the building of Denbigh could be simplified and cheapened; and on this plan he and Carey Thomas worked arduously whenever he could get to Bryn Mawr. It was the last year of his life; he was old and had a weak heart. Every now and again they were obliged to break off discussion for him to lie down, breathless. Digitalis, or whatever his remedy might be, was administered. A few minutes' rest, and again they began the heated shuffling back and forth of ways and means.

The financial problems involved in building Dalton Hall, completed two years later, 1893, were less obfuscated by being based on mere probability. As a scientific, not a residence, hall, it could not be expected to pay its own way. At least half the sum needed, about seventy-five thousand dollars, must be begged by alumnae and friends of the college; the rest might gradually be refunded from the profits of the residence halls. This time the trustees were grateful for Carey Thomas's zeal. Her youth, good looks, and quick wits, and especially the ardent assurance with which she spoke—her shyness forgotten in the enthusiasm of her purpose—made her an admirable beggar. Her victims were temporarily carried away by the privilege offered them of contributing to so large and useful a scheme. This begging for Dalton was an encouraging initiation into the business of soliciting funds, and was the easier since near-by sources had not yet been drained.[1]

Meantime, across the valley at the western end of the campus, on the crest of the hill along which runs Roberts Road, a number of houses for professors had been built. "The Greenery" and "the Betweenery," later moved to form Yarrow West and East on the southern edge of the campus, already stood, with the Deanery, on old Yarrow Road which, until it was closed in 1902, cut the campus along the hillside where the Deanery still stands. Carey Thomas was inclined to think of these two houses, in which male professors lived, as centers of high thinking and hard intellectual labor. That she herself had made a signal failure of communal life she felt to be the fault of the communities in which she had tried it—a large and disorderly household, Sage College and European pensions where the other inhabitants were neither of equal cultivation nor of like purpose. Here in the Greenery and Betweenery were two groups of individuals, scholars of similar education and aims, intent upon intellectual matters. They should be, she took it for granted, fairly congenial; at any rate, they should be so absorbed in their work as to be thankful to have the material framework of daily life ordered for them. The common human longing for privacy and independence, for elbow room both physical and mental, though it was so strong in herself, she overlooked. It was a disenchantment to her to learn that the professors were not satisfied with their way of life. She suspected that the presence of wives and children was the source of disturbance. In any case, as the faculty increased, the accommodation of the Greenery and the Betweenery grew cramped; and so, if it was with something of disappointment, it was with no objection that she approved of the college's arrangement for the building of professors' houses. Not that her approval was necessary; but her opposition would have been troublesome. The brown shingled houses of "faculty row" were begun at the western end of the campus, so familiar to generations of students, if somewhat dark and forbidding and very remote.

In all this building Carey Thomas had a finger. By the time a new hall of residence was needed, soon after the completion of Denbigh and before Dalton was entirely finished, Dr. Rhoads had become more and more inclined to leave all that did not demand the authorization of the official head of the college in the hands of the competent young dean. And the trustees, even those antagonistic to her by temperament, had grown to respect her pronouncements. After Francis King's death, too, she came into more direct contact with the chairman of the Buildings and

Grounds Committee, her cousin David Scull. In the building of Pembroke Hall, therefore, her voice was the effective voice; she had a more direct part in it than any of the trustees except David Scull, who worked with her.

Encouraged by the profitableness of Denbigh Hall, the trustees agreed fairly readily in September, 1892, to the proposed building of another hall for sixty students. But this did not satisfy Carey Thomas. She foresaw that no sooner was such a hall built than still another would be needed; though Bryn Mawr had been the only college to limit its numbers from the beginning—namely, to about five hundred undergraduate and one hundred graduate students—it had not yet reached that limit or even the number of students with whom its academic departments were already capable of dealing. In conjunction with Cope and Stewardson, therefore, she worked out a plan and drew up detailed estimates of cost for a double hall of two wings and a central tower, containing the joint kitchen and dining hall over an archway that would form the western entrance to the college. It would house twice as many students as a single hall and cost only two-thirds as much as two separate halls. She bombarded the Buildings Committee and other influential trustees with columns of figures and a multitude of arguments on reams of paper. Months passed in negotiations, followed by months during which she worked closely on details of the actual building, seeing that plans were followed and materials not scamped by contractors, making suggestions, and even advising the workmen as they toiled. By the opening of the college in 1893, in spite of numerous setbacks, the west wing and tower of the new double hall, Pembroke, was habitable and the east wing was well under way.

The success of this first of her buildings was concrete evidence to the trustees, especially to those who knew how entirely it was hers, of her ability in administration. To David Scull, who heretofore had accepted her as doubtless a competent dean and learned in her own particular subject, personally attractive and mildly endeared to him because he was fond of her family, the experience of his year's work with her was a revelation. She, for her part, was impressed by his distinguished appearance and by the gentle urbanity that permitted them to work together from the first without friction. Before Pembroke was finished their relations were cordial and their respect for each other high; and a few years later he joined the ranks of her father and uncle, taking the place of her other cousin Francis King, as her wholehearted supporter and would-be protector.

Even those trustees least in sympathy with her did not hesitate to advise her; nor was she reluctant to accept their suggestions. In many of them lay the germs, even sometimes the full outline, of schemes that later seemed to have sprung from her own brain. Her yearly commencement luncheon, for instance, was the result of careful planning on the part of a member of the trustees' Executive and Finance Committee. Impressed by the advisability of "seeking to interest the prominent and wealthy ladies of Philadelphia" in the college, he urged the dean to invite a group of ladies "selected, with some reference to congeniality, according to wealth, social standing, or intellectual superiority" to a luncheon in her house at the same time that Dr. Rhoads proposed to give lunch to all who attended the commencement exercises. He submitted to her a list of names and suggested that later she might invite even the great of New York, "the Vanderbilts and others." He thought, also, that it would be well for her to join one or two of the Philadelphia clubs, the New Century Club and the Contemporary Club, for instance, where she would be likely to make acquaintance with and to interest the influential members of Philadelphia society. These suggestions filled her with dismay. Shyness, interlinked with a combined sense of superiority and inferiority to the ladies of society, made the prospect of mingling with them formidable. And Mamie Gwinn, who cultivated with care her own ostensible contempt for society, was no support in such enterprises. Nevertheless, Carey Thomas saw their expediency. She allowed her name to be put up at the clubs and, encouraged by the success of being promptly elected, did her best to take part in their meetings and undertakings. As a result of these efforts her father, in arguing in 1893 for her election to the college presidency, could speak of "the popularity of the Dean in Philadelphia circles of intelligent and influential people."

If various trustees occasionally administered good advice, her father and uncle were her constant guides. Responsible for her not only as dean but as a person whom they loved and whose success was dear to them, they watched over her every step. Hardly a day passed without letters to and from them of instructive maxims of worldly wisdom. In view of her impetuous joy in combat these are largely exhortations to avoid friction. "The *quiet management* of difficult matters *before they come to a head* and *before oppositions crystallize* etc., is much the best way," James Whitall replied emphatically to her announcement that the students proposed to send a petition directly to the trustees. In connection with the dismissal of a member of the faculty who had made a failure of his work, he wrote, "When the business in hand is to get rid of an employe, it is always desirable if possible to keep the person in a *comfortable state of mind,* so that the parting will be peaceable and without any law suit. To this end, if the person has *any* talent or ability in *any field*, it does no harm to speak to them about that, and commend it." The wisdom of this nice balance of praise and blame Carey Thomas never forgot. Indeed most of her uncle's precepts took root and flowered. She accepted them with neither surprise nor indignation, for ever since she could remember "uncle James" in his kindly solicitude had rained advice upon her parents—and upon her, since she had entered his orbit in connection with Bryn Mawr. It was no less natural, no more to be resented than the rain from heaven, and equally useful. Besides, she knew that she could trust him as she could her father to defend her in face of criticism.

Sometimes, unwittingly, he overdid his part of protector. One of the trustees, he reported to her after a board meeting early in 1894, "made a motion that Beaumont and Fletcher be taken out of our library. I informed the Board that thou had told me that F. R. Cope spoke to thee about these books some time ago, and that thou had at once removed them. That quieted that subject. Was I right?" Unhappily, his niece was obliged to confess that he was not right, although the books were later put in the library "locked closet." To be sure, F. R. Cope, one of the original trustees, had pleaded with her to omit Shakespeare from her lectures and to remove his works from the library, but she had made it clear to him that she would not feel justified in doing so. Perhaps he had complained also of other Elizabethan dramatists.

In any case, the dean was immovable in her belief that, however at variance with Quaker custom, it was necessary for a student of English literature to have some acquaintance with Elizabethan plays. Toward the end of her deanship, F. R. Cope found her views so entirely in conflict with his own that he was constrained to resign from the board rather than appear to support her. She went so far, however, toward compliance with his views and those of even less exigent trustees as to choose the plays for student consumption with care, never suggesting to undergraduates that they read *Othello*, for instance, and always permitting certain scenes and lines to be omitted from the plays that she did require of them—a precaution that, needless to say, defeated its object.

Indispensable though her father and uncle were in posting her as to all the trustees' debates and decisions, and in warning her of their general temper, they were hardly less so as a proving ground for her own ideas. They showed her how to modify them to insure acceptance, or when, as they occasionally did, they disapproved of them entirely, they pointed out her error in no unmeasured terms. In reply to her proposal in December, 1888, that some form of faculty government should be instituted, her uncle wrote at some length advising her against sending a resolution about it to the board. He did not believe the trustees would adopt it. More likely, they would agree with his own opinion that college faculties should be advisory only, with no executive functions—like a cabinet consulted by the president. "I have," said he, "a great dread of government by talk. Give the faculty whatever power you please, dignify their position, but do not ask the Trustees to set them up over the head of the President." In all cases the decision and action should rest with the president. However little during her deanship she sympathized with this point of view, in the ripeness of experience and from her own position as president, when the subject was brought up again twenty-eight years later, she saw that government by the faculty if rashly instituted might work more harm than good.

Before the board meetings she took pains to prime her father with her point of view on every subject likely to be on the agenda. She agreed, she wrote him, to the trustees' permitting a certain member of the faculty to break his contract and resign, but "be careful *not* to make it a general principle. . . . Nothing could be more unfortunate than for the impression to prevail among the faculty that the Trustees would always release. Each special case should be considered on its own merits." Then, leaving nothing to chance, she framed a resolution for him to present on the subject. And sometimes she used her father, too, to influence Dr. Rhoads, who on occasion tried her sorely by not taking action immediately she pointed out to him the need for it. Time and again she thought that she had screwed him to the sticking point of unequivocally dismissing a housekeeper who was not only inefficient but "utterly unsuited to the care of young people." Each time he was won back to passivity by one of the trustees who befriended the housekeeper. Could not her father make him see that he must dismiss her?

2

For the most part, however, the dean and the president worked together without friction. Roughly speaking, the president, as deputy of the trustees, managed the finances and the appointments and announced the general policy of the college.[2] Since he was an ardent Quaker, as the dean was not, he was deeply concerned with the religious life of the college. To the dean the important point of Dr. Taylor's statement in regard to religion was his evident intention that the college be nonsectarian; to the president the fact that Dr. Taylor wished the college to be pervaded by the principles of Christianity held by the Friends was of far greater moment. Through the Quaker meeting held by him each working day and through his class in ethics, in which he dealt with Christian and chiefly Quaker principles, concentrating especially upon "the moral aspects of social problems," he attempted to guide the students. This one hour weekly class, the result of the experience and reading of a thoughtful Friend but not of a trained philosopher, was the one exception to the otherwise unbroken rule of permitting only specialists to teach in the college. Recognizing it not only as being dear to the heart of Dr. Rhoads but as possibly staving off more stringent action on the part of the trustees, Carey

Thomas averted her eyes and accepted it. She had no belief, in any case, in offending uselessly against feeling or convention, whether religious or other. The outward forms of religion should be kept. She became a member of the Haverford Meeting and, at least twice a week, held the college morning assembly. Only if religious feeling interfered with the progress of the college as an institution of learning did she find any need of opposing it.

After more than three years' teamwork in which to judge her qualities Dr. Rhoads wrote to Carey Thomas's father, "I wish you to know how highly I esteem the talents, learning and remarkable executive ability of Carey, as well as admire her many other noble personal traits." So evident, in fact, was his admiration that many onlookers felt him to be dominated by her. Looking back years later, she herself was rather inclined to feel that she had been the ruling spirit. In one sense doubtless she was, since the force of her zeal and her power with people counted incalculably in the partnership. He recognized her flair for promoting her ends and used it to the full, but never blindly. He weighed and questioned her decisions and had to be convinced before yielding. Though the president had charge of the appointments, carrying on the final negotiations with the candidates, the dean shared in the spadework, and from her contemporaries was often able to obtain information denied to Dr. Rhoads about promising young scholars. Though for him the scales were weighted by considerations of character and for her by those of intellectual attainment, in theory at least they agreed as to the qualifications to be demanded of candidates. He made no appointments, however, even upon her strong recommendation, without careful consideration. In 1891 a brilliant young Jew was made associate in biology largely because of recommendations obtained by Carey Thomas. Recognizing the fact that his brilliance outweighed any difficulties created by racial prejudice and perhaps also that Bryn Mawr would soon have to lose him to some other college—in point of fact it lost him in a year—Dr. Rhoads agreed to his appointment. But when Carey Thomas suggested appointing another Jew in the following year he opposed it, remarking that, though he had "no unkind feeling towards the Jews" and never forgot "our vast indebtedness to them," the effect of the presence of several Jews in the college would be to make difficult the inculcation of Friendly Christian principles and also, socially, to "repel many of the best Protestant families" as had happened at other places. Later, during her own presidency, Carey Thomas opposed more often than not the appointment of Jews to the Bryn Mawr faculty owing, it is sometimes said, to her personal prejudice. In reality her opposition, like that to a relatively undue number of appointments made from any single religious sect, was a reasoned policy founded in the first instance upon Dr. Rhoads's arguments in 1891. The years as dean were those of her apprenticeship.

The faculty, too, had their part in training her. Her relations with them as well as with the Board of Trustees demanded self-discipline. Though the professors had authority within departments to decide what the courses were to cover and how they were to be given, the dean saw to it that the departments' policies corresponded with the college policy and that the departments answered the needs of the college. Given her consuming interest in her job it was natural that she should not only become aware of almost every move in the faculty that affected the college but take part in it, frequently overstepping her legitimate duties, sometimes to the indignation of the other professors involved. More often than not, from their angle, their resentment was legitimate. Surely it showed no undue professional touchiness in Professor Hopkins to object strongly to her discussing and even deciding with Professor Smyth, head of the Latin Department, matters concerning the Greek Department that had never been broached to Dr. Hopkins himself, the head of the Greek Department. Nor is it surprising that the head of the Department of Physical Training should have been stirred to remonstrance by the dean's encouraging complaints of her department from students who should have made their dissatisfaction known directly to her. The dean took suggestions when and where she found them, saw their point in relation to the improvement of the college as a whole, often in her zeal exaggerated them, and acted upon them with lightninglike rapidity.

Such precipitate action naturally led her, even more quickly than is the case with many executives, into the appearance of despotism or of double-dealing, and sometimes into a reversal of her former position. She was overheard one morning, as she escorted a graduate student to the door of the Deanery, outlining the procedure that she thought the student should follow. Suddenly she paused: "No. I had forgotten the regulations. If you look up the rules, you will see that that is impossible. You might . . ." and she outlined an entirely different course to pursue. Had her change of mind been less immediate and obvious it might well have been attributed to baser sources than the quick, wholehearted interest and lapse of memory from which, in reality, it sprang. The enthusiasm generated by finding a new idea that seemed good to her quick mind, momentarily at least, carried her over obstacles otherwise insuperable, including matters of personal feeling and interdepartmental jealousy. Given warning of the need of it, she could be tactful; successfully so, since she was shrewd. But when she conceived a move to be for the advantage of the college she carried it through with deliberate ruthlessness. She did not hedge in reply to protest. Enjoying a good stand-up fight herself, she met the protester halfway and loosed upon him all her guns. In turn, she expected him to reply openly in kind. Anyone strong enough to do so, she respected. Only for the weak and the sulkers she had no use. If her opponent hit home she admitted it, for she was open to conviction since her whole energy was directed toward doing her best for the college. If her adversary could show reason that a move other than the one she had made or proposed to make would be of greater advantage to Bryn Mawr, when the heat of battle cooled, she welcomed his opposition, acknowledged his victory, apologized handsomely, and changed her position to accord with his. This sometimes appeared to her opponent as weakness or duplicity on her part, and attributing the victory entirely to his own prowess he continued to suspect her sincerity. Others, who understood her better, recognized her real open-mindedness and became her devoted adherents.

A characteristic of the dean less discussed, but of considerable influence, was her attitude toward social intercourse with the faculty and staff. She had no time and no use for casual chitchat. Compelled by courtesy to suffer it, the warmth of her manner chilled to bare civility, the heavy eyelids drooped slightly over the brilliant eyes, her face became a mask of controlled impatience and distaste. To the physical director, a schoolmate of the dean's, to Professor Scott, used to the easy intercourse of Cambridge common rooms, and to various other members of the teaching staff it was a source of bewilderment and some resentment to perceive by degrees that they were not encouraged to drop in for friendly gossip. For pointed discussion, however, of matters relevant to the dean's main interests—women's education, Bryn Mawr College—they were welcomed always. They found it difficult to understand that the interest in their lives that she sometimes showed was for the sake of their careers, part of her counsel of perfection for women and the college, not because of any special liking for them as human beings.

The formality in her relationship with the faculty and staff, on the other hand, was not without effectiveness. She was respected, even grudgingly admired, if not loved by those whom it confused and affronted; and her reputation as a brilliant young woman of scholarly experience unprecedented in the American world, as well as her good looks, her lovely voice, her dignity of manner, drew many eyes to her. Nevertheless, not until, with the passage of time, the evidences of her vigor of mind and action and her strength of purpose had accumulated did she win her later ascendancy over the administration of the college. The faculty, like the trustees, demanded proof of her power in leadership before following her, or refusing to follow. In the light of her later supremacy, however, much has been attributed to her as dean for which she was not responsible—the negotiations, for instance, concerning the resignation of Woodrow Wilson from the faculty of Bryn Mawr College. The story of Woodrow Wilson's place on the faculty and his departure is so widely known, and so inaccurately, that it is worth telling at length.

The current belief that Carey Thomas had some sort of quarrel with Wilson about his departure from Bryn Mawr is incorrect. In actual fact, she had little to do with him and nothing whatever to do with his leaving the college. To be sure, she had been with Dr. Rhoads in November, 1884, during his preliminary inquiry at the Johns Hopkins for a professor of history when Wilson, the most promising candidate, was disconcerted by being introduced to her as dean of the Bryn Mawr faculty and to Dr. Rhoads merely as one of the trustees. Wilson soon learned, however, that Dr. Rhoads was president and that he himself would be his own master under the president, not subordinate to a young woman. As Carey Thomas was staying in Baltimore she had two further interviews with him during which he explained his special interests and the salary he hoped for and she urged him to complete the work for his doctorate of philosophy. But the formal negotiations concerning his appointment were carried on and completed directly with Dr. Rhoads. Following the usual procedure, after two years' successful work at Bryn Mawr, Wilson was reappointed by the president; and again following the usual procedure, he tendered his resignation to the president. During his term at the college, the first three years of its existence, he had only the usual official contacts with the dean, purely routine affairs.

By nature they were antipathetic. Wilson's introversion, his intellectuality and narrow sympathy, his cold passion and his slow tenacity, were diametrically opposed to her extroversion and practicality, her impulsiveness and generosity of mind and heart. The very characteristics in which they were alike—strength of will and ruthless ambition and even, perhaps, a sense of superiority—were sufficient to keep them apart. Finally, they were at opposite poles in their attitude toward women. He, in proverbial southern fashion, liked women to be sweet and gentle and pretty, accomplished in the social graces, possibly in household arts. Woman was to be cherished as man's dear honored chattel. Of independent women he did not approve, least of all of women who meddled in the serious concerns of masculine life, such as scholarship. The dean, in short, was all that he disliked most in women. In so far as he thought of her at all, he probably thought of her with distaste. He dispatched routine business as quickly as was civilly possible and, for the rest, steered clear of her. For her part, she was well aware of his attitude toward women and scorned him for it. Among the few notes for her proposed autobiography are two scraps of paper on which, under the heading "Woodrow Wilson" are jotted in her large fist, "Coventry Patmore, 'The Angel in the House'" and Tennyson's "Put thy sweet hand in mine and trust in me"—acid little notes that give the measure of her disdain.[3]

When, in 1887, his position at Bryn Mawr was raised from associate in history to that of associate professor of history and political science with a corresponding increase in salary, he boggled at signing a three years' contract unless promised an assistant. He had come to feel his situation as a professor of women almost intolerable. At first he had been delighted by the prospect of building up a library in his subject; now he felt the Bryn Mawr library facilities so inadequate as to cramp his work. As the college grew his work increased, leaving too little time for his private writing. And the salary, although larger than he had been offered elsewhere, was quite inadequate to his wants. After considerable discussion of the contract with Dr. Rhoads, he agreed, however, to sign it if it contained the clause, "he shall have an assistant as soon as practicable," accepting Dr. Rhoads's interpretation of "practicable" as signifying chiefly financial ability. The following August President Rhoads, thinking eight hundred dollars could be spared for the purpose, had interviewed a prospective assistant. But as the young man did not wish to teach ancient history, the subject for which Wilson wanted him, and the trustees' Executive Committee thought eight hundred dollars a great strain on the budget, the matter was dropped for the time being. In the next March or April, 1888, the college appointed an associate in history to assist Wilson for the following year; and in that same April, Wilson told President Rhoads that he considered his contract with the college annulled because, in having failed to appoint him an assistant heretofore, the college had not carried out its side of the bargain. President Rhoads at once "repudiated the thought that the reasons assigned made the contract invalid."

During the three years since joining the faculty of Bryn Mawr, Wilson had applied for and been offered positions at various other colleges—offers that he had neither accepted nor mentioned to the Bryn Mawr authorities. Now, in mid-June, came a tentative offer of the Hedding Professorship of History and Political Economy at Wesleyan University which carried with it greater advantages to him than Bryn Mawr could provide. He announced his proposed resignation from the Bryn Mawr faculty on June 23 leaving President Rhoads amazed, since Wilson's contract had another year to run, and aghast, since the college was closed and it seemed unlikely that any suitable substitute could be found so late in the year. In an attempt to show Wilson that the contract was still binding, he went over the history of their negotiations during the past year. Wilson admitted that President Rhoads had urged the binding force of the contract when Wilson had said it was annulled and that, in reply to Dr. Rhoads's assertion that the college "expected him to continue next year with the same salary," he himself had expected to do so. He had regarded the engagement, however, as he explained to Dr. Rhoads, as terminable at any date before the actual work began in the autumn that "would *in his judgment* allow time for providing a successor." The time in which to do so seemed to him adequate, and he felt "perfectly justified" in resigning.

The misunderstanding was one that foreshadowed difficulties of far greater import in Wilson's later career. He had formed his own interpretation of events and words but had failed to make sure that it coincided with the interpretation formed by his partner in the agreement. Indeed he had failed to put his interpretation into words until the time to take action on it arrived, and was genuinely surprised to find that his partner had not drawn the same conclusions as he had drawn. The clash arose, as many of his later clashes were to do, from his difficulty in seeing a situation from any but his own point of view. "He holds," wrote Dr. Rhoads to Carey Thomas, "that he has acted as a man of honor, education and conscience should have acted throughout, but admits some indiscretion in not making sure that what was so obviously right to him was equally so to the Trustees." Finding Wilson impervious to arguments other than those that he had already weighed and rejected in solitude, President Rhoads advised the Trustees to release him since he would undoubtedly be "dissatisfied and exacting if retained." The trustees, however, took no such realistic view of the affair. They not only felt with Dr. Rhoads that Wilson had committed a serious breach of faith but pointed out with some heat that both students *and an assistant* were coming to Bryn Mawr in the autumn in the expectation of working with him. Meanwhile, Wilson obtained legal advice that the college contracts were merely gentlemen's agreements and not bind-

ing in law. The matter dragged on until the trustees, seeing that
Wilson intended to leave in any case, accepted his resignation.

Of all this, Carey Thomas, who had already left Bryn Mawr
for the summer, knew only what Dr. Rhoads and the other
trustees reported to her. But deeply averse to Wilson by nature,
resenting his attitude toward women and toward Bryn Mawr as a
woman's college, she took the matter much to heart. From that
time on she rarely failed to make it clear that she felt that he
had behaved ill to the college, and in private conversation made
no bones of her distrust and dislike of him. It is a mark of her
essential fair-mindedness that later, on various public occasions,
she paid tribute to his particular greatness. Speaking to the students of the Summer School for Women Workers in Industry at
Bryn Mawr in 1922, she named him among the five "great
leaders" of the American people—Washington, Lincoln, Theodore
Roosevelt, and, characteristically, Susan B. Anthony were the
others. He "voiced the universal desire for justice and fair dealing and made the people of all nations vibrate to his eloquent and
moving words." As was to be expected, she was called upon to
talk of "Woodrow Wilson at Bryn Mawr" with increasing frequency as he became more and more important in the eyes of the
world; and with repetition of the story combined with the strength
of her feeling she began to fancy that she had had a hand in the
college's final dealings with him. With the growth of her own
importance, too, it was assumed by others that the negotiations
had been carried on by her, and not by President Rhoads or the
trustees, of whom they had heard little or nothing.

3

In affairs of growth and gradual development, such as changes
in the curriculum and matriculation requirements, it is impossible
to know how much responsibility rests upon Carey Thomas, although both came within her province. Nor in any event is it important, since for many years few changes were necessary. As
entering class followed class, of course, more and more advanced
instruction was worked out and co-ordinated and the schedule
elaborated to permit its inclusion. The breadth of interest and

learning of many of the early members of the faculty was drawn on to fill the lacks in certain of the departments. Philosophy, for instance, was ably given for a time under the aegis of the Classical Department in default of a professor of philosophy; and the entire lack of any department of art was made up for, in part at least, by other departments.

When first planning the curriculum, the trustees had accepted without question, in discussing the possibility of starting departments in both the history of music and the history of art, the fact that students working in either subject should be given an elementary knowledge of the fundamental technique of these arts and could be given such knowledge only by a certain amount of practical training and demonstration. As good Quakers they were not loath to forgo a department of music on the grounds of no available money; nor at this time was Carey Thomas reluctant, since she took little interest in music with the exception of Wagnerian opera. As for the history of art, Dr. Rhoads, when enumerating the needs of the college in his inaugural address, named "an art building" along with laboratories and a library building. With this Carey Thomas was in complete accord and, during these early years, busied herself with begging money, books, photographs, casts, toward the establishment of the future department, meanwhile providing stopgaps in the form of single lectures or series continuing for some weeks, chiefly archaeological, and for short periods more extensive instruction. It is an odd break in her thought, though consistent with her belief in book learning and in accepted theory, that, believing in thoroughness, quarreling with the common superficiality of women's education, demanding laboratories for the sciences, she took no interest in providing either elementary practical instruction in art or examples of painting or sculpture. Sepia photographs and casts of masterpieces were as far as she went, since she respected only accredited masterpieces, and those the college could not afford to buy.

Against superficiality in all other departments she kept vigilant watch. Indeed few of either the faculty or the students would have condoned any slackening of standards. The women on the faculty, in especial, were inexorable. "I am glad to know," wrote the professor of mathematics austerely to the dean, "that it is not proposed to do anything for those conditioned [those students who failed in examinations]. I think they have shown themselves far too ready to rely on our supplying deficiencies for them." Among the men of the faculty, too, there were some who imposed standards of the highest excellence and contributed largely to the fame of Bryn Mawr's intellectual exigence; but there were also some who, like Wilson, were affected by an inbred attitude of so-called southern chivalry, or who were susceptible to the blandishments of young and pretty girls—weaknesses sometimes found endearing but scorned by the students. In theory, at least, the students were intent upon learning all they could of subjects that interested them, regardless of difficulty, and wished to be judged fairly according to the announced high standards. "Snap courses" were few, and popular only as padding to allow more time for work of greater interest. The early years were a time of determined academic virtue.

The first four classes saw themselves dedicated to the advancement of Bryn Mawr and, through it, of women's education. They felt Bryn Mawr's problems to be their problems and approached them in a spirit of solemnity. The president's reports of these years abound with commendation of their "earnest endeavour." With the entrance of the fifth class, however, missionary zeal somewhat abated since, obliged to struggle, as many of them still had been, against faulty academic preparation or parental opposition, they were no longer called upon to prove that women could undergo advantageously as arduous an academic career as men. That had been done. Certain traditions had grown up. Professors and classes had been tried, their gifts and their possibilities discovered. Most important, students had passed through the mill and emerged happier and, according to college statistics, healthier. No longer needing to prove the worth of a new way of life, the classes of the early nineties were freer to devote themselves to intellectual achievement. Moreover, they no longer came chiefly from within the Quaker fold and, as Carey Thomas had hoped, they brought from diverse backgrounds a fresh stimulus and variety into the life and work of the college. And, as these students in their turn were succeeded by those of the late nineties, the temper of the college changed still further, becoming more carefree and more worldly as it began to be "the thing" for young women of any intellectual pretensions to enter Bryn Mawr. If they began to regard their entrance as a right to be won by scholarship rather than an experiment to be put through for the sake of large moral principles, it was still entrance into paradise. That Bryn Mawr was reputedly as difficult to enter as is every paradise shed coveted luster upon them. And not only was the college well established, but it was growing; the possibilities of its development and of individual achievement there seemed unbounded. To its radiant inhabitants in these first fifteen years the world seemed fair and new and they alone, in the bright dawn, in a position to shape the destinies of men—and, of greater consequence to them, of women.

So at least it seemed to them as many years later they looked back upon their youth; and so it seems to the generations who have followed them and who find still burning, blazing sometimes, in their forerunners a flame lighted and fed, it must be, in a golden age. With whatever hardships and disillusionments life has scarred them, the fire of their belief in things of the mind remains undimmed. And for this good fortune they owe a debt to the young Carey Thomas. Perhaps in the more sensitive among them "the things that are worth while" have ceased to be limited, as she would have had them, to the more obviously intellectual manifestations of man's mind. It is nevertheless largely to her that these students of the past owe not only the intensity of their awareness of what they perceive but the acknowledgment of their obligation to weigh and distinguish its value. It was she by the clarity and assurance of her discrimination of values—largely inspired by Mamie Gwinn—who impelled them toward their own discriminations. And it was she who urged upon them the imperative need of integrity and courage of mind.

She took every means at hand by precept and example to influence them, and her double position at the college gave her ample opportunity. They were, after all, the guinea pigs of her experiments. But they were far more than that. They were the potential members of the army that it was Bryn Mawr's purpose—her purpose—to send into the world to spread her doctrines of true scholarship, freedom of the mind, equality of women to men. The intellectual atmosphere of the college, clearly, must be such as to set a standard; but the physical aspect and the social life, too, should have a certain graciousness and ceremony. Students must be shown as well as told of the things that she regarded as beautiful and desirable. From the smallest to the largest circumstance there should be as little as possible to mislead their intellectual or aesthetic perceptions, for they must be accustomed to the best, so that in the future they would recognize and demand and work for it.

Doubtless she could not have been entirely unconscious of the fact that her own career was the shining example of the sort of career she advocated, or failed to derive increasing self-confidence from her growing importance in the college. However that may be, she pointed out the merits and successful achievement of every member of the faculty or staff or students whenever possible and by reiterating the good points throughout the college markedly strengthened those good points, particularly since—though only when likely to be effective—she held up the faults to relentless objurgation. And she stated her views with a zest that temporarily swept all before her. During the morning chapel exercises, which she was called upon with increasing frequency to hold, she introduced a talk of five minutes upon some topic of current interest, whether a college problem or a national or international event. As she mounted the platform the shy reticence that made her seem aloof in private life dropped away with growing ease. Not for nothing did she come of a line of Quaker preachers, and of Whitall women who were willing to exaggerate, to expose themselves to jeers and misconception, in short, to run the risk of making fools of themselves in order to convince others. The ideas that she enunciated, even the points of view, might be—and often were—secondhand, but their direction, their vehemence, and the words in which they were couched were unmistakably hers. They forced agreement or disagreement, snapped her listeners to attention and made them think for themselves.

To the students whom she thought in any way outstanding her point of view was reinforced by direct attack. She spared no pains to push and prune, encourage or discourage, those in whom she saw the makings of leaders in one or another field of intellectual or administrative work. Though readily accessible to anyone who sought her out for serious purpose, many of the students she saw only at the formal interviews or social occasions called for by her position. But she knew in surprising detail what each student was like, what were her abilities and disabilities, failures and achievements. Though she might not recognize them in person, behind the scenes she followed their records tirelessly. Academic and health reports and reports from the head of each hall came to her ex officio; and, as professor of English, in the very early years she could herself estimate each student's intellectual capacity, for she taught them all for two years in "the required literature course" and had, moreover, the power of sizing up people quickly and shrewdly. She knew in what subjects they were most interested, how strong they were physically, what were their relations to other members of the college, even sometimes what they liked to eat. If she saw a student whom she thought worth advice making the wrong motions, or thought of some way in which a student might do better, she told her so. If a good student needed financial help, she arranged for her somehow to procure it. If another fell ill, she followed up her case in minutest details and against whatever odds, parental or natural. From the student's point of view to have Carey Thomas, so much admired and, above all, so aloof, suddenly concentrate with apparent single-mindedness upon her problems was flattering in the extreme. And Carey Thomas's words, whether or not they were precisely complied with, bit deep.

Paradoxically, even where compliance was not intended her advice was often followed. In the case of student self-government, for instance: the initial steps for a definite plan were taken in 1891 by a small group comprised not only of students devoted to the young dean but of others who were less so. The former saw in her stress upon independence of mind and freedom logical support for their effort; the latter, skeptical of her sincerity and perhaps more subtle, used her own words to forward the plan as a means of controlling what they regarded as her despotism. In point of fact, though out of sympathy with some of its promoters, seeing their motives clearly, Carey Thomas was from the beginning an advocate of student self-government. Her belief in it went hand in hand with her early belief in faculty government. She herself at the Howland Institute and again at Cornell had experienced modified forms of student government and found them success-ful. Besides, supported by Quaker training and later experience, she had too firm a faith in freedom and in the intelligence and serious purpose of the young not to encourage them to bear the responsibility for their actions. She also trusted, less reasonably, the justice as well as the effectiveness of mass opinion. For the students to govern themselves might be useful from the point of view of training and, moreover, would relieve her and others in the administration of the petty duties of regulating, watching, and penalizing. Perhaps most important of all, as she at once recognized—and here Carey Thomas showed her flair for promot-ing her ends—it would be a potentially great advertisement for Bryn Mawr College and her own ideas. That is, if it were a suc-cess. And from the beginning she saw to it that it should be successful, watching over each step in its growth.

Not only were the first officers of the association enlightened and full of zeal, but for ten years its presidents, holders of this proudest student office, were drawn from the cream of the under-graduates. Administrative ability and energy went hand in hand with high academic standing. But independence of mind was not one of the characteristics that administration of the association fostered; nor could freedom in its full sense be its aim. Highly as Carey Thomas lauded these qualities, she had long since seen the necessity of limiting both. In order to allow the college to ad-vance academically with as little friction as possible it must be un-hampered, she felt, by criticism of the conduct and social life and manners of its members. As she had disciplined herself severely in her own career in order to achieve her education with the least possible criticism that might harm the cause of women's advance-ment, so, she believed, the students must be disciplined. They must, moreover, learn to bear the responsibilities and to impose the self-restraints necessarily suffered by citizens of a democracy. She saw to it, therefore, that the rules of the Self-Government Association were made to conform with convention, and expected its leaders to subject their rulings to those whose experience in governing the young was recognized—to herself, in particular, and to the president and trustees—leading many students to suspect that "self-government" was only her sweetening of the pill of government by the college authorities and had little to do with real self-government. Within the conventional mold, nevertheless, the plan of the association and its rules of conduct were drawn up with such liberality that little change had to be made for forty or more years. Naturally, with the disappearance of oil lamps and gas jets, the fire rules were changed; and rules concerning smoking, drinking, and motoring were added. But the outlines of both the association and its rules remained the same, proving so successful as a way of government and as a method of training in self-discipline that most of the educational institutions in the country gradually followed Bryn Mawr in instituting similar forms of student government.[4]

The division between Carey Thomas's praise of independence of mind and freedom and her tendency in action to hark back to authorities is easily rationalized and condoned in matters of behavior from the point of view of the good of the college if for no other reason. In intellectual matters, however, it takes a subtler form, less evident and, when recognized, less readily overlooked. In her own field, English literature, the German training of her student days and especially the ascendancy of Mamie Gwinn, whose gifts were primarily critical, reined in her impulse to drive onward by the light of instinct checked by reason. As time passed, the influence of Carey Thomas and Mamie Gwinn upon each other led them in their teaching to stress the need of discrimination based on exact knowledge and to measure the work of students against works of established excellence. The advantage of this to their students outweighed, of course, its drawbacks for it disciplined their perceptions, taught them to balance and draw conclusions and to avoid regarding a mere amassing of facts as scholarship. But it also sapped the self-confidence of the more sensitive among them. It took many years for those who had most benefited by the emphasis on criticism and a counsel of perfection to regain that firm trust in themselves needed for original work. And no student escaped this exacting pressure. They drew it from the climate of the college which Carey Thomas, manifestly, and Mamie Gwinn, incalculably, had so large a share in tempering; and, more directly, they drew it from their instruction in the English Department.

4

As the only professor, indeed for the first year the only member, of the English Department, Carey Thomas lectured to every Bryn Mawr undergraduate in a two years' course in the English language and literature.[5] One of the first survey courses, if not the first, to be given in the United States, it was planned as a framework for the students' future reading and later was adopted by most of the other colleges and, eventually, by the schools of the country. She also conducted certain advanced courses in Anglo-Saxon and the work of various nineteenth-century poets. From 1888 on, when her own administrative duties increased and an associate in English was appointed, followed soon by the appointment of other instructors, she took less and less direct part in the work of the English Department. For a time, until the work was put altogether into other hands, one of the instructors read her lectures for her in the two-year survey course and held the weekly quiz on them. Long after she had stopped teaching, however, Carey Thomas, proud of her scholarly attainment, kept her name in the college catalogue as professor of English.

The extreme gusto with which, as long as she taught in the department, she delivered her lectures sharpened even well-worn truths, and the emphatic manner with which she put her questions aroused in her students a responsive mental energy. She bore with no nonsense, no vague "literary appreciations," no slipshod statements. Her own ability to spell she knew was uncertain and led to many jokes, but her characteristic exaggerations were not recognized by her as such. Through the doors that she opened she expected the clear light of informed intelligence to stream unimpeded by hazy thinking or incompetent expression. Needless to say, she soon found that few of the students "could write" and, with the innocent zeal of the tyro, attempted to remedy their faults by requiring each student to study and pass an examination in Abbott's *How To Write*. That failing to have the desired effect, she arranged in 1888 for Mamie Gwinn to give instruction in the art of "essay writing"—and at this point, as associate in English, Mamie Gwinn began to take a more active part in the life of the college.

From that time on in the early years of the college, behind the clearly spotlighted figure of Carey Thomas moves the shadowy form of "Miss Gwinn," lending depth and chiaroscuro to a picture otherwise somewhat unshaded. A curiously enigmatic figure, Mamie Gwinn, both repellent and fascinating: dark haired, dark eyed, white skinned, tall, elegant; physically indolent, languid in movement, studied in gesture; selfish, sometimes malicious; and mentally, brilliantly, subtly active. In intellectual matters, especially, Bryn Mawr could have lost her only to its detriment since she was largely responsible for its force and distinction. Her intellectual ideals were the same as those of Carey Thomas—had she not, indeed, taken a chief part in forming Carey Thomas's?— and she had influenced and helped her in almost every way behind the scenes in shaping the college. Although living with Carey Thomas in the Deanery from the time that Bryn Mawr opened, she held no official position in the first year save that of graduate student in the Department of English, and its first fellow. In her third year she received one of the two first degrees to be granted by the college, her doctorate of philosophy in English and Greek. Incapable of finishing any piece of work, she never succeeded in publishing her dissertation, "On the First Part of Beowulf," a lapse resulting in the later ruling that the Bryn Mawr degree of Doctor of Philosophy should not be used before the publication of a dissertation within a stipulated time.

As instructor in the art of essay writing Mamie Gwinn developed a method peculiarly her own. Partly owing to shyness, partly to boredom, she shunned people and carried on her instruction, therefore, at one remove. Each student was requested at fixed times to drop in a black tin box a note of the subject upon which she proposed to write her next essay: she then wrote the essay. In time it was returned to her, in its margins comments, often scathing, in Mamie Gwinn's Italian hand. No class instruction was given, no reading advised, no discussion held upon the student's work. But by the end of the course Mamie Gwinn intended each student to possess in the margins of her essays a complete rhetoric suited to her needs—a stand-by for life, according to Mamie Gwinn, who ignored the fact that by many students such lengthy commentary was unlikely to be read.

To be sure, she had from the beginning set aside three hours weekly in which students might consult her, but clearly she neither expected nor perhaps wished them to do so. Few undergraduates were of a hardihood to enter the Deanery and brave the penetrating glance and silence with which they knew they would be greeted. The tale of one who, bolder than the others and rendered desperate by the throes of composition, ventured to her study to ask "how to write an essay," discouraged other such attempts. Ushered into the dimly lighted room, she found Mamie Gwinn reclining on the couch where reputedly she spent the days in reading and, summoning all her courage, put her question with explosive clarity. Mamie Gwinn regarded her in surprised cold silence, her eyes seeming to burn in her white face. After a moment of puzzled thought, she arose, moved to the desk, and taking up a sheet of foolscap folded it down the middle: "You write your essay here on the right hand side of the sheet, leaving the left side blank for my comments."

It was not until 1892 that, abdicating in no measure her place behind the throne and still rarely encountered personally by any student, she emerged from the Deanery to lecture on "Critics of the Nineteenth Century: Arnold, Pater and Swinburne" and "English Critics of Life: Burke, Carlyle and Ruskin" and, later, to conduct several graduate seminars. So fascinating was she, so brilliant were her lectures, in which she seemed to her students, as did Paul Shorey to his, to bring the ends of the world together, that almost at once her fame spread throughout the college. The small seminary in which she lectured, unwilling to brave the platform of a larger classroom, was packed always not only with her students clustered around the big table but with "hearers," members of the faculty as well as students, making a circle round the wall. Her teaching, perhaps more than that of any other instructor of those days, left its mark upon her students and set the tone of Bryn Mawr's intellectual life.

Exceptionally stimulating though she may have been as a lecturer, upon social occasions Mamie Gwinn was inhibiting. A dinner at the Deanery was a trying ordeal. Apart from the fact that Carey Thomas made a practice in these early years of inviting together the members of the same college department who were all too familiar with each other's ways and opinions, she was so shy as to make talk difficult and Mamie Gwinn, apparently interested only in her food, remained almost wholly silent. When the odds were obviously against her, Carey Thomas's courage shone: as on the occasion when, faced with a dinner for a Frenchman, a visiting lecturer, who spoke no English, she plunged on in French, laughing heartily at her own mistakes, with an abandon that won his lifelong admiration. Meanwhile Mamie Gwinn, whose French was facile and perfect, spoke never a word, eating each course with concentrated rapidity and then regarding the guests with an expression of superiority while she waited for them to catch up. She made her calculated impression, always, of knowing all the answers had she chosen to give them and of thinking the struggling conversationalists a little dull.

Even in the summer holidays Carey Thomas and Mamie Gwinn rarely separated. Occasionally they were held in America by the claims of Carey Thomas's family and, in 1893, by the Chicago Exhibition. Recognizing the need of keeping well informed in their field, they wished to look over the educational exhibits and in especial to see how the Bryn Mawr exhibit, organized by Carey Thomas, compared with those of other institutions. Well satisfied on that score, they pushed on to Colorado. But the natural beauties and the history of the United States interested them little—the charms of the Southwest were yet to be discovered by American intellectuals—and it was with a sense of freedom and of moral gratification that usually they turned toward Europe.

However delightful and stimulating it might be, traveling was hard, for neither had much money and they went far afield: to Holland and Belgium (1887), to Greece and Constantinople (1889), to Russia (1890), to Italy and Sicily (1892). They intended in 1891 to visit Spain but cholera broke out there and they went instead to Denmark and Scandinavia putting off the Spanish journey till 1897. And, almost always, they began or ended in canonical fashion with London or Paris. It is a pity that there are few records of these summer travels. Most of the long letters have been lost that Carey Thomas dispatched to be passed about among the family and friends at home. One, written to her sister Margaret, gives at least their flavor. In London, she wrote, they had met "Dolly Tennant who is married to Stanley, Governor of the Belgian Congo. . . . She is said to be adorable and to come the nearest to having a salon of anyone in London." Then follow the vicissitudes of their journey to Copenhagen, "which is," she instructs her sister, "the capital of Denmark. . . . The great Thorwaldsen museum is there, with all the things he has ever done, mostly originals, and casts of all the others. . . . The Danes [are] almost as sweet as the Italians. We went to their great pleasure garden, Tivoli, and concluded they must be as a people far less complex than we, for the amusements were babyish. . . . We did see, however, a magnificent Mme. Tussaud done by their best artists and what was of thrilling interest the wax faces of dead authors lying along row after row in cases."

Rather less instructive than the family letters are her diaries, small untidy paper books at first, then imposing red morocco volumes, most of which contain only a few jotted lines. Only the journal of the summer when she and Mamie Gwinn went to Russia gives any consecutive account. Two days after reaching London, she records, they went up to Oxford where Logan Pearsall Smith took them to a garden party in the Fellow's garden at Balliol—an undated note of an earlier visit reads, "Saw Jowett at garden party in rain"—and a few weeks later they were steaming up the Göta Canal in Sweden: "Perfect day. Beautiful scenery. . . . Moon full and like enchantment on the water and the trees. Last July saw moonlight on the Bosphorus from our rooms in Constantinople." In Stockholm, of which apart from "moonlight splendid on water from window" she had little good to say, they stayed a week before going on to Helsingfors "capital of Finland. . . . We drove in one of the utterly absurd little droschkies with a delicious coachman in a blue coat that came to his heels with a calico belt and an indescribable hat over his ears for an hour and a half and saw all there was to see, which was 0. Dined very well at the Societetehus before leaving. Read three Academys, Bourget's 'Un Coeur de Femme'—his masterpiece so far. . . . Interest of book almost too great, one is dreadfully anxious." The following day they reached St. Petersburg where they at once obtained, through the chargé d'affaires at the American Legation—"more creditable than often"—permission to visit the Hermitage every day in order to have plenty of time to enjoy the works of art. They went, also, to the grand mass at St. Isaac's: "Two hours long. Very monotonous chanting but more tune than Catholic chants. Far less impressive than St. Peter's, for example, because no instrumental accompaniment. Parts of service read in overwhelming bass voice. All through service people bowing, crossing, kissing floor and hands of icons. Most idolatrous." She finished up some correspondence for Bryn Mawr College from St. Petersburg and, tired out by sight-seeing, in which she followed Gautier's itinerary closely, read as usual a great deal of fiction: "Mark Twain's 'Yankee at Court of King Arthur' intolerably vulgar. Could not finish it."

With their first view of Moscow they were "perfectly enchanted. It is unlike anything else and reminds one only of Constantinople and Brusa and not of them. The city is a sea of green and pink and yellow houses and within it is two cities, each with towers and walls. The Kremlin walls are most picturesque and the Italianated towers the most charming mossy green colour. The city is spangled in every part with the wonderful blue and gold domes of churches, blue, pale gold, red gold, copper gold, fantastic beautiful mosque-like. Seen from a hill or down a side street the view is wonderful—unique. Why does one say so little about it?" Here she reversed her opinion of the mass of the Orthodox Church. The singing was "nicer" than that at St. Petersburg. "It has an oriental wail in it and the absence of instrumental music makes it different and far more emotional than the Catholic service. The prostration of the people and the bowing adds to the effect." A week there and they were off to Warsaw, which bored them—"literally nothing to see." Then on through Germany to Paris where they had a concentrated bout of playgoing, especially at the Français, seeing, among other things, *Hernani* for the first time. "The effect was overwhelming." Then Cherbourg and Bryn Mawr again.

We look back upon them now—two figures, curiously isolated, hurrying across the picturesquely unreal European scenes of guidebooks, observing, gathering in, discarding impressions. In England, however, the stage was peopled for brief moments by the Pearsall Smiths and their charmed circle which held Carey

Thomas's imagination to the end of her days. She entered the circle as of right, a pre-eminently Whitall woman, especially since, the family story runs, she had been responsible for starting her cousin Logan on his career in England. Bored by his life in New York where, since finishing his studies at Haverford and Harvard, he had worked in connection with the family business, the Whitall glass factories, he had been in the right frame of mind to receive his cousin's characteristic admonitions. In the midst of her business she granted him a brief, hurried interview and urged him to return to England, to work at Oxford, to seek Culture and to write—which he accordingly did.

So the stage in England for Carey Thomas and Mamie Gwinn was filled with the color and movement of young people revolving about the ambassadors, as it were, of a Henry James novel—about aunt Hannah with her energetic interests in all sorts of people and her dry forthright judgments, and the cousins, the radiantly lovely Mary, lately married to a clever Irishman, Benjamin Costelloe, a Balliol man and London barrister, and the younger, fine-looking, earnest Alys, and the tall, lean and fastidious Logan. The American Pearsall Smiths, wonderfully, impulsively kind, immensely aware of but a little bemused by the mellow, elusive, and so desirable English scene, carried out with singular accuracy the international theme of Henry James. The spirit and amusement with which they sought experiences, the freshness of their observation, the pungency of their discriminations, and the warmth with which they embraced new loyalties, as well as their good looks and generosity, endeared them to circles upon whose doors many knock in vain. They exposed themselves, doubtless, to some misconception and some loss; a loss overestimated, perhaps, by those American onlookers intent upon guarding unimpaired their native inheritance. But the vivid interest with which they pursued their way in a wider, richer world than they could ever have known in America gave their lives a rare distinction. And to Carey Thomas and Mamie Gwinn it seemed as if through the Pearsall Smiths they caught glimpses of that exalted society of which they had read and, more important they chose to think, the very center of the intellectual stir of their time.

Sooner or later almost everyone of interest in art or letters or radical social reform seemed to them to impinge upon the life of the Pearsall Smiths. And at their houses, Friday's Hill House near Haslemere and 44, Grosvenor Road in London, Carey Thomas and Mamie Gwinn might meet the Sidney Webbs, Graham Wallis, the Gilbert Murrays, the lovely American Kinsella sisters, George Santayana, the paradoxical, desperately shy Bertrand Russell, whom Alys married in 1894, and his brilliant Cambridge group, the Alfred Whiteheads, Roger Fry, Lowes Dickinson. In 1890 aunt Hannah heralded to her niece from Friday's Hill the first appearance of Bernard Berenson, later to become Mary's second husband: "Today we have a great genius staying with us. He has been in Italy studying art for two years and he knows everything about it. He knows where every picture is, and all about the copies and the imitations and the owners. I believe he is really an authority on Art. And to hear him dethroning one idol after another with all our party listening open mouthed is something delicious. He utterly abhors Blake and Rossetti and Burne-Jones and all modern painters." If such iconoclasm startled Carey Thomas, the leisurely, careless, gay acceptance of values and satisfactions that she had sought with careful deliberation captivated her. It was the ideal of which she had dreamed. But it was not unalloyed delight. The skillful tossing back and forth of talk, the clever weaving of ideas and brilliant, half-fantastic half-serious theories, to which she listened during these rare days in England bewildered while they charmed her. She was too unaccustomed to conversational fireworks to take part easily, too conscious of her own position as the president of Bryn Mawr, the admired elder cousin whose attainments had been proclaimed and must be borne out, to be anything less than laboriously self-conscious. Her manner became a little portentous; her own talk, heavier, more serious. It is not surprising that sometimes, after all was over and England behind them, the effort of keeping it up bred in the minds of Carey Thomas and Mamie Gwinn personal strictures that had all the blunt impatience of a Henrietta Stackpole's.

The hospitality they offered in return, however, was generous. With the college to back her, Carey Thomas invited a good many

English acquaintances, recommended by the Pearsall Smiths, to stay at Bryn Mawr: among others, the Webbs—they sat all day on the Deanery veranda "chattering to each other like two eager birds," oblivious of the college and all its inhabitants—Lowes Dickinson, the Gilbert Murrays, Roger Fry, and in 1896 the Bertrand Russells for a number of weeks, arduous weeks for Carey Thomas, however glorious in retrospect. Bertrand Russell, then a young fellow of Trinity not yet widely known, lectured to the students on mathematics, and Alys, on "the payment of motherhood." With their markedly unconventional statements, radical theories, and probing questions, they set the college, and in particular the trustees, by the ears. However right she thought them— and their flaming indiscretions seem tame old saws now—and however much she approved the mental ferment they engendered, she was sorely put to it to explain and justify.

5

At Bryn Mawr the united surface presented to the world by Carey Thomas and Mamie Gwinn on their travels inevitably was broken by divergent duties and, as the nineties wore on, below the surface their attachment began to crumble. Carey Thomas's life was complicated by the bewilderment and heartache and the blows to a sensitive pride that the breaking up of personal relations always brings. At their best they are maintained only by mutual sympathy and care. Toward the turn of the century Mamie Gwinn, always an exigent partner, was becoming a disaffected one: she had fallen in love with the brilliant Associate Professor Alfred Hodder appointed from the Harvard Graduate School to the Bryn Mawr Department of English by Carey Thomas in the midnineties on the advice of William James. Not only were his interests like hers in literature and ideas, but to her he seemed a man of the world. Like her he was ruthlessly egoistical; unlike her he was not inhibited by fear of people. Clever, unstable, a good talker, experienced in the ways of women, exacting in regard to their charms, he was irresistible to most of them. Since he professed to scorn those with pretensions to intellectuality, his attentions doubly flattered Mamie Gwinn. She who had hitherto arrogantly eschewed acquaintance with any man succumbed wholly to his fascination.

Unfortunately—or, perhaps, fortunately for them, since the resulting intrigue doubtless added spice to an otherwise ordinary enough affair—he was already married, and his wife and child were in Bryn Mawr. Mamie Gwinn, moreover, had not the courage openly to avow to Carey Thomas her new love or her complete reversal of opinion as to the ideal life of a woman. And the affair between Mamie Gwinn and Alfred Hodder remained for several years clandestine, known to few within the college, least of all, in the entirety of its machinations, to Carey Thomas. Mamie Gwinn stayed on at the Deanery doing her college work, keeping up appearances for six years after the resignation and departure to New York, in 1898, of Alfred Hodder. Then, at last, the fire flared too bright for Carey Thomas to refuse to see it. Mamie Gwinn resigned from her professorship and married Alfred Hodder, becoming entangled in the legal proceedings between him and his wife and, more surprisingly, being drawn by him for a brief period into an interest in social and political work. She never, so long as Carey Thomas was at the Deanery, returned to Bryn Mawr; and after 1904 they never met again.

Without doubt Carey Thomas deliberately closed her eyes to the development in all its unlovely intrigue of Mamie Gwinn's infatuation, but certainly she was conscious of her growing estrangement and increasing absorption in Alfred Hodder. The strain these caused must have been too obvious in a hundred ways to be ignored. However that may be, and however great a blow the repudiation was to her affection and pride as well as to her faith, Carey Thomas carried herself to all outward view with equanimity. But she needed always an intimate companion with whom to exchange opinions unreservedly. Her sense of mission and the growing isolation that is so often the fate of an administrator put severe restraint upon her natural expansiveness. Instinctively she turned now to her old friend Mary Garrett.

In the last years of Mamie Gwinn's life at the Deanery, Mary Garrett's visits had become more frequent and extended, and not long after Mamie Gwinn's departure she came there to live. Though Carey Thomas's imagination, perhaps, was never caught, as Mamie Gwinn had caught it, by the upright, unromantic Mary Garrett, she was genuinely touched by her justice and generosity, and more and more warmly bound by her self-effacing loyalty and intelligent co-operation. Mary Garrett had shown herself a staunch friend all through the various important projects on which they had worked closely together during Mamie Gwinn's ascendancy.

During their youth in Baltimore the five friends—Carey Thomas, Mamie Gwinn, Mary Garrett, Bessie King, and Julia Rogers—had felt the need of a school in their city where such girls as themselves could obtain an education that would prepare them to enter a college of high standing, supposing such a one to exist. They often discussed plans for their school and on the return of Carey Thomas and Mamie Gwinn from Europe, when Bryn Mawr College had appeared as a goal worthy of preparation, they set about realizing their dreams. Under the leadership of Carey Thomas, owing in part to the wise advice of her parents and the fathers of Mamie Gwinn and Bessie King and largely to the financial generosity of Mary Garrett, they succeeded in opening, in 1885, the Bryn Mawr School for Girls in Baltimore. As a fairly recent pamphlet concerning the school says, "These women defined for all time, in the articles of incorporation, the uncompromising academic standards of the School."[6] Only those pupils "who passed the examinations for admission to the college or colleges of highest grade at any time existing in the country" were to receive its diploma.

So successful was the school that within five years it outgrew its first building, an old house on Eutaw Street. Then Mary Garrett, advised by the other four friends and consulting with Carey Thomas at every step, erected the building on Cathedral and Preston streets in which the school flourished for the next quarter of a century. With characteristic meticulosity and egged on by Carey Thomas, Mary Garrett not only financed the building and passed upon its plans and its furnishings but saw to it that the plans were carried out in detail. Legend has it that she might be found at any hour of the day, elegantly costumed, fastidiously climbing the scaffolding to see that the bricks brought from England were being laid "in a kind of patterning in masonry almost a lost art," or poking about the debris inside the half-finished structure, urging the workmen to greater haste or care. In a manner familiar to generations of students at both Bryn Mawr College and the school, the interior was decorated by her with casts and marble replicas of great sculptures, and sepia photographs of masterpieces framed in stained or gilded wood. She backed the school financially and in her will left it a country property used for many years as its playground. Naturally, she was interested, too, in its academic welfare, but here Carey Thomas, supported until her departure from Bryn Mawr by Mamie Gwinn, was the chief motivating force on the school's Board of Trustees. She, after all, was the authority upon academic matters and she seemed to generate fresh energy to oversee those of the school.

The school had not been long planted firmly upon its feet when these same women embarked upon another and more revolutionary scheme of public importance. From the time of its founding, in 1876, the Johns Hopkins University planned to include, as soon as it could be financed, a medical school in connection with its hospital opened in 1889. The university had called professors to teach the branches of scientific medicine in the premedical course already established in the university and doctors to the hospital to whom they gave the title of professors, with an eye to their future position in the school. All were men who wished to see founded in the United States a school that would demand as high qualifications for entrance and give as thorough and extended opportunities for learning as did the great institutions of Europe. They had come to the Johns Hopkins largely because of the promise of building up a medical school there in accordance with their theories. By 1890, however, they were becoming discouraged, and tempting offers were being made to draw them elsewhere: if the school ever was to be started it must be begun at once in order to hold them. Yet how to procure the special endowment necessary for it? Little support was to be had either from the medical profession or from the general public, that naturally in such matters followed its doctors. The standard of medical education was for the most part low and narrow, unbelievably so from a later point of view. Those who wished for experience and knowledge in scientific fields were obliged to study abroad as few could afford to do. But the medical profession could hardly be expected to turn in a body and condemn its own incompetence by demanding a kind of education for its future members of which it was largely ignorant. Opposition to the proposed school at the Johns Hopkins was, therefore, widespread.

Learning of the dilemma from their fathers, who were connected with the university and the hospital, the five friends saw their chance to open another door to women. It seemed to them that, if they could collect a sufficient sum of money toward the endowment of the school, the university trustees might be forced to accept with the gift the condition that women be admitted to the school on the same footing as men: in view of its ends, a highly respectable form of bribery. They formed committees for propaganda and the collection of money in the large cities, wherever they could find in the United States one or two women whom they could interest in the scheme.

All five friends were active on the Baltimore committee, which met usually at Bessie King's; with Mary Garrett as its secretary. Carey Thomas was secretary of the Philadelphia committee. But, whatever their official positions, the success of their work was owing to the immense effort put into it, especially by Mary Garrett and Carey Thomas and, though perhaps with more zeal than good judgment, by Bessie King. Doubtless Carey Thomas and Bessie King remembered their own youthful ambitions to become doctors. Fresh in Carey Thomas's mind, too, were the words of her fellow student at Zürich, the woman doctor from Boston, describing her experience of the iniquities and injustices undergone by women in both medical education and practice in the United States and the cruelties, born of lack of understanding, committed by men physicians in regard to their women patients, stupidities that might be avoided if there were a greater number of competent women doctors. Though Mary Garrett's interest sprang less from personal memories, it was no less keen. She threw all her shrewd business ability, all her social weight, and every ounce of energy into carrying through the scheme. She was ready, moreover, to use her large private revenues to support her words and tip the scales. But it was Carey Thomas's planning of the campaign, her gift of managing people, disciplined by experience at Bryn Mawr College, her wary foresight in holding back and driving forward at the right moments, above all her contagious zest and conviction, that insured success.

The position of campaign leader, held unofficially but none the less securely by Carey Thomas, was no sinecure. Not only did the various committees have to be co-ordinated and their members encouraged or restrained, but the general public had to be taught and conciliated by articles and pamphlets and speeches. On all this detail she kept her hand. Opposition to coeducation presented a special difficulty since it existed within the university itself among the very men who most strongly desired the medical school for men. The professor of pathology, Dr. William Henry Welch, whose vision and effort were largely responsible for the advanced character of the projected school, regarded the presence of men and women together in the scientific classroom with profound misgiving and distaste. And on the score of his attitude toward women, Carey Thomas had learned long since to mistrust President Gilman. Though his advice in connection with Bryn Mawr had been invaluable, he had harmed the college, she felt, by voicing his doubts of women's ability to profit by the education it offered. She spent much effort during the campaign, therefore, in circumventing his suspected opposition.

In the heat of battle she spoke frankly to her old friends. To Mary Garrett she wrote, "Your letter today is inexplicable. You had . . . a full list of subscribers. . . . I have asked you to send them back to me. Please be sure to do so by special delivery." Finding that the names of Philadelphia subscribers were not among the lists in the special-delivery package, she wrote severely, "What you sent is worthless." To her surprise Bessie King resented similar brusque treatment; and in order to gain her ends Carey Thomas was obliged to deal gently with her, recognizing the probable effect upon Francis King should his daughter be provoked to antagonism. "Please try to yield every possible point during the next month," she begged Mary Garrett, "or we shall have Mr. King against us. Personal dignity—nothing—matters, if we can get our money accepted when raised. . . . I feel that we had better let all non-essentials go. Let her do whatever she proposes even if strictly it ought to be done by someone else." Dealt with in this fashion, although her relations with

Carey Thomas never again resumed their former warmth, Bessie King proved an invaluable, however trying, ally. Through her, by means of her father, Dr. William Osler was persuaded to write an article in support of the women's effort, and the committees of Baltimore, Washington, and Philadelphia were invited to a tea given for them at the hospital, which was evidence, of publicity value, that the officials of the hospital supported the women.

Eight months after the committees started work, by the opening of the new college year of 1890, need for some tangible assurance that the medical school really was to be founded had become so acute that, advised by the three fathers, the ladies, as they were called, thought it a favorable moment to strike. They had succeeded in raising $62,593, which Mary Garrett now brought up to $100,000. On October 28 they offered this sum toward the endowment to the trustees of the university if they would agree to admit women "whose previous training has been equivalent to your preliminary medical course" on the "same footing as men." A demand for equal opportunities for women the trustees had expected, but to accept women on precisely the same terms as men—that was a horse of quite a different color. So well, however, had the fathers of "The Ladies" prepared the way and so evident was it that the money was unlikely to be obtained elsewhere that the trustees recorded a favorable vote, only guarding themselves against an incursion of women into other parts of the university.

For the first time in eight months Carey Thomas and Mary Garrett could breathe a little freely. But, as the school could not open until its endowment reached five hundred thousand dollars, they by no means relaxed. And six months later it was evident that a noteworthy step of some sort must be taken to keep up interest. Again, Mary Garrett offered the trustees, to be added upon certain conditions to the Woman's Fund, another hundred thousand dollars, which was accepted upon Mary Garrett's terms. But by February, 1892, the trustees themselves had added little to Mary Garrett's gifts, and it became clearer than ever that without the help of the women's committees the medical school could not be founded. Carey Thomas's carefully planned maneuvers had reached their intended climax and the women were at last in a position to dictate terms. They must, nevertheless, while dictating provide the money and, as usual, Mary Garrett came forward, this time with the whole remaining sum needed to make up five hundred thousand dollars accompanied by a letter in which the conditions of the gift were outlined unequivocally and the high standards of the school as well as the position of women in it thoroughly safeguarded.

The trustees already had made up their minds, some hardly convinced of their wisdom, to accept women on the same terms with men. But the requirements for admission to the school upon which Mary Garrett insisted dismayed them. It was unheard of in any medical school in the country that candidates for admission must possess a bachelor of arts degree or its equivalent and a knowledge of French and German as well as of certain premedical studies. Yet this was, in effect, what she demanded. The standards of few European medical schools were so high, none higher. Not that they were contrary to the ideals of the Johns Hopkins trustees—they were precisely in accordance with them—but, as Dr. Welch wrote later to Dr. Harvey Cushing, "it is one thing to build an educational castle in the air at your library table, and another to face its actual appearance under existing circumstances." Some years previously he had drawn up, at the request of President Gilman and the trustees, a list of requirements that they would like to see enforced in the school. "Miss Garrett got this document through her lawyer, Mr. Gwinn," Welch explained to Cushing, adding, "She naturally supposed that this was exactly what we wanted."[7] That Mary Garrett supposed any such thing was most unlikely. As Carey Thomas later recalled: "When it came to laying down requirements our fathers deserted us and joined the Trustees begging Mary not to insist. My father almost wept and told me it was incredible that two young women should take such a position. The Trustees called on us separately and together"—here she adds the significant parenthesis, "I was always present"—"but at the last critical moment Dr. Welch saved the situation."

The Ladies were well aware of what they were doing. Recognizing Dr. Welch's tentative requirements as admirable and know-

ing the advisability of setting the terms of admission at the outset
as high as was ultimately desirable, they persisted. In the end
Mary Garrett's stipulations with her gift were accepted and the
medical school was advertised to open its doors, with Dr. Welch
as its first dean, in the autumn of 1893. In the next year Mary
Garrett, knowing that the part women had played was likely to
be forgotten, insisted that the tablet commemorating it, inscribed
"Women's Fund Memorial Building," be placed over the outer
door rather than inside the new anatomical building. The trustees
were only persuaded to agree by Dr. Welch's counsel that it would
be a pity to alienate any further gifts that Mary Garrett might
choose to bestow. But, having won her points and set the school
financially on its feet, she gave no more to the Johns Hopkins
save the portrait now hanging there of the four great doctors
Welch, Halstead, Osler, and Kelly which she commissioned John
Singer Sargent to paint in 1905 and, in her will, the bequest to
the university, as the final legatee, of the Garrett residence in
Baltimore.

No one in 1893, least of all the trustees, took a cheerful view
of the probable number of acceptable candidates. "Welch," remarked Dr. Osler, "we are lucky to get in as professors, for I am
sure that neither you nor I could ever get in as students." In point
of fact seventeen candidates, three of them women, succeeded in
fulfilling the requirements, and in the following year forty candidates entered, of whom eight were women. Increasingly the school
flourished, spreading its influence wide through the country. Because of the foresight and determination of Carey Thomas and
Mary Garrett more than of any other factors, the beneficent reform of medical education throughout the country had advanced;
that it was now being led by example as well as by precept was
owing to them.

There was one cause, however, for which Carey Thomas and
Mary Garrett were not at this time equally enthusiastic. Mary
Garrett's situation as the inheritor of a large estate had brought
home to her the legal and political disadvantages under which
women labored. She had become deeply interested, consequently,
in the progress of the various movements to obtain the suffrage
for women that were flourishing with increasing strength. Theo-

retically Carey Thomas, too, being an ardent feminist, believed in woman's suffrage. And at the turn of the century she allowed herself to participate actively in the movement because by then it had achieved such velocity that its effect upon the problems of women's education and the intellectual position of women appeared to her to be crucial. To her the political and social aspects of women's struggle for "equality" commended themselves in particular as they were allied to the educational side. Occupied primarily with education she had not time, moreover, to throw herself wholeheartedly into work for them. She rarely took an active hand in supporting causes unless she could play a leading role, partly because she was by nature a leader, partly because she had to guard herself against dissipating her energies. In the nineties what time she had to give to anything beyond Bryn Mawr College and the two Baltimore projects was absorbed by her friends and, especially, her family. It is not, perhaps, surprising that in so taut and energetic a life as hers family problems were irritating and to be attacked with unwonted and sometimes misguided vehemence.

The family relationships were full of changes and shadows during the early years of Carey Thomas's life at Bryn Mawr. In the winter of 1888 Mrs. Thomas developed cancer and, depending on spiritual cures, refused to have the proper medical care and the necessary operation until too late for them to be effective. After a short, severe illness she died in the following summer. The family was plunged into grief, bewildered and distraught by the suddenness of the blow. Carey Thomas blamed her father for not having insisted as a physician upon her mother's receiving proper medical attention in time. Since her early youth when she had watched her mother struggling with household cares, fatigued by the birth of one child after another, she had resented what from her feminist point of view seemed her father's selfishness as the cause of it. She either did not see now or did not choose to see that the very independence which she so loved in her mother, and which she herself had benefited by and inherited to the fullest degree, exonerated her father. Her mother's life was of her own choosing. If she sometimes sighed for greater freedom, for a different life, who does not? When Mrs. Thomas made up her mind, she abided by her decision firmly, as Carey Thomas had ample cause to know. When she fell ill there was no way, except force, by which her husband, gentle and devoted and with a life-time habit of deferring to her, could overcome her decision to trust in a faith cure. She had grown to believe that bodily like spiritual ills might be cured without recourse to physical aid. Carey Thomas might have remembered her own experience of her mother's uncompromising attitude in regard to spiritual matters. But in her grief she forgot all these truths and the summer at Coombe Edge after her mother's death was a bitter one for her, and for all her family.

Some years later Carey Thomas was again assailed by frus-trated anger with her family. Her sister Grace, who with Margaret and their cousin Alys Pearsall Smith had entered Bryn Mawr with its first class, soon left the college to marry Thomas Worth-ington. Three children were born, but by the mid-nineties the marriage had proved so unsuccessful that a divorce was obtained in which, with commendable generosity if little practical foresight, Grace refused alimony. In fact, to Carey Thomas, it seemed that her sister agreed to a wholly unjust settlement. That she foresaw long years of helping out the situation financially was the least of her trouble. Her deep rancor was aroused by the fact that the woman in the case had not stood up for her rights. She did her best to stir the family and Grace's friends to support her point of view. To no avail. And the rift, though gradually it healed over, never ceased to smart in the family relationships.

There were other shadows, too: Bond's unsuccessful first mar-riage, ending in the early twentieth century in the suicide of his wife; and Harry's illness, which threatened to cut short his medical career. Harry fortunately recovered and became one of the most valued and best-known members of the staffs of the Johns Hopkins Hospital and Medical School. Doubly fortunate for Carey Thomas, whose favorite he was among her brothers, he married a cousin whom she grew to love. Margaret's later mar-riage, to her first cousin also, turned out happily. But it was in Helen's career that Carey Thomas took her greatest pleasure. Ever since the Munich summer in which she and Mamie Gwinn had taken charge of Frank and Nellie, she had been interested in her youngest sister's development. Now the beguiling little Nellie, so decorous in spite of her mop of red curls and her bright brown eyes, her earnest passion and ambitions, had grown up into the no less appealing young Helen, gratifyingly eager to follow her elder sister's intellectual paths. When, in the autumn of 1889, Helen, sad and bewildered after nursing her mother through her last illness, entered Bryn Mawr College, Carey Thomas watched over her with especial tenderness.

The presence at the college of younger members of her family was far less awkward than, on the face of it, it might have been. In actual fact, except for consuming extra time and energy, it proved to be an asset to Carey Thomas. The children were accustomed to being led by her and, since growing up, had seen so little of her that she had taken on for them something of a legendary character. They regarded her with almost as much awe as affection, and the discretion demanded of them they observed willingly if sometimes with difficulty. Rather than disrupting her influence in the college, they added to it, spreading the fame of her achievements, imbuing their fellow students with their own admiration. They were useful to her, also, both as a source of student opinion and as tests of the college that she could observe from beginning to end. Besides, she was fond of them. She protected them carefully, and especially Helen, for whose welfare since the death of her mother she felt doubly responsible.

Almost at once Helen made friends with her classmate Lucy Martin Donnelly, the beginning of a lifelong friendship that in time extended to Carey Thomas herself and her Pearsall Smith cousins. From the first Carey Thomas welcomed her sister's new friend. She was the daughter of a New York lawyer with a liberal background; sensitive, individual, and intensely alive, she stood out among an unusually gifted group of students. Besides, the inseparable pair both touched and amused Carey Thomas, they were so grave and innocent and eager to be up to date in intellectual and artistic matters—so very young.

After being graduated at Bryn Mawr, Lucy Donnelly, with her sister and a classmate, Louise Brownell, elected to go to England to continue her work in Greek at Oxford in spite of Carey Thomas's argument that Germany was the place in which to seek scholarship. When at the end of the year, in compliance with her advice, they went on to study comparative philology in Germany she saw to it that Helen Thomas should join them in Leipzig, recording in her diary after seeing her sister off, "I was blue, blue, blue because I can never be twenty-three and going to Europe for the first time. Never again." Another year and a half of Germany and France and the two friends returned to Bryn Mawr where they were taken into the English Department to read students' "essays." They soon began to form plans for a development of the English work in which they could have a share and, with the encouragement of Logan Pearsall Smith, hatched a course of their own in descriptive and narrative writing. It took a number of years' hard work and the threat of resignation, however, before they won a higher place on the academic ladder, for Carey Thomas, believing in the routine of German scholarship in which they were not primarily interested, mistrusted their lack of advanced degrees. They had, after all, followed a scholarly path for some years, though less systematically than if they had wished to achieve doctorates. In time their manifestly sound knowledge as well as their signal success in teaching dispelled in large measure her doubts and in the case of Lucy Donnelly, who continued her career at Bryn Mawr, at last cleared them away.

6

Meantime the status of the dean herself had changed: she had become president of the college. In the early nineties Dr. Rhoads, nearing sixty-five and perhaps tired of routine, sank more and more into the background of the college while continuing to keep his hand on its business. Though the faculty trusted and liked him and the students admired his fine appearance and felt his personal integrity and kindness, neither one nor the other recognized how important was his part not only in the administration but even in promoting the intellectual life of the college, in which they were especially interested. Carey Thomas was the daemonic focus of the life of Bryn Mawr. Increasingly the burden of action fell upon her. And, needless to say, she welcomed it, taking on with a will his work as well as her own. To all intents and purposes she was, during the years 1892 and '93, acting president, still advised by Dr. Rhoads and still communicating with the Board of Trustees through him, but making the college plans and carrying them through herself. The force of her administration caused considerable uneasiness in the minds of the trustees; even many of those among them who most esteemed her work felt qualms as to what she might do were the restraining hand of Dr. Rhoads entirely removed. Late in 1893, when at last they were obliged to accede to his repeated wish for retirement, they were assailed by grave doubts of her qualifications as his successor. Indeed a number of them seemed adamant in opposition. Carey Thomas herself, however, had no doubts—and rightly. She had proved to herself that she could carry the presidential work as well as the dean's successfully. The college had thrived under her rule and she had plans for its further development. Such restraint as she felt in her secondary office she regarded only as an unfortunate handicap better removed. She was determined to become president.

Her resentment against her father for his supposed neglect of her mother had cooled; surface relations had returned to their former affectionate terms. But, insensibly, father and daughter had reversed positions and her word rather than his had become the final one. He was saddened by his wife's death and was tired and old. But when Carey Thomas needed him, as she did in 1893, he rose valiantly to her defense. Her uncle James Whitall also rallied to her side, as, with perhaps most telling effect, did Dr. Rhoads. With these three she exchanged almost daily letters. When, on March 10, the trustees appointed a committee to nominate the new president they all counseled patience. "The committee to appoint a successor," Dr. Rhoads wrote her, "will probably soon exhaust all other alternatives and come to the conclusion that seems to me the right one. To this end we must wait and be patient." Patience was a virtue cultivated by Carey Thomas only with extreme distaste as her three mentors too well knew. James Whitall promptly cautioned her at least not to attempt threats. They would certainly turn the trustees against her. Her best means of persuasion was to carry on successfully in Dr. Rhoads's place. "When the captain of the ship is disabled," he pointed out for he was fond of parables, "the chief mate takes charge and proves

himself to the owners the very person to be elected captain. Be
swift to hear, slow to speak," he adjured. She might, he added,
effectively prove herself tractable by deliberately relinquishing her
cherished desire to be made a trustee as well as president. Above
all, she must try to establish agreeable working relations with the
trustees. She had been unable to impress herself directly upon
them during the past nine years; they in their turn had been unable
to express directly to her their many objections and criticisms,
which, in consequence, had swelled to undue proportions. To
remedy this, he arranged meetings between the dean and various
trustees. "I do hope you will have a quiet, calm and pleasant interview," he wrote nervously before one such meeting. "Remember
Dr. Rhoads's prescription of *patience*."

Rather to her surprise Carey Thomas enjoyed these interviews
with individual trustees, believing in the civilities of even the most
intransigent to such an extent as to alarm her uncle. "I cannot
agree with thy sanguine view," he wrote. "Trustees talk very
pleasantly *to thee* individually; appreciating as they do thy character, abilities, etc. But when it comes to putting the *reins in thy
hands*, some of them will *vote* differently." If the board should
refuse to make her president, would she, he asked, be willing to
continue as dean under a man as president? Carey Thomas
answered emphatically that she would accept only the office of
president. Finding her decision irrevocable, he wrote to each of
the trustees pointing out that she had been "given to understand
very fully by F. T. King that he expected she would succeed Dr.
Rhoads," that "the same view had been fully expressed to her by
Dr. Rhoads and has been definitely before the Trustees for more
than a year past." Not to elect her would be "a manifest injustice."
To reassure the trustees, he suggested that she might be appointed
for five or six trial years at the end of which she might, if they
desired, be deposed: a proposal that served only to alarm them.
Would it not mean that they could not terminate the agreement
for five years? And so letters flew back and forth, meetings took
place, and no decision of any sort was come to.

Meantime, Mary Garrett took a hand in the campaign. Her
experience with the Johns Hopkins trustees in regard to the Medical School had taught her that gifts, if large enough, were a

more powerful inducement to the acceptance of unpalatable conditions than were any reasoned arguments. Early in the year 1893 she had presented to Bryn Mawr twenty-six white marble busts of Zeus and Hera and "Emperors, poets and philosophers among the Greeks and Romans done by sculptors of merit." Somewhat later in the year, she offered to present, and eventually did so, the great classical library assembled by Professor Hermann Sauppe, a gift widely heralded in the press and joyfully accepted by the trustees since it gave Bryn Mawr possession of "one of the largest and best selected classical libraries in the United States." And on March 28 she showed still further her interest in the college—this time attaching a condition to her prospective gift.

She wrote the trustees a letter stating her intentions, which she had never expressed to Carey Thomas, in regard to her future financial support of Bryn Mawr. It had always been her plan, she said, "whenever Miss M. Carey Thomas should become President of your College, to pay into her hands the sum of ten thousand dollars yearly so long as I live and she remains President, to be used at her discretion, for the English department in the first instance, and then for other departments of the College, but not for buildings." She had intended also, as had the other members of the Board of Managers of the Bryn Mawr School in Baltimore, to help to establish "other preparatory schools for Bryn Mawr College, throughout the country" when proper opportunity offered and there were competent graduates of the college to conduct them. But—and herein lay the sting—her "interest in the College depended" upon Carey Thomas's "connection with it. . . . All the friends of the College who had watched its brilliantly successful career longest" would agree, she was sure, that "such a change of policy and administration" as would occur were Carey Thomas not made president would be "the greatest misfortune that could befall the education of women in this country."

Mary Garrett's letter was read to the trustees at their meeting on April 14. Dr. Rhoads, to whom Carey Thomas had shown her copy directly upon receiving it a fortnight earlier, had feared that the trustees might feel Mary Garrett's offer unacceptable since such a gift as she proposed would make the president so powerful as to be "wholly beyond the guidance of the Board" and, were the gift established and then cut off, the college would find itself organized on a scale demanding ten thousand dollars a year beyond its income. He himself, he added, had "no doubt these apparent difficulties could be adjusted by a conference with Mary Garrett." Whether or not the conference took place, the day following the trustees' meeting James Whitall wrote his niece that the letter had been well received. Having heard no unfavorable comment, he was "very much encouraged." The trustees, however, had gone no farther toward accepting the gift than to acknowledge Mary Garrett's "liberal offer." Nothing more was to be expected. The gift was too munificent for a small college to turn down out of hand; yet the condition attaching to it almost precluded its approval by some of the trustees. The meeting ended, therefore, with the board recording their continued desire to have Dr. Rhoads remain as president with a vice-president, as yet unnamed, to assist him and, presumably, Carey Thomas still as dean.

In a flurry lest this inevitable hesitation, however honest, provoke his niece to some ill-considered action, James Whitall cautioned her again emphatically: "In the present situation of affairs, it is *absolutely necessary* to *take time* and *exercise patience*. It is costly but we must do it; and it *will pay*. The Committee *must have time* to consult with Dr. Rhoads, and it is the best thing they can do. It will do them good. So we must not attempt to force matters but abide in the everlasting patience. I trust if we do, all will come out right. But indiscretion now may upset the whole business. The Committee will probably learn from Dr. Rhoads that their suggestion is impossible, and I trust they will soon be prepared to do the right thing; and our contribution toward this result is *silence*. Thus a harmonious and *united* result may be reached, which would be very desirable for the new administration. All things come to him who knows how to wait and be silent. I have written to thy father a similar note." Little as she liked it, his niece was quite astute enough to see the wisdom of this advice. It was not "soon," however, that the committee were "prepared to do the right thing."

In order to reinforce Mary Garrett's letter, a copy of which he, too, had seen before the meeting, Carey Thomas's father had written to each of the trustees a letter of his own, stating at length the arguments in favor of his daughter's appointment. The hand of Carey Thomas herself is to be detected in the points that he makes, for most of them are those that she was prone to note in later years as evidence of her early achievement. He spoke, also, of her success in securing money and other gifts for the college and in enhancing the popularity of the College by her own popularity in "Philadelphia circles of intelligent and influential people," and stressed especially Dr. Rhoad's belief in her, after years of close observation, "as the person eminently fitted to become his successor." In words that might have been Carey Thomas's own, he pointed out that as a woman she was peculiarly suited to head a woman's college: "It would be a poor commentary in establishing a college for the higher training of women to refuse to the Dean, because she is a woman, the recognition of her acknowledged gifts and ability for this position." His "personal relationship to the Dean," therefore, could not prevent his "earnestly advocating, as one of the Trustees originally appointed by Dr. Taylor, her election."

As the trustees were all well aware of these arguments, the letter did little more than harry them. They could not turn down Mary Garrett's offer; they could not dispute Dr. Thomas's arguments; but they wanted so little—oh so little—to comply with either. Like most committees in a similar dilemma, they temporized. For twelve weeks they took no definite step beyond sounding out vaguely possible candidates and reiterating their wish for Dr. Rhoads to remain in office. Not until July 7 did they at last express clearly, and record in their minutes, an objection to Carey Thomas upon which they could stand firm.

The trustees had observed that Bryn Mawr College was becoming less and less of a Quaker institution and with considerable justice they attributed this departure to the influence of the dean. Dr. Rhoads had warned her before the mid-April meeting that "the hesitation of those members of the Board who are doubtful about thy appointment is, I am sure, caused by two or three questions: (1) Several of the Board sincerely feel an obligation to make the College more Friendly than it is rather than less so, because of their responsibility under the will and charter. They think thou wilt make the College less Friendly, and practically discard the intentions of the Founder. (2) They think thou art too unwilling to respect the seriously expressed view of the Board, and that they will have responsibilities on their consciences which they will be powerless to fulfill, in short that the College will pass absolutely into the control of an officer, who, especially with $10,000 a year at her own control, will be independent of the Board. Now, thou knows, I believe Friends must change a good deal and am prepared to see those changes so made, slowly, as the *necessity* for them appears, yet I also think we are bound to respect the intentions of the Founder of the College and the terms of the Charter. Moreover I interpret thy very kind expressions of willingness to act in consultation with me as President of the Board as a deliberate purpose to have all due regard for the serious judgments and expressed wishes of the Board, and I shall take care (of course in a proper manner) to express my confidence in thy disposition to respect the properly formulated conclusions of the Board as to the management of the College."

With this warning and promise of mediation Carey Thomas accepted quietly the resolutions passed by the trustees strengthening the religious life of the college; and the even stiffer ones, passed by them five months later, she saw could be met without detriment to Bryn Mawr. They belied, however, the liberality shown heretofore by the trustees for, if carried out with stringency, they would undoubtedly lower its academic standing. Were the requirements of Dr. Taylor's will broadly construed, the trustees said, it would be possible to observe them by giving the preference to Quakers as Haverford did in choosing professors. They did not "suppose the Founder intended the standard" of Bryn Mawr "to be lower than that of Haverford"; on the other hand, neither did they suppose that he intended it to be higher. Shocking though this statement was to her, Carey Thomas thought that by tactful handling she could preserve Bryn Mawr's high standards. She persuaded the trustees to rule that every professor appointed to Bryn Mawr should have a doctor's degree. Later, when circumstances permitted, she induced them to enlarge the possibilities by basing the requirement upon quality and amount of work rather than upon a degree itself. But, for the moment, the more stringent rule enabled her to avoid the issue since few Quakers then possessed higher degrees. From the beginning she had taken in her stride, as she proposed to continue to do, the trustees' recurrent concern with the religious life of the college, sometimes drastically stated but rarely, she had found, drastic in action.

A much more important point, to her, was her belief that whoever might be appointed president must be made at the same time a member of the Board of Trustees. Again and again she brought up this point; again and again her three mentors headed her off from too definite an ultimatum. "Wait until you are appointed President, then work for the next step," was their repeated counsel. But she must, she felt, make her position clear. Early in November she indited a long letter to one of the more friendly trustees giving her reasons at length. "My conviction," she wrote, "does not rest on the custom or experience of other colleges but on facts that have come under my own observation. Both Dr. Rhoads and I feel—indeed he said only two days ago—that his being a Trustee has been essential to our successful management of Bryn Mawr. In no other way could we have carried with us the sympathy of the greater number of the Trustees. It has been of great importance too in establishing authoritative and cordial relations between us and the Faculty." She then listed the cases of which she knew where the head of an institution had found it necessary to demand inclusion in the Board of Managers. "Now," she continued, "although my conviction on this point could not be stronger, I am willing and anxious to do all I can to bring about a speedy and amiable settlement. I wish to be guided by thy advice, in which I feel the greatest confidence. I do not wish to force an issue, and if thee thinks best I will leave the matter for the present, until there is a vacancy in the Board, but under no circumstances could I consent to be President unless there were a distinct resolution of the Board providing that the President should attend all meetings of the Board—the annual election of Directors might be omitted if desired—the Executive Committee in its regular and special meetings, the Buildings Committee, the Library Committee and Committees that concern themselves with the College grounds, buildings or administration; and providing also that the President be the only authorized means of communication between the

Trustees and the Faculty and Students, and vice versa. This ought
to be put, I think, in the resolution electing the President."

By dint of tactful management on the part of her friends this
slight intransigence was smoothed over, temporarily at least, and
she was persuaded not to hold out on this point. On November 17
the trustees finally accepted Dr. Rhoads's resignation, insisting
only that he continue to hold his professorship of ethics and his
presidency of the Board of Trustees. And they elected in his stead,
by a majority of one, Carey Thomas as president, the election to
take effect on August 31, 1894.

At once her appointment was hailed as an advance for women's
education. "It is a great day for the higher education of young
women," President Isaac Sharpless of Haverford congratulated
her. The press made much of her youth—she was thirty-six. It
lauded her, as a Pennsylvania newspaper put it with more enthusiasm than grace, as "one of the brainiest women in this state and
one who is an honor to any state or country"; and some papers
spoke of the fact that she was in large measure responsible for
"the distinctive character of Bryn Mawr." The more sedate Philadelphia and New York papers noted Dr. Rhoads's resignation
with regret but found the appointment of Carey Thomas "peculiarly fitting." "Under the Presidency of Miss Thomas," said the
Public Ledger, "the future of Bryn Mawr is assured."

What pleased Carey Thomas more than almost anything else
was the satisfaction that the Bryn Mawr faculty in general seemed
to feel in her election. She had been sure of the ardent approval of
most of the students. Of the faculty's welcome she had felt less
certain. She wrote with manifest elation to David Scull: "I think
perhaps it might interest thee to know that the faculty have, one
and all, received my election *most cordially*"—the older professors
had told her privately that, had "almost any other appointment
they could think of" been made, most of the faculty would have
resigned. To this enthusiastic thanksgiving David Scull's reply is
characteristically tempered, the sort of warning frequently administered by her relatives on the board which served to put Carey
Thomas on her mettle. He could understand her satisfaction in the
assurance of support from the faculty, and hoped that, in time,
the board would be brought by her own "wise course of action"

to support her with equal loyalty. No one who followed Dr. Rhoads in the presidency, he pointed out, could fail to suffer by comparison with him; but "all evidence of a hearty purpose on thy part to follow in his steps" would meet, he felt sure, with a warm welcome. "Thy course and thy influence will be watched by many, with that closeness which positive characters are likely to attract."

CHAPTER VIII

President of Bryn Mawr College

I

DURING the first years of Carey Thomas's presidency the position was growing, taking on new outlines and a fuller form. In January, 1894, the trustees decided to merge, at least temporarily, the office of dean with that of president, raising her salary one thousand dollars above the three thousand that she had heretofore received. Since, during Dr. Rhoads's illness, the duties of dean and president had been carried on simultaneously by Carey Thomas, there seemed no reason why they should not continue to be united: an arrangement highly satisfactory to Carey Thomas herself and prolongd by her till 1908. She never wished to divide authority whatever the burden of work it entailed.

Her twofold duties as president and dean—her professorship of English had become a mere title—gave her direct control of an unprecedentedly wide range in college affairs and, more important, broke the conventional mold of the presidential office so that she could make of it what she would. With its expansion her own powers defined themselves. As she thrust down obstacle after obstacle that impeded the fulfillment of her vision and saw her widening ambitions and dreams materialize, her personality, always strong, lost any youthful uncertainty that it may have had. Through the pressure of external circumstances rather than spiritual struggle she achieved an inner harmony: the need for constant expense of energy in quick decisions and outward action left little time or power, little desire even, for inward searchings or for feeling the pain of grief or perplexity or disillusion. The readjustment after the deaths of her parents, the friction with her family, and the defection of Mamie Gwinn, as well as the exacerbating delays and hindrances in her work for the college, all resolved into immediate action. And action was to her the breath of life; the conflict that breeds action, its salt.

She had been gratified that the trustees, shortly after electing her president, passed the resolution which she had been persuaded only reluctantly to abandon as a condition of her acceptance of the office: "She shall be expected to attend the regular meetings of the Board, the meetings of committees hitherto attended by the President and also special meetings when invited." She regarded this, nevertheless, as a mere stopgap, by no means discouraging to her campaign for the trusteeship itself, for which she continued to strike a blow whenever opportunity offered. At their meeting after Dr. Rhoads's death in 1895, she surprised even her closest friends among the trustees by addressing them directly: "Now Friends," she began, "there is something that I feel it my duty to say. After I have told you what is on my mind I shall then be satisfied to leave the decision to you. What I have to say will take only a few minutes. I shall then withdraw so as not to embarrass any discussion; and next month I shall do the same." On this ominous declaration, she reminded them of Dr. Rhoads's belief that the president of the college should also be a member of its governing board, and of the list that he had drawn up of the colleges and universities of good standing in the eastern and middle states in which the president was a trustee. Bryn Mawr alone among the women's colleges, along with its Quaker neighbors Haverford and Swarthmore colleges and Lehigh and Clark universities, could not be included in this list; and these four institutions suffered by the curtailment of their president's powers. Moreover, she herself especially needed the added authority of trusteeship to give her counsels greater weight with the Bryn Mawr faculty and staff.

The trustees, to a man, opposed her request. David Scull at once wrote begging her to withdraw it. It threatened, he felt, the harmony existing both within the board and between her and the board: "If harmony is maintained all really best results are obtainable; but without harmony!—oh my—well, *I* would get out." And he reminded her of the fact that the trustees had considered ejecting Dr. Rhoads from the board when he became the president of the college. In the end, perforce, she withdrew her request and Henry Tatnall, destined to be a thorn in her flesh, was elected to the vacant seat. Within a year, however, she again took the offensive, this time by letter, pointing out that, although her position as administrator of a largely male faculty was proving easier than she had feared, she had found it difficult to beg money for the college: people preferred to give money to her when she asked for it rather than to a board of which she was not a member. David Scull pronounced the letter "a temperate and suitable expression of the case"; but it had no marked effect upon the trustees.

After her father's death, David Scull was obliged to warn her that she was mistaken in trying to persuade him or any of the other members of the board to plead with the trustees who were definitely in opposition to her: "Positive advocacy to a greater extent than thee is aware has heretofore aroused an adverse sentiment." Nevertheless, her yearly attempt by one means or another to win over the board continued unabated. One weary trustee remarked after her annual attack in 1897, "I *had* thought that with the last election of a Trustee the subject was permanently settled." But finally, of course, she won. Early in November, 1902, she sent about, again, Dr. Rhoads's list of colleges and universities in which the president was also a trustee and at the end of the month was elected one of the thirteen life trustees of Bryn Mawr College.

This matter of the trusteeship was not the only bone of contention between Carey Thomas and the board during the first years of her presidency but it was the only very serious one.[1] It is a tribute to both her valiant efforts and those of most of the trustees that their accord suffered no more than it did through the deaths of those loyal, hard-working interpreters of each party to the other, Dr. Rhoads, James Whitall, and Carey Thomas's father. Dr. Rhoads's death not only deeply grieved Carey Thomas but robbed her, she realized, of a most effective counselor and upholder at a time, not many months after her election to the presidency, when she needed both. No one else could have such intimate and comprehensive knowledge as Dr. Rhoads upon which to base advice in regard to the college. The deaths of her uncle James in 1896 and of her father in 1897 removed her other two most valued and staunchest advisers. More than that, their deaths, particularly her father's, cut at the foundations of her life, destroying in a bewildering way the continuity of her early associations and accustomed supports. With the death of her mother had fallen upon her shoulders, at her request, the administration of Mrs. Thomas's estate, especially Coombe Edge; now, with the death of her father, she felt herself to be the head of the family with all the responsibilities such a position entailed. Yet in spite of the difficulties and burden of work, the grief and grave losses she suffered, the first six years following her appointment to the presidency were among the freest and happiest of her life.

Having attained to the trusteeship she, as president of the college, had achieved the highest position possible in the administration of Bryn Mawr. Moreover, the first days of creation for the college, both material and intellectual, had passed. The lines of its development had been laid down, in large part by Carey Thomas herself, certainly in the direction she would have them go. It behooved her now to apply her ingenuity to ways and means within an already clearly foreshadowed shape.

The fund of two hundred and fifty thousand dollars collected during the second semester and announced in the president's commencement speech in 1902 provided enough money at least to begin—though, unfortunately, not to complete—her building program. She herself had done most of the collecting, making begging calls and writing begging letters innumerable, never missing the opportunity of even a chance meeting with a possible donor, young or old, male or female, to put forward the needs of the college. By May 3, as she wrote her young niece Mary Worthington, she still had to find "sixty thousand to give us those beautiful buildings I hope you will enjoy." The last month, a frenzy of telephone calls, telegrams, and special-delivery letters had clinched her argument that she needed to belong to the Board of Trustees in order to beg efficiently. Once over the line, on the very morning of Commencement, she began immediately to set in motion the machinery for carrying out the building plans.

The plans themselves had already been laid. The architect

Walter Cope, in conjunction with Carey Thomas and the trustees' Buildings Committee, had drawn them up and established the sites for the sorely needed new dormitory and library. For the most part, Cope had his own way with the plans for the residence hall. In designing the library, however, he had adapted his plans closely to the wishes and dreams of Carey Thomas. During her past summers' travels she had collected photographs and measurements of the great halls and windows, stairways, porches, and cloisters, of the Oxford colleges that especially caught her imagination; indeed, with Mary Garrett's help, she had herself measured "with a flexible steel tape measure" many cloisters elsewhere in England and on the Continent. Why, she asked, should not an American college have a hall as beautiful as those most beautiful of academic halls if such specifications were composed into a harmonious whole? A naïve enough conception on the face of it, and one that posed peculiarly difficult problems to an architect working in another country under entirely dissimilar conditions, restrained by limited finances and the needs of a modern library. And yet, when Walter Cope completed his adaptations, he had designed a charming building and one capable of fulfilling its purpose.

Not very large, of square-cut blocks of rough brownish gray stone—machicolated and turreted, to be sure, but lacking the fussiness often attendant upon pseudo-Jacobean erections—the building rose from the green lawn with dignity and simplicity. From the entrance through the porch of Oriel College Chapel the wide stairway led to a reading room, the great hall of Wadham College with its two huge stone fireplaces, tall windows, and vaulted roof. Below the reading room were the open stacks; and forming with it the sides of a quadrangle—one side of which was not built till 1940—were professors' offices and seminars. At the four corners of the quadrangle rose turrets from which on high days the banners of the college flaunted; and enclosed within it, the arched cloisters, of lovely proportions, surrounded their square of smooth turf, pointed in the center by a low fountain from which sprang a single jet of water. For generations of students the cloisters were to hold, as they did most of all for Carey Thomas, a kind of enchantment, a cool peace, the distillation of academic quiet.

There were flaws in the building's interior design which, with the growing stress upon functional efficiency, were to become increasingly obvious. Perhaps the most glaring and most characteristic of Carey Thomas in its contradictions was the arrangement of the reading room. No books were to be kept there, not even a dictionary, for students to refer to though, in order to protect readers from the noise of the main entrance, a sort of inverted storm door, a wooden boxlike structure, was erected around the doorway, protruding into the hall and breaking its line. That Carey Thomas clung to these idiosyncrasies of the reading room in spite of criticism and remonstrance can be set down only to the inexplicable and obvious deviation from common sense to which the autocratic temperament is subject. She, who had insisted that the stacks be open to students as they are in few college libraries, might above all others have been expected to envisage students working in alcoves shelved with reference and reading material, not in a great hall bare of books.

Walter Cope died in the autumn of 1902; but the following spring his plans and proposed sites were accepted and the two new buildings were to be begun under the direction of the firm of Cope and Stewardson during the summer. Carey Thomas sailed to England for a few weeks of needed holiday with Mary Garrett, confident that all building matters were for the moment in fair train. Within a short time, however, she received a cable from Isabel Maddison, secretary to the president of the college— later recording dean and assistant to the president—saying that the treasurer of the Board of Trustees, Henry Tatnall, the ultimate authority on the spot for the summer, had ordered all work on the library held up. He did not approve of its proposed site. Amazed, Carey Thomas wrote him at once: the site had been confirmed by the board early in May at a meeting at which he arrived late and he had made no objection either then or in the remaining weeks before her departure for Europe; besides, it was exceedingly risky to act against expert advice in the matter of building sites. Walter Cope had determined the position of the library after painstaking consideration of the lay of the land and the other buildings on the campus. To move the site back even the fifteen feet desired by Henry Tatnall would be to run into a series of difficulties enumerated by Cope as being insuperable except at great cost.

Though Carey Thomas's letter was long and explicit, hitting every nail a clean clip on the head, but with perfect good temper and civility, it neither convinced nor mollified the treasurer. Replying to her letter, he reiterated his objections, adding the two-edged observation that he had expected her to return by August 1—David Scull had urged her to prolong her holiday—as the college was "a distinct loser" by her absence. He "considered" her secretary, moreover, to have exceeded her duties in reporting to the president that he had stopped work on the library; a strange giveaway of his attitude, since he had himself already notified most of the other members of the board, some of whom, like David Scull, had lost no time in disagreeing with him.

There followed a succinct correspondence. In the end, though delayed many weeks, the library was built on the site determined by Cope. But Carey Thomas never forgave Tatnall his devious implacability in opposing her plans. Nor had their mutual bitterness been lessened in any way by an episode that occurred when the building neared completion. Returning from the summer vacation the trustees found that, against their expressed wishes, teak had been used in the woodwork of the main stairway and reading room by order of the president. Before going away they had voted against its use as an unnecessary expense; elsewhere the building was put up at minimum cost. But Carey Thomas had taken matters into her own hands. In her opinion it was fitting that the entrance to the library, the heart of the college, should be especially dignified.

Temperamentally Carey Thomas and Henry Tatnall were doomed to mistrust and condemn each other. And matters were not helped by the occasions on which one was obliged to concede the other right. In many cases, such as that of the library site and, especially, in daringly conceived financial plans, Carey Thomas was shown to be wise. Sometimes, however, events proved Henry Tatnall well advised, as in the case of the fire that gutted Denbigh Hall in March, 1902. In the previous winter, when one of the professors' houses had caught fire, the Ardmore fire company had arrived late and, according to Carey Thomas, demonstrated base inefficiency in contrast to the masterly competence of the college workmen and the students' fire brigade. She proposed that fires be dealt with thereafter only by the college men and students. Henry Tatnall quashed this jejune idea with biting, if civilly veiled, scorn—fortunately, since without the Ardmore and Philadelphia brigades Denbigh Hall would probably have burned to the ground. As it was, the damage could be repaired quickly. And, since the fire had been caused by a carelessly placed oil "student's lamp," Carey Thomas was at last permitted to install the electric lighting system for which she had argued vainly for years. The only troublesome mark left by the fire was the opportunity it had given the students of making excuses to their professors for several years to come of lecture notes, essays, even Ph.D. theses burned or lost in the scuffle.

Meantime, in the summer of 1903, the cost of the new residence hall was proving greater than had been estimated. Young Mr. Rockefeller had voluntarily added five thousand dollars to the large sum already given by his father for the hall's—Rockefeller Hall's—construction. No more help, therefore, could be counted on from that quarter. There seemed nowhere else to turn to make up the increasing deficit. The following year was consequently one of great stress for the president of the college, especially in view of the personal strain existing between her and some of the trustees led by their treasurer. One trustee, unable to bear the tension, resigned. The treasurer himself threatened to resign but was persuaded, largely by David Scull, to continue in office. It would have been awkward, even Carey Thomas reluctantly agreed, and "caused speculation detrimental to the College," had two trustees resigned within a year.

By the summer of 1904 the college deficit ran to thirty thousand dollars—a debt generously defrayed, as were lesser deficits in other years, by Mary Garrett—and the new hall was accumulating a like sum in excess of all available funds. In exact proportion, nevertheless, as the spirits of the trustees sank in face of the ominous situation, of work proceeding though there was no money to pay for it, Carey Thomas's own spirits rose.

To cut the cost of the library in order to lend part of its building fund to that of the new residence hall, the trustees decided against attempting to build the fourth side of the library quadrangle. They clung to the theory that the incompleteness of the building would be a constant appeal to some rich alumna to finish it. Realizing this hope to be forlorn, impatiently feeling that she might as well hang for a sheep as a lamb, and convinced within herself that whatever sum must be procured could be procured, Carey Thomas pleaded to be allowed to beg an extra one hundred and fifty thousand dollars in order to build the entire library at once. The trustees refused, perhaps wisely, since she was put to sore shifts to carry on even the three wings. Selling securities to do so, backed by Mary Garrett, she herself assumed responsibility for the payment of certain pieces of work. But the deficit remained.

In April, 1905, as a desperate and, on the face of it, ill-advised resort, she wrote to young Mr. Rockefeller, submitting statements concerning the deficit on the new hall and asking for help. The reply, a discouraging one, came in June followed by other equally disheartening letters. Then, suddenly on Christmas Eve, into her depressing, foggy holiday with Mary Garrett at Newport, dropped a brilliant light: a letter and check from young Mr. Rockefeller completely reversing the situation. The check, which Carey Thomas forwarded to Henry Tatnall with a long letter of thanksgiving, cleared Rockefeller Hall of every debt including the twenty-six thousand dollars borrowed from the library fund. The residence hall could begin on a fair slate to pay for itself, the sum advanced by Carey Thomas to the library be repaid, the library stacks and furnishings be completed, and ten thousand dollars, Carey Thomas reckoned, be left over toward the fourth, unfinished side of the library. For an instant, at least, Carey Thomas gazed into a future in which Bryn Mawr College flourished, rich and fully developed, in a benign glow of academic perfection. The Students' Building designed by Cope even Carey Thomas was unable to force through either at this time or later against the opposition of the trusteees. But the power house and the long and charming shingled house, Low Buildings, the first hostel to be put up by any college for the female members of its faculty usually relegated to life in dormitories with the students, had already been built. And with the building, in 1908, of a new gymnasium, on the site of the old, large enough to contain a swimming pool and in harmony with the other Jacobean buildings, the college was established physically for another quarter of a century, only the infirmary being rebuilt and enlarged in 1912 as the gift of the class of 1905.

2

Carey Thomas was not one to rest on her oars. The new buildings had been permitted neither to swamp the college in debt nor, by preoccupying her with their finances, to turn her into a mere money-raising executive. She was aware that Bryn Mawr's prestige had been won and must be maintained by excellence of intellectual achievement. Yet she recognized that a small college, guided by trustees all drawn from one circle, the Society of Friends in this case, ran a grave danger of becoming parochial. Dr. Taylor's will, stipulating that the thirteen trustees not only should be Quakers but should form a self-perpetuating board, effectually prevented the election to trusteeship of members having diverse interests, until the desire of the trustees to appoint Mary Garrett to the governing board and the pressure of the alumnae who wished to appoint one or more of themselves, not necessarily Quakers, led to an amendment to the charter. The legal device was hit upon by John G. Johnson, then legal adviser to the college, and was incorporated in the charter in 1906, of merging the Board of Trustees in a larger Board of Directors of whom thirteen must be Friends.

It devolved upon herself, Carey Thomas felt, to offset provincialism by keeping herself intellectually alive and bringing the college into connection with the outside world. She must keep up with what was doing in the arts and sciences, in politics and social movements as well as in education. It was a policy entirely compatible with her temperament, one indeed that she had pursued from the beginning of her deanship; and the troubled period concerned with the new buildings was no moment to relax it.

In making academic appointments she tried to see to it that men and women be appointed who were both good scholars and teachers, or showed promise of becoming so, and who were interesting persons from wider points of view. To find such she spared no effort, traveling far and combing the faculties and the alumnae of other institutions as well as the alumnae of Bryn Mawr. She had the power of gauging under what circumstances special capabilities might flower most fully, and was willing to give a candidate in whom she saw promise—even though he saw little in himself in the field for which she destined him—every chance and encouragement to develop his abilities. Her early advice to Dr. Rhoads regarding appointments had proved peculiarly successful; and the appointments negotiated by herself alone were equally so. An extraordinary proportion of the men who were brought to the Bryn Mawr faculty were called to large universities which could offer them greater inducements than could a small college and where their names became well known throughout the academic world; and from the more restricted field of women scholars and teachers a number were appointed who, since no other institution offered women larger opportunities, remained at Bryn Mawr for long periods and won great distinction.

When left to herself—as she was, in the early days, only in making appointments to the staff—Carey Thomas sometimes ran risks that might at the time have been thought fantastic: in the choice, for instance, of a young woman as secretary who had interested her by taking the Bryn Mawr examinations in 1885 although without hope of gratifying her desire to enter the college. Carey Thomas sent for her and asked if she knew stenography. "No," said the candidate. "Can you typewrite?" "No." "Do you write a good hand?" "No, a very poor one." "Well," said Carey Thomas, who had picked her woman and was undaunted, "I think it will take you five years to get your degree, for I shall need you three hours a day." And, upon that basis of no apparent secretarial qualifications but many others visible to the dean, the young woman, Abby Kirk, was installed as a student in Bryn Mawr and Carey Thomas's secretary, proving so successful that after taking her A.B. she was appointed to the staff as reader in the Department of English and, later, as instructor in elementary Greek. With equal success her elder sister, Sophia Kirk, although boasting neither college degree nor any training or experience in such a position, was made mistress of Merion Hall by Carey Thomas, who believed that an exceptionally keen mind and high intellectual standards would carry her through; as they did, triumphantly.

Years afterwards, when Bryn Mawr needed a classical archaeologist and none suitable appeared to be available, Carey Thomas, then president, discovered a young Rhodes scholar teaching Greek at Columbia who impressed her as possessing to a distinguished degree the qualifications needed. He himself had never contemplated entering the archaeological field. After an interview in which she put to him that he could, if he would, change the direction of his work, he found himself so fired by her words and enthusiasm that he accepted her appointment and plunged into archaeology, reaching in a few years a position of marked eminence in the field. It was a reward for her brave acumen and encouragement that Rhys Carpenter remained at Bryn Mawr to become one of the most brilliant of its faculty, and to support Carey Thomas staunchly during a difficult period later when her adherents among the faculty were few and unpopular.

Sometimes, to be sure, in her eagerness to obtain the best for Bryn Mawr she overplayed her hand. In a moment of aberration she appointed to the same post in the same year two promising young men, afterwards to become well-known members, respectively, of the Princeton and Yale faculties. Only after much stress and scheming, by arranging for one to fill the vacancy that had occurred and tactfully persuading the other to finish the work upon which he was engaged for his doctor's degree until a second post should fall vacant in the next year, did she manage to obtain them both for the Department of English, albeit in different branches of the subject. Sometimes, too, the high standard of both scholarship and teaching and the amount and variety of work that she demanded of young, inexperienced instructors gained her bitter opprobrium, as did her insistence that no instructor should lecture elsewhere than at Bryn Mawr either during the academic year or in the summer lest his best energies be lost to the college or, in the vacations, to research. Many good stories grew up of her autocratic ways; many people, like the physicist Rutherford, heard of her as "a lady dean who is an autocrat of the toughest type."[2] But few—though those few were later vocal in disparagement—who have been members of the Bryn Mawr faculty have failed to laud the unusual encouragement and freedom of development given them at Bryn Mawr, largely through Carey Thomas's influence.

It was indisputable, at any rate, that however high the standards by which she measured the faculty, she held herself to standards no less high; and however heavy the work she expected of them, she herself worked no less hard. The list of meetings of associations and societies in which she took part in these years seems interminable. Usually she was the chief speaker at them and, almost without fail, the speaker who aroused most comment and discussion of ideas.

She worked over these speeches, not only their composition but their delivery. From the time of her early youth when her mother had called her attention to the niceties of public speaking and to the sound of her own voice, a slovenly enunciation or muffled tones had greatly irritated her. After attending the ceremony, followed by a luncheon of dignitaries, at which the University of Pennsylvania bestowed, in 1905, honorary degrees upon President Theodore Roosevelt and, in the person of his ambassador to Washington, the Kaiser Wilhelm II, she commented crossly in her journal not on what Roosevelt had to say, although she became a great admirer of his, but on the way in which he said it: "Spoke very badly, Amurrica etc."

When, at the turn of the century, she at last found a teacher of elocution, Samuel Arthur King, whom she thought excellent, she at once established him at the college and in as many schools as she could persuade to employ his services. Each address, moreover, that she herself was to deliver she made beforehand, if possible, to him. He listened, criticized the delivery, the enunciation, the rise and fall of her voice, its carrying power and clarity, even the relative arrangements of major and minor points in the argument, making her repeat the important passages over and over again. Her voice had always been clear and beautiful. It hardly needed his training to carry effortlessly and pleasingly to the farthest corner of the largest hall, but she valued it as the backing of authority which unconsciously she always sought.

In these early years of the century she spent much pains, too, upon the matter of her speeches. Many of them, consequently, make interesting and lively reading even now. They are not always wholly accurate in statement of fact, even in the statistics upon which she trustingly depended for support; but they are provocative and show flashes of brilliant insight. Two, in particular, stand out, both made to the Association of Collegiate Alumnae. The first, delivered in Washington in 1902, on "The Future of Women in Independent Study and Research," for which she drew on the material of one of the most readable of her pamphlets, *The College Woman of the Present and Future*, gives an inspiriting view of the time when women shall have obtained equal opportunities with men as teachers and scholars as well as students in the field of advanced education. The other, delivered in New York in the same year, is a better illustration, when read forty-four years later, of the validity of her reasoning. It is a vehement denunciation of "the free elective system," advocated by President Eliot of Harvard, which prescribed little work in any particular subjects, permitting every student almost unrestricted choice of subjects and courses.

In this speech, tracing her own varied, successive decisions in regard to a career and pointing out that many children are born intellectually lazy, she showed that the swift and early individualization of the human intelligence is not a sure indication of future development and that all subjects, even though equally well taught, are not of equal disciplinary value. To her the ideal system, of course, was a judicious modification of that supported by President Eliot, such as "the group system" of Bryn Mawr College, which requires specified basic studies of every student but permits a certain amount of freedom and may lead to further specialization. But, in order to make such a desirable system possible, she was careful to stress, the colleges must oppose too early specialization in the schools and insist upon thorough general preparation.

What is notable about this speech, and what sets Carey Thomas well in the vanguard of educational thinkers, is that time has vindicated her point of view. The points that she makes in 1901 are similar in basic conception to those made by "the Harvard

Committee on the objectives of a general education in a free society," published in 1945.[3] She knew her subject well in all its aspects and did not hesitate to speculate on the conclusions that she drew. There was no corner of the field of women's education that she did not explore. Occasionally a pleased note sounds in her diary to the effect that she shocked her audience by a frankness to which they were unaccustomed. The vigorous blast of fresh air took their breath away; but, in the end, they savored the pleasant righteousness of feeling themselves to be emancipators, and were won over. In her more public speeches, of course, she was careful for Bryn Mawr's sake to avoid such a risk. Nevertheless, they too had an invigorating quality.

For many of the addresses that she was called upon to make to graduating schoolgirls she drew on the history of her own struggle to obtain a first-rate education. In memory the struggle grew more and more strenuous and, retailed to far distant schools by teachers rallying their pupils, had a most bracing effect. The various memorial addresses, also, that she made during these years throw an interesting light upon her character in showing the personal qualities that aroused her admiration: physical beauty, assurance, high spirit, ingenuity, intelligent efficiency; willingness to admit error when faced by proof; "the quality of faithfulness, without which I sometimes think all other qualities are ineffective. . . . I think I should be almost satisfied if fairness and truthfulness could become the future preeminent Bryn Mawr virtues." These notes, and always the virtue of loyalty, are struck again and again by Carey Thomas.

To most people the travel necessitated by much public speaking is the bane of existence. Not to Carey Thomas. She was a born sight-seer and seized with avidity her chance to visit "all points of interest," all natural phenomena, exhibitions, plays, and operas everywhere she went. Her business visits to New York in December, 1905, were timed to allow her to see almost all Sarah Bernhardt's performances there: "Saw Bernhardt in Victor Hugo's *Angelo*. She was wonderful. A vision of grace and charm. Her death ecstatic killed by her lover. Her acting was very quiet. . . . Heard *Fédora*. Sarah was glorious. . . . To see *Phèdre* in afternoon. Sarah was most wonderful. It is her most glorious part."

On the latter occasion and at Bernhardt's evening performance, however, her attention was divided, for she saw for the first time, and almost the last, since their departure from Bryn Mawr Mamie Gwinn and her husband among the audience and watched them, as well as Sarah, through her glass.

At the St. Louis Exposition of 1904 the exhibitions of countries that she had not yet visited interested her almost as much as the educational exhibits, even that of Bryn Mawr College, which she herself arranged. They did not always please her: "Saw Japan, China, Cairo, Siberian railway, and Hagenbach's animals. All wretched." Exhibitions of pictures she greatly enjoyed, especially those recalling her years abroad with Mamie Gwinn and those connected with her friends or family. When the Naples Round Table—a committee of which she was one of the chief executives —met in Boston, she "spent hours" in Mrs. Jack Gardiner's Fenway Court. It interested her not only because of the collection but partly because Bernard Berenson, the second husband of her cousin Mary Pearsall Smith Costelloe, had had so large a share in forming it.

Meantime the refreshment to her spirit as well as the experiences themselves were reflected in the college. Designedly she opened door after door to many unsophisticated students in her chapel speeches, giving them new interests, making real to them delights they had hardly dreamed of. Nor did she fail to stimulate the efforts of the students themselves, promoting their clubs and magazine and dramatic performances so long as they did not interfere with academic work and accorded with her own high standards built up and kept alive largely for this purpose. Though she encouraged athletic contests arranged by Constance Applebee, the redoubtable and popular director of physical education, she rarely attended and took only perfunctory interest in them; but at college plays she made a point of being present. Even more than these, perhaps, she enjoyed the rites—unusual at that time in the United States but since become quite common—in celebration of May first. She liked the color and ordered pageantry of the Elizabethan plays and masques and dancing on the green of the "Big May Days," habitually celebrated every four years after the first, in 1900, organized by Evangeline Andrews (Bryn Mawr,

1893); and, almost better, the "Little May Days" when the seniors in caps and gowns, carrying their May baskets, followed by students of other classes, greeted the sun with the Magdalen hymn from Rockefeller tower and then danced about the maypoles on Merion and Denbigh greens.

But dearest to her heart were academic ceremonies. She saw to it that academic dress was worn whenever fitting, that academic processions moved with decorum, that the bestowal of academic honors was attended by suitable fanfare. And above all Bryn Mawr occasions she loved "Lantern Night," so academic in flavor and, in her view, so characteristic of Bryn Mawr. She urged all who could come to Bryn Mawr on the autumn evening when Lantern Night took place each year to join the silent audience ranged on the roof of the cloisters. Below them the dark procession of black-gowned sophomores, each carrying a lantern and singing their lovely Greek hymn to "Pallas Athene Thea," marched slowly beneath the arches to hand on their lanterns to the waiting semicircle of freshmen, capped and gowned too, shadowy in the bright autumn starlight of the open court, and responding with their grave song of acceptance. It seemed to Carey Thomas, as to others, a solemn, infinitely touching and beautiful ceremony.

To hold any of these performances in the absence of Carey Thomas was to feel it somehow lacking in point. To see her enter the gymnasium, where in those days plays were given, and lead with quick uneven gait her party of guests to the front row where chairs awaited them—for her, an armchair on the aisle more stately than the others—was to experience the tension felt at the entrance of a royal party. Her presence on all such college occasions made the air electric for both audience and actors, and in the actors awoke the desperate determination to do or die. They longed for the dizzy pride of being singled out with approbation in the next morning's chapel speech; or, if that were beyond hope, looked forward to the satisfaction of hearing the deeds of their fellow students dissected and measured by a standard which they revered.

Not many students were willing to miss the quarter to nine chapel meetings even on cold, stormy winter mornings. And not many ever forgot the picture of Carey Thomas swiftly mounting the platform in Taylor Hall, gown billowing, cap well to the back of her beautiful head and at a preposterous angle pointing straight up into the air, opening the Bible on the square block of the speaker's desk, reading some great passage—her favorites were from the Book of Isaiah—of which her lovely voice made music, then closing the book and speaking with all the gusto of which she was so capable of some item that had caught her interest in the day's news, some cause dear to her, some book that she had read, some exhibition or play that she had seen, some ceremony in which they themselves had taken part, holding the students agog, making them feel and think, by the liveliness of her own interested reminiscence and by the vividness of her statements.

Carey Thomas followed in the vigorous tradition of her family, especially as exemplified by her aunt Hannah, who in the early days of the college, a dignified, fine-looking lady in Quaker bonnet, already famous as a religious teacher of whom the students expected quiet reverence, had mounted this same platform and accidentally knocked the Bible to the floor: "Never mind, Friends, it's only the Bible." One of the stories most often told of Carey Thomas herself when, in the interests of the college, she had come to defend marriage is that, in enumerating the statistics that had been gathered concerning the employment of Bryn Mawr alumnae, she finished with a flourish: "Thirty-three percent of the Bryn Mawr alumnae are married, and fifty percent of them have children." Later, during the Versailles Congress after World War I, in discussing possible peace settlements, she remarked that the suggestion had been made of putting Constantinople under the joint rule of Britain and the United States. She paused, thinking—then, "It would be a pity to put Constantinople under the rule of too *sanitary* a nation." Often she was unaware of what she had said; for a moment the inevitable laughter of the students would bewilder her; then, suddenly, she would understand, flinging back her head to laugh with them. But her remarks lost none of their edge, her penetrating comments none of their force, through occasional absurdity of statement.

In her unremitting effort to arouse the students' perceptions of the various fields of human concern, Carey Thomas invited to

Bryn Mawr many guests, both American and foreign. She took pains, as she urged the faculty to do, to prepare the way for these visitors by speaking to the students beforehand of their work and importance. Wires often had to be pulled to arrange the visits and readjustments made in the already crowded schedule of the college. Sometimes in order to include the students in the ceremony, visitors were greeted with considerable naïveté: President Taft was met by Carey Thomas accompanied by his daughter and the highest student officers, all in cap and gown; Vincente Ibáñez, after the publication of *Four Horsemen of the Apocalypse*, by four students on horseback; Queen Elizabeth of the Belgians was hailed on the library steps by the entire student body shouting in unison, "Rah! rah! rah! the Queen of the Belgians!"

When Duse acted in Philadelphia in 1901 she visited the college, taking tea at the Deanery and walking about the campus. She won Carey Thomas's heart: "Duse entrancing. Very, very attractive and clever and lovable." But Duse herself afterwards confided to her Philadelphia hostesses that she was scandalized by the freedom of the students' life and by their having men as instructors. About that same time, William Butler Yeats paid his first visit to the college, delighting the students and young literary instructors but not sparing the feelings of Carey Thomas as hostess. As was her wont with visiting poets or other speakers, she gave a dinner in his honor to which she invited a number of the faculty, trustees, and "Main Line" worthies. Warmed at first by the satisfaction of seeing a poet who looked and spoke the part, they were amused, then bewildered, then affronted by this gravely dark and lanky young man who talked with arrogant insistence about things beneath their contempt. Turn the conversation as his hostess would, all through dinner and afterwards he persisted in discoursing to this wholly uncomprehending audience on fairies and Celtic magic. The air grew chill with ironic disapproval and then with flat boredom. By the evening's end Carey Thomas was exhausted, torn between laughter and annoyance. To her reproachful question, "Why did you do it, Mr. Yeats?" he replied only, "They needed to hear about fairies." He might have retaliated that she herself had not started the dinner off happily, for when the guests were being served grape juice, the usual beverage at Deanery dinners of that time, she had turned to Mr. Yeats on her right hand: "You, Mr. Yeats," she had said in tones that rang in the ears of her other guests, "*you* may have claret."

The positivist Frederic Harrison, then a vigorous and practical old man of seventy, after speaking at Bryn Mawr in the spring of that same year, published an account of the visit in his *Autobiographic Memoirs*: "I am to dine and sleep," he had written his wife, "at the College—oh! the 700 girls! I am advertised to address them on 'the famous men and women I have known in the last fifty years'—so they will expect me to be a tottery old man. What I am going to say—God knows!" Some days later he continued: "The lecture at the Girls' College was very successful. Miss Thomas, my hostess, a very able woman—do you remember in the Academy last year Sargent's portrait of her, a quiet lady in *black*, one of his best? She lives in an elegant villa in the College grounds. I went off at once, and talked for an hour and a half about all the people I had known. The women quite full of excitement over stories about George Eliot, Ruskin, Tennyson, etc. etc. . . . In the morning she took me all over the College." And he describes with zest his impression of the "elegant" buildings and the "pretty free and easy" life and manners of the students.[4]

Even more important, for he was at that time the literary god, "the master," of many on the campus, were Henry James's two visits in 1905. At once on learning that he was coming to America Carey Thomas had written asking him to speak at the college and offering him the fee of fifty dollars usual in those days. His reply was characteristic, a civil letter with many involutions in which he regretted that he had no speech "up his sleeve" suitable to deliver to young ladies. The crux of the matter was appended as an apparent afterthought: "To be lucid, the honorarium that you offer is not sufficient." The difficulty being overcome, on a mid-January evening in Taylor Hall Henry James spoke on "The Lesson of Balzac," spending a night at the Deanery and "walking about the College grounds for two hours" on the following day. Carey Thomas found him "charming, direct, simple" and was much struck by his "well-balanced judgments." He commended, she said later, the beauty of Pembroke arch.

The faculty and students urged her to ask him to speak at Commencement. On June 7, therefore, he returned to the Deanery. "In a gentle rain," accompanied by Carey Thomas, he walked again about the college, seeming to be "delighted by the buildings"; attended the seniors' garden party, which unfortunately had to be held in one of the residence halls and was crowded and noisy; and, the next day, delivered the commencement address on "The Question of Our Speech," later published in book form. The gymnasium, where the exercises were held, was packed. Although Carey Thomas's own speech, she felt, "went much less well than usual," and the luncheon in the Deanery afterwards was "utterly uneatable," she was satisfied that the day had been memorable in the college annals. Henry James had been received with enthusiasm. Students and faculty alike had been stirred by him. Two days later, again accompanied by Carey Thomas, he repeated the address in Baltimore at the Commencement of the Bryn Mawr School.

3

Whether or not Carey Thomas followed with any consistency the Quaker tradition, which she occasionally urged upon the students, of setting aside a portion of each day for meditation, is to be questioned. The quick constructive thinking now required of her about immediate problems she was apt to do under the stimulus of discussion rather than in quiet intervals reserved for the purpose. Since she was carrying out policies long since formed at least in outline in regard to herself, the college, women—all life, indeed—she had both a mold into which to press impending circumstances and a standard against which to measure their value. Things would fit or would not fit, were to be snapped up whole or in part, followed or discarded or ignored. Steadfast purpose and decisive speed were indispensable; and these, like her temperament itself, lent themselves to seeing the world in black and white as well as to continual activity. Moreover, in her boundless energy, she attacked her pleasures with no less dispatch than her business.

When she gave them rein, her tastes often were oddly unsophisticated. Strong colors and contrasts, adventure, romance enthralled her. She especially delighted in a good story, reading with zest the works of the Duchess or Mrs. Humphrey Ward, E. Phillips Oppenheim or H. G. Wells. It was the libretto hardly less than the music that interested her in her favorite Wagner operas. Above all, she liked to feel herself well informed. Not to be "in the know," not to be acquainted with the latest book or play, with the latest idea or theory regarding intellectual and, increasingly, social and political matters, with the name and deeds of the latest person to come into fame, was to her humiliating—inevitably, perhaps, since the wider her knowledge the better she could fulfill her academic duties as she conceived them. Good, bad, or indifferent, any book or journal or play, any opera or ballet on the face of it interested her. She fell upon them all with equal concentration, "tearing the heart out" of a book, "getting ideas from" a newspaper or impressions of society from "a talky-talky play." Her desire to know what was in them sometimes warped, though it did not kill, her critical sense. If conducive to missing the finer shades, it made the second-, even the third-rate bearable and led to omnivorous consumption.

A pace so quick, so unendurable had her activities been less various, meant that even with these many diversions, added to her manifold academic duties, Carey Thomas had a margin of time to spare. Especially now that Mary Garrett had come to live with her in the Deanery, freeing her of many of the domestic cares which formerly she had borne for herself and Mamie Gwinn, she could throw herself into social and political movements that hitherto she had had neither time nor inclination to take part in. Gradually, as her influence grew, Mary Garrett's way of life took precedence in the Deanery. It was on an elaborate scale, far more so than that of Carey Thomas and Mamie Gwinn, since she was the daughter of a railway magnate and even at this time, in early middle age, lived something of a valetudinarian's life. She was able to provide the financial backing and the fitting domestic hierarchy to support it without strain on Carey Thomas.

On coming to live at the Deanery Mary Garrett transferred there many of the Garrett treasures—silver, linen, works of art —from 202 Monument Street in Baltimore. And the Deanery itself was enlarged for the second time, in fact almost wholly re-

built. Its most important changes were the large wing thrown out
to the west of the main house and, especially, the great room
built where Mamie Gwinn's little study had been, opposite Carey
Thomas's "blue study." This room, with its large fireplace and
rectangular bays of leaded, small-paned windows, its panelings,
its timbered ceiling and tiled floor, was designed in some part
after a room much admired by Carey Thomas in Haddon Hall
and is now known as "the Dorothy Vernon room." Although
the ceiling, covered between the great beams with beaten copper
brought from India, was not high, the room had an air of spacious-
ness; and people looked well in it.

In fact, this sprawling new Deanery, awkward as its brown
shingled exterior appeared before vines and shrubs cloaked it,
and impractical as it was within because of the long distances to be
traveled, proved admirable for the sort of entertaining for which
it had been planned. And, in the singleness of its decorative taste,
it was beautiful. Taken separately, the combination of styles in
its furniture—carved chests and chairs and tables from India or
China or Italy cheek by jowl with those painted to match the
woodwork or older turned mahogany—might appear a hodge-
podge; the Tiffany stenciling of cornices and ceilings and even
floors might seem nightmare inducing; the multitude of Tiffany
and Venetian glass ornaments and bronze replicas of museum
pieces, an ornate clutter; the numberless sepia photographs in
stained wooden frames of famous places or works of art, de-
pressingly cultural.[5] Yet everything was pulled together, given a
kind of harmony and life, by the vision of the Deanery's creator.

It was unmistakably Carey Thomas who had envisaged the
Deanery with an imagination almost Renaissance in its exuberant
love of color, splendor, elaboration, but thinned by the sight-seer's
eclecticism and by early training as well as by the taste of the day
—the American taste for Tiffany irrelevancies and gingerbread,
toned down by a remote uncomprehending admiration for the
work of William Morris. Mary Garrett, swept away as she
almost always was by Carey Thomas's enthusiasm, aided and
abetted her plans in every way, not least in providing the money
with which to carry them out. The house as a whole possessed
the fairy-tale quality of an extravagant dream that is character-

istic of Carey Thomas's vivid though immature imagination and seemed astonishingly alive with life derived from her.

The Deanery garden laid out at this same time, on the other hand, cast its own spell. Green throughout the year, enclosed by a wall and high hedge, it followed the fall of the land closely, its different levels outlined here by an ivy-bordered bank, there by flowering shrubs. Though gradually Carey Thomas brought ornaments to it from the ends of the earth—dogs of Fo from China, Byzantine birds and Venetian lions to guard the steps, Persian tiles for the wall fountains, bronze figures from Italy for the rim of the pool, wicker chairs and taborets from India and Singapore, and though she set an electric bell in the pine tree with which to summon tea or after-dinner coffee, she exercised in its decoration a restraint unknown in the furnishing of the house itself. Sensitive, as always, to atmosphere, she subordinated her taste to the peculiar magic of the garden. It seemed a secluded, intimate, and charming place.[6]

The plans for all this reconstruction were discussed for a number of years before building began.[7] Carey Thomas, eager as she was for the imagined grandeurs of the Deanery to materialize, was reluctant to destroy the old house. In preparation for radical change she had the latter photographed from top to bottom in 1904. It was associated with many people and events dear to her, most poignantly with Mamie Gwinn and with her father and Uncle James Whitall, Dr. Rhoads and Francis T. King, as well as with various memorable meetings and parties—recently with the marriage in 1903 of her sister Helen to Simon Flexner, the distinguished first director of the Rockefeller Institute for Medical Research. It had been necessary, also, as the Deanery belonged to the college, to obtain the consent of the Board of Trustees before changes in it could be made.

The remodeling, finally begun in 1907, took far longer than was expected and cost more than the estimated fifty thousand dollars. "Well under way" in September of that year, it was still only under way a year later. To hasten progress, Carey Thomas and Mary Garrett, who had been staying in Dolgelly, another college house in Merion Avenue, until the worst should be over, moved into the Deanery, torn up and uncomfortable though it still was. Two months afterwards, when it at last seemed to be nearing completion, the contractor in a huff "destroyed everything, even the soapstone hearths of fireplaces. He chipped up every bit of moulding," wrote Carey Thomas despairingly in her journal, "so that it all had to be made and stained over again." The house seemed hardly habitable; the garden, too, was troublesome: banks washed away, turf refused to grow, shrubs died. Carey Thomas and Mary Garrett stuck it out as best they could in the midst of "terrible confusion."

The new Deanery provided Carey Thomas with an added amusement, allowing her to indulge her innate love, long suppressed by the combined pressure of her own and Mamie Gwinn's ideals and lack of money, for amassing material possessions. Not that Mary Garrett encouraged lavishness, but she came of people to whom collecting was habitual. She knew something of both crafts and arts and could afford to indulge her interest in them; and the empty spaces of the Deanery cried out for more and yet more decoration.

Mary Garrett, however, though she could at times spend freely, was almost always frugal in personal matters. The Garrett fortune was not to be carelessly squandered; it carried with it high philanthropic responsibility. She gave large sums to causes that were to her satisfaction demonstrably worthy, but her own petty expenditures she totted up daily with unbelievable exactitude and saw to it that Carey Thomas did likewise, often keeping Carey Thomas's accounts for her, as is shown by the sporadic appearance of neat entries in copperplate hand among the otherwise untidy jottings of Carey Thomas's splashing fist. Mary Garrett had a natural aptitude for finance and, carefully trained from infancy, not only was an astute businesswoman but enjoyed balancing up the most insignificant as well as the most complicated accounts. Carey Thomas, on the contrary, chary as perforce she had been in spending money, had never been systematic in figuring debits and credits. Even the weight of Mary Garrett's displeasure, added to her own anxiety to do the correct thing, could not make her follow such orderly procedure.

Many were the agitated evenings they spent during their summer travels, straightening out their respective—and especially

Carey Thomas's—records of petty cash. In the winters at the Deanery the matter was less to the fore since secretaries took over for them both. In the winter, too, Carey Thomas escaped another pitfall: in Bryn Mawr the temptations to spend money were infinitesimal; abroad, they were vast. Besides, it rather went to her head to see Mary Garrett buy two dozen pairs of white kid gloves and three dozen pairs of stockings all at once at the Bon Marché. In the end, they would be needed and they came cheaper by the dozen: a doctrine useful to the very rich but unsuitable for Carey Thomas, as Mary Garrett pointed out. Oddly enough, however, Mary Garrett abetted Carey Thomas in her tendency to buy Christmas gifts in quantity for her family, especially from Liberty in London—twenty-seven scarves, or four cases of "silver and stone spoons," or seven leather blotting pads, or eight shawls, all at once; paperweights, flashlights, clocks, umbrellas, handbags by sixes and twelves—and souvenir spoons to be used as prizes for Bryn Mawr school and college girls, and baubles such as the "silver and enamel headdress" from Chipping Campden to be bestowed upon the college May Queen.

The embellishment of the college, too, concerned them both. After lunching at Oxford with her cousin Logan and two friends and listening to them discuss "Henry James, spiritualism, and American corruption," Carey Thomas walked about the colleges —"shocked to find them looking so shabby"—in order to satisfy herself that none of them had nail-studded doors which should be copied in Bryn Mawr's library. At Nuremberg, she and Mary Garrett found in the Germanische Museum a fourteenth-century wall fountainhead, a woman's face crowned with oak leaves, that they had copied in bronze for the Deanery garden, as well as bronze tablets which, though probably intended for tombs, would do nicely as models for memorial tablets in the cloisters. In Venice they "decided to copy the grotesques on the columns outside the Ducal Palace for gargoyles in the Library—just the right size." Three years later, however, on a visit to Chipping Campden, to see the co-operative arts and crafts shops there, they met Alec Miller, whose work struck them as so delightful that they arranged for him to carve the "gargoyles"—the corbel heads in the cloisters.

In general, life with Mary Garrett was more placid than that with Mamie Gwinn. By temperament and discipline she was incapable of the hysterical tempests in which Mamie Gwinn had indulged. The respective provinces, also, of Mary Garrett and Carey Thomas were separate and well defined: in financial and social matters, even in matters of art, Carey Thomas deferred to Mary Garrett; academic and intellectual matters were wholly her own. In whatever concerned the organization and the publicizing of their various joint schemes, also, Carey Thomas took the lead, for Mary Garrett, if not shy like Mamie Gwinn, was self-effacing. She had a sense of social obligation, too, and was hospitable, not least toward Carey Thomas's family. There was more coming and going at the Deanery during these years and a good deal of entertaining in spite of the fact that Mary Garrett's frequent illnesses slowed the pace of their lives, especially of their summer travels.

Many weeks of each summer were devoted to taking the cure at Marienbad or other watering places as well as, regularly each August after 1905, at Kaltenleutgeben near Vienna. To be sure, Carey Thomas usually contracted evil ailments at these cures—a case of ringworm annually at Kaltenleutgeben—and Mary Garrett found her ills were far more numerous than she had suspected. Nevertheless, they were entertained by the fuss of treatments. And if the remainder of their holidays lacked for Carey Thomas the tang of her youthful journeys, they were still full of interest and much more comfortable. There were, of course, a certain number of accidents: a runaway during a drive from Innsbruck when "the powerful brute" of a horse bolted, frightening the driver to helplessness, and was only stopped by Carey Thomas herself managing to turn the brake on the carriage wheel; and various mishaps owing to Mary Garrett's susceptibility to blood poisoning, as when in Naples the doctor treated her arms, which had been badly bitten by mosquitoes, with alcohol and tight bandages so that they became raw and painful for weeks. And later in Cairo she fell seriously ill. After debating what might give her pleasure, Carey Thomas bought her a small mummy case containing the embalmed body of an infant princess. Intensely sympathetic with her friends in illness or sorrow, Carey Thomas was inclined to cheer them by means that she felt might cheer herself; a method that was sometimes irritating, sometimes ludicrous, almost always endearing. Many years later, longing to comfort another friend who learned of the death of her father while they were traveling together in France, Carey Thomas presented her as she left Paris for America with half a dozen pairs of white kid gloves—and her own, not her friend's, size.

For the most part Carey Thomas and Mary Garrett returned on their travels to places already known to them. In 1911 as tourists in Egypt they found the country such a paradise that their enthusiasm was aroused for English rule, especially since they made out for themselves that the Egyptians are "one of the untrustworthy, untruthful races, totally ignorant, superstitious, and without any intellectual curiosity. Like our negroes," wrote Carey Thomas in the astonishingly long circular letter to her family, "they seem unable to sustain intellectual work": an opinion in line with her later pronouncements such as, "The Arabs have contributed nothing to civilization." In spite of her scorn of Germans, she shared their mistrust of all other than the white races, spending much time, especially after reading the books of Lothrop Stoddard, in fulminating against the Japanese in particular. Nevertheless, Egypt itself, with its temples and tombs, its desert and fertile corn land, and its brilliant colors delighted her; and the Egyptians, "who are a wonderful and unique example of a people preoccupied by providing themselves with immortality," made her "feel that we pay too little attention to our dead." She enjoyed sight-seeing there as she always did, "astonished" to find other tourists "wasting their time on hotel terraces," though she went about it now in the grand style, beyond her means in the old days, issuing from "the best rooms" at Shepheard's or the Mena House or some luxury hotel farther up the Nile to be accompanied by a dragoman "in beautiful blue robes with splendid sashes about his waist" and "trained not to speak unless spoken to."

In Paris, too, she led a very different life from that of earlier days. Her diary still records trips to the Louvre and to smaller galleries; but at the exposition in 1900 she saw on display her monograph on the *Education of Women*, upon which had been bestowed a medal, as well as her own portrait which the Alumnae

Association of the College had commissioned John Singer Sargent to paint in 1898 and which had been awarded the Grand Prix. Though she still went to the Français and other theaters—in 1909 she notes, "Saw Isadora Duncan in Beethoven dances and thought her really objectionable, but very beautiful"—she made many expeditions now, also, to dressmakers and fashionable restaurants. Even London saw her doing things undreamt of heretofore: going to suffrage meetings; attending a swimming meet arranged by Ray Costelloe to make money for the Cause; and, in 1904, accompanying Mary Garrett to sit for her portrait by Sargent.[8] He could not understand Mary Garrett's combination of elegance and primness, and had some difficulty in composing the picture until Carey Thomas found a soft frilled white fichu at Liberty's to put round her shoulders. Caught at the waist with a red rose, it helped the color scheme. With Carey Thomas in her academic gown he had been more successful, especially in painting her fine alert head and her hands, small and ruthless looking, a little talon-like as they curl about the dark arm of the chair.[9]

During the travels of Carey Thomas with Mary Garrett chance meetings with Bryn Mawr students and alumnae became more and more frequent and dinners and luncheons to dignitaries such as she and Mamie Gwinn could not have contemplated. But after 1912, when Mary Garrett's chronic illnesses were diagnosed as being the result of leukemia, their journeys were curtailed, seldom extending beyond England where Carey Thomas was in the habit of visiting for a few days her sister Grace Worthington in her cottage at Fernhurst in Sussex and her Pearsall Smith cousins. Leaving Mary Garrett in London she went up to Oxford to stop with them at Court Place, Iffley, a lovely Georgian house with "enchanting views, especially of Iffley church, and a garden that ran down to the river." The Berensons were there, too, and the Bertrand Russells were living at Bagley Wood where Lucy Donnelly was staying with them. They rowed on the Isis, motored or drove about the countryside, and sat talking in the garden gathered about Aunt Hannah, who now, though she seemed as energetic and full of dry fun as ever, was confined to a Bath chair.

Perhaps partly because Mary Garrett was lonely as well as hospitable, she enjoyed being with Carey Thomas's family. When any of the young relatives were at the college, she often joined Carey Thomas in entertaining them and their friends at the Deanery. She followed the career of young Harold Worthington, whom his aunt was shepherding through Yale, with interest second only to Carey Thomas's own. And at the yearly parties in the Christmas holidays—luncheon and buffet supper to sixteen or forty members of the family—Mary Garrett shared the role of hostess. December 19, 1908, was the date of the great Whitall family gathering when the Berensons and the two Costelloe girls and Grace Worthington and her children were in America and "twelve first cousins, seven husbands and wives of first cousins and twenty children of first cousins were entertained at the Deanery." Together, Carey Thomas and Mary Garrett sent out a card wishing "A Happy New Year to the seventy-two Whitall cousins and to the oldest Whitall of us all, our beloved Aunt Hannah," enclosing a copy of the song that had been sung at the New Year's dinner with the Whitall grandparents in 1876. The song contained a verse about each Whitall grandchild and was sung again by the great-grandchildren at the Deanery in 1908.

By this time Carey Thomas had developed the method of conducting parties that is well remembered by all her guests. Her cousins in England had impressed upon her the fact that general conversation should be the focus of importance and that the hostess should lead it, holding it to the proper standard and permitting no one to be left out. In order to keep the talk at a high level she planned the subject and course of talk beforehand and drew out the opinion of each guest in turn by direct questions: a method which might result in fireworks or boredom. In fact, her dinners and receptions came to be conducted, as her cousin-in-law Bertrand Russell once observed, in the manner of a committee meeting. No matter how coveted the distinction of an invitation to one of them, they were likely to be harassing.

It was not wholly the draftiness of the Deanery—Carey Thomas liked fresh air and open windows—that set her less sophisticated and younger guests shivering. Awaiting their own turn, as the question was put first to one and then another of their fellow guests, their nerves were apt to quiver and their forces to dissipate themselves, particularly since Carey Thomas, becoming interested in the talk, was inclined to fall heavily upon replies with which she disagreed. To be told succinctly, however inaccurately, before an assembled company of dignitaries, in answer to the innocuous remark that African art was of considerable interest, "There is no art in Africa" tended to shatter even steady poise; to reply to some of the larger questions stretched ingenuity as well as knowledge. Perhaps the only adequate answer during a Thanksgiving dinner to "What is your belief about immortality?" was that given by a formidable English lady: "It is a subject unsuitable for discussion at the dinner table." None the less, few people refused an invitation to a party at the Deanery, and few failed to enjoy it at least in retrospect.

Nor is any Bryn Mawr alumna likely to forget the receptions given every year to first one and then another of the college classes: the half-circle of students in the subdued light about the fire in the big room, Carey Thomas in evening dress, eyes brilliant, color high with the effort of leading the talk, seated at its head in a great carved chair; the despair or happy excitement, according to temperament, of awaiting their turn to comment on the subject posed for discussion; the gong ringing at intervals to summon another group to the dining room for refreshments rich and abundant as food at the Deanery always was. The grave ceremony of these occasions stamped them on the minds of the young as being, whether enjoyable or not, memorable, a glimpse of an ordered life full of color and warmth and interest, on a plane higher than that of their own higgledy-piggledy lives in the halls.

4

For many years Mary Garrett had been a wholehearted adherent of women's struggle for equal suffrage. Carey Thomas, too, following the tradition of her family as well as the interests of her friend, had long been sympathetic with the suffragists; their work and her own were parts of the same struggle toward achieving an opportunity in life for women equal to that of men. In the first years of the century a College Equal Suffrage League, modeled on that founded in Massachusetts in 1900 by Maud Wood Park, a graduate of Radcliffe College, had been started at Bryn Mawr, but Carey Thomas was too busy in those early years with academic matters to devote herself zealously to "the Cause." Gradually, as habit eased the pressure of business and a comfortable, equable life gave her greater leisure, she was drawn more fully into the movement. To contribute to women's political efforts, she saw, would be the logical expansion of her endeavors in regard to women's education. It might, on the one hand, increase Bryn Mawr's prestige by making its president better known and, on the other, broaden and freshen her view of the college. She had a lively understanding, also, of the value that the passionate support of a cause has in awakening the young to interests beyond their own little daily concerns.

At the Baltimore convention in 1906 she entered the ranks of the movement's active participants. In this, as in most cases, there was no question of her entering merely the fringes of the movement or of toiling in obscurity. She had become the most eminent woman of her time in her own field of women's education and was recognized as that most coveted asset to any political movement, an effective orator; and the elder statesmen of the national association, Susan B. Anthony and Julia Ward Howe, were her friends—indeed it had been old Mrs. Howe who, while staying with her at the Deanery, first warned her of Mamie Gwinn's defection. Susan B. Anthony Carey Thomas had long admired, saying of her sixteen years later, "She was the Moses that led the women of the United States into the promised land of political freedom. She was the greatest person I have ever known. If she had been born a man with a man's opportunities she, like Abraham Lincoln, would have been recognized as one of the world's great leaders and one of the two greatest Americans."

Her friendship, as well as Mary Garrett's, with Miss Anthony had begun in 1902 when the latter visited the college,[10] and they had seen a good deal of her as well as of other suffrage leaders at the International Suffrage Convention at Berlin in 1904. But Carey Thomas had been too troubled then by her final parting from Mamie Gwinn, whose wedding to Alfred Hodder was taking place at the very moment of the congress in Berlin, to feel much more than a perfunctory interest in the suffrage movement. In the following year, she and Mary Garrett determined to respond to the best of their ability to Miss Anthony's plea, made during a second visit to Bryn Mawr, to make the convention to be held in 1906 in Baltimore a success in that stronghold of conservatism. Mary Garrett opened her house in Baltimore, asking Miss Anthony and Mrs. Howe and other suffragist leaders to stay there with her and Carey Thomas, and gave a series of entertainments —a formal lunch and dinner daily to Baltimorean dignitaries and national and state leaders of the movement, and two large receptions—to add to the social luster of the occasion. And Carey Thomas initiated and managed "the College Evening," presided over by the president of the Johns Hopkins University. One of the three great meetings of the congress to which Susan B. Anthony was able to go, it was among the most successful since, as Miss Anthony said, it typified the intellectual triumph of the cause. She had fallen ill in Baltimore—she was eighty-six and frail. Carey Thomas and Mary Garrett saw to it, as daughters might have done she said, that every care and attention was given her.

Early in the convention week Dr. Anna Howard Shaw, the president of the association, had explained to Carey Thomas and Mary Garrett the financial difficulties of the association; and in reply to their question as to the greatest service that could be rendered to the movement, Susan B. Anthony had said: the gift of a large sum of money which she herself had hoped to raise. They at once concocted a scheme to solicit from a number of women, unable like themselves to give their whole time to active work in the association, contributions to a "guarantee fund" of twelve thousand dollars for five years. When, shortly after the convention, Miss Anthony died, the fund was renamed "the Susan B. Anthony Memorial Fund" and a committee formed by Carey Thomas and Mary Garrett to raise the necessary money apart from Miss Anthony's residual estate—about forty-five hundred dollars—which she had requested in her will be applied to this fund. By early May the sum had been raised; and the fund was continued until 1912.

Most of Carey Thomas's early suffrage work, naturally, was done in connection with the colleges, in speaking either at the College Evenings of the national association or at meetings of the National College Equal Suffrage League founded in 1908 with her as its first president. Though she delivered many suffrage speeches that were greeted with acclaim, the most important was "A New Fashioned Argument for Woman Suffrage" made first at the College Evening of the national association in Buffalo in October, 1908, repeated at three other suffrage meetings and at the Bryn Mawr Club of New York in April of the following year when one distinguished guest and speaker pronounced it "the most masterly address he had ever heard" and another said that he had "followed every word with emotion and sympathy and thought it splendid." So seriously effective, as well as entertaining, was the speech that the Equal Franchise Society of Pennsylvania in 1909 and, two years later, the National College Equal Suffrage League printed and distributed it.

The old arguments based on justice and "no taxation without representation," said Carey Thomas in this address, were losing their appeal. From the students of Bryn Mawr she had learned that interest lay less in theory and more in practical means of protecting women from unnecessary and unjust hardships. Women could not secure protection without the ballot, nor could they help the human race—so much in need of help—to "right the terrible wrongs of the present social system." With characteristic ardor she replied to the question, Is it good for women to work after marriage?: "The question is simply and solely this, is it not better for these myriads of unborn children to have married working mothers, than to have no mothers at all?"[11] Point by point, she took up and answered the antisuffrage reasoning, supporting her replies with conclusive statistics and illustrations, often reducing to absurdity her opponents' arguments: "If women are really not intelligent enough to know whether they wish pure or foul food and water, clean or filthy streets, good or bad schools, honest or dishonest laws, judges, policies . . . then in heaven's name let us veil women's faces and bind up their feet again and return them to the harem; and if they as mothers are not intelligent enough for us to regard and register their opinion in matters of such primary importance to themselves and their children, then they are wholly unfit to bring up their sons to be voters." The only true objection to woman suffrage, she concluded, is that women's enfranchisement is "the symbol of a stupendous social revolution and we are frightened before it."

By 1909, Carey Thomas had become chairman of the Committee on Publication of the National College Equal Suffrage League as well as its president; Mary Garrett was chairman of its Finance Committee. Carey Thomas set about organizing chapters in Philadelphia and Baltimore and making out a constitution for the national league. She was still hard at work for it in 1917, when as president of its Executive Committee she sent out in January a manifesto, addressed in particular to the graduates of sixteen colleges, pleading for five thousand dollars to be raised by the end of May in order to meet necessary expenses. Somewhat later in the same year, however, at its annual meeting held at the convention of the National American Woman Suffrage Association, the league voted to disband since its objects had been accomplished— its debts, amounting to about six and a half thousand dollars, were paid off by its president, still Carey Thomas. The subject of woman suffrage, in 1908 when the League was started, could hardly be mentioned in gatherings of college students and was forbidden at the annual convention of the Association of Collegiate Alumnae; in 1917, that same association had not only reaffirmed its belief in woman's suffrage but urged its members to work for the federal amendment.

Long since, Carey Thomas had been drawn beyond the college field, into intensive work for the National American Woman Suffrage Association. When the association convened at Chicago, in 1910, she was a moving force in managing the old conservative bloc, which, jealous of the lively appeal of the more liberal element and alarmed by Jane Addams's espousal of the new Progressive party in presidential politics, threatened to create an open split in the councils of the association. Carey Thomas herself, needless to say, sympathized with the liberals in the suffrage association as well as with the Progressive party. She wrote sadly to Jane Addams that, though she had spoken eloquently to the students of Bryn Mawr in favor of Roosevelt, they had voted, in their dummy presidential election, "two to one for Wilson—and Roosevelt only won over Taft by four votes."

The following year she took part in the convention of the

association at Louisville leading, with Dr. Anna E. Blount of Chicago, a conference on the proper function of the national association, acting as toastmistress at a luncheon for college and professional women, and presiding over the College Women's Evening at which she spoke on "What Woman Suffrage Means to College Women." On the return journey to Bryn Mawr she stopped at Cincinnati, attending a street suffrage meeting and speaking at a luncheon given by the College Equal Suffrage League of Cincinnati. And in March, 1912, when the national convention met in Philadelphia its national board convened in Bryn Mawr at the Deanery. Carey Thomas was by this time deep in the policies of the association, countering the machinations of difficult members and helping to plan campaigns. As chairman of the Ways and Means Committee, she prepared and sent out in 1913 a comprehensive plea for the fifteen thousand dollars needed at once by the association—"And it could use twice fifteen thousand. . . . The sun of equal suffrage," she explained in closing, "is above the horizon and suffragists everywhere must redouble their efforts until it is full day."

By the next year, 1914, Mary Garrett's long illness had become critical and Carey Thomas took less and less part in the counsels of the association. Nevertheless, at the great meeting in Philadelphia in 1915 in honor of Anna Howard Shaw, who, resigning the presidency, was made honorary president with a seat on the governing board, she took a leading part both in the somewhat rococo ceremonies themselves and in announcing that an annuity had been raised which would give Miss Shaw an income of thirty-two hundred dollars a year as long as she lived, "in order," said Carey Thomas, turning to present the basic fund of thirty thousand dollars to Miss Shaw, "that you may work without stopping to think of finances. . . . Every mill in the thirty thousand represents a heart you have won or a mind you have converted to woman suffrage."

For Miss Shaw's sake alone, probably, Carey Thomas attended this convention since Mary Garrett was very ill. On April 3, 1915, she died. Carey Thomas had devoted the last months to her, lavished the tenderest care upon her. Everything had been done that could be done: doctors of the Johns Hopkins Hospital had been called in, consultations had taken place with scientists of the Rockefeller Institute for Medical Research. Prepared as Carey Thomas was for the blow, courage failed her. She was desolate. The fact that Mary Garrett had left her almost her entire property comforted her not at all. She sank into bleak despair from which nothing appeared to rouse her. Even those who most admired and loved her found no way to bring her back to a sense of reality and could only regret her neglect of all the important interests to whose welfare she seemed indispensable. Then one day an acquaintance, meeting her by chance in Philadelphia and stirred to sudden impatience by her melancholy aspect, remonstrated frankly: it was not worthy of her to sink into herself, to neglect her duties, and to go about depressing others by her grief. With that extraordinary flash of understanding with which Carey Thomas accepted unpalatable truths when faced with them, and that startlingly quick action upon acceptance, she pulled herself together and began, at least outwardly, to carry on existence as before, bearing as she might her own burden of loneliness. Many years later she wrote to an old student of hers whose husband had died that after Mary Garrett's death, "I never let myself be a moment without a book. I did not dare. And in time, wonderful, incredible as it seems—life comes back and peace and even joy in life. . . . Travel is a help in filling one's thoughts and in tiring one out physically." She seemed at the time, however, to find her anodyne in turning back again to work for the college and for the suffrage cause.

Perhaps the person most closely associated in Carey Thomas's mind with Mary Garrett at the time of her death was Anna Howard Shaw, with whom in the course of their suffrage work since 1906 they had become firm friends. They had exchanged many visits, Miss Shaw had often spoken at Bryn Mawr, and in 1910, when Carey Thomas and Mary Garrett set off for Norway, she had sailed with them as far as England, writing with somewhat awed admiration of Carey Thomas's efficiency in making them all comfortable aboard ship, procuring them the best table in the dining room and chairs in the most sheltered spot on deck. Miss Shaw possessed something of the downright common sense and incorruptible honesty that Carey Thomas admired and loved in her aunt Hannah; and besides being an accredited minister of the Methodist Church, she, like Hannah Smith, was an evangelist as well as a feminist. Perhaps, too, the fact that she had been born in England impressed Carey Thomas; certainly, her possession of a degree as Doctor of Medicine carried weight.

With their growing friendship Carey Thomas's admiration for Miss Shaw had become almost unbounded. In her need of companionship she now turned to her frequently—or as frequently as possible in their two busy lives—and the more easily since Miss Shaw lived at Moylan within short motoring distance of Bryn Mawr. She had been ill with pneumonia at the time of Mary Garrett's death and unable to travel to Bryn Mawr. But, in May of the following year, she attended a meeting of the Suffrage League there and was the first person to occupy, since Mary Garrett's death, her room. Sometimes they made expeditions together, occasionally driving in Carey Thomas's car to Atlantic City. On one such trip Carey Thomas asked Helen Taft, who had lately been appointed dean of the college, to accompany them to the Hotel Marlborough-Blenheim where, she said, "we always go when I take my nephew Harold Worthington to Atlantic City." Arriving at the hotel at about three-thirty, she asked a flunky in gold lace to direct them to the grill: "It's down there, lady, but you can't go there without a man." Knowing her distinguished companions' feminist sensibilities, Helen Taft braced herself for combat. But the two dignified, stocky figures, in their long skirts and flat-heeled shoes, turned quietly away. "That," observed Carey Thomas, "is because they are afraid we may be prostitutes." "Really, Miss Thomas," cried Helen Taft, aghast, "I think they ought to be able to tell the difference." "No," said the Reverend Anna Howard Shaw, "it is very difficult to distinguish."

In 1919 Miss Shaw accepted Carey Thomas's invitation to travel with her as her guest that summer in Spain. But the struggle to persuade the United States to enter the League of Nations had begun and ex-President Taft and President Lowell of Harvard asked Anna Howard Shaw to go on a speaking tour to arouse public opinion in favor of the League. The Spanish trip had to be abandoned—perhaps fortunately, since Miss Shaw fell ill shortly after the tour began. She never fully recovered and soon after-

wards died. Many years later a memorial tablet designed by Paul
Manship was set in the wall of the cloisters of the library in
Miss Shaw's honor. Its unveiling in November, 1934, was one of
the last formal occasions in which Carey Thomas took part at
the college.

As she suspected might happen, the suffrage work had widened
Carey Thomas's interests. Though in her youth, in her austere
pursuit of academic learning, she felt a certain impatience of her
mother's preoccupation with alleviating the hardships of less fortunate women, gradually, under Mary Garrett's influence and the
enlightening knowledge gained in suffrage work, she herself
became interested in social questions. The most concrete evidence
of this new concern was the founding of the Carola Woerishoffer
Department at Bryn Mawr College in 1915.

Emma Carola Woerishoffer, the granddaughter of Anna Otten-
dorfer, who with her husband had started the liberal *New Yorker
Staats Zeitung*, had devoted herself after being graduated from
Bryn Mawr in 1907 to social work. She had lost her life in a
motor accident in 1911 while inspecting labor camps as a special
investigator for the Bureau of Industries and Immigration of
New York and in her will left Bryn Mawr College seven hundred
and fifty thousand dollars. The trustees established this sum as
the Carola Woerishoffer Endowment Fund, of which only the
income was to be spent. For two years the income from the fund
accumulated in the general expectation that eventually the directors would allocate it to the already established Department of
Economics.

Suddenly, early in 1915, to their surprise, the faculty of the
college learned that the directors, upon Carey Thomas's advice,
had resolved to use the fund for setting up a new department, the
Carola Woerishoffer Graduate Department of Social Economy
and Social Research, "in order to afford post-graduate women
students an opportunity to obtain preparation for work in social
economy, as nearly as possible of the academic standard of the
other graduate departments." They also established two relatively
large fellowships in social research. The school was to train its
students by means of field work as well as academic instruction
and was to exist quite apart from the Department of Economics

of the college, its separation from the purely academic departments being further emphasized by awarding to its graduates a certificate of accomplishment rather than the usual college diploma.

Great was the consternation among the faculty and the graduates and friends of the college, who upheld Bryn Mawr first and foremost as a college of liberal arts, at the foundation in its midst of a semiprofessional school. For many years the schism was wide, and perhaps never healed, between the new school and the older wholly academic departments; and the bitterness felt on this count never entirely ceased to smart. Nevertheless the directors, under the fire of Carey Thomas's enthusiasm, opened the school in the autumn of 1915 with Professor Susan M. Kingsbury as its director. And with their support the Carola Woerishoffer Department continued to flourish, training many useful graduates and bringing many persons of interest in social work and politics to the college. At the time of its foundation there were only five independent schools for social workers in existence in the United States and it was the first school of advanced teaching in social economy and research to be established as an organic part of any college or university in the country. This pioneering gesture of Carey Thomas's did much to give the study of social economy and research academic standing and to make of social work a serious and honored profession, removing the stigma previously often attached to it of being work done in more or less haphazard fashion by untrained volunteers.

This period in Carey Thomas's life, in fact, was one in which the creative energy of her early years reasserted itself. Four years before the founding of the Carola Woerishoffer school she had drawn the college into another venture which also bore upon professional training, though perhaps more legitimately since Bryn Mawr College had been founded by Dr. Taylor largely to train women to be teachers—a Department of Education and, in connection with it, a secondary school. No primary department was started until 1919. The Phoebe Anna Thorne Open Air Model School was to be, not a training school for teachers, but an observation school, "a laboratory experiment in modern methods of teaching."

When the school opened in 1913 it incorporated the best

methods then known, and the most progressive, in regard to the
equipment, administration, and teaching of a secondary school.
It was intended to "demonstrate in a practical way that by such
methods enough time might be saved to teach the children both
the fundamental studies"—for each pupil was to be prepared to
pass the matriculation examinations of Bryn Mawr College—
"and the other so-called accomplishments which add to the interest
and pleasure of life." To read its prospectus and the contemporary
accounts of those who visited it is to read of a school in Utopia.
It was a counsel of perfection brought into being and, as such,
bearing the sign manual of Carey Thomas.

Recognizing the fact that education should be all of a piece as
well as that secondary and college education were inseparably
allied, Carey Thomas interested herself deeply in the scheme and
worked closely in fostering it with Mathilde Castro, its director, a
disciple of John Dewey and professor of education in the newly
established department of the college. The best progressive teaching seemed to be carried on in the open air and, as Carey Thomas
had recently traveled in Japan, it occurred to her that pagodas,
such as those of the Geisha School in Tokyo, might be built with
sliding walls which would open in order to permit the teaching to
take place virtually out of doors. Erected on the land opposite
Pembroke between the Students' Inn and the old stone houses,
Dolgelly and Cartref, where the Department of Education was
housed and the school administration might be managed, they
would look charming. Never having lost her youthful pleasure in
paraphernalia, the arrangements necessary to keep the children
warm—the hoods and extra coats and boots, or "esquimaux
suits"; and the sleeping bags, blankets and cots for periods
of rest—delighted her. She liked, too, the comprehensive nature
of the school's program and of its various departments: the
Music Department, for instance, directed by the first teacher
to come to America from the Jacques Dalcroze School of Rhythmic Gymnastics near Dresden, proposed to train each child in the
ability to recognize and reproduce sounds, in the rudiments of
musical composition, and in rhythmic movement, the co-ordina-
tion of ear and muscle.

Since the income from the Phoebe Anna Thorne fund even

plus the tuition fee could not meet the expenses of the school and the college could not afford to assume the debt, Carey Thomas worked out with the financial adviser of the Board of Trustees a plan to vest the business management of the school in "the Phoebe Anna Thorne Model School Association," a corporation of Pennsylvania, in which by buying shares the members contributed to the upkeep of the school. It was an arrangement similar to that which she had inaugurated in connection with Low Buildings and employed again at the time the Students' Inn was turned over to the college, in 1913, by its first promoters, Marion Reilly—Bryn Mawr, 1901—and Martha G. Thomas—Bryn Mawr, 1889.[12] In the end, the school proved too expensive to be maintained and was closed in 1931. But it had already served a purpose in the history of secondary education as a testing ground of methods. The astonishing thing was that it should have been possible to carry out for so long so idyllic a scheme; but Carey Thomas often, by the force of her belief in its possibility, achieved what on the face of it seemed impossible.

CHAPTER IX

Presidency Continued; Woman Suffrage and Other Interests

I

IT WOULD be folly to suppose that so successful a career as Carey Thomas's should not meet grave setbacks. So bright a medal must have its obverse side. And, naturally, the sharpest check followed a period of imperious activity on her part and, by chance, at a moment when she was grieved and lonely. It was not, however, her first reverse. She had weathered many minor ones, and an exceedingly serious one in 1906. After twenty years, the reaction against her dominant personality and occasionally high-handed activities first came to a head in the one group in connection with the college strong enough at that time to express itself effectively, the Board of Directors. Little by little Carey Thomas had become sensible of the growing hostility of certain members of the board, and of the faculty and Alumnae Association. "Very blue," she noted in her journal for May, 1906. "Have decided to hold on at College in spite of reactionary movement"— and, in opposition, she unconsciously permitted herself to take measures more and more openly despotic. Rumors and circumstantial stories that reached the directors concerning her autocratic methods took on for them fresh color from their own experience of her behavior during the building of the library, which many of them thought obstinate, and a few, even unscrupulous. An able letter written in 1906 by an instructor dropped from the English Department, accusing Carey Thomas of what amounted to dishonesty, brought their dissatisfaction, and especially that of their treasurer, who was antipathetic to her at best, to a climax. In response to his request, the Board of Directors appointed a committee to investigate all the charges brought against Carey Thomas in the performance of her duties and in relation to the financial condition of the college.

By mid-October the committee had amassed a great number of tales—both offered and solicited—particularly from the upholders of two students who had been dropped from the college and whose cases were thought by their adherents to have been unfairly dealt with, owing to the president's influence. Carey Thomas's request for a chance to answer the charges of the report before it was read to the board was refused. In fact, such a hornet's nest had been stirred up that almost everyone connected with Bryn Mawr had heard the broader outlines of the charges before they reached Carey Thomas herself. In most cases the accusations brought against her were ill founded; in others it was understandable why those who made them, not knowing all the circumstances, should have believed her to be "untruthful" and "unscrupulous." One trustee, she recorded, said that "the charges were of so definite a nature he feared I could not clear myself"; another, that "he had almost been made to believe in my untruthful character." After reading the report the Board of Directors refused, so serious were the allegations, to consider it until the documentary evidence had been submitted to Carey Thomas for refutation.

Meetings between Carey Thomas and three of the trustees followed and long talks with other trustees. Seldom pausing to consider how her precipitate actions, taken, she believed, for the sake of Bryn Mawr, might appear to others, she was shocked, for she set "truthfulness and sincerity above all other virtues"; and she was alarmed, lest her "character for truth and honesty" be taken away. She wrote at once to various alumnae and members, past and present, of the faculty and staff, asking if they believed the accusations to be well founded and urging them "for the good of the College" to reply frankly. This most of them did, pointing out, sometimes, actions that seemed capable of unfavorable interpretation but, for the most part, vindicating her on particular charges and always on the inclusive charge of working for her own good rather than for that of the college. At the meeting of the board at which, finally, she was permitted to answer the charges, she pleaded her own cause with such strong supporting evidence and sincere feeling—unprecedentedly, she broke down once—that the directors dismissed the case. They refused only to expunge the record of it from their minutes as she begged them to do.

Convinced that the case had been rightly dismissed, believing that Carey Thomas had learned a lesson from it, and having expressed their fears and resentments, the directors were ready again to uphold her. And with their support and their willingness to turn a slightly deaf ear to further complaints, her rule over the college returned to its normal routine. She herself, with courage and an exceptional power to weigh all in the balance, carried on her life proudly, outwardly ignoring her humiliation and her knowledge of both what had been said of her and the harm it had done her reputation.

For nearly ten years the college prospered, celebrating during that time its twenty-fifth anniversary on October 21 and 22, 1910. After the performance of "Lantern Night" in the library cloisters, a dinner was given in the gymnasium over which Carey Thomas presided, introducing sixteen speakers for five-minute addresses on the subject of "liberal *versus* vocational college training." The next morning a series of round-table discussions was held in Taylor Hall followed by a luncheon in the Deanery; and in the afternoon the academic exercises took place in the gymnasium. Following the invocation by Professor George A. Barton, ten speakers addressed the assembled college and the visiting dignitaries, extolling both Bryn Mawr and its president. Carey Thomas spoke in conclusion, sketching the history of the college and dwelling, as the occasion permitted, upon its triumphs.

But such happy equilibrium could not last forever. Gradually, in the ensuing ten years, the susceptibility of the directors to irritation returned; gradually, disgruntlement grew in the faculty and, especially, among the alumnae. In 1908 they had persuaded Carey Thomas to appoint a dean, Marion Reilly—the first such appointment since she herself had held that office—in order to reduce the centralization of power in the president's hands. But, on that score, the change had little effect. Four years more and disapproval and bitterness flared and smoldered; there were difficulties between the administration and the Academic Council of the Alumnae and dissatisfaction, on the part of one instructor in particular, made known to former students and friends who brought pressure to bear upon the administration. Disturbances, temporarily ironed out, left scars. The situation wanted only favorable conditions and a pretext to burst into steady flame; and in 1916 those occurred.

The opposition in the Alumnae Association found a leader: one of its own most energetic members. Wife of a former Bryn Mawr professor and known widely in the association as one of its former presidents, she had had unusual opportunity to become acquainted with many aspects of the college, though she was often ignorant of the particular reasons for the actions of the administration and of the proceedings behind the actions. Unsympathetic to Carey Thomas—in broad outlines of character they resembled each other too closely to get on well together—she was unable to understand the president's point of view or even, in many instances, to arrive at the full facts. And the alumnae were given pretext to revolt by the dismissal in 1915-16 of three instructors, friends of the instructor whose case they had already espoused and from the same department.

Simultaneously, the faculty were stirred to anger by the dismissal of an associate professor, friend in particular of an influential professor who took up his cause, inciting other members of the faculty to support it. In mid-March an article appeared in the Philadelphia *Public Ledger*, the information for which had been supplied to his friend the city editor by the professor in question, charging the president of Bryn Mawr College with despotism and unjust dealings with her faculty, and stating that the faculty believed the possibility of such despotism should be obviated by the introduction into the college of some form of faculty government. The fat was in the fire. Faculty and alumnae worked upon each other; the ball of dissatisfaction rolled up to overwhelming dimensions.

Two days before the *Ledger's* first attack was to appear, the professor chiefly responsible for it called on Carey Thomas to say that, if she "would promise to recommend" that the associate professor who had been dismissed "be retained, the whole *Ledger*

attack would be called off." Naturally, Carey Thomas would give
no such promise. The next day she saw the city editor of the
Ledger, who "refused to listen to any statement but said that if
the Associate Professor was retained there would be nothing
printed." Although the paper sent to Carey Thomas the proofs of
a later article—to be followed by a series of articles attacking her
in March and early April, 1916—it took no public notice of the
civil letter with which she thanked the editor for giving her an
opportunity of correcting certain misinformation. She pointed out
that she had herself long felt the faculty should bear some responsibility in the administration of the college—a fact corroborated
by her efforts toward "faculty government" in the early days of
the college—and that recently, after watching sympathetically
the progress of faculty government at Yale and the University
of Pennsylvania, she had brought the matter up before the Board
of Directors of Bryn Mawr and had led a one and a half hour's
discussion of the subject at a meeting in New York of sixteen
trustees of colleges where women study.

Meantime the *Public Ledger* had sent letters of inquiry to
members of the Bryn Mawr faculty and professors at other universities who had served at Bryn Mawr, as well as to leading
alumnae, publishing the replies from them with embellishing
headlines and comment. Although, according to a member of its
staff friendly to Carey Thomas, the paper was "snowed under"
by letters from subscribers protesting against the attack on her,
the staff was forbidden to write anything in her defense. The
attack had resolved itself chiefly into an assault upon her personally. The directors were innocent, either not informed by the
president or misinformed in regard to the college—or, vice versa,
the college was misinformed as to the attitude of the directors.
The faculty were serfs beaten down by a tyrant who, on personal
grounds, worked against them at every turn. Such replies as were
received to the *Ledger's* inquiries make unpleasant reading now,
most of them full of personal bitterness and, often, of frustration.
Of them all only three show disinterested consideration of the
problems; only two, cool judgment. These two point out that such
injustice as may have been wreaked upon the faculty of Bryn
Mawr was no greater, perhaps less great, than that suffered by

the faculties of other institutions. They argue, none the less, that, whatever the faults or virtues of the president, such power and responsibility as she held should be vested in no one person: it should be shared by the faculty.

The situation had become hopeless from the point of view of Carey Thomas. That faculty government should be instituted did not alarm her, as is proved by a review of all the documents bearing on the case, including her letters and journals. On the other hand and rightly, she thought it dangerous to institute such a reform as a concession to attack and in the midst of bitterness on all sides. Worst of all, this airing of dirty linen did not only her but the college incalculable harm. Yet the situation could never be straightened out—the separate charges answered fully—without doing the college even greater injury. In an attempt to solve the difficulties, she called a meeting of the full professors of the college and took up with them each case, giving the reasons for each dismissal. But by that time matters were out of hand, judgments were blurred, to such an extent that the professors would not grant even proved immorality of behavior which threatened the college with a public law suit sufficient grounds of dismissal of a member of the faculty.

The report of this meeting that Carey Thomas sent the directors, though too long and repetitive, is a model of good temper and ability to understand opposing points of view. The professors, on their side, wrote her a letter giving their reasons for profound dissatisfaction, asking to be more closely associated with the management of the college and requesting her to send the letter on to the Board of Directors—as she did, enclosing with it a statement of her own "entire sympathy with the general movement" toward faculty government. A committee of five directors was thereupon appointed by the board to confer with the professors. Finally, a plan of government was drawn up for the college curtailing the provinces and duties of the president and increasing those of the faculty. Among other provisions, it arranged for direct communication, under certain conditions, between the faculty and the directors. It outlined, also, the rules of appointment, dismissal, and tenure of office and established the position of the Board of Directors as the final authority on all action taken by the faculty, council, or senate of the college. On May 19, 1916, the plan was approved by the directors, including the president; on May 23, communicated to the faculty, who took action on it. Subsequent action was taken in the following December and January.

On the surface things quieted down. But, however much the College political scene may have improved, however much of a relief the explosion may have been to some of its participants, irreparable damage had been done. The city editor of the *Ledger* was dismissed, chiefly, it was reported, because of the part he had played in the attack. The president of the Board of Directors of the college had resigned because by failing to defend its action in closing its engagement with the associate professor about whom the struggle had started, the board had not stood behind its deputy, the president of the college. Many of the faculty and alumnae felt that, by the justice of their arguments and methods, they had forced through a beneficent plan of government against a tyrant now justly humiliated. And Carey Thomas herself had suffered punishment beyond all proportion to any misdeeds or mistakes with which she may legitimately have been charged. There was no redress for her. It would have been impossible to kill the effect of such calumny as she had borne, even if the charges made against her could have been publicly answered in full. "It was a terrible experience," she wrote seventeen years later, "and I cannot help being still sensitive about even joking references to it."

Reviewing the affair thirty years later, it is not easy to see what other outcome of the situation there could have been. Carey Thomas was the most "human" of human beings and admittedly an autocrat, largely because her extraordinary vitality forced her to take the quickest and most direct action toward a desired end. That the end, in the matter under discussion, happened to be the good of the college made ruthlessness no more palatable. That the inevitable slips and mistakes to which any person is liable and the evasions upon which all busy executives fall back resulted in individual heartburning or even hardship, made them no more easily condoned. That Carey Thomas, both ex officio and owing to her singular ability in collecting it, possessed information unknown in its entirety to others ameliorated her action not at all in the eyes of its subjects and their friends. That again and again, when they were under attack, she stood behind members of the faculty for whom personally she cared little, that repeatedly, in her determination to protect the freedom of thought, speech, methods of teaching of the Bryn Mawr faculty, she was charged by those more conservative than herself with imperiling the good name of the college made the fate of those whom she did not support no less unwelcome. Difficult as it is to sympathize with the hysterical attitude of many of them it is easy enough to understand the point of view of her faculty and alumnae opponents. Undoubtedly they had much of which to complain; undoubtedly the administration of the college was too centralized. Few colleges have escaped agitations similar to those that shook Bryn Mawr in 1906 and 1916; less spectacular they may have been since the persons involved were not of Carey Thomas's stature.

The conclusive vindication of Carey Thomas's rule is, of course, that Bryn Mawr College throve under it and that an extraordinary number of exceptionally able scholars and teachers were willing, even eager, to become and to remain members of its faculty. On the other hand, it is evident that, in principle, faculty government follows the Quaker tradition of Bryn Mawr and was an inevitable development in a college which had long fostered student self-government. Some form of faculty government, moreover, had become imperative in answer to the democratic spirit of the time as well as to offset the natural dissatisfaction with Carey Thomas. Only the method, not the fact, of its accomplishment was to be deplored.

2

After the establishment of the new plan of government of the college, Carey Thomas, her vision cleared by the insight she had gained into human motives and reactions, took up the reins of office again determined for the sake of the college to make the new arrangements work. Though she never forgot the way in which certain members of the faculty whom she had thought her friends and for whom she had done much had turned upon her, she never showed it or in any way used her position, powerful as it still was, to their detriment. She sometimes noted a little dryly

—she was only human—certain failures and difficulties of the new mode of government but she was careful for the good of the college, as well, doubtless, as to sustain her pride, to acclaim publicly its successes. "Never," she said in her opening address to the students in the fall of 1917, "never has our faculty been stronger or more able to help our students to do scholarly work. Our new plan of democratic government which went into effect at the beginning of last year has been a splendid success. We all of us believed in it then but it has justified itself now even beyond our utmost expectations. It is a world movement to associate together in government and control everyone who is working for the good of a college." And, she continued, with perhaps some malice and with even more than her usual determination to see through to its inevitable sequels the accomplished fact, she hoped that the college would associate the students more closely with the teaching of the college—the faculty had already granted students the privilege of conference with them on academic matters.

She never voiced any public disapproval of the form or success of Bryn Mawr's new government until thirteen years after her retirement, nineteen years after its establishment, on the occasion of the fiftieth anniversary of the founding of the college. By that time most of the members of the faculty itself were willing to grant the justice of many of her strictures. They had suffered from numerous responsibilities, a multiplication of committees, a multitude of petty, nagging details. Many of them had come to realize, too, that there are certain advantages in clear-cut opposition and decisive action. Carey Thomas's greatest admirers at the celebration of the fiftieth anniversary may have regretted in her censure the breaking of her long, admirable self-control; her enemies may have recalled their past bitterness. Softened by experience, however, and even more by the occasion and the sight of the old lion returned, shorn of official power but none the less proud and passionate and worldly wise, even those who were averse to her listened to her denunciation with a certain sympathy.

But in June, 1916, the triumphs of 1935 were still far in the future. Though she bore herself with assurance and dignity, admitting no bitterness or hurt, the experiences of the past months inevitably took their toll. Though she in no way neglected the college, in which her interest continued to center—indeed she kept her finger firmly always on its administration—she was less often to be found in her office in Taylor Hall, or absorbed in college affairs. She occupied herself more often with personal concerns. The shock of the attack and all its circumstances had come at a time when she had hardly rallied from the heavy blow of Mary Garrett's death. She missed not only Mary Garrett's companionship but her support and advice, which would have been invaluable while she was under fire. Her brothers and sisters, even her favorites Helen and Harry, had been preoccupied with their own family affairs. Lucy Donnelly, for many years past and until her retirement in 1936 chairman of the English Department of the college, of whom she had grown increasingly fond and whose advice she relied on, had been far away in Japan and China in 1915-16. There had been no one for her to turn to during the time of the attack or immediately afterwards. Henceforth, therefore, she was to value companionship very highly.

Luckily now, since in travel she found an anodyne, she was able not only to make long journeys in the most comfortable fashion but to take her friends with her as her guests. Mary Garrett had made Carey Thomas her residuary legatee. The estate, to be sure, amounted to much less than the great fortune generally believed. Depleted by certain business reverses and by gifts of large sums to good causes during Mary Garrett's lifetime, the property came to somewhat less than five hundred thousand dollars. There was much speculation at the time as to why Mary Garrett had left everything to Carey Thomas, and considerable bitterness on the part of those who thought the fortune should have gone to some member of the Garrett family or to some cause or institution. But the explanation is self-evident: she loved Carey Thomas deeply and was sure that she would spend the fortune in ways of which she herself would approve. If in the end the fortune was dissipated because Carey Thomas continued to live on Mary Garrett's scale although the financial state of the world had changed, it is surprising in view of its comparatively small size that it did as much good of which Mary Garrett would have approved and, through Carey Thomas's generosity, made as many people happy as it did. For many people and certainly for Bryn Mawr the very lavishness with which Carey Thomas lived lent color and richness and ceremony to life.

In the summer after Mary Garrett's death, Carey Thomas voyaged to Japan with her nephew Harold Worthington, of whom she was fond and through whom she felt that she gained an intimate understanding of the young masculine mind and its point of view. The journey left upon him the impression that, had she permitted it, her travels would have been royal progresses, for they were met on the docks in Japan by a delegation of three of four hundred Japanese women led by Miss Tsuda, formerly a student at Bryn Mawr, and wherever they went were welcomed with marked deference. On their way home, stopping in California, he essayed to teach her to drive a car. Mary Garrett had not liked motoring, but after her death Carey Thomas turned to it as a chief means of enjoyment, finding in its speed and hazard relief to pent-up feelings. In spite of her nephew's instructions and the promptings of her chauffeur, she drove by inspiration rather than by skill. As, long ago, she had dashed about Baltimore with her father's horse and carriage and, more recently, about the Bryn Mawr countryside in a dogcart, now she dashed at what seemed a perilous speed in a Ford or Franklin car. Reckless as had been her driving of horses, her driving of a car was more so. Straight and masterful she sat at the wheel, the chauffeur, relegated to the rear, gripping the edge of the seat, apprehensive and unhappy as out of the Deanery driveway, across the campus and through Pembroke arch the car surged, jerking at each change of gear, cutting corners, scattering students from the roadway like frightened rabbits. Her companions clung to the knowledge that she had not yet had a serious accident—she never had one when driving herself, though her car broke down with even more than the usual inexplicable frequency of cars in those days.

In 1918 instead of to South America as they at first planned —South America never caught Carey Thomas's imagination— she went with Lucy Donnelly out West, meeting her car and chauffeur in Denver. Often driving herself, Lucy Donnelly beside her managing the map, the chauffeur as usual on the back seat, she covered a wide territory. The wilder, less inhabited the country, the less good the roads, the more she enjoyed herself. Starting from Casper, Wyoming, at 9 A.M. to go to Thermopolis, losing themselves in the sagebrush of trackless desert, obliged to take their direction by compass, scorched by the sun and wind, and with no food, they arrived by mistake among the oil wells of Salt Creek and had to turn back to Casper, reaching it again, dust covered and hungry, lips cracked and eyes smarting, at 9:30 P.M. Of this day Carey Thomas wrote enthusiastically: "The most beautiful thing we did on the trip. Gorgeous day."

She made many other journeys with Lucy Donnelly—notably in the immediately following years, from Italy westward to Carcassonne and north to Paris in 1920—and saw much of her in the summers in London and Paris. They went to innumerable plays together, attended the Grand Prix at Longchamps and, at the insistence of Carey Thomas, who liked her sight-seeing to be thorough, packed themselves with her sister Grace and cousin Alys into a small fiacre in which they trundled uncomfortably around Paris tracing the sites and relics of its various ramparts. She traveled, too, with her brother Harry and his wife in England and on the Continent and, in 1917, to China and Japan; and with her cousin Logan Pearsall Smith to Italy and Egypt and, in the early spring of 1920, to Syria. In Damascus they were called on by a delegation of "twenty-seven sheites from northern Palestine and Lebanon who were guests of the new King Feisul of Syria" and who wished Carey Thomas and her cousin to tell President Wilson that "they were putting their faith in his fourteen points and wanted to be free too."

Late in April she returned to Italy where Georgiana Goddard King joined her and they journeyed for a month and a half to Constantinople and Greece. While an instructor in the English Department, Georgiana King—Bryn Mawr, 1896—had become interested in art because, she said, of a visit in London to the National Gallery with Lucy Donnelly, who awakened her suddenly to pleasures she had missed. As there was at the moment little prospect of advancement for her in the Department of English, Carey Thomas, encouraging her particular bent, presently made her an instructor in the history of art and, later, when the Department of History of Art broke away in 1913 from that of

Archaeology, its chairman. In time, her gifts fostered by Carey Thomas, she became a recognized authority on Spanish painting and a companion whom for a number of years Carey Thomas found both interesting and enlivening.

In 1919 the college gave Carey Thomas a year's leave of absence —her first absence of such long duration. That summer she went with Helen Taft to England and France and Italy. Helen Taft, distinguished among the students as the daughter of the President of the United States, had not long been at the college before making her own mark on both students and faculty. Carey Thomas had watched her progress with interest, especially because she was one of the few undergraduates who could, and would, hold their own in argument with her. Since 1917, two years after her graduation, when appointed dean of the college—the youngest dean Bryn Mawr had ever boasted—she had won Carey Thomas's admiration by her assured judgment, her integrity of character, and her loyalty. When granted leave of absence Carey Thomas, with the directors' consent, appointed her acting president. All her life Carey Thomas maintained complete confidence in youth. She did not, perhaps, fully realize how heavy a burden she was placing upon so young and, in spite of her two years as dean, relatively inexperienced a woman—doubly heavy since, as substitute, she would be measured by the exacting standards of Carey Thomas herself as well as be obliged to act on her own responsibility. In any case, Carey Thomas's opinion that Helen Taft, however young, could administer the job, however difficult, was justified.

After Helen Taft returned to the United States, Carey Thomas was joined in Paris by her cousin Alys Russell, with whom after two months' motoring in Spain she crossed the Mediterranean to spend November and early December in Morocco and Algeria. She was charmed by the beauty of North Africa and particularly pleased by the difficulties of some of their journeys: on the boat from Tangier to Casablanca she was obliged to "sleep on the floor of the cabin with about ten Moors—not so terrible"; they had to take a police guard with them on their motor trip to Moulay Idris, a holy city in the Zerhoun Mountains where "no European has ever slept"; they drove through snowstorms in the Atlas Mountains and searing heat in the Sahara; and for eight or nine days they made a caravan trip into the desert from Touggourt to Nefta.

She had always imagined the desert, she said later, as "endless stretches of grey sand like the sands of the New Jersey seashore, but our desert was a great tawny ocean rolling from horizon to horizon. When you cross this ocean, as we did, you must go round, or over, these great billows of yellow sand, winding far below in their golden troughs, or climbing over their golden crests. It is indescribably beautiful." Theirs was, to be sure, a caravan de luxe with "one sleeping tent each, with a bed; one dining tent; five camels; four Arabs; one cook; two horses for three men; and two mules and a hot water bath every evening for us." Even so, it was no mean feat for Carey Thomas, at the age of sixty-two, lame and unaccustomed to such exercise, to ride over sand dunes through all sorts of weather for nine days. One night the camels got left behind and they had no food but dates and stale bread and were obliged to sleep under saddle blankets in the open—"very cold and frightfully uncomfortable." Five days later they arrived at Nefta in bright moonlight: "Heavenly view from camp over oasis with red mountains to left and mirage of sea to right." Again and again she remarks in her journal on the beauty of desert mirages, one of a sea, "blue and white water, deep blue islands and palms, more lovely than anything I have seen except the Japanese inland sea."

All these travels, except those in North Africa, were to places known to Carey Thomas and, for that reason, seemed doubly interesting and sometimes dear. Greece, in especial, recalled to her as nothing else could do the ambitions and loves of her youth, inspiring her to write a series of nostalgic poems. And on all these travels she liked to manage things as she had managed them in earlier days. At Nîmes on the motor trip to Carcassonne she appeared at Lucy Donnelly's door dressed for dinner, equipped, as usual, with stick and large velvet bag containing footstool, book, and other paraphernalia and carrying a lighted candle. Behind her stood her maid with another candlestick, which she handed to the astonished Lucy Donnelly. "The dining room here is always very dark, Lucy," said Carey Thomas, "we shall need these to read by." Uninterested in watching the scene about her, she always read at hotel meals and expected the friends who traveled with her to do likewise. Down the great staircase of the newly renovated "modern" hotel went Carey Thomas holding her candle before her and followed by Lucy Donnelly with hers. Met at the door of the dining room, brilliantly lighted with electricity, by an astounded maître d'hôtel, Carey Thomas observed, "This dining room is always dark." And past the gaping guests, down the long room they marched, candles flaming valiantly.

On these journeys, too, she was constantly on the lookout, as she had always been, for suggestions and objects that might be useful at Bryn Mawr. Behind the Capello Mayor in the Cathedral of Avila she found "a lovely renaissance tomb" finished in 1518, of Bishop Fernandez de Madrigal, called El Tostato, by Domenico Sarcelli or by Vasco de la Zazza, which "might serve as a model for my cloister tomb"—she intended to be buried in the cloisters of the Bryn Mawr library. "It could be copied exactly except for the medallion behind the head on which is the adoration of the Magi." The college buildings, she thought, might be carved in low relief as a substitute on the medallion.

From China she brought home not only crateful of exquisite parchment lanterns for evening receptions in the Deanery garden but a startling proposal to hold examinations at Bryn Mawr on the model of the famous Nanking examination school. She proposed to have the students in different courses all take their examinations at the same time in the big reading room of the library, instead of at various hours and in separate classrooms in Taylor Hall. The reading desks, each screened as they were on three sides, would do nicely as substitutes for the individual booths in which Nanking students were imprisoned for days to write their papers. Following the Chinese example, proctors would perambulate the aisles. And to make the sorting of the papers easier, she added an innovation entirely her own: the examinations in each different subject would be written in a book of special color —English in blue, history in pink, and so forth. After a semester of frenzied trial, the new fashion was abandoned.

Most important of all, on the caravan trip in Morocco, as she sat in her camp chair in the desert "watching the sun set and the moon rise while the tents were pitched and the prehistoric camels snarled and groaned as their packs were rolled on the sand," a plan occurred to her of holding during summer months at Bryn Mawr College a school for women workers in industry. The idea of such a school came, doubtless, from her talks with Susan Kingsbury, director of the Carola Woerishoffer Department— as the idea for the Phoebe Anna Thorne Model School had been suggested by Mathilde Castro, chairman of the Department of Education—and had lain in her mind until as she sat brooding in the desert it recurred to her and fell into perspective and she realized what such a project might mean to the advancement of women. Speaking later to the students of the school, she said, "Rejoicing that British women had just been enfranchised and American women would soon be politically free, and wondering what would be the next great social advance . . . suddenly, as in a vision, I saw that out of the hideous world war might come, as a glorious aftermath, international industrial justice and international peace, if your generation only had the courage to work as hard for them as my generation had worked for woman suffrage. I also saw as part of my vision that the coming of equal opportunity for the manual workers of the world might be hastened by utilizing the deep sex sympathy that women now feel for each other before it has had time to grow less. . . . Then with a glow of delight as radiant as the desert sunset I remembered the passionate interest of the Bryn Mawr College students in fairness and justice and the intense sympathy with girls less fortunate than themselves, and I realized that the first steps on the path to the sunrise might well be taken by the college women who, themselves just emerging from the wilderness, know best of all women living under fortunate conditions what it means to be denied access to things of the intellect and spirit."

3

Carey Thomas talked over plans with Alys Russell and, later, with the other friends whom she met on her travels. On her return to Bryn Mawr in the autumn of 1920 she discussed the project with Susan Kingsbury and with Hilda Worthington Smith, who had been dean of the college during her absence and who was already familiar with many of the problems of women workers in industry. At Carey Thomas's request, Susan Kingsbury drafted a plan for the administration, instruction, and financing of a school "to aid in the extension of education by granting the use of certain parts of the college equipment during eight weeks of the summer (mid-June to mid-August) for the instruction of women engaged in industry." Together they went on to Washington to talk with Mary Anderson, chief of the Women's Bureau of the United States Department of Labor, who had herself been a worker in industry. Filled with wonder and excitement, Mary Anderson endorsed the project wholeheartedly, and promised to take part in organizing the school and in finding support for it among other influential women workers. Susan Kingsbury consulted other women leaders in industry, particularly Rose Schneidermann, head of the New York Women's Trade Union League and later president of the national league, finding among them eager concurrence with the scheme. A similar project, in fact, had long been in their minds, though only as a dream: the national convention of the Women's Trade Union League had passed a resolution, as long ago as 1916, that "women's colleges should be asked to open their doors to women workers for a study program."

Meantime, Carey Thomas took up the plan with members of the Bryn Mawr Alumnae Association and faculty and with the Board of Directors, kindling them with such enthusiasm—and not without odds against her—that the final vote of the Alumnae Association at their meeting in December, 1920, was unanimously favorable to the opening of such a school as was that of the directors at their meeting on January 17, 1921. The college faculty, conservative and skeptical as any such academic group is apt to be in regard to educational experiments, also, in the end, voted to approve the plan. Nine workers in industry were invited to Bryn Mawr to form with nine representatives of the college and seven of its alumnae a Joint Administrative Committee, later enlarged to include a number of industrial workers equal to that of the college and alumnae representatives combined.

To the women of this first joint meeting it seemed "like the first day of creation." Seated in a wide semicircle around the great room of the Deanery, they toiled all day, stopping only for lunch, to form a plan for the proposed school. The astonishing flexibility and sympathetic eagerness of the college women, in what was suspected of being the stronghold of intellectual aloofness, to solicit their help toward a common end filled the labor members with ebullient hope; and the intelligence and quick grasp of the problems involved shown by the labor members increased the enthusiasm of the academic women. Nor were the latter least inspired by the sight of Carey Thomas, side by side with Mary Anderson, patiently, skillfully leading the discussion of a program for a new educational institution. Hearing the emphatic tones of the familiar, beautiful voice upholding intellectual standards, accommodating them to fresh circumstances, it seemed to the Bryn Mawr members as if the college itself were being reborn—in a surprising new form. Few of her faculty and alumnae had thought of Carey Thomas as taking so intimate and informed a part in social progress. The detailed plan that emerged that day and from immediately subsequent meetings, though it underwent successive modifications, remained the basis of the school's organization. And the first year began under the leadership of Hilda Worthington Smith, who resigned her position as dean of the College in order to become director of the new school, a position which she held for the following decade until appointed in 1933 to be specialist in workers' education of the Federal Emergency Relief Administration.

The object of the school, according to the original statement made by the Joint Administrative Committee, was "to offer young women of character and ability a fuller education, in order that they may widen their influence in the industrial world, help in the coming social reconstruction, and increase the happiness and usefulness of their own lives. The Summer School shall not be committed to any dogma or theory, but shall conduct its teaching in a broad spirit of impartial inquiry, with absolute freedom of discussion and academic freedom of teaching." Worked out on the basis outlined by the first committee, the curriculum was revised year by year. Its subjects of instruction, carefully co-ordinated in order to press as much as possible into a short time, were economics and English, both required, as was a series of lectures in hygiene, and courses chosen by each student from several given in literature and in history; and, in connection with the program of recreation, informal work in the appreciation of music and singing. In time, courses in art, psychology, and science were added. All were taught by means of small classes, tutorials, and special lectures, and adapted to the particular experience of industrial workers. The students, women between the ages of eighteen and thirty-five, must be workers with the tools of their trade, not supervisors in industry. Since the school was intended to be of national scope and, naturally, few women workers would apply voluntarily for this hitherto unthought of experiment, the students were recruited from all over the country by district committees set up on the basis of the seven districts, later subdivided, of the Bryn Mawr Alumnae Association.[1]

By the end of the first session, the summer school had already proved itself of significance both in the history of adult education and in that of labor relations. "It began a unique development in education," wrote Hilda Smith in 1928, which had in seven years affected "more than eight hundred women workers in this country and is beginning to interest women workers abroad. Certain college alumnae and teachers attribute to the school and their contacts with it fundamental changes in thinking which have reacted on their whole lives. Other educational institutions, as the result of the Bryn Mawr Summer School, are opening their doors for new experiments in new fields of teaching." It was carried on—with the exception of the summer of 1935 at Mount Ivy, New York—at Bryn Mawr until 1939. In that summer it moved to a permanent residence at the estate on the Hudson leased from its former director Hilda Smith. There, constituted as before but with a few more labor representatives on the committee, it could hold winter as well as summer sessions and experiment to meet the changing needs of labor.

It remains a tribute to the directors of the college and its faculty and alumnae that they started and supported the school in the face of dire predictions, even threats of ruin by more conservative-minded and shorter-sighted opponents. To have done so was, of course, in line with the liberal tradition of Bryn Mawr, just as to inspire the school was in line with Carey Thomas's enlightened vision of the progress of women's education—a vision which did not end with the first opening of the school: "If all the colleges in the United States," she observed at its opening for a second year, "would turn over for eight weeks every summer their buildings and equipment . . . to joint committees of education and labor, organized on a fifty-fifty basis like our Bryn Mawr Joint Administrative Committee, the rapid advance towards industrial peace would astonish us all." Not only would a wider range of instruction be achieved but a bond of sympathy would be created between winter and summer students, preparing them "to work together for common ends" and "to direct the course of the coming social readjustment."

Even more important here than such speculations is the fact that the school put into practice in a new field the educational beliefs that Carey Thomas had long held, bringing them into startlingly high relief and vindicating them afresh. It is in connection with the school, in her speech at the opening of its second session on June 14, 1922, a week after her retirement from the presidency of the college, that the most complete and characteristic statement of her educational credo, especially in relation to social movements, is to be found: "We [at Bryn Mawr college] believe in the most liberal possible teaching, in the fearless search for truth, and in entire freedom of discussion and of expression of opinion by teachers and students. We hold it to be the duty of teachers not only to state clearly both sides of controversial subjects but to say without hesitation what their individual opinion is. We think that students have the right to know what their teachers believe but we also believe that students who are properly taught will not accept their teachers' opinions as final, but will realize that such opinions represent one point of view only and that they must make up their own minds for themselves. It is our hope that the teaching you receive here will lead you to think things out for yourselves and to revise your opinions continually.

"We do not know that our present opinions are true. Opinions change from generation to generation, and even from decade to decade. . . . Cut and dried propaganda, undigested masses of applied scientific information, or applied social phenomena taught as unchanging facts have no place in schools or colleges. . . . Our colleges . . . should teach the unchanging principles of scientific and social research on which such theories are based from age to age, and the perpetual growth of knowledge.

"No real social advance can come without a great change in public opinion, but it must be enlightened public opinion. The opinion of people who are not familiar with the history of the world and with the development of thought, who are not trained to think straight, is not worth much. Their opinion can produce no permanent impression. No lasting change can be made by uneducated, ill-informed leaders." It was therefore, she pointed out, the duty of the summer students to study and to gain as much knowledge as they could in order to follow, in the conflict of opposing opinions, a sane course. "You will," she said, "not only be able to think straight yourselves but you will be able to help other people to think straight." But, besides this "altruistic reason for getting an education, there is no greater insurance against unhappiness than to learn to care for reading and study. The pleasure it gives is something that no one can take away from you. Nothing that happens in your personal life, not even great unhappiness, such as may easily come to any one of us at any time, can take away from you the joy of reading, of thinking, of comprehending things better, of satisfying the intellectual curiosity that is one of our strongest cravings. . . .

"Education, even a little of it, will make you more competent to do whatever you want to do, and the more education you have, the more generally competent you will be. The more you know, the more you will wish to know, the more interested you will be in everything and the happier you will be, and consequently the happier you will be able to make everyone around you.

"No country worthy of the name wishes its citizens to be slaves. A nation that does not think is doomed to destruction. All of us in the United States must be thinking as intelligently and as clearly as we can over the many problems that confront us as a nation. After we have taken time to prepare ourselves by study and reading it is our duty to reach the best conclusions we can and then to try to bring about what we think is right. It is not enough to think. We must act. But we must keep our minds continually open to new ideas. We must all of us be willing to revise our opinions until we die."[2]

4

That Carey Thomas stuck to her guns when she continued to think it advisable, no one can doubt. She never ceased to uphold the established subjects, including the old "disciplinary" studies, against newer, more "practical" interlopers in the curriculum of the liberal arts college. One of her most convincing addresses in regard to this controversy is that made to the Association of Collegiate Alumnae in 1917. But she also followed her own precepts and revised her opinions as need appeared. Many years after her retirement, toward the end of her life, she writes despairingly of the difficulty of finding a villa on the French Riviera that has any suitable quarters for the servants: they are all holes in the basement. She had been brought up at a time when servants had been treated in a similar benighted fashion in the United States, and had never thought much about it—the quarters arranged for servants in the Bryn Mawr buildings were deplorable—until public opinion began to veer toward treating them like human beings in need of light and air and comforts like other people and she herself had undergone the enlightening experience of associating, also under the impetus of public interest, with women workers in industry. Then she faced the facts and acted upon them, changing both opinions and actions.

One of her most radical changes, not to culminate until after her retirement from the college, was her gradual swing away from the National American Woman Suffrage Association, which she had supported sincerely and heartily for many years, toward the more radical National Woman's Suffrage party. Possibly at the end of her life she regretted this change, but at the time she suspected that only the National party, the extreme left wing of the suffrage movement in the United States, was likely to be as uncompromising in its feminism as she deemed necessary. Such changes, however, were merely developments of her former attitude, not an about-face. The National party had not been started until 1913 and was in the first instance an offshoot, a committee, of the national association. And her own feminist point of view was becoming more uncompromising as she grew older.

On the face of it, her speech at the round-table discussion which she led at the first meeting of the International Federation of University Women in London in 1920 might seem revolutionary in one who had devoted the better part of her life to building up a separate woman's college. In it she said: "The very first step [that university women should now take] seems to me to be the demand for unqualified, true, out and out coeducation. Only by having the schools and universities coeducational can we ensure the girls of the world receiving a thoroughly good education. There is not enough money in the world to duplicate schools and universities for women, and if we could duplicate them they would soon become less good. It requires endless vigilance to keep women's universities as good as coeducational universities. It would be tragic if now, after coeducation has been tried on a tremendous scale, we university women should accept separate universities for women. We must uncompromisingly refuse an offer so vicious and reactionary as that made by your great University of Cambridge for the establishment of a separate women's university." But such a position did not mean that women should relinquish the separate women's colleges. Although, as she had long ago said at the St. Louis Exposition in 1904, she foresaw a time when the need for them would pass, when women would gain more than they would lose by entering the more fully endowed great universities, such a time would never come to women's advantage if the universities, and the funds supporting them, were split. The education of men would deteriorate; and that of women—always more hardly won—would worsen twofold. Women all over the world must stand together to prevent such a calamity; and this was a chief reason for her helping to organize the new international federation.

Her support of the plan put forward by a number of alumnae, following a suggestion of Caroline Slade's, to introduce the study of the history and theory of music into the curriculum of Bryn Mawr was another such development. She had never opposed music at the college; indeed, she had accorded it perfunctory encouragement, welcoming the Kneisel Quartet when they gave several concerts in the gymnasium and interesting herself in any musical talent that might show itself among the undergraduates—providing it did not interfere with academic work—just as, to perhaps a greater degree owing to her love for the play, she encouraged any dramatic talent among them. Though she knew little of music herself, she respected the opinion of authorities in this as in other fields. And more and more she felt it impossible to be "really cultivated" without some knowledge and appreciation of music. The trustees of Bryn Mawr would support the introduction of music into the college curriculum. The first board, after all, had contemplated including music among the fields of study. Since then music had become increasingly a subject of popular enthusiasm—the first of the arts, as always, to catch public interest—and few Quakers, to whom it presented an outlet less objectionable than the drama, felt any hesitancy in indulging in its appreciation or its practice. Carey Thomas did not, of course, any more than in the history of painting or sculpture, believe in the introduction into the curriculum of any practical training in the art. But, always sensitive to public opinion, she welcomed the chance when it came to open a course in the appreciation of music under the supervision of Thomas Whitney Surette, already known in America as the director of several such courses elsewhere as well as of a summer school of music at Concord. When, in 1921, the alumnae formed a committee to support a Department of Theoretical Music until in 1925 they established its permanent endowment, she encouraged them warmly although taking no active part in the campaign.

She had long since lost her early zest for raising money. Since 1910 when she had been indefatigable in helping the alumnae to collect an endowment fund to increase the salaries of the Bryn Mawr faculty, she had promoted by speaking and writing in their favor other alumnae drives for money—from 1917 to 1920, for instance, the Mary E. Garrett Memorial Fund of somewhat over one hundred thousand dollars for the establishment of a chair of English—and had gathered privately considerable sums in support of this or that project for the college. In these last years of her presidency she spent untold effort, under pressure from the alumnae, to enable the college to contribute a sum equal

—if not exceeding 5 per cent of the teacher's salary—to the amount invested by any of its teaching staff in purchasing annuities or endowment insurance against their retirement from active work. For this purpose, largely owing to Carey Thomas's efforts, a gift of fifty thousand dollars was made to the college by the Carnegie Foundation for the Advancement of Teaching. And she furthered the alumnae under the leadership of Caroline McCormick Slade and while Helen Taft was acting president, when they set out in 1920 to collect the salary endowment fund of two million dollars completed in 1922, one hundred thousand of it to be set aside in "the M. Carey Thomas endowment fund as a testimonial of appreciation of her devoted service to Bryn Mawr College."

In 1920-21 Carey Thomas was much occupied, also, both in helping the efforts of American women to raise a fund to provide a grain of radium for the experiments of Mme. Marie Curie and in making arrangements for Mme. Curie to visit the United States. In connection with this visit Carey Thomas made one of the few entirely disappointing and ill-judged speeches of her career. Appointed to deliver the address of welcome to Mme. Curie at the great meeting held by the American Association of University Women on May 18, 1921, at Carnegie Hall, she discoursed under the heading "The Woman's Program" at what seemed endless length on the way to achieve future progress for women. The audience grew tired and restless. Finally she had to be stopped. It was a unique, misguided attempt to spread the gospel to an uncommonly large and varied audience which she could not resist. Later, Mme Curie visited Philadelphia where, falling ill, she retired to the Deanery with her daughters for a few days' quiet in the mad whirl of speeches and dinners that is America's welcome to visiting "celebrities." Even at Bryn Mawr though too ill to remain at it long, she was given a reception in the Deanery garden so that members of the faculty and students and a few friends of the college could see her.

Carey Thomas's begging—owing in part to the fact that Caroline Slade had shown herself capable of shouldering the burden effectively—indeed, her work for the college in general and her outside speeches, such as the successful "Present Day Problems" made on Founder's Day at Mt. Holyoke in 1921, was less intensive than it had been in earlier years. This lapse, which would have seemed comparatively slight in any other person, was due less to diminishing interest than to the fact that she had lost much time from active work in 1918 by an operation on her foot, and even more in the next year by a recurrence of her old trouble with the scar tissue of her burn for which she was obliged not only to have a serious operation but to spend two months or more in the Johns Hopkins Hospital. These illnesses only temporarily sapped her vitality but, with the following year's sabbatical leave, diverted her energy from the college. Moreover, as her time for retirement approached, she became, not unnaturally, engrossed in the question of her probable successor.

She foresaw that many of the alumnae, even some of the trustees, would wish to put in a man as president. Some of them, she knew, sincerely believed that a man would be more effective. To her indignation, even some of those who supported her, feeling that she, superwoman as they regarded her, was unique, were in favor of appointing a man. And a good many, she was equally well aware, wished a change from the present régime and above all to appoint someone who neither was her friend nor would be influenced by her. No disaster could be greater, she felt, than for Bryn Mawr, which had stood always for the advancement of women's opportunities, to repudiate a woman for its highest office. Not only did she believe that women were the suitable heads of women's institutions, as men were of men's, but that women quite as capable as men could be found for such positions —otherwise women's advance and achievements, for which Bryn Mawr had fought, meant nothing. Not to appoint a woman because none could be found who was satisfactory from every point of view would show singular lack of judgment. She had known most of the presidents of the men's colleges and held no very high opinion of many of them; and yet no one had thought of putting in a first-rate woman to head a man's college in place of a second-rate man. Why should the process be inverted, she asked, or even made worse by appointing a third-rate man in preference to a second-rate woman?

It was a temptation to try to prolong her own term of office as the struggle went on of men against women candidates, of candidates known to be first-rate who would carry on her work as she would like to have it carried on against those suspected by her of less secure standards and abilities. But if the Bryn Mawr regulation, which she had been instrumental in establishing, that members of the faculty must retire at the age of sixty-five, were a good rule, as she believed it to be, then she must stand by it. Besides, she knew that she was tired of office however much she might dread relinquishing it, however interested she was in carrying on all the projects still, she felt, hardly begun. Then, suddenly, at last her successor was appointed, a woman as she had hoped and a woman with high standards of scholarship— Marion Edwards Park. Retirement was actually upon her.

All the celebrations attendant upon the last commencement during her administration went off with an apparent smoothness and happiness almost unprecedented. To her list of honorary degrees were added an LL.D. from the Johns Hopkins University and an LL.D. from Swarthmore College. The sun shone upon the seniors' garden party on the lawn under the trees; the moon shone upon the cloisters, so dear to Carey Thomas's heart, giving many of the audience at the concert of Russian music afterwards, as Norman Hapgood said, "an odd feeling of exclusive poetry." And the commencement exercises themselves on the morning of June 8, 1922, were a triumph of present and retrospective glories. As it wound its way from the library under the maples of senior row and across the green turf in brilliant sunlight to the gymnasium, the long academic procession was a medieval pageant—the yellow and white, scarlet, blue and green of academic hoods, the few vermilion gowns and velvet caps of foreign universities set off by the sober black gowns and mortar boards of American institutions. The speaker of the morning, Dr. William H. Welch, Director of the Johns Hopkins Medical School, reviewed the advances made by Bryn Mawr for women's education owing in greatest part to Carey Thomas's vision and effort and placed the college justly in the vanguard of educational institutions.

But if the commencement speech was gratifying, the dinner given that evening in her honor by the directors, faculty, and alumnae of Bryn Mawr College was even more so. The guests, with the exception of a small group of students from the graduating class, were hardly less distinguished than the speakers. During the dinner, following the introductory speech of the presiding officer, Professor Rufus M. Jones of Haverford College, for many years the colleague of Carey Thomas on the Board of Directors of Bryn Mawr College and then its president, and the spirited presentations by the toastmistress, Mrs. Louise Brownell Saunders—Bryn Mawr, 1893—the fifteen speakers followed one another in rapid, brilliant succession. They had been chosen from among "fathers of Bryn Mawr daughters, husbands of Bryn Mawr wives, present and former Bryn Mawr professors, Bryn Mawr alumnae and women distinguished in education." Pre-eminent in their own fields, bearing names to be conjured with, most of them were accomplished speakers. Eloquently, the praises of Carey Thomas were sung again, this time with a note of delighted appreciation for her very human qualities as well as of admiration of her heroic stature and distinguished achievement, especially at Bryn Mawr. To her, in particular—to her taste and power and intellectual standards—Bryn Mawr owed both the charm of its campus and its academic distinction; and, still more to be treasured, to "her passionate conviction that the things of the mind are the things that matter" Bryn Mawr owed its flaming intellectual ideal which kindled in each student a desire to pursue the truth with integrity and courage.

Carey Thomas, speaking last, replied that what had been said had been said of her "as a symbol of Bryn Mawr College, which we all love so much, which has become what it is now, because of the many lovers of perfection who have devoted themselves, and are now devoting themselves, to its service." If she also felt that she had "experienced what I imagine must be the sensations of a departed spirit accidentally present at the ceremonious laying away of its own ashes," she was quite evidently touched to the heart and, also, surprised by the tributes paid her, especially as all the speakers, it could not be doubted, knew whereof they spoke. Most deeply of all the announcement by Caroline Slade touched her, of a prize established by the alumnae in her honor and bestowed for the first time upon her. A fund, the M. Carey Thomas Prize Fund, raised by the alumnae was to be kept in perpetuity by

the trustees of Bryn Mawr College to enable a committee constituted by the Alumnae Association to award from time to time
a prize of five thousand dollars to an American woman in recognition of eminent achievement. "I can think of nothing," Carey
Thomas said, "that I should care for as much as just such a gift
as this." It delighted her to think that the alumnae in her name
had taken this means to reward women "for excellence in any
form of human endeavour"—"women must do all that can be
done to develop the genius and ability of other women."

Her speech ended not on a note of sadness but on one of characteristic triumph and happy prophecy, turning to the students of
Bryn Mawr College for hope. "In closing I wish to say that, in
spite of being a pioneer, my life has been so happy that I often
wonder whether many other people have been as happy as I have
been. In looking back as I do tonight I realize that one of the
chief causes of my happiness has been the many children of the
spirit that have gone out from Bryn Mawr in whom I feel that I
have a little share and shall have a share as long as I live. It is
infinitely satisfying to feel that whatever work one has been able
to do will go on and be perfected by those who are themselves the
product of the work itself. And so, in leaving Bryn Mawr, it is
a very great joy to me to feel that the College is strong in the love
of her graduates and former students and that they are here in
their thousands to help our new President build the new Bryn
Mawr greater and fairer than our dreams, and that those of us
who have served her in the dawning of her fame can look forward
to a kind of vicarious immortality as the work of our hands
prospers and lives through the years to come."

CHAPTER X

Retirement and Last Years

I

WHEN challenged as to the wisdom of the college rule compelling members of its faculty and staff, including its president, to retire at the age of sixty-five, Carey Thomas always fell back upon the argument, which she continued until her death stoutly to maintain, that it was well to retire at an age when freedom from routine could be enjoyed. She had foreseen, however, that to lose familiar academic responsibilities after thirty-seven years must be, inevitably, a severe wrench and that to build up the different perspective on old interests needed in new circumstances, as well as to feel enthusiasm for the new, might demand painful effort. So she had promised herself, before buckling down to the new life, an interim year during which she would travel—and travel to some far country which she had never seen—to fill her mind with fresh scenes and ideas and, imperceptibly, to heal the breach. It would be only fair, too, she thought, to give the new administration a chance to develop its own policy unhampered by her presence.

The summer, of course, could be treated like any other summer's vacation. She would go to Paris and then to Constantinople, where she had taken a villa on the Bosporus and Georgiana King with her friend Edith Lowber were to be her guests. It proved an entertaining month and one to which she liked to refer afterwards, for she took a certain pride in "my villa" and its lovely views. She found the bazaars and palaces, mosques and churches, though many of them she had seen before, endlessly interesting. She sailed around the sea wall of the city in a caïque and out into the sea beyond the Golden Horn to look back at the domes and walls and dark trees of Istanbul and the tall shabby houses piling up the hill of Pera, many-colored in the glow of the sunset, and to dream of ancient Byzantine glories and wickedness and Turkish magnificence, all crumbling now in dilapidation, honeycombed by the modern city. An excursion to Brusa crowned the holiday weeks. Its picturesque valley, dusty, noisy bazaars and cafés where old men sat smoking and sipping their coffee in the checkered shade under ragged trees and arbors, and its mosques, above all the Green Mosque, seemed to her more unspoiled, more Turkish, more romantic than anything she had seen that summer.

This visit to Constantinople gave rise to one of the stories most often told to illustrate Carey Thomas's imperious, exigent manner, a story repeated far and wide, even in print, and so inaccurately as to arouse her hot resentment. The story ran, according to her account, that reading among other current novels Hutchinson's *This Freedom* and horrified by its reactionary tone and statements, particularly concerning women, she took it with her one afternoon and dropped it quietly over the side of the caïque into the waters of the Bosporus. She did it, she maintained, not as an outraged gesture of distaste but as a precaution. Turkey, that summer, was making rapid strides in its program of "westernization," especially in freeing its women, and she feared lest this shockingly retrograde book should fall into the hands of her landlady with disastrous effect. So she destroyed it—a step not taken lightly by one who revered the printed word as did Carey Thomas. To her annoyance the story was spread, doubtless innocently enough, by one of her companions and in numberless retellings took on many strange forms: she had hurled the book into the water in rage; she had ordered a servant to dispose of it; even, she had read it in the dining saloon of an ocean liner and affronted by its religious enthusiasm commanded the steward to fling it out the porthole—all most undignified versions and missing, she felt, the point. That she herself entirely failed to see the characteristic humor of her own version was but to be expected.

Though the excitement of the Bryn Mawr commencement and her new freedom, as well as the joys of sight-seeing, buoyed her up through these weeks, the summer was hardly a happy one, for Carey Thomas was tired and her nerves frayed easily. As the summer drew to a close and the fatigue of traveling mounted, weariness took its toll. Her sister Helen and Lucy Donnelly joined her in Paris early in September for a motor trip through Spain and another visit to North Africa to be followed by the year's great journey to India with Lucy Donnelly. The repacking and separate arrangements necessary for these various travels were a nightmare. Carey Thomas had long since abandoned the art of traveling light, learned years ago with Mamie Gwinn. With Mary Garrett she had made a practice of taking everything with her that "might be needed" in the way of clothes, books, even light warm cashmere shawls to cover their beds in place of hotel blankets. Now, her ideas of necessary comforts grown more elaborate and her power to eliminate irrelevancies weaker, in her mistrust of Spain and North Africa and especially of India producing everyday articles that she might want, her luggage achieved monumental proportions. There were not many clothes, for Carey Thomas still held to the Victorian belief that only simple and useful costumes were suitable for traveling; but there were enough electrical appliances to be sent on to India—lamps, fans, heating pads—enough coffee and tea equipages, enough linen, stationery, and gadgets of all sorts, as well as books innumerable, to fill even more trunks and hampers than she possessed. The trunks for India were finally dispatched, but the night before she was to start for Spain the packing for the preliminary trip was still to be done. Few containers were left. Things were stuffed at the last moment into baskets, two of which burst open on the Quai d'Orléans, tumbling their contents over the pavement in a humiliating exposure.

The two months' drive in an open car through Spain and then in North Africa, beautiful and interesting as it was, and a delight in many ways, was fraught with difficulties and some danger. Tired, and distracted by thoughts of Bryn Mawr and what was happening there, Carey Thomas dallied over newspapers and letters, never ready to start betimes in the morning, so that the day's drive would extend, dinnerless, far into the evening over dark, sometimes precipitous Spanish roads. Moreover, the determination cultivated long ago with Mamie Gwinn to obtain at however great effort the rooms that she thought best in each hotel at which she stopped, with balconies if possible, had grown upon her. At the end of a long day she would canvass the hotel, turn down proferred rooms, command and cajole the manager into giving her the rooms she desired. As the opening date of the college and the inauguration of its new president approached during the North African trip, more than half her mind was far away in Bryn Mawr. Yet she wanted her companions to enjoy themselves, sending them out to see the sights while she rested or wrote letters and composed a long congratulatory telegram to Bryn Mawr's incoming president. To penetrate beyond the frequented path, they drove to Biskra in order that Helen Flexner and Lucy Donnelly might experience several days' caravan trip southward into the desert—Carey Thomas wanted them to have the experience she herself had gloried in two years before—and to the holy city of Kairouan.

By the end of the first week in November they had returned to Marseilles where Carey Thomas and Lucy Donnelly took ship for India, arriving in Bombay on November 27 and sailing down the west coast to Ceylon. Shortly before leaving Bryn Mawr in July, Carey Thomas had fallen down two shallow steps in the Deanery and dislocated her shoulder. On the voyage to India she put it out again by flinging her arm up over her head as she habitually did in sleep. The pain was excruciating; but, having swallowed one of her "silver pills"—silver-coated marbles the size of the end of her thumb of cannabis indica in which she had faith as a panacea for any ill—she bore the anguish stoically until the ship's surgeon came, by chance a specialist from Harley Street. He snapped the shoulder back with such skill and apparent ease that Carey Thomas at once requested him to teach Lucy Donnelly the art, much to the latter's dismay. Then, if the shoulder slipped again in the jungle or some equally inaccessible place, it could be put right immediately. Happily no such misfortune occurred.

In fact most of the accidents that might have happened did not. Though the car in which they drove from Colombo across Ceylon broke down and had to be pushed two miles to the next resthouse by a swarm of Senhalese who in the nick of time rose up out of the jungle, they caught no glimpse of the trick elephants with which they were threatened and of which their chauffeur went in terror as they drove seventy miles through dense jungle. Though on leaving Java where they went next and where Carey Thomas liked neither the food nor the great temple of Boro Budur— "disappointing; everything architecturally wrong about it; carving crude and rough"—they were thrown during a storm from a tossing barge into the side of the big steamer for Singapore as it rose and fell on the waves, they suffered no harm. And though Carey Thomas, who liked to read under all circumstances, lighted candles that flared dangerously in the draught on the little table between the windows of the dimly lighted railway carriages, no dry woodwork or swinging coat ever caught fire—and this, in spite of the fact that she often had mishaps with candles, the last when traveling with Logan Pearsall Smith in Syria in 1920. Then, too, she balanced her traveling candleholders, silver at that time, on the railway carriage table, on either side of which she and her cousin were comfortably reading when suddenly "a long, thin, brown, Mediterranean hand" thrust through a window and withdrew first one of them and then the other, leaving the astonished readers open-mouthed in darkness.

From Singapore, where they spent Christmas, they went up to Saigon in French Indo-China and thence by boat up the Mekong River to Angkor, at that time little visited by tourists. The rivers were in flood and the end of the journey had to be made by sampan, floating among the treetops of the jungle. They arrived by the new year in time, as they always managed to do in especially beautiful places, for the full moon. They rode on an elephant round the walls of Angkor Wat and Carey Thomas, lame as she was, climbed through the series of galleries and up the precipitous staircase to the holy of holies at the very top. Unexpectedly timorous, always, about women venturing out unprotected, especially in strange lands, she exacted a promise from Lucy Donnelly, who had visited the temple by herself at twilight when it was haunted by clouds of bats and a few yellow-robed Buddhist acolytes, not again to risk going there alone. To celebrate Carey Thomas's birthday a special performance was given for them by

eight Cambodian dancers—one a "lovely dancer from the King's
palace"—lighted by three Bengal lights and by torches held by
thirty little Cambodians, the moon shining full on the vast temple
behind them.

Returning via Singapore to Ceylon, they started at last for
India proper. Carey Thomas spent much of her time on the voyages in her cabin reading, in the breeze from two electric fans,
the morning and evening daily papers of Philadelphia and New
York which she had forwarded to her, always, all over the world,
in great bundles. From Madura, Tanjore, Madras, up the east
coast they traveled to Calcutta and thence to Darjeeling at the
northernmost tip of Bengal. They reached there on the Buddhist
New Year and, among the intent crowds in the market place,
watched the strange, tempestuous devil dancers from Tibetan
monasteries. The next morning before dawn they started, each in
a dandy with drunken, wild-looking Tibetan bearers, on the expedition up the sharp-pitched side of Tiger Hill, hoping to catch
the promised glimpse of Mount Everest. The sun rose gold and
orange, splendid, on Kinchinjunga but the white crest of Everest
remained swathed in clouds. Two mornings later as they were
turning away disappointed for the third time, suddenly for a
short moment Mount Everest stood out remote and clear and
noble in the early light, though far less lovely than the nearer
Kinchinjunga.

From Calcutta, again, they went westward to Benares and Agra
and Delhi, making various excursions to distant cities on the way.
The Taj Mahal was "supremely beautiful by moonlight," though
Carey Thomas preferred to it the Pearl Mosque at Agra, distracted as she was in that city by the "wild license" of the Hindu
New Year festivities. Toward the end of March they traveled up
the Indus Valley to Srinagar for the spring in Kashmir where
the irresponsible people and the flowering land are gay and gentle
and lovely to look upon—save for the scolding fishwives. Thence
to Bombay and the P. & O. steamer to Marseilles where they
arrived at the end of April.

They had carried letters of introduction to the highest in the
land, including His Excellency the Viceroy and the Mahatma
Gandhi, but only once during the six months of the trip to India

did Carey Thomas of her own free will consent to talk with anyone other than Lucy Donnelly, and that was with a British
officer and his wife with whom she made acquaintance in Kashmir. She was too tired, too fundamentally bewildered and depressed to make the effort. The business and fuss of making travel
and hotel arrangements interested her, of engaging and dismissing unsatisfactory servants—Don Juan of Ceylon and Francis, a
meek Indian Christian—and of managing their thirty-eight pieces
of luggage. Such occupation stood substitute for the old familiar
administrative details, and she spent much time over them. Even
her zest in sight-seeing had somewhat waned. She preferred to
stay in her room reading the guidebooks and novels or writing
innumerable letters while Lucy Donnelly went about and returned
to describe what she had done and seen. None the less, with her
remarkably quick power of appreciation, she had caught sharp
impressions, and the strange new sights that she had inevitably
seen turned her mind a little into different channels. The journey
had done its desired work. It had refreshed her, given her time
unconsciously to recruit her forces. When she reached Paris on
May 31, after another short trip into the northern neck of Spain
with Alys Russell, who had met them in Marseilles, she was
ready to take up ordinary life again as it was to be.

Apart from a week in June during which she toured Normandy
and drove to Mount-Saint-Michel with Helen Taft Manning and
her husband Frederick Manning—who stayed on with Carey
Thomas for a few days in Paris after his wife's departure—and
a short trip in mid-July with her brother Harry and his wife to
visit the Berensons at their Villa I Tatti in Settignano, followed
by a month or so with them in Switzerland, she spent the summer
quietly enough in Paris. Various members of her family and
various friends visited her there and were royally entertained by
her at the Plaza Athénée, then famous for its kitchen and cellar.
Soon after arriving in Paris she began her sittings to Paul Manship for the white marble bust which now stands in the reading
room of the Bryn Mawr College library: lovely in itself and yet,
as a portrait, somehow lifeless and prim, giving little sense of
her energy and power, partly because her hair, which was itself
so full of vigor, is stylized out of recognition. She attended meet-

ings of the House Committee, of which she was a member, of Reid Hall, the American Women's University Club in the rue de Chevreuse and went the usual round of shopping and theaters. Its high point was the gala of the Russian ballet at the end of the season, Diaghilev's first presentation of Stravinsky's *Les Noces* arranged and danced by Nijinsky, to which she took Adolphe and Edith Borie—Bryn Mawr, 1895. All her zest flared up anew and her guests were impressed by the youthful, keen enthusiasm with which she watched both performance and audience, a brilliant audience of the great, panoplied in jewels. And as a steadying, continuous background to all that went on she worked on her "Peace plan," calling her young cousin Ray Costelloe Strachey over from London to help her, finishing it just before she sailed for the United States in early autumn.

2

"There are few causes that I have more at heart than that of international arbitration," Carey Thomas had remarked long ago in her speech at the second session of the Eighth Annual Meeting of the Lake Mohonk Conference on International Arbitration in May, 1902. "I sometimes think that the strength of my conviction of the good that will follow from the general acceptance of the principle of international arbitration is only second to my belief in the beneficent revolution to be wrought in human affairs by the result of the higher education of women." It was a conviction about which she had often spoken—a few months before, for instance, at a peace conference in Philadelphia as well as often to the students of Bryn Mawr College—hoping to correct the attitude which seemed to her general in the United States, that "international arbitration is in some mysterious way a treasonable and unpatriotic doctrine." She had followed with interest and frequently discussed the various moves that were made toward international peace. On the other hand, she was never an upholder of "peace at any price."

Though she sometimes held curiously impractical notions concerning the perfectibility of man—such as that "geniuses" could be bred by the segregation and eventual mating of children born of parents whose qualities if combined should produce ideal men and women—usually she reckoned firmly with evil in the world. To the end of time, she inclined to think, wars would probably be fought but they must be controlled as far as possible and mitigated. When war broke out in 1914, in spite of her Quaker affiliations as well as her doubt of its being "a war to end war," she believed that America should and, ultimately, must take part on the side of Great Britain and France.

Her long-standing antipathy to the Germans added sharpness to her attitude and led her during the war to act with regrettable harshness toward any Germans who had the misfortune to cross her path. Nevertheless, she preserved a clear-sighted balance on larger questions of policy. Under the weight of her own prejudice as well as popular feeling, she made no objection to the substitution during the war of an examination in Spanish or Italian for that in German which students were usually required to pass before graduating from Bryn Mawr College. But, sympathize though she did with those students who longed, especially after America's entrance into the war, to throw over their college careers and devote themselves to some form of war work, she urged upon them repeatedly and forcibly the fact that it was their "patriotic duty" to complete their studies. They must stick to their job; the world would need more than ever after the war such trained intelligences as theirs.

Fought the war must be, she was convinced, until Germany's complete defeat was accomplished, and she encouraged every effort that seemed to her likely to be effective toward that end. Hysterical or merely showy efforts, however sincere they might be, she did not countenance. And her own keen dramatic sense was confined by a hardheaded estimation of what it might achieve to those occasions when it could be used legitimately to arouse enthusiasm or to relieve the strain. When on November 7, 1918, the bells rang and the siren blew, waking the college to the rumored armistice, Carey Thomas hurried out, speaking to the students from the steps of Taylor Hall, announcing a holiday to follow the thanksgiving service to be held early in the morning as well as bringing home to them the significance of the occasion. Four days later, when the bells again rang at four in the morning to announce the real Armistice, Carey Thomas once more was among the first to appear on the campus and at the great bonfire burning on the hockey field, speaking the right words to the students. The next morning she mounted the chapel platform holding tiny flags of all the Allied nations, saving what might have been a somewhat jaded thanksgiving—the second within the week— by a gesture that in itself, had she not carried it off with so sure a hand, might have descended to bathos. She knew how to rejoice as well as how to inspire effort.

The war had but added urgency to her work for peace. People must be educated to demand peace, means must be found to establish international law and to uphold it, through negotiation if possible, through force if necessary. When the League to Enforce Peace under William Howard Taft, its first president, made itself known to the world at large in June, 1915, she took up its cudgels enthusiastically, speaking in its behalf whenever chance afforded and before long becoming a member of its Executive Committee, discussing and ironing out the difficulties in the way of its final support of President Wilson's plan for a League of Nations. Early in 1918 she attended the Congress of the National Security League in Chicago and helped to launch a Patriotic Speaking Bureau at the Women's University Club of Philadelphia. Later, she followed the proceedings of the Versailles Conference closely, often explaining them—in so far as they were then explicable— and her own sometimes unfavorable point of view upon them. The repudiation of the League of Nations by the United States Senate to her mind was disastrous. There remained a possibility, however, that public opinion could be aroused against isolationism to force the government to assume its rightful international responsibilities.

When she could, she took part in this education of the public. While she was preoccupied with her retirement from the college she had little time to devote to it. Now, after her travels in the south of Europe and in India, she returned to the charge. And when the announcement reached her of the American Peace Award—a prize of one hundred thousand dollars founded by Edward W. Bok to be bestowed upon the author of "the best practicable plan by which the United States may cooperate with

other nations to achieve and preserve the peace of the world"—
she not only commended it as a means of awakening public interest but herself determined to work out a plan of her own.[1] Composed with the help of Ray Strachey, who had considerable experience of English politics and a good knowledge of international
politics, her plan appeared in *Ways To Peace* in 1924 as one of the
twenty plans, including the winner, "most representative of those
submitted to the American Peace Award."

Carey Thomas's plan was a proposal, stated with clarity and in
detail, "to outlaw war : A Declaration of Interdependence by the
United States," which announced "that all aggressive warfare,
against whomsoever directed, is an international crime, greater
than any other whatsoever, and that any nation judged guilty of
such crime shall be held by us to be an outlaw among nations; that
no matter what the provocation, no matter what the material
interests involved, our country will never henceforth commit this
crime; that law shall be the ultimate arbiter of all our policies, and
that from this day forth all our disputes with other nations shall
be submitted by us to due process of negotiation, arbitration, con-
ciliation and international law; that we pledge ourselves to pursue
now and hereafter the following policy for world peace." Then
comes a thorough exposition of the policy and the mechanism by
which it is to be made effective. Finally, as soon as the government
of the United States shall have adopted the declaration, it shall
issue an invitation first "to the democratic peoples of Great
Britain, France, Italy and Japan" and, ultimately, to those of Germany, Russia, and China, to unite with the United States "in
calling an International Conference of Interdependent Nations"
to make a treaty to insure the maintenance of peace between
nations.

As Carey Thomas observed in her "Argument for Plan," her
proposal was "simple and practical," "based on two popular
slogans—the outlawing of war and the World Court"—and,
though definite and detailed, had some flexibility. With skill, she
avoided "political controversies and ancient grievances," guarding
from foreign interference the Monroe Doctrine, questions of
tariff and immigration, and other problems dear to many American hearts, providing for the co-operation of the United States

with the League of Nations without obligation to participate in it, and for the establishment of an international police force—but only if such should prove necessary. More comprehensive than most of the other plans, which dealt usually with one or another aspect of the problem, hers set up a Commission of Jurists "to codify and extend international law" and a Permanent Council of Vigilance and Inquiry "to furnish findings of fact to the world court and to take independent action to prevent war"; provided for a system of universal training in world citizenship and other means of education in international matters; as well as arranged for means of international economic and financial reconstruction. Naturally, it included women among the reconstructors—approximately one-third of the Permanent Council were to be women, and at least one-third of the Standing National Commission on Limitation of Armament; and in the system of universal training "due consideration" was to be "given to child-bearing women." Sound and practical, though hardly practicable, the plan was, and would have made an admirable basis of action. It was too all-embracing to be accepted as it stood and in tone was not so conciliatory as the less far-reaching winning plan. It was provocative, a clarion call.

No hint of the disappointment that Carey Thomas may have felt in failing to win the award appeared in any way. She took her part in politics, though she hoped "never to serve on another new committee, never to eat another public dinner and never to make another public speech," partly because "elder statesmen are a great mistake. I believe that if the men in control of affairs in this country and abroad were under forty instead of well over sixty the world would not be in its present desperate condition." One could not travel for a year and a half, as she said, seeing different countries and peoples, "reading their newspapers from day to day" without gaining "an imaginative conception" and a new "understanding of their special problems." She wrote in the *Bryn Mawr Alumnae Bulletin*, "I have come back more anxious than ever before to try in every way that I can to get the United States to take the position that belongs to her at the head of the peaceful economic and industrial reconstruction of the world. For her own sake she can no longer stand aside. It is all right for us to feed the starving children of the world, but it would be still more right for us to grapple with the causes of war and of physical and moral collapse and to pour out our millions to build up an enduring economic prosperity and lasting peace. The world needs the United States, but even more the United States needs the world." Again and again she reiterated the fact that "we should at once enter the League of Nations"—at various meetings of the college alumnae associations and of the American Association of University Women, and, at the request of her friend Caroline Slade, at a mass meeting of the New York State League of Women Voters' Annual Convention. By 1931 a new note of something like despair about the international situation creeps into her letters : she had hoped, she said wistfully, that she would not have to see the world crumble though she had long realized that crumble it must. And two years later she writes darkly, "How can we have deserted the wonderful and splendid Chinese? If we had been in the League of Nations it could not have happened and the sinister Sir John Simon could not have worked his wicked will."

One bright ray had shone into the desolate waste of what seemed to her largely misguided policies : the appointment in 1932 of Mary E. Woolley, President of Mt. Holyoke College, to the Disarmament Conference in London. Carey Thomas had long admired President Woolley as able and right-minded on the subject of women and in her political thinking, and she at once urged her to recommend "to the Nine Power Pact Nations and to the League of Nations" that they enforce economic boycott— above all in the matter of war supplies—upon all nations using force rather than arbitration to settle an international dispute. She had been shocked by the United States traffic with Japan after Japan's aggression upon China. She pointed out to Miss Woolley, also, that it would be as "impossible for Great Britain and the United States to disarm before we have the economic boycott and the international police force as it would be for citizens of Chicago and New York to dismiss all the city police and sit down to be robbed and murdered while waiting for the gangsters to have a change of heart."

Not only had she liked President Hoover personally when she had dined at the White House, but her opinion of his astuteness

was confirmed by the appointment of Miss Woolley and she had
been delighted the year before by that of Charles Rhoads, the
son of Bryn Mawr's first president, and of Henry Scattergood—
both members of the Board of Trustees of Bryn Mawr College—
as Indian commissioner and assistant Indian commissioner: "Ever
since my two motor trips to the Far West when I saw a little of
the mistreatment of our Indians and the good treatment of the
Indians of Canada, I have been very unhappy about the whole
situation. Now I feel that at last they will have fair treatment."
Not least among Mr. Hoover's policies did his attitude toward
prohibition commend itself to her, since the opposition of "the
liquor interests" to woman suffrage, as well as her family's tradition, aligned her solidly with the upholders of prohibition. For
eighteen months she stopped her subscription to the *Nation*
because of its ridicule of Mr. Hoover and its opposition to prohibition. Though she herself when abroad occasionally drank wine
—she liked *Asti spumante* and other such sweet and sparkling
wines—and always served it to those whom she knew to be
accustomed to it, at home she was an ardent prohibitionist. As a
lifelong reader of its pages, she wrote to the *Living Age* objecting
to its publication of an antiprohibition article and at the same time
dispatched to Commander Evangeline Booth of the Salvation
Army a letter warmly commending her strong stand for prohibition.

With the presidential defeat of Herbert Hoover she felt that
the domestic political scene had lost some of its brightness. "Since
Al Smith was so ignominiously defeated at Chicago," she observed shortly before the general election, "I have drawn a breath
of relief. At least the disgrace of having a Tammany Sachem
and the man who put Jimmie Walker in the New York mayor's
chair has been spared. Governor Roosevelt is at least civilized
although not a strong character and he has a rotten anti-prohibition plank. The pious wish that the States may not introduce
the saloon is fantastically ridiculous whereas the Republican plank
gives Congress the power to stop it. I am convinced that the great
industrialists and bankers are financing and carrying on this bitter
anti-prohibition propaganda in order to keep down the working
men and it will do it if carried for a half century or more. After

our masters have got the workers and everyone else to drink again (I am satisfied that now three fourths of the United States does not drink at all) they will proceed with violent propaganda against Congress which, silly as it is, almost always has immunity to say what it thinks of bankers and stock brokers. None of the rest of us have. It is already beginning. Then we shall have a dictatorship. This is my prophecy. Remember when you see it come."

In the next year, none the less, she was to be found supporting the policies of Franklin D. Roosevelt. He was in office: she made the best of existing circumstances; and she had been much gratified by the appointment as Secretary of Labor of Miss Frances Perkins, not only a woman but "a college woman." "The United States is at last beginning to organize socially," she told the guests at the dinner given in New York in her honor by the Affiliated Schools for Women Workers. "The NRA codes of President Roosevelt and his advisers are necessary social reforms of great significance. American men and women workers are to be given for the first time, not as a temporary concession but as an inalienable right, some hours of leisure every day, a longer week-end holiday, and fairer, if not yet adequate wages."

During the decade since her retirement Carey Thomas carried on, if at a much reduced tempo—after all, women had by that time been nationally enfranchised—her work for woman suffrage, attending various functions and conventions to forward it. She had turned toward the National Woman's party away from the National Association for Woman's Suffrage—or the League of Women Voters, as the association became in 1920—largely because the latter wished to enforce protective laws for women in industry. She herself stood for the complete equality of men and women both in and out of industry. "On so controversial a subject," she chided one of the promoters of the league, "where almost all English women and all the leading continental women are against preventing women from making a living by restrictive labor legislation, I think that the League of Women Voters ought to present to its members for study and consideration *both sides*." Her feminism had become even more exacting than it had been formerly. During her presidency of the college she had eschewed smoking and annoyed the women members of the faculty by requesting them also to give it up, at one point even causing them to rebel by having their agreement turned into a formal pledge. Now that Bryn Mawr could no longer be harmed by it, she determinedly smoked, and urged other women to do so, puffing gingerly a certain number of cigarettes a day, making great play with holder and ash dish, going to remarkable lengths to procure her favorite "Ward's Russians"—all in order to prove women's emancipation.

She worked with particular vigor over the plans for a woman's hostel at the American School for Archaeological Studies at Athens —having many a disheartening tussle over it with the men of the committee and especially with the director of the school—as well as over an older and dearer project, the Bryn Mawr School in Baltimore. The school had been a source of anxiety to her for several years before her retirement and its financial and adminis-trative difficulties occupied her energies again during the late nineteen-twenties. As is apt to be the case in an institution run by a determined and interested Board of Managers and an inde-pendent and brilliant chief executive, there long had been friction between Mary Garrett and Miss Thomas, the strongest members of the board, and the school's headmistress. Matters reached a climax a few years after Mary Garrett's death when Carey Thomas had taken her place as president of the board. Shortly before Carey Thomas's retirement from the college the situation threatened to get entirely out of hand; the patrons and alumnae of the School took acrimonious sides, chiefly against Carey Thomas; and the headmistress resigned. But under a new head, the school rallied—a tribute to both its value and its fundamental vigor—and for a time prospered until toward the end of the decade its finances reached a dangerously low ebb. It needed a new headmistress, and needed, also, to follow the general exodus of the better schools and their patrons from the heart of the city to the suburbs, as well as an endowment fund. Toward the latter Carey Thomas offered to contribute one hundred thousand dollars; and about the former two necessities she debated and worried, and wrote long letters.

She continued, also, to take part in certain educational move-ments, in the Association for the Advancement of Scientific Study for Women and, above all, in the American Association and the International Federation of University Women, attending their conventions whenever possible. The meeting that most entertained her was, of course, the opening of Crosby Hall, the fine old Tudor Hall and its modern dormitories and sitting rooms, as a hostel for foreign students in London in June, 1927. On this occasion, since she was not only a founder of the International Federation but a sponsor of one of the rooms in the hall which alumnae of Bryn Mawr had furnished in her honor, she was presented among other dignitaries to the Queen. For days beforehand she amused herself by practicing her curtsy and, in case she might have to kiss the Queen's hand, kissing the hand of any available friend. After the ceremony she wrote, "The opening of Crosby Hall went off perfectly in sunshine with a very distinguished audience filling the courtyard and the Queen in the best of good humour and in a charming sky blue gown and a bouquet of romantic climbing pink roses so huge that it almost covered her gown."

She had made up her mind upon retirement to withdraw entirely from matters concerning Bryn Mawr College. But such abnegation she found too difficult a counsel even for her to follow. She stoutly refused to speak at the Bryn Mawr commencement exercises and more often than not at alumnae gatherings; but she was still a trustee of the College and, besides, until the early thirties carried certain responsibilities which had been her own, not ex officio, such as the headship of the Low Buildings and the College Inn and the Phoebe Anna Thorne Model School associations. Fortunately for her peace of mind, since detailed planning had come to worry her though she still appeared to tackle it with the old zest, the trustees consented to take over the management of these associations.

It seemed, in these years after her retirement, as if she were beset by the vicissitudes of the projects that she had launched in the last decade of her college presidency and for which she felt a special responsibility: the Phoebe Anna Thorne Model School, which collapsed in 1931 from want of financial underpinning; the Carola Woerishoffer School, which, though it came through sound, if shaken, floundered in deep waters in 1924-25; and the Summer School for Women Workers in Industry, which had its ups and violent downs and had changed its policy in a way that disappointed her. Early in the thirties, as she wrote bitterly two or three years later to her friend Frances Hand—Bryn Mawr, '97— a director of the college and a much sought after and conciliatory adviser in all these matters, she discovered "after it was an accomplished fact, that the course of study had been changed from a liberal to a strictly practical course: English composition on economic subjects; history not cultural but economic; English literature not for its own beautiful sake but as it affected economics. From this time on it has seemed to me that the glory of the Summer School's teaching has been gradually growing dim."

In earlier days she had accepted change enforced by unavoidable circumstances and made the best she could of however unwelcome a bargain; but now, since she was no longer in a position to feel all the blows of circumstances, she could ignore their urgency and sometimes did so where old loyalties were concerned. Like many parents who cannot restrain themselves from interfering in the lives of their children, she observed changes in the policies of the college with pain. Temperamentally addicted to setting things straight, she could not refrain from stating her objections to those concerned, though unfailingly supporting the administration of the college to the public at large. Had she not been a trustee, or had she not continued to live on the campus or near it for some part of almost every year, possibly she might have divorced her mind from college problems. As it was, she suffered.

The charming homogeneity of the Bryn Mawr buildings, in particular, and its smooth green lawns were dear to her. The sight of Carey Thomas limping quickly across the campus at the head of the Buildings and Grounds Committee, pointing out with her stick errors in planting or needed repairs in the halls, had been a familiar one during her administration. As plans were submitted to the Board of Trustees for new buildings not to be built in the established Jacobean Gothic style of Bryn Mawr halls and not to be situated on the sites designated for them on the old carefully worked out plan of the campus, she was roused to vehement protest. Just though her remonstrance may often have been, since the new architects were inexperienced in the kind of buildings needed, it was too often reiterated and too obviously in line with her past policies to meet with sympathetic consideration. To be sure, her plans were sometimes uncomfortably revolutionizing, but that was because she was still resourceful and fearless in her desire to impel the college toward the ideal academic institution rather than to help it to conform with the accepted pattern of women's colleges.

In spite of these vain struggles, to the results of which she never became reconciled—although contributing, little as she approved of its architecture, fifteen thousand dollars toward one of the buildings—her devotion to the college remained unimpaired. She was undaunted by such natural but none the less dispiriting experiences as being turned away from the library door for lack of a ticket, unrecognized by a freshman guard during the May Day festivities two years after her retirement. Her relations with the college alumnae grew, if anything, warmer than ever. When she was abroad, messages of affection and admiration reached her from classes returned to the campus for June reunions, and appreciation of their enjoyment of the Deanery garden. She opened the garden to them even in her absence, arranging for it to be turned, in the evening, into a magic place by the dim glow of the lanterns that she had brought from China—small, pale globes of light strung above the lawns; huge dragon-embossed parchment lamps on the terrace—and later by smaller, brighter glass globes blown from special designs at Murano. Still less forgettable, in the minds of the alumnae, were those rarer occasions on which the presence of Carey Thomas herself heightened their sense of life and perception of a great tradition. As she stood under the pine tree in the garden, leaning on her stick, a short figure of immense dignity in her full, soft French suit of black satin, her broad-brimmed hat of straw shading her strongly marked features, they watched her vivid gestures and gracious manner, recognizing suddenly with a rush of pride that here was a very great lady indeed.

But as the years passed, she occupied the Deanery less and less. Both the care and the expense of running so large a house became too heavy a burden. Most of the year she spent in travel or in living in England or on the French Riviera; even in the United States she preferred to take a flat in some near-by hotel to troubling with all the pother of opening and managing a house. Yet she loved the Deanery. Though she saw that, for the very reasons she wished to give it up, no other president of Bryn Mawr would be likely to wish to live there, it seemed too delightful to stand empty and idle. Some way must be found to put it to use for the college. And she hit upon the perfect solution: she would give it—in so far as it was hers to give—to the alumnae to be their particular center upon the campus. The house and the land belonged to the college. She requested the trustees to turn the Deanery over to the Alumnae Association on the same terms upon which she held it, proposing herself to give them all its contents save only her personal belongings, a small amount of furniture, and certain books and treasures too valuable to be left in a house open for all sorts of entertainments and which she could sell at a high price.

The trustees agreed, but the Alumnae Association, touched and delighted by the gift though its members were, feared the responsibility such possessions would entail. A satisfactory arrangement at last was worked out: the contents of the house were given to the trustees, who held it in trust for use as an alumnae center to be managed by a group of alumnae known as the Deanery Committee. Foreseeing that the operation of the Deanery as an alumnae house and a place where the college could entertain its official guests would require at least five thousand dollars a year beyond any income that could be derived by renting its rooms or serving meals, Carey Thomas gave the committee a fund of twenty thousand dollars to tide it over its first years, stipulating only that not more than sixty-five hundred be used yearly. In her will she left the Mary E. Garrett and M. Carey Thomas Fund, a trust fund of one hundred thousand dollars—amounting in fact, after the sale of her Baltimore property, to somewhat under eighty-three thousand—to be administered by the trustees of the college, its income to be used for running the Deanery as an alumnae center.

On October 21, 1933, standing before the windows at the end of the great room, strikingly handsome with her white hair and high color and in a white lace dress, flanked by the head of the Deanery Committee, Caroline McCormick Slade, the alumnae directors of the college and the president of the Alumnae Association, she received the alumnae for the last time at the Deanery.

The occasion was a gay one. Carey Thomas's vitality still filled the Deanery with life, her taste still ruled there. To envisage a day when that would no longer be true was beyond the power of most of her guests as it was outside the wish of them all. That this was a real parting of Carey Thomas from the college and from them seemed to the alumnae, for all that the knowledge weighed upon them in its certainty, impossible to believe. In spite of the underlying "sense of loss," which all reports of the reception note, it seemed to mark, as did most occasions presided over by Carey Thomas, a beginning rather than an end, a hopeful beginning that would lead to happy and great things.

In fact, it marked the end of an epoch for the college. Disliking gossip about herself as she always had, and unrelenting as she was toward offenders who spread tales of her doings and opinions, about no one connected with Bryn Mawr was such a web of stories spun. Though the undergraduates and the new members of the faculty rarely saw her—occasionally at a college lecture, sometimes at a meeting such as the opening of the summer school—the glimpses that they had, added to the reports of the small fortunate number who for one reason or another were invited to the Deanery, gave particular color to her legend. And there was always the chance that they might meet her on the campus. The stories about her enriched college tradition; and her presence lent richness to its life. There was still "little need to ask if Miss Thomas is there; you feel her when she is." When she left the Deanery, though her few old friends among the faculty by the loyalty of their memories kept her legend alive, even enhanced it, they could not make up for the loss of her quickening presence—and by so much the college remained the poorer.

3

As Carey Thomas announced in the *Bryn Mawr College Alumnae Bulletin* early in 1924, she planned to write the history of the college and, at the same time, her autobiography as well as to read some of the many books that she had "never had time to read," to see her friends, and to travel. All these things she did, save only the history and autobiography. The aggregation of material, large as it was, that had accumulated for her autobiography might have been manageable had she remained in one place for any length of time or found any reliable person to help with its sorting. There was no one, however, well enough acquainted with the circumstances to sort intelligently who was free to give time to what obviously would take several years. There were boxes and trunks tight packed with journals and notebooks and letters—copies of Carey Thomas's own letters, family letters "crossed" in fine spidery hands, letters from friends, business letters, and notes of little consequence; there were telegrams and fragments of paper on which were jotted plans for travel, prescriptions, even laundry lists; there were newspaper clippings, theater and opera programs, and lists of art exhibitions. Much of this was undated and it covered a period from her earliest childhood and before; but it was packed away more or less in the order in which it had gathered. There were, also, trunks of data relating in particular to the college. To all this Carey Thomas's love of paraphernalia and of documents and statistics led her to add books, pamphlets, and articles on anything that touched, sometimes only remotely, herself or her family or her interests. The whole was overwhelming.

Though she made valiant efforts, and was helped for a short time by Ray Strachey, she was never able to bring order out of the amorphous mass. It was a dreary occupation, and often painful, to review past ambitions and setbacks, loves and adventures, some of which she could hardly bring herself to face. Logan Pearsall Smith and Lucy Donnelly repeatedly urged her to try writing down episodes as they sprang into her mind, not troubling about framework and final organization until she had it all down on paper, to which she would reply severely, that was not her way of working. The sense that she must have solid documentation, make a "scholarly" approach, prevented her writing her memoirs freely as they occurred to her; and she had been too long a busy executive to bear the solitary drudgery of writing. Perhaps realizing that she had always been a speaker rather than a writer, someone at a luncheon in the Deanery, after she had been reminiscing in especially vivid fashion, suggested that she talk her memories into a dictaphone. The suggestion delighted her: "I will get two dictaphones." And get them she did, two ediphones and a receiving instrument. Unfortunately, her eloquence tended to vanish in face of mechanical contrivances that were not only unresponsive but, to the unaccustomed, bewildering and tiresome to manage. Only one disk remains, and that scored by a mere business letter, catching sometimes, however, her emphasis and the tones of her voice.

Even to the time of her death she was replying to importunate publishers that she expected to finish the autobiography—the history she soon abandoned—and have it ready for publication "by next June." In private her tone grew less certain as the years passed. From her villa on the Riviera in 1931 she sent word to an anxious friend that she was "writing regularly four hours a day and here if ever I can write my autobiography—but I am not yet sure that I can"; and two years later in France she remarked that she was, she feared, "too comfortable. I ought to be in an attic overlooking the Seine to write a good autobiography—but I will at least do my best until the vanishing dollar sends me home." By the next year she had succeeded in writing four short chapters which she read to Caroline Chadwick Collins—Bryn Mawr, 1905 —then director of publicity at the college upon whom with other friends she depended now for much loyal advice in college matters. But seeing herself that these chapters did her no justice, she destroyed them. At the time of her death all that remained of her work were a few scraps of paper on which she had jotted varying versions of several early episodes, and a formidable disorder among the material upon which she had proposed to base it: torn and separated parts of letters and documents stirred up, higgledy-piggledy as if with a stick; portfolios whose contents rarely corresponded with their labels; clippings, manifestoes, and bits of speeches with neither date nor provenance.

Yet what else was to be expected? It had been from the outset a slender hope that she could write her life—one to which her friends clung only because they wished her to write it and had known her often to accomplish the impossible—and the distractions of her years of retirement were greater than even her friends expected. Her family and her friends, though they paid her frequent visits, were for the most part too absorbed in their own lives to be able to companion her for any length of time and the older among them no longer had enough stamina wholly to enjoy traveling with her. Delightful as journeys in her company were, they were exhausting, particularly since the exigencies of her requirements in accommodations and equipment had increased and she countenanced on the part of her companions no more readily than in earlier days the usual relaxations of travel: talks with passing acquaintances, aimless strolls, hours of watching the world wag by a café table. Carey Thomas's own vitality, moreover, magnetic and revivifying though it seemed, was in itself apt to wear out her fellow travelers.

More and more she sought the movement and flurry of travel to guard against unadmitted boredom and to turn her mind from the college and other more personal anxieties. Accompanied most often by Edith Lowber, she journeyed in the next years to most of the places—to some of them, as to Venice, repeatedly—that she had visited long ago with Mamie Gwinn and more recently with Mary Garrett and other friends. From Palestine she made her first airplane flight, to and from Bagdad, finding the experience as satisfactory as Bagdad itself was dull. Urging a friend who had never flown to take the same flights, she remarked: "You could hardly be killed doing it only twice." As always, travels began and ended with Paris or England where for several summers she rented a little house, Kilnmeadow, to be near her family at Fernhurst.

In the autumn and winter of 1927 she took a small villa, *Les Acacias*, between Monte Carlo and Menton on the French Riviera where Grace Worthington and Alys Russell visited her and were alarmed to find her sad and discouraged. They had never seen her so before. It had always seemed to them that, as she had once observed to Alys Russell, she "enjoyed even buttoning her boots." But she had been by herself for several weeks reading old letters in preparation for the autobiography and was disheartened and lonely. The only diversions that her dairy recorded were drives in solitude along the Corniche and, occasionally, her delight in the melancholy sweet song of the nightingale which "sings at noon in the garden." Later she wrote from another villa on the Riviera, "A nightingale has come to live in my garden and sings delightfully for a mate who makes me anxious by not arriving."

It reminded her of the cardinal that long ago found a mate each year in the Deanery garden until one winter it appeared, all dressed in brilliant hue for courting, but with no female bird, and for days pecked angrily at the windows thinking that its destined mate was held a prisoner within.

Now and again, assuaging her restlessness by frequent trips to New York and elsewhere, Carey Thomas would return to the Deanery as she did following the death in June, 1925, of her brother Harry who had been seriously ill for a long time and whom she had seen much of in the last years. In the summer of 1930 she spent some months with her sister-in-law, Harry's widow, at Coombe Edge, the old house in which the young Thomases had enjoyed their summers at the time of Bryn Mawr's opening. And the next winter, staying in a hotel near Bryn Mawr, with the help of several younger members of her family and, also, of Edith Lowber, she began to inventory and to set in order and clear out the contents of the Deanery. In this winter, too, she saw more than usual of Millicent Carey—Bryn Mawr, 1920—her sister Margaret's elder daughter, who was at this time acting dean of Bryn Mawr College while Helen Taft Manning again acted as its president.

Carey Thomas had always taken much interest in her little nieces and nephews. She liked children—especially spirited, naughty ones—and usually got on well with them and with older young people since she took them seriously. The career of anyone who caught her interest was a matter of consideration to her, and she enjoyed especially mapping out with them the futures of young people who were full of ambitions and zest. Many a student emerging from Carey Thomas's office at the college found that she had committed herself to following a career which before she had hardly thought of as a possibility. One young woman who, like others, had entered Bryn Mawr not knowing what she intended in the future to do heard herself say in reply to Carey Thomas's searching questions that she would like to be a doctor; before she left the office a career in medicine had been sketched for her: she is now a distinguished New York surgeon. Carey Thomas still had this gift to a marked degree of awakening young people to new concerns, of making them believe that they could do what they had never contemplated doing and that it was worth the effort involved.

Another young woman arriving to visit Carey Thomas in England in the late nineteen-twenties was told at dinner that Carey Thomas would like at breakfast the following morning to hear her opinion of the six or seven books that she would find in her room—they were interesting, delightful. It did not occur to the young person in question, as it rarely did to any of the young whom Carey Thomas so chose to flatter, that she had been set a preposterous task. The night went in concentrated reading; and the next morning she was primed and cocked to discuss the books, if hollow-eyed and too shaky to deal efficiently with the breakfast apple and egg. Carey Thomas, proud of her skill in both accomplishments, cut off the top of her egg with a single clip and peeled her apple in one long curling red ribbon. In her letters to young people, also, Carey Thomas was careful to discuss matters that were interesting, never either talking down or, though often grave, solemnly preaching. She was great fun and liked a joke as well as they. Besides, she did not seem to them old-fashioned. Indeed, she was often far ahead of them in her interest in the latest happenings—the development of the movies, for instance, which she watched with zest.

Naturally, Carey Thomas followed the careers of the younger members of her family with more than ordinary attention. Long ago her hopes had centered in her sister Grace's daughter, Mary Worthington—Bryn Mawr, 1910—a fine-looking, intelligent, strong-minded girl, interested in science, whom Carey Thomas thought would go far and do credit to all college women. But Mary Worthington had died while a student in the Johns Hopkins Medical School in 1912. Now, gradually, Carey Thomas came to admire the qualities of Millicent Carey, particularly after observing her success in the English Department and in the administration of Bryn Mawr College. Disappointed though she was at first when Millicent Carey left Bryn Mawr to become headmistress of the Brearley School in New York and, not long afterwards, married Dr. Rustin McIntosh, Professor of Pediatrics at the College of Physicians and Surgeons, she soon rallied, seeing as always the possibilities—to be admirably fulfilled in this case—in accom-

plished fact: "She can do a great deal for the CAUSE," wrote
Carey Thomas, "by proving that she can hold down a husband
and a job like the headmistresship of a big school." She already
had another niece—her nephew Henry Thomas's wife—of whom
she was exceedingly proud as an example of a married woman
following a successful career in medicine.

In May, 1931, with Edith Lowber, Carey Thomas returned
to Europe, finally settling for the winter—and the three following winters—on the Riviera in the "villa of my dreams," where
her sister Helen and brother-in-law Simon Flexner soon visited
her. It had not been easy to find the villa since Carey Thomas
wished a view, central heating, decent servants' rooms, hot water
for baths, flyscreens, and open fireplaces and, as she said, "the
French run to white marble staircases, parquet floors, tapestry
walls and incredibly uncomfortable Louis XIV furniture." However, once found, it was entirely satisfactory even in ways apart
from what she considered the necessities: it "has a large terraced
garden overhanging the sea. My working room opens with four
great windows on the sea and the mountains. There are four large
balconies on the sea and all the rooms, balconies, and garden face
south." And every night, "except during one week of each month,"
moonlight bathed the garden.

Her many journeys were not all accomplished without accident.
In Berlin, in 1931, she slipped on the steps of the old museum and
put her shoulder out again. Two years before in Brittany, as she
and Edith Lowber were driving in the outskirts of Saint-Malo,
their chauffeur went to sleep, drove into a telegraph pole, snap-
ping it off three feet from the ground, and overturned the car
in the ditch. Miraculously, four American women appeared almost
at once and, with the help of the rudely awakened chauffeur,
pulled Carey Thomas and Edith Lowber out through the window
of their wrecked car, cut and bruised and badly shaken but not
seriously injured and apparently with zest only temporarily abated
since the next day they continued their tour. In 1924, however,
an accident grave in its consequences had overtaken Carey
Thomas. She was at Delphi with Ray Strachey when one of the
mules they had been riding up the slope of Mount Parnassus
kicked her in the thigh and knocked her down, bruising and cut-

ting her shoulder. The drive back to Athens was painful. Nevertheless, she insisted upon stopping in Thebes to see, as she had promised to do, the archaeological work there of two Bryn Mawr graduates, Hetty Goldman—Bryn Mawr, 1903—and her assistant Dorothy Burr—Bryn Mawr, 1923. In Athens she was given antitoxin injections and her shoulder was bound up. From the combination of the injections, which produced an agonizingly itching rash, and the tight bandages, she arrived in Paris suffering tortures and by the time she reached the United States had become seriously ill. The following two months she spent in the Johns Hopkins Hospital, undergoing in the course of them an operation to extract a splinter of bone—probably caused by the mule's kick—from her thigh.

Again, in 1931, she was obliged to spend many weeks in the Johns Hopkins Hospital when another splinter was extracted. This time, however, her illness was not owing to the splinter and consequent operation, and it alarmed her. She asked her nephew Henry M. Thomas to be her "consulting physician," instructed him as to what she wished done if she should become paralyzed or lose her mind. She had come not only to be very fond of him but to put great faith in him, a doctor like his father and an assistant professor at the Johns Hopkins Medical School.

In the course of these and other illnesses she sometimes advised her physicians, even her surgeons—and helpfully—as to their treatment of her. The intelligent, well-informed layman, she believed, who put his mind on the history of his own illnesses and their circumstances could give his doctor useful suggestions as to the treatment of his own particular case. Her interest in medicine had always been considerable: she not only took in but read the leading medical journals. She liked to read through and revise any paper that young Dr. Henry Thomas might write for a medical journal, because, she said, if she could not be made to understand it, it was not clearly or well written. Barring, of course, special terminology which could be looked up, scientific articles should be intelligible to laymen who cared to apply their minds to them. To make them so was one way to insure clarity of thought.

Carey Thomas appeared to others to be full of vigor: she

looked a little older, possibly, but "really much the same": as handsome and commanding as ever. Perhaps, from living so long in France and England, her clothes had become more Continental, hung in more graceful folds, but they were still cut to the same general pattern, especially the voluminous skirts, the front of which she still lifted, with an absent, scrabbling gesture, to fish her large handkerchief or theater or opera ticket or other important odds and ends from the pockets in her petticoat; and the layer upon layer of straight, loose coats—silk, velvet, and fur—in which she wrapped herself for motor drives. In spite of little change in her outward appearance, she felt herself much older, tired and less certain. And though she saw the members of her family almost as often as heretofore and her old friends in Bryn Mawr, she had come more and more to rely upon Edith Lowber.

Twenty-one years younger than Carey Thomas, tall and handsome, Edith Lowber had been in the beginning the friend of Georgiana King. She was an agreeable and sympathetic companion and foot-loose, loved travel and delighted in the luxury with which Carey Thomas surrounded her. She was, also, not strong—a fact that provided Carey Thomas with a certain amount of interest, for she enjoyed prescribing and arranging cures for her friends, not always successfully, and occupied herself with caring tenderly for Edith Lowber. In 1934 they were living in the villa on the Riviera where Grace Worthington and Alys Russell had just paid them a visit, staying in the *villino* in the garden, and Mary Berenson had motored up from Italy to see them. Edith Lowber as well as Carey Thomas had seemed quite well. Suddenly, in mid-March when the visitors had gone, she fell ill; six days later she died. Her death was a shock to Carey Thomas, grieved to the heart and left to cope alone with the sordid circumstances attendant upon the death of anyone in a foreign country. With the help of her maid Marie, kindness and loyalty itself, she got through the days, interviewing American consul and French authorities, making all the arrangements involved. The shock had affected her eyes and turned her knees to water; and she could not sleep. The members of her family living in England and Italy, near enough to reach her quickly, offered to join her, but she preferred to be alone. Little by little she pulled herself together, distracting her mind by all the entertainments available —drives into the hills or along the coast, *Tristan und Isolde* at Nice, the Monte Carlo Ballet, detective stories, even the movies. And in April she went for a month to Venice where she took a fresh grip on herself before going on to England for the summer.

Among the things that she had found hardest to bear after the death of Edith Lowber had been the grief of Edith Lowber's dog. He "mourned her like a person." Carey Thomas loved dogs. For many years, because both Mamie Gwinn and Mary Garrett preferred cats, she had had a series of cats, all with the best of manners: a handsome cat from Maine, third in the series, scratching on her dressing room window for admittance, brought in a mouse and laying it at her feet looked anxiously at the door. For a moment Carey Thomas failed to realize what was wanted. Then she opened the door; the cat rushed through, bearing the mouse with it, down to the dining room where it placed the mouse upon the little table on the hearth on which it was customarily served its meals. At last it was able to consume its feast with, as Carey Thomas proudly observed, due decorum. After Mary Garrett's death Carey Thomas had a series of spaniels one after another named Lady Ching, finding comfort in their companionship. The one dearest to her died in 1919. "I wept for a long time," she wrote. "She had given me her whole heart just recently and had mine in return. I shall miss her terribly." Now she regretted parting from Edith Lowber's dog, but it was out of the question for her to keep him.

Returning to America in October, she did not again go abroad. Her winters were spent, with the exception of a short time in Washington, at a hotel in Philadelphia—anxious winters since she was disturbed about the state of the world and the changes at the college and even more by her own finances, which during the last years abroad had gradually diminished. In the twenties she had subscribed to many good works—among those not already mentioned, to the Caroline Spurgeon Scholarship, and to a tombstone and memorial to Emmeline Pankhurst, whom she had admired greatly during the militant days of the English suffrage movement and had entertained several times at the Deanery. But as the thirties drew on she could give less and was obliged to refuse to contribute the full amount, as she might have done earlier, needed by the Bryn Mawr Summer School to carry on its work in 1930. Now, in 1934, her fortune had reached a harassingly low ebb. Much of her time was given to planning how to increase her income, how to settle her mother's estate advantageously to all the heirs, how to live on a far smaller sum of money than she was used to doing without lessening the charm of her life either for herself or for others.

For many years she had made and remade her will at frequent intervals. Now, once more, she took it up, perfecting it point by point in long sessions with her lawyer, forgetting no one for whom she cared and nothing in which she was interested, until it attained to the formidable length of ninety-odd pages, and was based upon what she wished to do rather than on what, in fact, she could do—as if the words in themselves might magically conjure up the wherewithal for their own accomplishment. Perhaps she foresaw the truth, that her wishes would be valued as a mark of her esteem, whatever the impossibility of carrying them out or the awkwardness of the situation this sometimes created. She had too often seen the college, in what had appeared hopeless financial crises, profit by some last-minute gift not to half-believe that she herself might receive a windfall.

4

It was a solitary winter that Carey Thomas spent in Philadelphia in 1934-35. Friends and family came and went; theaters and operas entertained her every so often and movies more frequently; she took short drives to Bryn Mawr and along the Schuylkill or Wissahickon rivers and about the countryside. But much of the time she was alone. She still kept up the show of writing her autobiography, though her zest for it had waned, and still was interested in the news of the world and in a variety of books that she ran through with great rapidity. Yet all this left, sometimes, an uncomfortable amount of time for reflection.

Long ago she had deplored "the half-happiness" with which many people seemed to be content while calling themselves happy. There were Christians satisfied "with a half Christianity, lovers with a half love, poets with such little poems." She had been impatient with this pusillanimity and oppressed, too, in her youth, by the unhappiness in the world, "most of it useless, but without remedy." Now, she had achieved a sort of equilibrium: unhappiness, her own and others, no longer was so sharp a grief; half-happiness had become acceptable. She wondered if she herself had squeezed the last drop of experience from the past seventy-eight years. Had she, perhaps, deliberately cut herself off from more of life than she need have done? Would she have had a fuller, more varied, useful and successful life if she had encouraged and married any of the men whom she had known were fascinated and half, perhaps wholly, in love with her—and she ran over the list in her mind; or had there been interests and causes to which she might have devoted herself which would have taken her into wider fields? She thought not, and in any case such speculations were pointless; but they were diverting and no longer painful.

Her friends were disappointed that she failed to receive the prize founded by Edward Bok to be awarded every so often to a citizen of Philadelphia for important contributions to its life. She had done much for Philadelphia and stood, certainly, among its citizens of more than parochial eminence; and her friends knew that she liked honors that betokened fame. From earliest youth she had believed that the desire for fame was the most important force in the achievement of great deeds and its reward the most to be desired. It incensed her that women were so rarely elected to the American Hall of Fame; it was one of the injustices that she urged her younger friends to right.

As the spring drew on, Carey Thomas was caught up again in the affairs of the college. The alumnae of Bryn Mawr were engaged in raising a fund of a million dollars, the achievement of which was to be announced at the celebration of the fiftieth anniversary of the college in the autumn. The fund would be used for building the fourth wing of the library and for building, equipping, and endowing a new science hall. Carey Thomas discussed and argued vainly with her fellow directors and with members of the faculty about the design and, especially, the site of the new hall. That the college library, including the new wing, was to be named for her—and an announcement made to that effect at the anniversary exercises—gratified her; and the matter of the correct lettering in which her name should be carved over the entrance caused her to search anxiously for examples of lettering that corresponded with Jacobean Gothic architecture. She consented to speak, this time over the radio, to help Bryn Mawr in its "drive."

Many years before, in complaining to Hannah Smith of the indignity of begging funds, she wrote: "Although I disapprove of the principle I should like to leave Bryn Mawr one million dollars more endowment and one million dollars more in buildings than when I became President. It would spread a kindly warmth through my ashes in my niche in the library cloister to know the College will be able to go on and not close its doors on account of the high prices." So she responded once again as effectively as she could to the distasteful call to obtain money. To speak over the radio, which she had never before attempted to do, filled her with apprehension; yet it would be a fresh adventure and, as such, was not to be rejected. She referred to the coming experience as "the ordeal," and began to write her speech, having difficulty in compressing all that she wished to say into the allotted ten minutes. In the end, the unaccustomed strain of dealing with mechanisms and strange conditions, worst of all the necessity to begin and end on an exact dot of time, made the speech less successful than she had hoped it might be. A sense of failure depressed her. None the less, as a member of the small central committee for organizing the celebration of the college anniversary, she set about laying plans with undiminished ardor.

When she was able that summer, spent again at Coombe Edge, she worked on her own speech for the anniversary exercises. For years she had saved clippings and bits of information that might be useful for this purpose. She felt that this was to be her final appearance before a Bryn Mawr audience—certainly before so large a one—and she must make many points, yet not so many as to mar their salience. The task was harassing and before many weeks were out was interrupted for a long time by illness, a heart attack, so serious that it seemed as if she would never be able to make the speech. With surprising resiliency and determination, however, she rallied and by October, when she returned to Philadelphia, appeared to be restored. To her friends, few of whom knew how gravely ill she had been since she never liked her illnesses spoken of, she looked older and less vigorous, her face with its heavy-lidded eyes and deeply carved lines had taken on a Rembrandtesque beauty, but her interest was as keen as ever and her mind quite unimpaired.

Her nephew Dr. Henry Thomas and her Philadelphia physician prevailed upon her to give up thought of attending the dinner and entertainment on Friday, November 1, the evening before the anniversary exercises. Her determination to march in the academic procession the following day was not to be questioned. Though she sat at home on Friday evening, she worked over her speech, reading it, in spite of losing her voice at intervals, to her sister Helen and brother-in-law Simon Flexner who helped her to cut it somewhat and to tone down the most vehement passages. She had determined, if will power could do it, to take part in the celebrations of Saturday, agreeing only—and this she did thankfully—to rest quietly after the morning exercises and in preparation for those of the afternoon, while everyone else lunched in the gymnasium.

In the chill of the gray autumn morning of November 2, the long procession in caps and gowns and many-colored hoods, interspersed with marshalls carrying the white and yellow batons of their office, formed at the library: under-graduates, graduates, staff, faculty, and alumnae of the college lined up; presidents and deans of other colleges and universities; other distinguished guests and directors of Bryn Mawr College—and finally, the president and president emeritus of the college. Slowly, decorously, it made its way, no longer to the gymnasium as on former academic occasions in which Carey Thomas had taken part, but past Pembroke, through Rockefeller arch to Goodhart Hall, between groups of alumnae and guests standing under the trees waiting for the procession to pass and then scurrying quietly away to take their places in Goodhart. As the procession moved down the aisle of the somber, high-vaulted hall, separating right and left, then mounting the platform, only the solemn music to which it marched and the rhythmic shuffle of feet on the stone pavement broke the quiet. The audience seemed to hold its breath, standing tense with expectation, each member wrapped in memories, recalled by passing figures, of her own experiences at Bryn Mawr and of Carey Thomas herself for whom they waited. Those who were too young to have known her at Bryn Mawr were filled with curiosity to see this, to them, almost mythical person; those who had been her students waited half-exultant, half-anxious lest there be some change in her.

Suddenly from near the entrance came the sound of applause. The two presidents of the college had appeared. The younger with thoughtful courtesy stepped back, applauding her predecessor, recognizing that this occasion belonged less to the last thirteen years than to the past, to Carey Thomas, who for thirty-seven years, from the college's earliest days, had held the highest offices in Bryn Mawr's administration. The audience turned and saw them. The tension snapped in a swelling burst of applause, a great wave of emotion that surged toward the familiar, imperious figure in gown and mortar board far to the back of the fine white head. Carey Thomas hesitated, buffeted by the applause, then started forward through the tumult of enthusiasm. Whatever the past may have held in the relations of any single person to Carey Thomas, no member of the audience but was carried away by the emotion of that moment. There were few dry eyes among them as Carey Thomas, old and distinguished, bearing herself proudly, moved limping down the aisle.

There were tears in Carey Thomas's own eyes. She had not dreamt of such an ovation. She had been full of nervous dread, feeling that she might be too tired and old to pull through. She was quite aware both that there would be many among the audience who in the past had been her severe critics as well as many to whom she was a symbol of the college and of an ideal. But this spontaneous burst of personal acclaim which for a moment swept the audience had been as unexpected by her as it was afterwards surprising to a number who had felt it. For an instant it had overwhelmed her; then given her heart. The color had come into her cheeks, her eyes had brightened, she had straightened, moving down the aisle unfalteringly, mounting the platform with as vigorous and quick a step as of old.

After the invocation by Rufus Jones, president of the Board of Directors of Bryn Mawr, the presiding officer, President Marian Edwards Park, introduced the speakers: President Conant of Harvard University, who spoke on the role of the privately endowed colleges in this country in the coming years; President Comstock of Radcliffe College, on the colleges for women; President Bowman of the Johns Hopkins University; President Emeritus M. Carey Thomas; and, in conclusion, Caroline McCormick Slade, presenting the Fiftieth Anniversary Fund raised, under her leadership, by the alumnae and accepted by President Park. None of the speakers failed to laud Carey Thomas, identifying her with the college. There are, said President Comstock, many women who call Bryn Mawr blessed who have never set foot in a college for women. "If this great army of women might be conceived of as converging upon Bryn Mawr today . . . there would be . . . an image of a person as well as of an institution in their eyes. . . . In honouring Bryn Mawr today we honour also a woman whose mark upon the higher education of women is characteristic and ineffaceable." President Comstock's speech reminded many of her listeners of past addresses by Carey Thomas herself, for it ended as hers often did by pointing out problems still to be solved.

Carey Thomas arose. The clear voice sounded into the far corners of the hall as few voices ever had done, emphatically pointing out Bryn Mawr's triumphs and mistakes as from her long firsthand experience and later observation she adjudged them. It was true, as she wrote a few days later, that "her alumnae and her past and present faculty have always been to me the twin glories of Bryn Mawr and I realize more and more as time goes on that Byrn Mawr has a right to be proud of them," but she did not spare them on this occasion. Neither they nor the college were perfect. Bryn Mawr must again lead the way. Women had won advanced education and much else, but they had not yet been given the positions of honor in academic institutions for which their ability and training fitted them. Among other advisable reforms, Bryn Mawr must whenever possible appoint women to her faculty, giving them preference to men of equal stature, and must urge other colleges to follow its example. If her audience regretted some of Carey Thomas's strictures, it recognized the truth of her claims that Bryn Mawr in certain ways had led other institutions and might do so again in the future. Most of all, it admired the courage with which she spoke her mind. Again, it acclaimed her power.

The exultation of the morning buoyed up Carey Thomas through the afternoon's ceremonies, the awarding of the M. Carey Thomas Prize given for the first time to herself in 1922 and for the second, in 1931, to Jane Addams. Fortunately on this occasion, for she was very tired though her spirit seemed unflagging, Carey Thomas had only to sit upon the platform. The speakers were President Park, who presented the award, its recipient, Dr. Florence Sabin of the Rockefeller Institute for Medical Research, and Dr. Simon Flexner, retired director of the Institute. It was with thankfulness that Carey Thomas welcomed the end of all the proceedings, not only relieved to have come through safely but inexpressibly happy. The occasion had been a great personal triumph. Many years before, rebuking the writer of a piece in the *Bryn Mawr College Alumnae Bulletin*, she remarked that she had detected in it "a slight nuance of sentiment—not exactly sentimentality but something approaching it. . . . I may be mistaken but I think it is something that women have to be very much on their guard against." Thinking over the happenings of November 2, it seemed to her that all trace of sentimentality had been avoided. The feeling had been strong and sincere. She need have no regrets. And she was filled with deep gratitude.

But for all the triumph and the pleasure Carey Thomas had risked much. She was too old, her heart too unpredictable, to bear such exertions lightly. Years before, she had written Hannah Smith, that other Whitall woman whom in many ways she resembled, regretting bitterly that the old must die and their wisdom learned through experience and discipline be lost. For herself, however, in November, 1935, she neither expected nor dreaded death. Life could hold for her no greater satisfaction than she had experienced; and by taking care she might live for unnumbered months, even years.

If careful precautions irked her or the heightened awareness of the uncertainty of life saddened her, no shadow of it was allowed to appear in her relations with her family or her friends. Her own physical ills, she felt now as she had always felt, should not be permitted at whatever cost to obtrude themselves. The month following the fiftieth anniversary passed outwardly much as other months. She replied to the many messages of congratulation, received occasional visitors, drove sometimes into the country—the last drive the day before her death along her favorite, romantic stream near Bryn Mawr with Lucy Donnelly. Apparently with all her old zest, she laid plans for the future.

Suddenly, unexpectedly, early in the morning of December 2, 1935, Carey Thomas died, a month after her great triumph, a month before her seventy-ninth birthday. In the following week a service, simple, as is the custom of the Society of Friends, was held in the Deanery for her family and the friends whom she had mentioned in her will; in May a memorial meeting was held in Goodhart Hall at which President Park presided, and Rufus Jones spoke for the directors, of whom he was president, Helen Taft Manning for the faculty, of which she was dean, and Caroline McCormick Slade for the alumnae; and her ashes were buried in the cloisters of the Bryn Mawr College library—all according to her wishes.[2]

Carey Thomas may have felt that with the fiftieth anniversary and her death would begin a new era in the history of Bryn Mawr College. Perhaps she was right. "To the making of Bryn Mawr," she said in concluding her address at the exercises in celebration of Bryn Mawr's quarter centenary, twenty-five years earlier, "the very stars in their courses seem to have worked together.; from her cradle no good genius, no fairy godmother has been absent. Beautiful exceedingly, dowered with gifts of intellect and spirit, strong in the love of her faculty and students past and present, with the tradition of success behind her, the College stands at the beginning of her second quarter century. We commit her future to those who love her, to the many friends who have gathered about her in the dawning of her fame, to her foster children who have received her best gifts of education." They were words that with equal justice might have been uttered at the time of her death. And, with one short addition, the words with which she concluded express the attitude of many of these "foster children," the alumnae whose careers she watched with interest and hope and pride: "In endowing colleges and helping them we are in a peculiar but very real sense continuing our own existence beyond our own lives. If it is possible to build on earth a heavenly house not made with hands, it is possible in the creation and perfecting of a college such as this. An immortality of remembrance and gratitude belongs to the past and awaits the future directors and faculty and benefactors of Bryn Mawr College." Before all, the alumnae would add, it awaited Carey Thomas.

NOTES

Chapter I

1. The quotations from the diary of Ann Cooper Whitall [1716-1739 O.S.] are taken from the essay "Ann Whitall" in *Reperusals and Recollections* by Logan Pearsall Smith, by permission of Constable & Co., publishers, London, 1936. There is also (1) a leaflet compiled by the Daughters of the American Revolution, who have an Ann Whitall Chapter in Woodbury, New Jersey, consisting of excerpts from an article written by Ralph D. Paine and entitled "The Battle of Red Bank. A Battle Whose Deeds Match the Beauty of Romance," published in 1907 and again in 1926; (2) a pamphlet: "The Heroine of Red Bank" by Isabella C. McGeorge, as read before the Gloucester County Historical Society, January 11, 1904.

2. For the Whitall ancestry of M. Carey Thomas see *John M. Whitall. The Story of His Life* written for the grandchildren by his daughter, H. W. S., printed for the family in Philadelphia, 1879; and *Memoir of Mary Whitall* by her granddaughter, R. N. T., printed for the family in Philadelphia in 1885.

3. For the Thomas ancestry of M. Carey Thomas see *The Thomas Book* by Lawrence Buckley Thomas, D.D., printed by the Henry T. Thomas Company, New York, 1896.

Chapter II

1. For stories concerning M. Carey Thomas's childhood holidays see *Small Adventures of a Little Quaker Girl* by Rebecca Nicholson Taylor, published by the Friends' Bookstore, Philadelphia, 1937.

Chapter IV

1. For accounts of Hannah Whitall Smith and Robert Pearsall Smith see the reminiscences of their son, *Unforgotten Years* by Logan Pearsall Smith, Little, Brown & Co., Boston, 1938. See also two books by their granddaughter Ray Costelloe Strachey: *Religious Life; extracts from the papers of Hannah Whitall Smith, edited with an introduction by Ray Strachey consisting of an account of the author of these papers, and of the times in which she lived; together with a description of the curious religious sects and communities of America during the early and middle years of the nineteenth century,* Faber & Gwyer, Ltd., London, 1928; and *Shaken by the Wind* by Ray Strachey, Faber & Gwyer, Ltd., London, 1927, a novel based on material drawn from the experiences of her grandparents.

2. For an admirably concise account of the founding of the university and especially the part played by Daniel C. Gilman in its establishment and growth, see *Daniel Coit Gilman, Creator of the American Type of University,* by Abraham Flexner, Harcourt, Brace & Co., New York, 1946.

3. There is an amusing story often told even by herself, it is said, of Carey Thomas being permitted to attend certain lectures at the Johns Hopkins Univer-

sity—occasionally a German university is named instead—only if she would sit behind a screen in order not to distract the attention of the men students. I have been unable to verify this story in any of her diaries or contemporary letters.

Chapter V

1. For an account of this trip abroad as well as of other experiences of her childhood see *A Quaker Childhood* by Helen Thomas Flexner, Yale University Press, New Haven, 1940.

2. Joseph Wright Taylor was born in March, 1810, in Monmouth County, New Jersey; took his doctorate of medicine before he was twenty at the University of Pennsylvania; gave up the practice of medicine in 1835 and moved to Cincinnati to join two of his brothers in a tannery business from which he made a considerable fortune that he increased by shrewd investment and cautious husbanding. He retired in 1850 and moved with his sister Hannah to Burlington, New Jersey, where in the following year he bought the estate "Woodlands," two miles outside the town, in which he lived as a country gentleman until his death in January, 1880. He was an ardent member of the orthodox Society of Friends, interested in various philanthropies and especially in education. In 1854 he became, and remained until his death, a member of the Board of Managers of Haverford College and, on his fairly wide travels in the United States as well as on his two visits to England and Europe in 1849 and 1861, observed educational projects and institutions. Early in the seventies he began to think of leaving his fortune to found an institution "for the advanced education of our young female Friends" in which they might be given "all the advantages of a college education which are so freely offered to young men." In the will written in February, 1877, quoted above, bequeathing the bulk of his fortune to such an institution he states his belief "that the effects of a guarded advanced Christian education of females, by expanding mental resources, would strengthen character and elevate them above the foolish fashions, now so prevalent, and would fit for usefulness and influence. Should they become mothers—to train infant minds and give direction to character, and to make *home* the centre of interest and attraction, and thus to preserve youth from foolish follies, or haunts that lead to ruin!" For a full account of his life see *Joseph Wright Taylor, Founder of Bryn Mawr College,* by Margaret Taylor MacIntosh with an introduction by Rufus M. Jones, Charles Shoemaker Taylor, Haverford, Pa., 1936.

Chapter VI

1. Dr. Taylor and some of his advisers, later appointed trustees, wished the new college to be situated near Haverford College so that the same water and heating system might be employed for both. Francis King, however, did not approve of this plan, fearing that it would mean that the woman's college would become a mere annex of the man's. Independently of Dr. Taylor he drove about the countryside with his daughter Bessie, looking for a suitable situation for the new college. At last he found it at Bryn Mawr—"High Hill" in Welsh—the highest point within a ten-mile radius of Philadelphia, with a good water supply, conveniently near the Pennsylvania Railroad, and near enough Haverford College to share its library and instructors if necessary but not so near as to become its annex. Dr. Taylor approved the situation and by the time of his death had bought a little over thirty-nine acres, most of the land now constituting the college grounds. In 1882 the college bought 1.2 acres on which

stood "Cartref" and now stands the infirmary as well. Between 1893 and 1895 about nine and a half acres, on which stand "Yarrow" and "The President's House" and also Goodhart Hall, was bought and the old road, the continuation of Yarrow Street which ran along the side of the hill separating the old from the new land, was closed. Somewhat later the college bought the plot of land, a little less than one acre, on the corner of Merion Avenue and Lombaert Street on which was situated "Dolgelly" and where the Phoebe Anna Thorne Model School pagodas were built later. In 1913, the 1.5 acres on which stood the College Inn was transferred from Miss Marion Reilly and Miss Martha G. Thomas to the trustees of the college. Finally, "Wyndham" and somewhat over six acres were acquired in 1925-26. By that time the college property amounted to a little more than sixty acres. Carey Thomas was disappointed in 1889 to have the trustees refuse to buy land offered them to the north of Gulph Road, including the little Baptist cemetery. James Whitall wrote her that "our beautiful distant views will have to be surrendered for building purposes and beautiful distant views are not *essential* to the success of a first class college. Only the *very rich* can in a crowded locality afford to pay for the preservation of such views." The trustees have held consistently to this policy of buying only such land as they felt to be absolutely necessary for building purposes. Nevertheless, so varied is the configuration of the land, so skillful has been the location of buildings and of plantings, that the extent of the campus is usually estimated by Bryn Mawr alumnae as much larger than it is, somewhere between one hundred and three hundred acres.

2. Taylor and Merion halls were designed by Addison Hutton, a Philadelphia architect and member of the Society of Friends. Merion Hall on its present site was to form one side of the quadrangle that the trustees planned to build to the north of Taylor Hall and about which they intended to dispose a gymnasium, laboratory buildings, and a library.

3. The elective system, as envisaged by President Eliot, was accepted at Harvard by 1878-79, by which time, with the exception of the study of rhetoric and the writing of themes and forensics in the last three years, only freshmen were obliged to follow a set curriculum of "required studies." For a discussion of the elective system at Harvard see *Charles W. Eliot, President of Harvard University 1869-1909* by Henry James, 2 vols., Houghton Mifflin Co., Boston, 1930. The group system first instituted by President Gilman at the Johns Hopkins and adapted by Bryn Mawr comprised a course of studies that would not only permit some freedom and flexibility but would insure a thorough knowledge of one or two subjects as well as a knowledge of those subjects deemed necessary as a foundation for all advanced studies. It differed from the Bryn Mawr adaptation largely in the fact that it was less flexible and its "groups" comprised fewer subjects than its Bryn Mawr counterpart. For a discussion of the group system at the Johns Hopkins University see *The Life of Daniel Coit Gilman* by Fabian Franklin, Dodd, Mead & Co., New York, 1910.

4. Of this faculty, Professor Scott remained at Bryn Mawr until her retirement in 1922; Professor Hopkins resigned in 1894 to accept the professorship of Sanskrit at Yale University, and was succeeded by Professor Herbert Weir Smyth as head of the Classical Department and by Paul Elmer More as associate in Sanskrit and classical literature; Professor E. B. Wilson resigned in 1890 to go to Columbia College, New York, and was succeeded by Professor Thomas Hunt Morgan and, for a year, by Jacques Loeb; Professor Keiser resigned in 1898 to go to Washington University and was succeeded as head of the depart-

ment by Professor Elmer P. Kohler; Professor Sturzinger resigned in 1890 and was succeeded by Professor Thomas McCabe; Professor Gregory resigned in 1888, and botany as a separate study was dropped from the curriculum; Professor Paul Shorey resigned in 1891 to go to the University of Chicago and was succeeded by Professor William C. Lawton; Professor Woodrow Wilson resigned in 1888 to go to Wesleyan University and was succeeded for a year by Professor Williston Walker and then by Professor Charles Maclean Andrews.

Chapter VII

1. Owing chiefly to the energy and success of Carey Thomas, somewhat over thirty-one thousand was contributed. The remainder of the sum necessary—a little less than forty-two thousand dollars—the trustees felt justified in paying from the college principal.

2. Although Carey Thomas had brought back from Smith College recommendations for the college furniture, Dr. Rhoads himself journeyed to Smith to look into the matter for himself and to obtain final specifications. His findings, in turn, he reported to her. The Bryn Mawr furnishings were the result of their joint effort. Sometimes the suggestions of one of them balanced those of the other: in return for advice from the dean concerning the undergraduates' "course books," the president advised the preparation of a half-yearly report by the professors on the work of the fellows. The yearly programs were, theoretically, compiled by the dean but Dr. Rhoads went over them with a fine-tooth comb, changing them considerably even in proof. The schedule, also worked out by the dean, was annotated closely in successive drafts by Dr. Rhoads; and its final composition was in many respects owing to his suggestions. In regard to the entrance examinations, the various professors submitted their papers to the president, but both president and dean criticized them. The mathematics papers, in especial, caused them both anxiety—for different reasons: "I feel pretty sure," wrote Dr. Rhoads to Carey Thomas, "that the mathematical papers are too difficult"—and, in the event, they caused an uproar of remonstrance in the schools because they demanded a knowledge of circulating decimals unheard of in most American schools; but the dean worried only lest the professor of mathematics be obliged to lower her standards and wrote at once urging her to hold them high.

3. With his other colleagues Wilson's relations were also superficial. They respected him intellectually, and those who shared a table with him at the Betweenery found him a pleasant, entertaining companion. He told a good story delightfully. His pretty wife they accepted as an amiable acquaintance though her southern manner misled them into thinking her too frivolous to command much attention. In point of fact she was, of course, serious minded and a very positive help to Wilson. But she was not strong and became absorbed by domestic tasks, especially after the birth of their first child in April, 1886; and when in the following year, a few months before the birth of their second daughter, they moved to the brick parsonage next the little Baptist Church in Gulph Road opposite the campus, she had less time than ever for social intercourse. Wilson himself was, if possible, even more preoccupied than she. In addition to his college duties, although he grudged what seemed to him a waste of time, he completed the work for his doctorate of philosophy, taking his degree at the Johns Hopkins in May, 1886; and after moving into their new house, he had to tend the furnace and the pump and to eke out his salary by giving a series of lectures at the Johns Hopkins University and by writing

numerous articles for the *Atlantic Monthly*, the *Political Quarterly*, and other journals. He tried his hand, too, at a number of short stories, none of which was accepted by any publisher. And he made plans for a vast future work, as well as began *The State*, published in 1889 after he left Bryn Mawr.

Meanwhile the necessary social amenities were observed with punctilio though without enthusiasm by the Wilsons, who had as little desire as time for closer contact with the college community. Indeed, Wilson regarded his colleagues with some disdain since he inclined to think that all professors were out of touch with the world and, hence, as one-sided as those others whom he scorned, men purely of affairs. With no liking, moreover, for "intellectual women" and no belief in their intellectual power or wish to foster it, he felt teaching in a woman's college to be beneath his dignity. His willingness to have his wife's cousin live with them in order that she might attend the college is a break in his logic which shows the strength of his family feeling. However that may be, in measure as he felt himself degraded, he felt his colleagues so; but he, at least, recognized his shame—a fact that somewhat assuaged and bolstered his sense of superiority.

Naturally his relations with the students were also distant. Unlike many of his colleagues who made warm friends among the students in spite of strictly observed proprieties, he was hardly aware of them as individuals; and as representatives of the genus woman student they were, of course, suspect. His sense of duty, nevertheless, was scrupulous, if limited by narrow sympathy; and it would have been beneath his pride to shirk any part of the work to which he believed he had set his hand. His lectures were good, clear, and polished—a finished performance. The theoretical plan of his courses was excellent. In the course in modern history he required each student to prepare a biographical notice of a leading historical character that was read and criticized in the class, and he allowed the students time to ask questions—though, given no encouragement, they rarely availed themselves of it. Even the conferences that he held meticulously as was the custom with each of his graduate students tended to become lectures delivered before an audience of one. If he expected and therefore got little work out of his students, his indifference to them, the assurance with which he delivered his lectures, and the perfection of their form impressed them. His fortnightly lectures on public affairs were well attended even by those who were not students of history. Lectures day in and day out, however, are an anodyne. His students, whom he had thought at the very first "interested and intelligent," soon became too docile to be stimulating—they were lulled to passivity. Only years later, when he became a great figure in the world, did they struggle to remember all they could about him. Even in the eighties, nevertheless, in response to his interest in English parliamentary government they formed, as had his fellow students at the Johns Hopkins and Princeton and later his students at Wesleyan, a parliament modeled on the House of Commons. During his professorship at the college this parliament, with a prime minister, home and foreign secretaries, a speaker, a clerk, and a sergeant at arms—the tallest of the students—met fortnightly to debate according to parliamentary usage bills dealing with questions of current public interest such as the abolishment of capital punishment, the restriction of foreign immigration, and the prohibition of the sale of alcoholic liquors.

I am indebted for much of the material upon which this sketch of Woodrow Wilson at Bryn Mawr is based to Mr. Henry Bragdon, who has been engaged for some time upon work concerning Wilson's academic career, as well as to

Woodrow Wilson; Life and Letters by Ray Stannard Baker, Doubleday, Page & Co., New York, 1927-29.

4. Even before the Self-Government Association was started the students governed themselves under the supervision of the dean. In her speech on "Present Tendencies in Women's College and University Education" at the quarter-centennial of the Association of Collegiate Alumnae, 1907, Carey Thomas spoke of the surprise evinced by the president of Harvard when he visited Bryn Mawr College one year after its opening and found that the students virtually governed themselves, going away whenever they saw fit for the night or the week end. "If this continues," he remarked, "I will give you two years, no more, in which to close Bryn Mawr."

5. In this course she lectured for three or four hours a week, during the first year on the history of the language and on Anglo-Saxon and Middle English literature from the time of Chaucer through the early nineteenth century including, the president's report to the trustees stated, "a brief excursus on Italian and French literature." One hour a week—a terrifying hour to the apprehensive, exhilarating to the bold, and the source of many a good story—she quizzed the students on the reading that they were required to do in connection with her lectures. A certain number of more advanced students who were majoring in English she instructed in Anglo-Saxon or in the development of modern poetry—that is, chiefly, the work of the Lake poets and Shelley, Keats, and Byron; and to a small number of graduate students she gave classes in Browning's poetry or, again, in Anglo-Saxon. No graduate seminar in English was given in the college until its seventh year when Carey Thomas alternated with the associate in Anglo-Saxon, appointed in 1888, in conducting a seminar on Chaucer.

6. *The Bryn Mawr School. Its New Country Site and its Financial Need,* 1929-30.

7. This and the quotation from Dr. Osler on the following page are taken from *William Henry Welch and the Heroic Age of Medicine* by Simon Flexner and James Thomas Flexner, by permission of the Viking Press, publishers, New York, 1941. See both that book and the Appendix to the Catalogue of the Johns Hopkins University Medical School for further details about the founding of the school.

Chapter VIII

1. Discord threatened at one point because Carey Thomas went over the heads of the trustees' Buildings Committee in a matter concerning the strengthening of the running gallery of the gymnasium. Carey Thomas soothed the affronted chairman of the committee, only to disturb the trustees' equilibrium again by her sudden objection to submitting the budget to the Finance Committee and by her demand, a month later, that the Executive Committee should report upon the budget, a request greatly resented by the chairman of the Finance Committee.

2. From *Rutherford. Being the Life and Letters of the Rt. Hon. Lord Rutherford, D.M.* by A. S. Eve. By permission of The Macmillan Company, publishers, New York, 1939.

3. *General Education in a Free Society; Report of the Harvard Committee* published by the Harvard University Press, Cambridge, 1945,

4. From *Autobiographic Memoirs* by Frederic Harrison, by permission of Macmillan and Company, publishers, New York, 1911.

5. Mary Garrett in 1894 had the president's and secretary's offices in Taylor Hall decorated and furnished in similar style for seven thousand dollars. In the Deanery the oriental rugs were, almost without exception, of great beauty as were the brocades which covered some of the chairs. Except for Holman Hunt's oil painting of "Isabella and the Pot of Basil" and a series of etchings by Whistler —both of which were disposed of later by Carey Thomas herself—and "Endymion Recumbent" carved in white marble by Thorwaldsen, such original works of art as there were had little interest. In recent years, since a group of young men guests spending the night at the Deanery, now an alumnae guest house, decorated the Endymion with mustache, pink cheeks, and clothing, the statue has been relegated to the basement. Owing to the difficulty and expense of cleaning them, many of the books and ornaments which formerly lent character to the Deanery have also been removed. Lack of money to keep it in its former state has enforced other changes in its decoration and furnishings. Similar changes have robbed Taylor Hall of much of its nineteenth-century distinction— its only asset. To obtain a little more space as well as to satisfy contemporary taste for "simplicity," the white marble busts which for half a century looked down from their tall golden oak pedestals upon the students in the corridors have been removed and the decoration of some of the offices has been altered.

6. The architect of the garden was Frederick Law Olmsted, who was responsible, also, for the planting done at this time on the campus. In a speech at the supper of the Alumnae Association at Bryn Mawr College, June, 1912, Carey Thomas said, "Olmsted, the leading landscape gardener of his time in the United States, made the first comprehensive study of the Bryn Mawr Campus. In consultation with Cope and Stewardson, he put on his first map of the College all our buildings both those existing and those planned for, except the power house which is wrongly placed."

The green secluded charm of the garden was only enhanced during Carey Thomas's lifetime by the tulips, hyacinths, and daffodils that sprang up beneath its shrubberies and in its ivy borders in the spring. In recent years, however, it has been greatly impaired by the cutting down of the high enclosing hedge which in large measure gave it its particular character.

7. The architect of the Deanery was Lockwood de Forrest, who for some years was retained as the college architect.

8. The portrait now hangs at the head of the steps in the William H. Welch Library of the Johns Hopkins University Medical School. A copy of it by Gabrielle de V. Clements hangs in the Deanery, Bryn Mawr.

9. This favorable view of Carey Thomas's portrait is not held by everyone: some, who dislike Sargent's painting, will go no farther than to call it "one of his best"; others, who wish the portrait not only to be a likeness but to give their personal impressions of Carey Thomas, are dissatisfied.

10. In 1902 Miss Anthony attended the presentation to Bryn Mawr College, by Dr. Howard A. Kelly of the Johns Hopkins Medical School, of a medallion of herself sculptured by Leila Usher and, after a formal dinner to distinguished guests at the Deanery, spoke in Taylor Hall to the students about difficulties encountered by the pioneers of the suffrage movement such as they would never meet. In 1905, while visiting Anna Howard Shaw in Mount Airy, she inspected the new library and residence hall of the college.

11 Speaking on this subject years later to an audience in London, she said that she believed in women marrying and continuing their careers. "A short time ago a married woman member of the faculty of Bryn Mawr College came

to me and said, 'I am going to have a baby, Miss Thomas. Must I give up my position on the faculty?' And I replied, 'Not at all. Have it in the summer.'" Carey Thomas paused a moment to let this sink in; then added reflectively, "She had to have leave of absence because she did not have the baby in the summer. I forget for the moment the reason why." Unfortunately, I heard this story too late to include it in the text.

12. For the plan to finance the Students' Inn—now the College Inn—see Carey Thomas's speech reported in the *Alumnae Quarterly*, June, 1912. Much of the building of which she dreamt in connection with the Students' Inn she was unable to achieve. She wished the Inn to be the central building in a grassy court around which were to be built, between the inn and Gulph Road, two double professors' houses and an apartment house of six housekeeping flats. "If our teachers are to give their best work," she said, "to the College as they get older they must be able to live near our library and laboratories in better built houses and in more healthful and pleasanter surroundings than their salaries would make possible for them to secure in open market. If Bryn Mawr cannot pay larger salaries than other colleges it can at least continue its present policy and provide for its professors more reasonable and more civilized living arrangements than they can obtain in other colleges."

Chapter IX

1. These committees were not only to select suitable candidates and to prepare them when possible for the school, but were to raise scholarships and to help former students of the school to continue their education and, of course, to publicize the school. The directors of the college had placed the buildings, grounds, and summer personnel of the college, as far as they might be needed, at the disposal of the school provided that the Joint Administrative Committee assumed responsibility for running expenses. The sum needed for the first summer was raised by a few enthusiastic women; but thereafter the district committees were responsible for the budget. Funds had to be provided for the usual expenses of a school, including salaries of instructors and other running expenses, as well as scholarships of two hundred and fifty dollars for each student and a sum for traveling. The workers, especially after relinquishing two months' pay in order to attend the school, had no money for any journeys, even of the hitchhiking variety, let alone long ones from the southern or middle states or the west coast. Toward the budget, too, something over one thousand dollars was contributed annually by the undergraduates of Bryn Mawr's "winter College," as it was known among the summer students.

Among the most difficult problems were not only choice of students but that of the eight instructors and fifteen tutors. Since Bryn Mawr refused to permit any member of its faculty to teach in any summer school, on the theory that teachers needed the summer for research and a change of pursuit, the instructors were brought from other colleges and universities and private schools. It was fairly easy to find trained teachers in the various subjects, but far from simple to find such teachers who also understood something of the special problems of teaching women industrial workers and who had the courage and ability to experiment wisely. Those who were appointed, however, never ceased to be grateful, finding the experience enlightening and stimulating beyond anything they had encountered in their teaching careers.

For the students themselves the experience was revolutionary not only because of the academic instruction, though that in itself opened doors to them into undreamt of interests and delights, but because of the beauty of the place—many of them had never before seen green lawns, never noticed trees or stars, never encountered comfortable living conditions—and, perhaps most of all, because of the variety of co-workers of diverse backgrounds and affiliations with whom they came in contact as fellow students. One hundred workers—eighty, the first summer—from every trade and of every extraction—Scotch, Irish, Pennsylvania Dutch, Canadian, Russian, Italian, Lithuanian, Polish, Scandinavian, Czechoslovakian, Hungarian, any number of others—were gathered together in the halls of Bryn Mawr. Some were union members, some were not; some could hardly speak English, let alone write it. The living, as well as the academic, arrangements were carefully prepared. "The general plan," wrote the director, "is to give every girl some new contacts, and at the same time not to place her in a position where through too pronounced antagonisms or differences in experience she will be unhappy and out of her element." Even extracurricular activities—sports, picnics, excursions, speakers, debates, evenings of music and poetry, a school magazine—had to be arranged with greater care than those for regular college students, since leisure was unknown to most of the summer students and they did not understand how to use it. Indeed, the women workers on the Joint Administrative Committee disclaimed any ability to advise in regard to the recreation program, never having indulged in recreation themselves.

2. For further details concerning the summer school see *Women Workers at the Bryn Mawr Summer School* by Hilda Worthington Smith, from which this and the quotations concerning the school not noted as being Carey Thomas's own words are taken by permission of the joint publishers: the Affiliated Summer Schools for Women Workers in Industry and the American Association on Adult Education.

Chapter X

1. The following quotations from Carey Thomas's plan are taken from *Ways To Peace* with an introduction by Esther Everett Lape and a preface by Edward W. Bok, by permission of Charles Scribner's Sons, publishers, New York, 1924.

2. In 1942 a Victory ship was launched from the Baltimore yards of the Bethlehem Shipbuilding Company named after "Mrs. [sic] Martha C. Thomas, formerly President of Bryn Mawr College."

INDEX

336

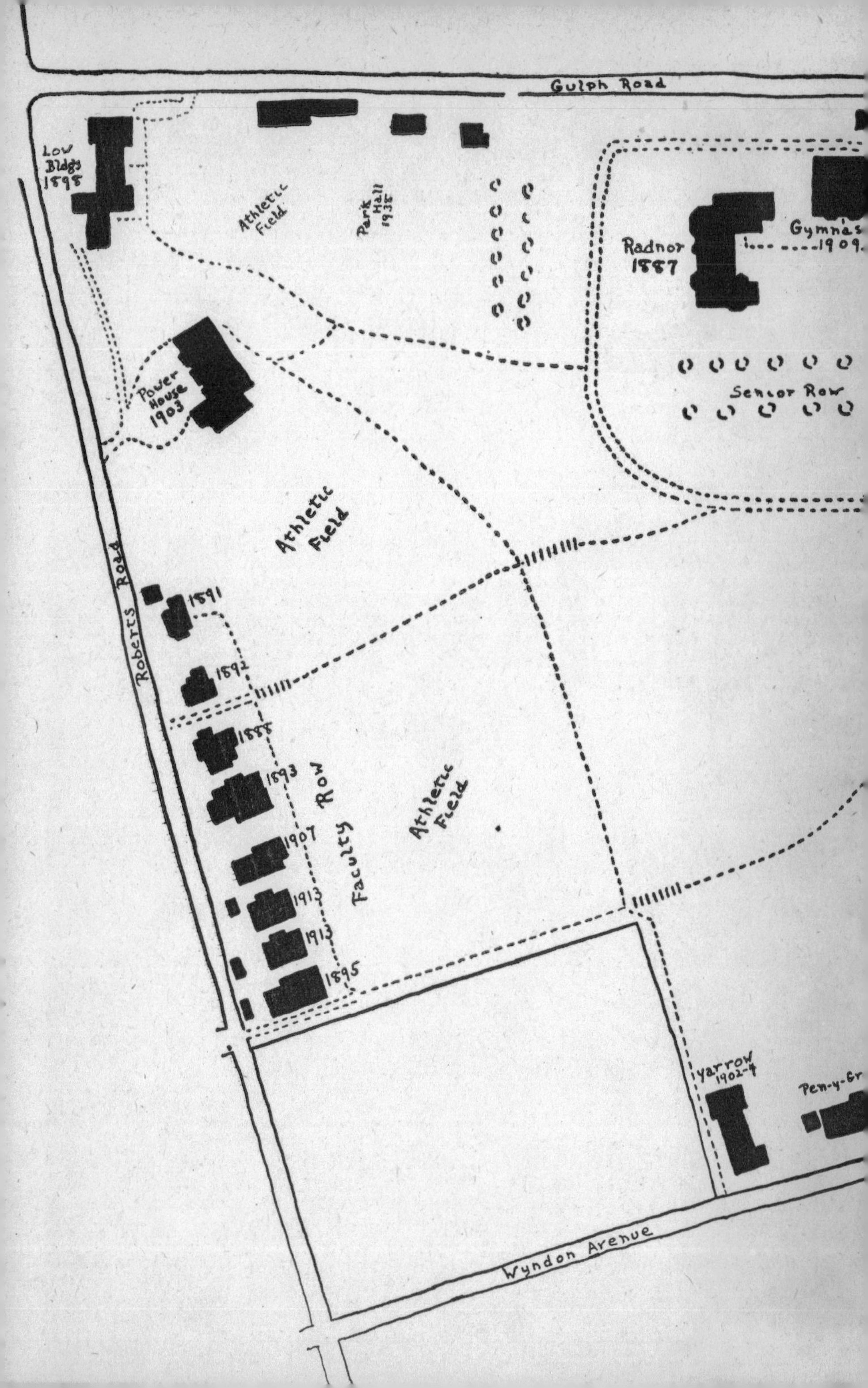

Gulph Road
Low Bldgs 1898
Athletic Field
Park Hall 1935
Radnor 1887
Gymnas 1909
Power House 1903
Senior Row
Athletic Field
Roberts Road
1891
1892
1888
1893
1907
1913
1913
1895
Faculty Row
Athletic Field
Yarrow 1902-4
Pen-y-Gr
Wyndon Avenue